The publisher gratefully acknowledges the generous support of the AMS 75 PAYS Endowment of the American Musicological Society, funded in part by the National Endowment for the Humanities and the Andrew W. Mellon Foundation.

Music Makes Me

Music Makes Me

Fred Astaire and Jazz

Todd Decker

UNIVERSITY OF CALIFORNIA PRESS

Berkeley · Los Angeles · London

University of California Press, one of the most distinguished university
presses in the United States, enriches lives around the world by advancing
scholarship in the humanities, social sciences, and natural sciences. Its
activities are supported by the UC Press Foundation and by philanthropic
contributions from individuals and institutions. For more information, visit
www.ucpress.edu.

University of California Press
Berkeley and Los Angeles, California

University of California Press, Ltd.
London, England

Library of Congress Cataloging-in-Publication Data

Decker, Todd R.
    Music makes me : Fred Astaire and jazz / Todd Decker.
        p.   cm
    Includes bibliographical references and index.
    ISBN 978-0-520-26888-3 (cloth : alk. paper)
    ISBN 978-0-520-26890-6 (pbk. : alk. paper)
    1. Astaire, Fred.   2. Jazz musicians—United States—
Biography.   3. Dancers—United States—Biography.
4. Motion picture actors and actresses—United States—
Biography.   I. Title.
    ML420.A896D46   2011
    781.65092—dc22   2011004809

Manufactured in the United States of America

19 18 17 16 15 14 13 12 11
10 9 8 7 6 5 4 3 2 1

This book is printed on Cascades Enviro 100, a 100 percent postconsumer
waste, recycled, de-inked fiber. FSC recycled certified and processed chlorine
free. It is acid free, Ecologo certified, and manufactured by BioGas energy.

For Kelly, David, and James

You can't say to a jazz performer, whose talent is worth anything, that he plays avant-garde, or that he plays Dixieland, or that he is modern or a proponent of the Chicago style. A substantial musician will say, "I just play."

—Jazz musician Bud Freeman, quoted in Burt Korall, *Drummin' Men: The Heartbeat of Jazz, the Swing Years*

When you come to the evolution of the dance, its history and philosophy, I know as much about that as I do about how a television tube produces a picture—which is absolutely nothing. I don't know how it all started and I don't want to know. I have no desire to prove anything by it. I have never used it as an outlet or as a means of expressing myself.

I just dance.

—Fred Astaire, *Steps in Time*

Dick Cavett: Do you dance every day?
Fred Astaire: I don't usually dance. Oh, a piece of music might set me off.

—*The Dick Cavett Show*, November 1970

Goodman cherishes a remark by Fred Astaire, who said: "I'd rather play like Benny Goodman than dance like Fred Astaire."

—*New York Post*, 6 June 1973

Contents

Illustrations

TABLES

MUSICAL EXAMPLES

Introduction

Fred Astaire filmed his first dance solo in a Hollywood musical to the sound of a live jazz jam session. The occasion, a momentous one in hindsight, was by Hollywood standards a genuine jazz encounter. The date was 7 September 1933; the film, *Flying Down to Rio;* the song, "Music Makes Me (Do the Things I Never Should Do)." The musical and choreographic content of this routine, when put beside archival evidence for how the number was made, provide a foretaste of Astaire's remarkable four-decade career dancing on screen. "Music Makes Me"—the finished film dance and the process behind its creation—also encapsulates the larger themes of this book, which details how music of a particular kind—for now, call it jazz—lay at the heart of Astaire's creative life as both dancer and dancemaker on film. Astaire's first film solo offers a prism for his creative life, a life as much about music as it was about dancing and filmmaking.

Astaire danced two "hot" instrumental choruses of this Vincent Youmans tune. Edward Eliscu and Gus Kahn's lyrics had been sung in an earlier scene by Ginger Rogers. The chorus describes how popular music might affect a susceptible listener.

> I like music old and new,
> But music makes me do the things I never should do.
> Oh, I like music sweet and blue,
> But music makes me do the things I never should do.

My self-control was something to brag about,
Now it's a gag about town.
The things I do are never forgiven,
And just when I'm livin' 'em down;
I hear music, then I'm through,
'Cause music makes me do the things I never should do.

Astaire's dance solo—a syncopated rhythm tap routine performed on a small dance floor—has no significant place in the film's plot. It's a specialty that says more about Astaire's already well-defined music and dance persona than it does about the film. Set against an exotic South American background, *Flying Down to Rio* served as a colorful excuse for a variety of musical numbers, and the reviewer for the trade paper *Variety* understood the merits of Astaire's work relative to the rest of the picture: "But *Rio*'s story lets it down. It's slow and lacks laughs to the point where average business seems its groove. From the time of the opening melody ('Music Makes Me'—and hot) to the next number, 'Carioca,' almost three reels elapse and anybody can take a walk, come back and be that much ahead. Those who keep on walking, however, will muff Astaire's specialty, which is down next to closing, where it belongs."[1] *Variety* describes *Flying Down to Rio* as if it were a vaudeville show, with "Astaire's specialty" to "Music Makes Me" "down next to closing," the best spot on any bill. By the standards of the time, the film was an excuse for the numbers. *Variety*'s approach to the film musical as a commercially viable host genre for musical numbers operates as the norm throughout this study of Astaire's creative work. He was not a maker of film musicals: Astaire made filmed song-and-dance routines. The distinction is crucial.

The setup for the dance to "Music Makes Me" begins with Astaire's character, self-referentially named Fred Ayres, rehearsing a group of chorus girls for a nightclub show. The shooting script generally reflects what happens in the film.

At this point, Roger [played by Gene Raymond], a little bored by all this, starts the orchestra playing the vamp of Fred's number. Fred begins to get fidgety feet. He waves the orchestra to silence. It stops.

FRED: Boys wait a minute will you? Now, as I was saying, before—

The orchestra repeats the vamp. Again Fred succumbs to the music and does a few steps and then waves the Orchestra to silence.

FRED: Hey Rog—listen will you—listen girls—How do you expect me to teach these follies girls if you—if you don't keep your mind exactly on the jib, you can't do a thing—because

Orchestra begins again. Fred resigns himself and goes into his number.[2]

The laconic designation "his number" is about as specific as most Hollywood screenwriters got when putting the musical and choreographic content of a dance number into words. In Astaire's case, such content remained firmly under the control of Astaire himself and a trusted set of collaborators. However, differences between the lead-in to the number in the script and in the film are worth noting. All are musical in nature.

The script calls for the music to stop and start: in the film, however, the music never stops. Instead, the musical structure of the tune is integrated into the larger conceit that music compels Astaire to dance. In the lead-in to the dance the script suggests the band play a vamp, a short rhythmic idea that can be repeated indefinitely and easily started and stopped. Vamps are typically associated with vaudeville and Broadway. In the film, the band instead plays once through the chorus of Youmans's song, which is thirty-two bars long and in standard AABA form (four phrases, each eight bars long). When the band falls silent for a two-bar break at the end of the second A phrase, Astaire finds himself compelled to fill the empty space, just as any improvising jazz musician might. Being a tap dancer—a kind of jazz percussionist—Astaire fills the break with syncopated rhythms. Breaks formed an integral part of popular music and jazz for decades, making room for solo improvisation in the midst of a hummable tune. Astaire's use of the breaks—a lifelong practice deployed to varied ends—serves as but one indication that he thinks in jazz terms. Astaire the dancemaker—and not his screenwriter—used the song structure of "Music Makes Me" and the common practices of jazz musicians to express the internal narrative of the routine, which in this case nicely connects with the lyrics. Again and again in his output, the conventional structures of popular music and jazz compel Astaire to dance. Paying close attention to musical form—in effect, listening to the dance—reveals much about Astaire's approach to both dance and music making.

The Hollywood studios of Astaire's day were filmmaking factories, and, like all such monumental enterprises, the studios kept meticulous records. In some cases—and, fortunately, at RKO and MGM, the two studios where Astaire made the bulk of his films—many production records have survived. A variety of production files from the RKO collection at the University of California, Los Angeles gives a glimpse of when and how Astaire's solo to "Music Makes Me" was made. Like most of Astaire's solos, "Music Makes Me" was filmed at or near the beginning of production, or shooting, on the film. On that September day the twelve actors playing the members of the Yankee Clippers dance band reported to the set for the first time. The players on screen are faking it—they make up a fairly convincing group of what the industry called sideline musicians—while off camera a second set of players, actual musicians, made the music to which Astaire rapped out his solo. Sound and image were captured together. The very beginning of Astaire's long career overlapped with the transitional period between silent and sound film.[3] Within months of filming this routine, live music on set would be a thing of the past and the playback system would become standard for Hollywood musicals. The playback system replaced live music with a prerecorded soundtrack captured in the more controlled environment of a recording studio. Film musical performers pretended to sing to the recording while filming the image track, and sound and image were then wedded to each other during postproduction. Film musicals, for most of Astaire's career, were entirely synthetic products, made using a methodical process and nothing like a live performance captured on film. As will be shown, Astaire was directly involved in every step in the laborious process of making moving pictures that sang and danced, and he exercised considerable control over the technical process in almost all of his films. But in September 1933, filming the image track and recording the sound track simultaneously was still a possibility, and Astaire took advantage of this practice for as long as it lasted.[4] Coming as he did from the world of live stage performance in vaudeville and on Broadway, having actual musicians on the set—if not on-screen—may have provided one familiar element for Astaire, who found himself in the midst of a still unfamiliar technical process, lacking any audience response to gauge his overall success putting over a song-and-dance routine.

Musicians were important collaborators for Astaire, and archival research sometimes reveals who was playing on his films. The musicians playing on "Music Makes Me"—six in all—were the responsibility of the RKO music department. Bob Morrow on violin, Gene La Franiere on trumpet, Eddie Sharpe on saxophone, A. Gifford on banjo, and Jack Barsby on tuba were hired by the hour for the gig. Joe Heindl was paid for contracting the ad hoc group. Uncredited on the film itself—typically only heads of departments were listed in the abbreviated screen credits of the studio era—some of these players left traces in the history of recorded jazz.[5] Hal Findlay on piano joined this group of five jazz players. Astaire's rehearsal pianist on *Flying Down to Rio,* Findlay had been close to the dance to "Music Makes Me" from its beginnings in the rehearsal studio. Astaire's regular accompanist at RKO would be a different Hal—Hal Borne—but Findlay was on the job in this case, filling an essential role in Astaire's creative process. Rehearsal pianists played the music that made Astaire dance while he was making up his dance steps. (On occasion a drummer was also present.) Of all the musicians on the lot, Astaire's rehearsal pianists knew the musical structure and special requirements of Astaire's dances most intimately. Rehearsal pianists collaborated with Astaire and his dance assistants on the musical arrangement, and, once the dance was set, wrote out a short score indicating all the important musical points of emphasis for the arrangers and orchestrators in the music department, who would, in turn, clothe the number in the sounds Astaire wanted. In the case of "Music Makes Me," Findlay would have been the de facto leader. Only he knew when the small jazz combo should lay out in order to get out of the way of Astaire's solo breaks. Musical collaborators such as Findlay were essential to Astaire's working methods, and these behind-the-scenes creative actors play major roles here. Their expertise and experience—frequently brought directly from the worlds of jazz and popular music—inform Astaire's output in substantial, even defining, ways.

The actual music played by this small jazz combo does not survive. Instead, there is only a folder listing the name of the song, the names of the six players, and their phone numbers: essentially, a call list.[6] This was clearly a pickup group, not a regular RKO ensemble. Did anyone bother writing out parts for Astaire's solo to "Music Makes Me"? Probably not. None of Astaire's moves are matched (or "mickey moused") by the band, and the breaks occur in predictable places. All six players would have been perfectly capable of improvising from a lead sheet or after hearing the chord changes on "Music Makes Me" a few times. The sound of the music does not suggest arrangement. It's a jam session in a popular early 1930s style, exactly as the setup suggests. The sextet swings hard, sounding like such contemporary jazz ensembles as Joe Venuti's Blue Four and Blue Five, a prominent violin-centered combo.[7] Jazz critic and historian Gary Giddins has described Venuti's Blue Four as "white jazz at its best, providing the most distinctive alternative to the very different kind of chamber music represented by Louis Armstrong's electrifying Hot Fives and Sevens."[8] The sideline violin player faking it on-screen plays with his bow tied around the instrument, engaging all four strings at once so that chords are played throughout. This novel approach was used often by Venuti, and violinist Morrow plays in the same style on the soundtrack.[9] Someone on the set matched sound and image as faithfully as possible. Such care would have delighted jazz play- ers and lovers who went to see *Flying Down to Rio,* and the views of such musically oriented moviegoers will be heard throughout this book. Their always musically biased opinions bring a surprising new perspec- tive to the story of the Hollywood musical in general, and the work of Astaire in particular.

Why does Astaire start dancing in "Music Makes Me"? This is a fo- cused version of the larger question at the center of this book. Taking my cue (and my title) from the title of the song, I will argue that music made Astaire dance. And not just any music: popular syncopated music, which for most of Astaire's long career meant some variety of jazz, whether swing, boogie-woogie, the blues, soul jazz, or, in this case, a collective improvisation aesthetic typical of the 1920s (and reaching beyond that to the roots of the music in New Orleans). Astaire's danced response to the music of a fictional jazz band, ghosted offscreen by ac- tual jazz musicians, is joyful, seemingly involuntary, slightly out of con- trol, and completely of its early 1930s moment. It starts in the feet, inter- rupts his thought process, and is not yet all that refined. In her influential book *The Hollywood Musical,* Jane Feuer builds a short reading of Astaire's career on "his trademark 'reflex' dancing." Feuer writes, "The involuntary dancing motif not only serves to associate dancing with ut- terly spontaneous impulses; it also implies that for Astaire the dance is a life process like breathing."[10] Feuer detaches the word *dancing* from all historical context—there are many different kinds of dancing—and omits the key point that Astaire required music of a certain type before his "utterly spontaneous impulses" kicked in. He didn't just dance: he danced to music. And only certain kinds of music had the power to set him off. This book zeroes in on the varied musical stimuli that made Astaire dance, always with an ear and an eye to the historical context that gives specific meaning to the capacious categories of dance and music.

The internal narrative to "Music Makes Me"—syncopated popular music making the dancer dance—occurs again and again in Astaire's enormous output. It's the most common narrative device he drew upon to provide internal cohesion for his dances. In "The Continental" from *The Gay Divorcee* (1934), his second film and first leading role at RKO, music briefly pushes Astaire into the dance in the middle of Ginger Rogers's vocal chorus. Attentively listening to Rogers sing, Astaire suddenly starts tapping when she gets to the suggestive lyric "a certain rhythm that you can't control." Astaire embellishes the rhythm of the tune itself, tapping a pattern that matches the melody being sung, adopting a practice jazz drummers call "playing the stems."[11] In the case of Astaire (or any tap dancer), this approach can be usefully termed "tapping the stems." The overlap between drumming and tapping can be found in such parallel practices. From the start of his screen career, Astaire was a jazz drummer without a drum kit. Several times he remedied this lack and danced with drums as his partner. All rhythm tappers were drummers in spirit, and Astaire was far from being the only tapper. Indeed, tap dance was everywhere in American popular culture between the World Wars, as ubiquitous as sampling in current popular music. Tapping the stems with a rhythm-referencing lyric in "The Continental" was no aberration. Astaire did this often, as will be shown. He gravitated toward syncopated, tappable moments in the melodies of the popular songs that came his way, and songwriters soon enough began to write songs with exactly those kinds of syncopated patterns. As singer Barbara Lea noted, "The composers who wrote for him wrote light rhythm songs, because he was a dancer, and a circular thing took effect. Their songs probably made him even more that way, which made them produce more of the same sort of songs, and so on."[12] The chapters that follow frequently highlight Astaire's search for "light rhythm songs," as well as his songwriters' not-always-successful attempts to meet his demands.

The theme of music making the dancer dance turns up everywhere in Astaire's work. It is his most fundamental creative impulse. Following this theme also helps connect Astaire to trends in popular music and jazz, highlighting his desire to meet the changing tastes of his audience. His comic partner dance with Marjorie Reynolds to the Irving Berlin song "I Can't Tell a Lie" in *Holiday Inn* (1942) provides a revealing example. Performed in eighteenth-century costumes and wigs for a Washington's birthday–themed floor show, the dance is built around abrupt musical shifts between the light classical sound of flute, strings, and harpsichord and four contrasting popular music styles played on the soundtrack by Bob Crosby and His Orchestra, a popular dance band. Moderate swing, a bluesy trumpet shuffle, hot flag-waving swing, and the Conga take turns interrupting what would have been a graceful, if effete, gavotte. The script supervisor heard these contrasts on the set during filming to playback. In her notes, she used commonplace musical terms to describe the action: "going through routine to La Conga music, then music changing back and forth from minuet to jazz—cutting as he holds her hand and she whirls doing minuet."[13] Astaire and Reynolds play professional dancers who are expected to respond correctly and instantaneously to the musical cues being given by the band. In an era when variety was a hallmark of popular music, different dance rhythms and tempos cued different dances. Competency on the dance floor meant a working knowledge of different dance styles and the ability to match these moves to the shifting musical program of the bands that played in ballrooms large and small. The constant stylistic shifts in "I Can't Tell a Lie" are all to the popular music point. The joke isn't only that the classical-sounding music that matches the couple's costumes keeps being interrupted by pop sounds; it's that the interruptions reference real varieties of popular music heard everywhere outside the movie theaters where *Holiday Inn* first played to capacity audiences. The routine runs through a veritable catalog of popular dance music circa 1942. The brief bit of Conga was a particularly poignant joke at the time. A huge hit in the late 1930s, the Conga during the war became an invitation to controlled mayhem, a crazy release of energy in a time of crisis when the dance floor was an important place of escape. A regular feature at servicemen's canteens, the Conga was an old novelty dance everybody knew, so its intrusion into "I Can't Tell a Lie" can perhaps be imagined as something like hearing the mid-1990s hit "Macarena" after the 2001 terrorist attacks—old party music echoing from a less complicated time.[14] If today we miss these finer points, in 1942 audiences—who flocked to this movie—certainly got them all. "I Can't Tell a Lie" was funnier then, and for specifically musical reasons that had everything to do with the larger world of popular music and dance. As subsequent chapters will demonstrate, many such musical jokes or references can be recovered by listening to Astaire's films in the context of the popular music marketplace.

It's not so easy to miss the musical jokes in Astaire's last big solo, a recasting of his signature tune "Top Hat, White Tie and Tails" in a late-1960s rock style that closed his final television special in 1968. Astaire danced on television for a full decade after the film musical in its studio-era incarnation disappeared. His four television specials (1958, 1959, 1960, and 1968) were consistently acclaimed by the television industry and critics.[15] In the mid-1960s, Astaire guest hosted several episodes of *The Hollywood Palace,* a revival of vaudeville entertainment values that gave him further opportunities to make dance routines for television.

All his TV dances looked to the popular music moment, giving Astaire the chance to engage creatively with contemporary musicians whose music made him want to dance. Often these were African American jazz players, some with roots in the swing era, others exploring newer but still popular jazz styles. For the 1968 "Top Hat" finale, Astaire went out on a limb musically and brought in The Gordian Knot, a rock band enjoying a brief season of popularity on the Hollywood scene. After doing a bit of "Top Hat" in his understated manner to a swinging beat provided by the Neal Hefti Orchestra, the house band on the special, Astaire pulled the proceedings into the pop music present, saying, "That was then. But now, if we were to turn on with that groovy sound of The Gordian Knot . . ." A dissolve put Astaire—still with top hat and cane but now wearing a turtleneck and trendy medallion—in a brightly colored cube-shaped set with a group of similarly attired male dancers. Perched high above on a scaffold, The Gordian Knot wore beads and flowing garb echoing The Beatles' contemporary fascination with all things Indian. The band plays a simplified version of Irving Berlin's sophisticated tune. Moving across the pre- and post-rock divide, the musical contrast between then and now is extreme. And unlike the shifts back and forth between classical and popular styles that worked to comic effect in "I Can't Tell a Lie," once "Top Hat" lands in the land of rock and roll, there's no going back to swing time.

Astaire's initial sung version presents "Top Hat" in an articulate and complete manner, respecting the structure of the tune. The Gordian Knot—working with Astaire, of course—takes a much freer approach, in the end reducing the melody to a two-chord groove and singing a largely incomprehensible lyric.

> I'm putting on my top hat (yes I am)
> Brushing off my tails
> I'm putting on my top hat (yes I am)
> Really gonna wail

This transformation of a well-known song—done with the permission of the still very much alive Berlin—demonstrates the extent to which Astaire's songwriters let him do absolutely anything he wanted with their songs. However, Astaire's rock version of "Top Hat" carefully preserves one element of Berlin's tune: the bridge (see example 1). Every time Astaire danced "Top Hat," he tapped the stems on Berlin's syncopated bridge (also known as the release and the B in this AABA tune). Astaire tapped the bridge on all three dance choruses in the original

EXAMPLE 1. Astaire "tapped the stems" on the bridge of Berlin's "Top Hat, White Tie and Tails" every time he danced the song.

1935 film version and on the pop record made the same year for release with the film. The bridge ends up being the only syncopated moment in the 1968 rock version. The roots of Astaire's creative identity in a pre-rock, jazz-oriented, syncopated rhythmic style briefly rise to the surface.

Astaire tries hard to be "with it" while dancing with The Gordian Knot and the routine is not played for laughs. He had the idea of bringing the band onto the special, and this shared production number was meant to be taken at face value as the big finish to the show. The original "Top Hat" production number would have been familiar to many viewers in Astaire's 1968 audience from television and revival cinema showings of *Top Hat*. Indeed, without this reference point the rock version would have lacked resonance. And what Astaire proclaims about his musical identity in the 1968 version is essentially the same message he delivered in the more iconic 1935 version, in his solo to "Music Makes Me," and in virtually all the dances described in the pages that follow. This dancing man moves to the beat of the times while remaining faithful to an underlying syncopated rhythmic sensibility. He makes music—makes rhythm while dancing—and responds to the sounds of the moment. *Music Makes Me: Fred Astaire and Jazz* examines Astaire's identity as a rhythm- and dancemaker attuned to the changing beat of American popular music from the 1920s to the 1960s. For most of that time, jazz was in the ascendant as popular music. The high point for jazz as popular music—the so-called swing era, narrowly defined as the mid- to late 1930s and early 1940s—coincided with Astaire's prime. After the coming of rock and roll in the mid-1950s, jazz did not leave the popular music mainstream—and neither did Astaire. In enduringly popular forms, jazz tunes, techniques, rhythms, and sensibilities from the swing era maintained their presence—albeit a diminishing one—in all parts of the popular culture establishment, on film, television, records, and radio. With the inevitable impediment of his advancing age, Astaire survived the rock-and-roll transition along with several other swing-era jazz figures who found a way to stay both in the groove and true to the wellsprings of their art. Among these survivors were Count Basie, Lionel Hampton, Buddy Rich, and Frank Sinatra. This study places Astaire in these performers' eminent company, surrounding him with the many creative individuals with jazz credentials who made specifically musical contributions to his work as a dancemaker on film, television, and records.

Music Makes Me considers the full breadth of Astaire's "camera career" as a singer and dancer on film and television, plus his work on record.[16] (Table 1 is a quick reference guide to the span of Astaire's career encompassed by this book.) The earliest example drawn upon is a 1926 record, on which Astaire sang and tapped with George Gershwin at the piano; the latest is Astaire's dance to three choruses of the twelve-bar blues on *The Dick Cavett Show* on television in 1970. I do not delve deeply into the sources of Astaire's creative persona in the early phases of his career on vaudeville, Broadway, and West End stages. Nor is this a conventional biography. Beyond Astaire's 1959 autobiography *Steps in Time,* a cluster of popular biographies from the 1970s and 1980s and Peter J. Levinson's recent *Puttin' on the Ritz: Fred Astaire and the Fine Art of Panache* (2009) all provide fairly reliable narratives of the events of Astaire's life.[17] John Mueller's extraordinary *Astaire Dancing: The Musical Films* (1985) is the essential monument of Astaire scholarship. Mueller's meticulous parsing of every dance number in every film provides uniformly detailed coverage of Astaire's cinematic output, and his introductory chapter remains the best summary of the facts of Astaire's career.[18] What I hope to add to Mueller's work, beyond integrating Astaire's television dances and recordings into the story, is a specifically musical perspective that is, inevitably, selective where Mueller's dance-oriented analysis is comprehensive.

Astaire has often been characterized as inimitable, and I have no intention of denying this. But I want to describe his uniqueness in historical rather than critical terms. Part 1—"Astaire among Others"—provides the broadest comparative context for Astaire's career. Chapter 1 places Astaire among four types of show business peers. In such varied company, Astaire's uniqueness can be seen to flow from specific industrial, social, and aesthetic contexts, extraordinary opportunities enjoyed by

TABLE I   FRED ASTAIRE'S FILM AND TELEVISION WORK DISCUSSED IN THIS BOOK

Studio-Era Films (1933–1957)

Year	Film	Studio	Music	Lyrics	Costars	Dance Collaborators
1933	Dancing Lady	MGM	Various	Various	Joan Crawford	
	Flying Down to Rio	RKO	Vincent Youmans	Edward Eliscu and Gus Kahn	Ginger Rogers	Hermes Pan
1934	The Gay Divorcee	RKO	Various	Various	Ginger Rogers	Hermes Pan
1935	Roberta	RKO	Jerome Kern	Irving Berlin	Ginger Rogers	Hermes Pan
	Top Hat	RKO	Irving Berlin	Irving Berlin	Ginger Rogers	Hermes Pan
1936	Follow the Fleet	RKO	Irving Berlin	Dorothy Fields	Ginger Rogers	Hermes Pan
	Swing Time	RKO	Jerome Kern		Ginger Rogers	Hermes Pan
1937	Shall We Dance	RKO	George Gershwin	Ira Gershwin	Ginger Rogers	Hermes Pan
	A Damsel in Distress	RKO	George Gershwin	Ira Gershwin	Joan Fontaine	Hermes Pan
1938	Carefree	RKO	Irving Berlin	Irving Berlin	Ginger Rogers	Hermes Pan
1939	The Story of Vernon and Irene Castle	RKO	Various	Various	Ginger Rogers	Hermes Pan
1940	Broadway Melody of 1940	MGM	Cole Porter	Cole Porter	Eleanor Powell	Eleanor Powell
1941	Second Chorus	Boris Morros[1]	Hal Borne, Artie Shaw, Bernie Hanighen	Johnny Mercer	Paulette Goddard	Hermes Pan
	You'll Never Get Rich	Columbia	Cole Porter	Cole Porter	Rita Hayworth	Robert Alton
1942	Holiday Inn	Paramount	Irving Berlin	Irving Berlin	Bing Crosby, Marjorie Reynolds, Virginia Dale	Danny Dare

Year	Film	Studio				
	You Were Never Lovelier	Columbia	Jerome Kern	Johnny Mercer	Rita Hayworth	Val Raset, Rita Hayworth
1943	*The Sky's the Limit*	RKO	Harold Arlen	Johnny Mercer	Joan Leslie	
1944	*Ziegfeld Follies*[2]	MGM	Various	Various	Lucille Bremer, Gene Kelly	Robert Alton, Gene Kelly
1945	*Yolanda and the Thief*	MGM	Harry Warren	Arthur Freed	Lucille Bremer	Eugene Loring
1946	*Blue Skies*	Paramount	Irving Berlin	Irving Berlin	Bing Crosby, Joan Caulfield, Olga San Juan	Hermes Pan, Dave Robel
1948	*Easter Parade*	MGM	Irving Berlin	Irving Berlin	Judy Garland	Robert Alton
1949	*The Barkleys of Broadway*	MGM	Harry Warren	Ira Gershwin	Ginger Rogers	Robert Alton, Hermes Pan ("Shoes With Wings On")
1950	*Let's Dance*	Paramount	Frank Loesser	Frank Loesser	Betty Hutton	Hermes Pan
	Three Little Words	MGM	Harry Ruby, André Previn	Burt Kalmar	Vera-Ellen	Hermes Pan
1951	*Royal Wedding*	MGM	Burton Lane	Alan Jay Lerner	Jane Powell	Nick Castle
1952	*The Belle of New York*	MGM	Harry Warren	Johnny Mercer	Vera-Ellen	Robert Alton
1953	*The Band Wagon*	MGM	Arthur Schwartz	Howard Dietz	Cyd Charisse	Michael Kidd
1955	*Daddy Long Legs*	Twentieth Century-Fox	Johnny Mercer	Johnny Mercer	Leslie Caron	David Robel, Roland Petit (on the dream ballets)

(continued)

TABLE 1 *(continued)*

			Studio-Era Films (1933–1957)			
Year	Film	Studio	Music	Lyrics	Costars	Dance Collaborators
1957	Funny Face	Paramount	George Gershwin, Roger Edens	Ira Gershwin, Leonard Gershe	Audrey Hepburn	Eugene Loring
	Silk Stockings	Arthur Freed Production[3]	Cole Porter	Cole Porter	Cyd Charisse	Hermes Pan (on Astaire's numbers), Eugene Loring (on everything else)

Television Variety Career (1958–1970); Specials Starring Astaire and Produced by Ava Productions

Title	First Aired	Rebroadcast	Sponsor	Guests
"An Evening with Fred Astaire"	17 October 1958	11 February 1959; 20 December 1964	Chrysler	Barrie Chase, Jonah Jones
"Another Evening with Fred Astaire"	4 November 1959	9 May 1960	Chrysler	Barrie Chase, Jonah Jones
"Astaire Time"	28 September 1960	20 February 1961	Chrysler	Barrie Chase, Count Basie and His Orchestra, with Joe Williams
"The Fred Astaire Show"	7 February 1968	9 February 1969	Full-service bank industry group	Barrie Chase, Young-Holt Unlimited, Sergio Mendes and Brazil '66, The Gordian Knot, Simon & Garfunkel (billed as "special guest stars")

Additional Television Appearances

Show	Date Aired	Description
"Bob Hope presents the Chrysler Theatre 'Think Pretty'"	2 October 1964	A one-hour comedy-drama ending with a dance number for Astaire and Barrie Chase
"The Hollywood Palace"	2 October 1965	Astaire dances to the music of jazz organist Jimmy Smith
"The Hollywood Palace"	22 January 1966	Astaire as dressmaker and Chase as mannequin come to life share a dance in a high-fashion dress shop
"The Hollywood Palace"	12 March 1966	Astaire sings a medley with Ethel Merman, dances a version of "Bugle Call Rag"
"The Hollywood Palace"	30 April 1966	*Dance Magazine* noted, "Fred Astaire capered with Barrie Chase in one of those dances that looked disarmingly improvised, but probably took loads of rehearsal"
"The Academy Awards Telecast"	7 April 1970	Astaire coaxed by host Bob Hope into dancing several blues choruses
"The Dick Cavett Show"	11 November 1970	Astaire interviewed about his career; ends the show dancing to several choruses of the blues

[1]Distributed by Paramount.
[2]Released 1946.
[3]Distributed by MGM.

no other figure, and personal creative sensibilities shaped by the times in which he lived and came of age as a dancemaker and musician. Astaire was an entertainer by profession, working near the center of a vibrant entertainment economy. The many performers laboring in the same commercial vineyard were doing substantially different work from Astaire. Defining his differences from his peers is a needful first step before Astaire's work can be discussed on its own terms, a task that occupies the remainder of the book. Astaire was a popular entertainer, and chapter 2 defines the product he sold and how he made it. Astaire worked within a popular music culture that relied on songs, originating as sheet music and presented to the public in a variety of routined forms. From Astaire's position in Hollywood, the entertainment industry was a realm where songs both old and new were sold by professionals with distinctive, personal styles who were eager to please their audiences and keep them wanting more. In an interview with Joseph McBride in 1981, Astaire described his life's work as "trying to make a buck and make it look good and knock a lot of people on their ass in the aisle."[19] Chapter 2 considers in general terms how he went about doing this, looking briefly at Astaire's relationships with the songwriters who wrote specifically for him and his collaborative work with several kinds of show business professionals who assisted him in routing songs for film, television, and records. Astaire's primary creative focus on making musical numbers, rather than musical films, is laid out in chapter 2 as well.

Part 2—chapters 3, 4, and 5—locates Astaire as maker of musical numbers within the studio-era production system. Connections to popular music and jazz prove important wherever one looks. Films set against jazz-friendly backgrounds outnumber those in theatrical contexts. Jazz bands, real and imagined, play a major role both in front of the camera and behind the scenes. Draft scripts contain clues to how musical style was understood by Astaire's screenwriters. And music department archives reveal the extent to which the arrangements and orchestrations for Astaire's routines drew upon popular music and jazz trends and talent. Hollywood was never deaf to popular music. There was tremendous overlap between popular music and the film musical. Indeed, it is nearly impossible to understand what is happening *musically* in an Astaire number without situating the number within a specific historical popular music context.

Part 3 contains four chapters, each taking up a different pattern or theme in Astaire's output relating to jazz and popular music. Chapter 6 looks at Astaire the maker of partner dances. Links between Astaire and his various partners in the idealized realm of the film musical and real-life couples in actual American ballrooms are explored through the named dances Astaire frequently introduced in his films. Named dances were intertextual by design, intended to translate beyond the screen. By looking behind and around the screen image, we can gain a sense of how Astaire tried, often with little success, to insert himself into the realm of social dance. In 1952, Astaire remarked that "jazz means the blues," and chapter 7 explores this comment in practical terms by detailing Astaire's varied use of the twelve-bar blues progression as a musical scaffold for dance making. All the important popular blues-based idioms turn up in Astaire's work, from boogie-woogie and swing blues (use of the blues progression by big bands) to 1950s rock and roll and 1960s soul jazz. Chapter 8 analyzes three idiosyncratic routines from the late forties, a period of aesthetic and commercial uncertainty in popular music, jazz, and the film musical alike. Insights from production documents and close analysis of musical and choreographic content reveal how these three routines express Astaire's creative sensibilities with particular sharpness. This triptych also demonstrates his ability to work without the formal "net" of conventional song forms. Chapter 9 moves to questions of casting and content by examining Astaire's film and television routines made in partnership with African American musicians. I read this substantial body of work as an ongoing project in Astaire's creative life, placing five representative examples in historical context. Spanning more than a thirty-year period, these dances trace not only Astaire's ongoing engagement with black jazz and popular musicians, but also the changing possibilities for interracial performance on big and small screen alike. While each can be read on its own, the chapters in part 3 are ordered with a purpose. Details and references accumulate from chapter to chapter, with the last in the group—chapter 9, concerning Astaire's work with African American musicians—offering the broadest perspective on the span of American life covered in this book. In all four, close analysis of musical, choreographic, and visual content helps bring out a pattern of bright threads tying Astaire to jazz and popular music. The book concludes with a portrait of Astaire as sideman, surveying select recordings made with jazz musicians that put Astaire as both dancer and singer into thoroughgoing jazz contexts.

Many books have been written about Astaire, and many of his collaborators, friends, and admirers have been interviewed. Interviews can provide much in the way of useful information, but memories of the past are not the same as evidence from the past. As far as possible, my conclusions are grounded in sources from the period: studio production files, musical scores, correspondence, and contemporary print media. These sources afford a fresh look behind the scenes at the Hollywood studios where Astaire did his creative work. By putting musical, cinematic, and production matters of a sometimes technical nature at the center of my story, I have endeavored to reconstruct as fully as possible the process behind Astaire's work, gaining some measure of access to his closely guarded rehearsal studio. In this way, I hope to place Astaire's body of work in a rich historical context that reveals the inevitably intertwined industrial, social, and aesthetic origins of his singular contribution to American popular culture from the 1930s to the 1960s.

Along the way, Astaire's engagement with varied jazzmakers suggests an inclusive view of the music, one that brings jazz into the too often separately told histories of popular music, the film musical, and variety television. I view these narratives as one big story, a tale with much to say about how American artists worked out the complexities of race relations in the twentieth century in the creative realm of commercial popular culture. Astaire's creative life forms an important chapter in that larger story, and it is my hope that any reader with an interest in how the process of racial reconciliation played out in American popular culture will find something of value in the story of Fred Astaire told here.

PART ONE

Astaire among Others

CHAPTER I

"There's a difference and Astaire is it"

He's distinctly likeable on the screen, the mike is kind to his
voice and as a dancer he remains in a class by himself. . . .
There's a difference and Astaire is it.
—*Variety*'s review of *Flying Down to Rio* (1933)

Fred Astaire was incomparable. There's no more succinct way to describe him or his career. He arrived in Hollywood an established Broadway star and almost immediately became a legend, movie business jar-
gon for an irreplaceable screen presence with indefinable magic. It didn't
hurt that Astaire did something no one else was doing in any comparable way: he danced. Astaire stayed at or near the top for a quarter century, never dropping off the radar entirely or experiencing a genuine
slump. The critics generally adored him and he was admired by men and
women alike (not an easy feat, especially for a dancing man).[1] When the
studio system collapsed and the film musical as Astaire had known it
folded, he transitioned seamlessly onto television for a final decade of
successful song and dance. He danced on camera into his seventies.

Astaire's path as dancer, singer, movie star and icon is incomparable.
Still, comparisons need to be made, if only to understand exactly how
Astaire managed to carve out and sustain a uniquely empowered position as a dancer and dancemaker on film, television, and records, the
signature creative media of the twentieth century. Astaire didn't work in
a vacuum, and this chapter begins the work of surrounding Astaire with
a creative context by considering his peers in four categories: dancing
leading men, singing leading men, tap dancers, and musicians. The first
three situate Astaire in the Hollywood film industry; the fourth inserts
him into the realm of popular music, specifically among jazz musicians

of the swing era. That Astaire finds a meaningful place in each of these categories testifies to the breadth of his talents. And yet, in the entertainment industry as Astaire knew it, the musical content of these four areas might easily overlap. Astaire's uniqueness lies in his historic ability to be, at once, dancer, singer, tapper, and musician.

This context-setting chapter explores large patterns, using synoptic views of the careers of select entertainers as the unit of comparison. Subsequent chapters descend to a greater level of detail.

DANCING LEADING MEN

Variety's review of *Roberta* (1935) saw Astaire's ascending star as potentially opening a bold new world for dancers. After noting that Astaire was adept at "light comedy," which might come in handy if his audiences "ever tire of the stepping," the reviewer looked toward the future: "Meanwhile [Astaire] can consider himself a Christopher Columbus who has discovered for the boys and girls on the hoof a new world—Hollywood. There are other dancers around who can troupe as well as dance, and now that Astaire has led the way, they may follow."[2] *Variety*'s prediction proved off the mark: movie audiences never tired of Astaire's "stepping," and he had almost no followers. With the exception of Gene Kelly, no male film star made much of a mark as a dancing leading man. Several male stars took on dancing lead roles, but all, including Kelly, appeared in both musicals and nonmusical genres. No other male star hung his entire reputation on the musical the way that Astaire did. And he never stopped making pictures. When Astaire as Tony Hunter in *The Band Wagon* (1953) says he "hasn't made a picture in three years," it's a line that distances Astaire from the character he's playing. In the three years before *The Band Wagon*, no fewer than four films starring Astaire hit the nation's theaters; all but *The Belle of New York* met with success at the box office. Between his screen debut in the early 1930s and the general drop-off in musical pictures in the mid-1950s, Astaire never went more than seventeen months between the release of his pictures (that includes his supposed retirement between *Blue Skies* and *Easter Parade*) except for a two-year gap caused by World War II and Metro's tardy release of *Ziegfeld Follies*. Over the full length of his studio career—between 1933 and 1957—a new Astaire musical premiered on average every nine or ten months. Relentless filmmaking over the course of decades was not unusual for a studio-era star. It was, however, unheard of for a musical star. Most strictly musical stars lasted about a decade, then either stopped making movies (Al Jolson, Alice Faye, Ruby Keeler) or extended their careers by switching to nonmusical genres (Dick Powell's transformation from boy singer to noir detective). The search for Astaire's peers in the dancing leading man category yields a short list of short careers and modest filmographies: George Murphy, James Cagney, George Raft, Ricardo Montalban, Gower Champion, and Gene Kelly. The screen-dancing careers of these six men are briefly considered here as a means to define both Astaire's unique place within the Hollywood system and his supremely good historical timing.

A not overly talented but always game guy, George Murphy was a 1930s peer of Astaire's. Murphy could sing and dance passably well. (Metro director Charles Walters said, "I couldn't stand the way [he] danced.")[3] Musicals never dominated Murphy's career; MGM mixed in dramatic and comic roles for him from the start. And despite appearing in a fair number of musicals, Murphy never had a well-defined song-and-dance identity. He could keep up with real dancers, like Astaire and Eleanor Powell in *Broadway Melody of 1940*, but his career never depended on his doing so. Murphy later claimed to have taken a creative leadership role on the set, but there's no distinctive mark to his work.[4] The ideal contract player, Murphy played the role of the requisite male who danced a bit when required to do so. He was not a creative force in musical production.

Murphy's willingness to let Metro shape his less than distinctive persona contrasts strongly with Warner Brothers' James Cagney, whose reputation as a dancing star rests on his Oscar-winning performance as George M. Cohan in *Yankee Doodle Dandy* (1942). Cagney came to Hollywood in 1930, just a few years before Astaire. The two were friends, and Cagney was on the set the day Astaire committed "Top Hat, White Tie and Tails" to film. Despite his roots in vaudeville as a song-and-dance man, only four of Cagney's fifty-seven studio-era films were musicals in which Cagney danced two or more numbers.[5] Musicals are time-consuming and expensive to make. Cagney could turn out three gangster films in the time it took Astaire to complete one musical. Warner Brothers knew where the profits from their star lay, so musicals appear infrequently in Cagney's filmography, which is dominated by his tough-guy persona applied to both comedies and dramas. And yet Cagney did have a distinctive song-and-dance style. Like Astaire, Cagney was responsible for his own choreography, although it hardly seems to matter, as he performs similar straight-legged, bent-at-the-waist moves in all his musical pictures. And so, despite having his own way with the dance,

Cagney did not create a series of musical numbers that can be evaluated as a group (beyond their sameness). There is no body of musical work to set beside Cagney's gallery of film characters, just as Astaire doesn't have a gallery of film characters to set beside his anthology of musical numbers. Cagney struggled to exercise control over the parts he played, in the late thirties going so far as to break his Warner's contract and set up an independent production company. (The first film he made on his own was the 1937 musical *Something to Sing About*.) But Cagney soon returned to Warner's, with only modest control gained over his career, such as a limit of two pictures per year.[6] Astaire was never forced to play a role he didn't want to play.

The only dancing leading man to attempt serious partner routines in the 1930s was George Raft, Paramount's resident tough guy. Astaire remembered Raft as "the fastest dancer . . . I've ever seen, doing the Charleston in his solo act at Texas Guinan's night club" in Prohibition-era New York.[7] Raft danced himself out of poverty in the 1910s and '20s, winning dance contests and working in tearooms partnering women for pay. Astaire, of course, was the toast of Broadway and the West End in these years. Graduating to nightclub and vaudeville specialties, Raft described his dancing in the 1920s as "very erotic. I used to caress myself as I danced."[8] He brought this dangerous sexual style to film when he went to Hollywood in 1931, his arrival, like Cagney's, just a few years prior to Astaire's. Raft never made a musical. Instead he played hardened underworld characters who also happened to dance. Raft's big breakthrough was *Scarface* (1932), in which he did not play a dancer and resisted the danced come-on of a brunette in a long, clinging gown who does a tap lick that calls to mind Ginger Rogers. Seen today, the shadow of Astaire and Rogers hovers over the encounter. Raft didn't sing or tap, and some of the long shots of lifts in his dances were doubled. He often wore a top hat, white tie, and tails, but he projected a cold, threatening persona as slick as his shiny "patent leather" hair. His dancing characters hailed from the lower classes—scam artists and gigolos who sometimes died in the final reel.

Raft danced opposite Carole Lombard in two films released just as Astaire and Rogers were getting going; *Bolero* (1934) and *Rumba* (1935) are penumbral companions to the sunny silliness of *The Gay Divorcee* and *Top Hat*. If Astaire and Rogers were destined always to fall into each other's arms, Raft and Lombard were mismatched by fate and doomed to separation. Their dances are always desperate. Raft's dances were often deeply integrated into the plots of his films. In *Bolero* he stops dancing in the middle of the title routine to announce to the on-screen audience his intention to join the army. In *Rumba* the big number with Lombard is danced under the threat of a mob hit man shooting Raft down midroutine. The generic focus of Raft's films remains firmly on the story, even during the dances. By contrast, Astaire's dances are always the primary reason for his films; the plot remains secondary, a necessary "hanger" for the musical numbers.[9] Astaire was a dancer, first and foremost; Raft, only secondarily. But whatever their differences, Raft and Astaire alike embodied the unassailable masculinity of the dancing man who lived his life in nightclubs, dressed with consummate taste, and listened to jazz. Raft's 1930s films both counter and corroborate Astaire's more familiar output from the decade.

Like Murphy in black-and-white MGM musicals of the 1930s and early '40s, Ricardo Montalban was the necessary man for a diverse group of women in Technicolor musicals of the late 1940s and early '50s. Color was a major draw in the immediate postwar era, and exotic locations and characters were favored by MGM, Montalban's home studio. His Latin lovers display tremendous physical confidence, his dancing presented as the natural expression of a Latin man's desire for a woman. This persona proved remarkably flexible, and Montalban's range of partners was diverse. In *On an Island with You* (1948) he played a dancer in love with Esther Williams, herself falling for an ardent Navy pilot played by Peter Lawford. Cyd Charisse, in turn, loves Montalban. After Charisse and Montalban rehearse an Apache dance for a bad girl and a sailor, Montalban finds his desire for Charisse awakened. They end the routine in a kiss that continues after the lights come up. This dance (created by Jack Donohue) sets a precedent for Charisse's later tough-girl dances with Kelly in *Singin' in the Rain* (1952) and Astaire in *The Band Wagon*, but its choreographic content is more technical than either. Indeed, Montalban executes demanding lifts unlike any that Kelly, much less Astaire, ever did.

Montalban's ethnically grounded dancing persona was subtle, as demonstrated by a pair of films from the early 1950s in which he starred opposite very different leading ladies. In the nostalgic period film *Two Weeks with Love* (1950), with Jane Powell in her last adolescent role, Montalban is all chivalry. He appears in full operetta regalia for a waltz in one of Powell's girlish dreams and initiates her into womanhood in a safely chaperoned tango. In *Latin Lovers* (1953), a contemporary story with Lana Turner as his love interest, Montalban exudes a more adult sexuality. The film's setting on a Brazilian ranch provides plentiful opportunities for passionate embraces and hungry kisses. At a dance in the open air, Montalban teaches Turner the samba and other "native" dances. The music, arranged by jazz arranger Pete Rugolo, captures early 1950s Latin dance trends in the United States. Montalban and Turner's dances were created by Frank Veloz, of Veloz and Yolanda, the most famous Latin ballroom team of the era. (Similar links to popular music and dance are shared by Astaire's work in the same period, but in decidedly less sensual modes.)

Fiesta (1947), Montalban's first leading role in Hollywood, suggests Metro started out shaping his star persona in expansive terms, presenting him as a sensitive leading man who was more than just a Latin lover. Montalban plays the son of a legendary Mexican bullfighter who does not want to follow in his father's footsteps. Instead, he hopes to attend the national conservatory and become a great composer, expressing the soul of his country in classical music. Getting the father to acquiesce to the son's desires forms the substance of *Fiesta*'s plot. The musical climax occurs when Montalban, fleeing both father and music, comes upon a live radio broadcast of his only orchestral work being performed by the Mexican national symphony. (Such things happen in Hollywood films: it's useless to shake one's head at them. How such coincidences create character and inflect the meaning of music making in a film narrative is, however, well worth exploring.) Montalban hears the broadcast in a restaurant. He moves slowly to a nearby piano, seating himself at the keyboard in time to play along with the broadcast. The camera stays on Montalban at the piano in a medium shot for a long time; the entire keyboard is visible. Montalban is not heard on the soundtrack—which features a young André Previn—but he gives an exceedingly convincing visual performance of the virtuoso piece, an arrangement by MGM music director Johnny Green of Aaron Copland's *El Salon Mexico* as a piano concerto. (Astaire worked closely with both Previn and Green around this time.) Montalban has visually authentic piano skills and the sound/image illusion—an elaborate technical confection—works to good effect. Here, then, is a screen hero who dances, plays piano, and fights bulls, all packaged with an exotic masculinity and a movie-star handsome face and physique (something Astaire never had going for him).

Montalban's convincing turn in the ring for the boxing picture *Right Cross* (1950) was exactly contemporary with his work in musicals. As with Gene Kelly around the same time, MGM explored the link between action films and musicals by casting physically strong leading men in both genres. (The physically slight Astaire wasn't built for this genre-crossing strategy.) Montalban was equally at home in the water, partnering Williams in two of her "swimmers," *On an Island with You* and *Neptune's Daughter* (1949). In the latter Montalban sings as well, courting Williams on dry land in exactly the manner Astaire had pioneered: first a song, then a dance. Their dance duet in formal wear to "My Heart Beats Faster" is as close as the 1950s came to re-creating the 1930s equation of contemporary song and dance with sexual foreplay pioneered by Astaire and Rogers. Montalban is completely convincing in the part.

The multitalented Montalban filled a particular Hollywood niche at a particular moment, and Metro, a star-making studio, was able to make him into a versatile dancing leading man. When the moment passed, Montalban's career in musicals ended. The essential element lacking in Montalban's case, beyond simple longevity, is self-starting creative work as either dancer or musician. Montalban was always taking direction. It is impossible to speak of him as a creative figure. He is a performer playing roles assigned by the studio, learning dances from others, pretending to play a piano part ghosted by someone else. Astaire danced and played pianos as well, but always under the audience assumption that the creative work was authentically his.

Only two male dancers doing their own choreography attained anything close to Astaire's creative position as a dancing leading man capable of putting a mark on their films. Both were a generation younger than Astaire, grew up in very different music and dance contexts, and had quite different opportunities as dancers. Yet Gene Kelly (born in 1912) and Gower Champion (born in 1919) must be read beside Astaire in any account of Astaire's Hollywood peers. They provide needed contrast, if only because Kelly and Champion were more like each other than either was like Astaire. Narrative and character, rather than music, made Kelly and Champion dance. For both, this concern for narrative and character expressed in dance led to a desire for control over the entire film (or stage) musical product. Kelly and Champion both aspired to direct, extending their creative energies and time beyond the making of musical numbers. By contrast, Astaire's interests stayed within the bounds of his own numbers and, to a large extent, his own body. His creative ambitions were, by comparison with Kelly and Champion, narrower in both focus and scale. Historical circumstances also played a role in setting Astaire off from Kelly and Champion. In different ways, Kelly and Champion were somewhat out of sync with the historical trajectory of the musical as a genre. Astaire, out of sheer luck and a propensity to stay close to the musical side of things, was remarkably in sync with historical trends from the beginning to the end of his long career.

Gower Champion, like Astaire, was a largely self-taught, self-choreographing dancer who came to Hollywood after gaining renown in live performance venues—in Champion's case, nightclubs and early television.[10] At the height of Astaire and Rogers's mid-1930s fame, Champion and his partner Jeanne Tyler were a leading exhibition ball-room dance couple, still in their teens and all the rage in New York nightclubs. After the war, MGM signed Champion on his own. He part-nered Charisse in a specialty in *Till the Clouds Roll By* (1947), but laughter at his performance during a preview showing led to Champi-on's only number being reduced to thirty seconds of screen time. Dem-onstrating his professed ambivalence toward the studio system, Cham-pion promptly bought out his Metro contract and left Hollywood. He teamed with and married Marge Belcher, and in 1949 the Champions achieved television fame on *The Admiral Broadway Revue* (later *Your Show of Shows*). For each of sixteen weeks, Champion created an origi-nal partner dance, performing it live on television with Marge. The new national phenomenon of television launched the Champions, landing them on the cover of *Life*. Soon Metro was calling, and Champion re-turned to Hollywood, this time part of a team. Marge, who had played supporting film roles in the 1940s, turned down Louis B. Mayer's offer to play the female lead opposite Kelly in *An American in Paris* (1951). The Champions would succeed or fail as a couple. Gower's insistence on dancing with Marge contrasts sharply with Astaire, who was frus-trated by having a steady partner in Rogers in the 1930s and relished dancing with different partners in the 1940s and '50s. The Champions played second-couple roles in *Show Boat* (1951) and *Lovely to Look At* (1952). Their first chance to play the leads, *Everything I Have Is Yours* (1952), was a box office failure despite Gower's creative dances, which used the resources of film inventively. Evidently with little room to grow at Metro, they returned to television, where Ed Sullivan fea-tured the team for a full hour in June 1953. A critical and popular hit, the telecast predictably rekindled MGM's interest, so the Champions returned to Hollywood for three more musicals before the genre died.

Always reluctant to commit himself entirely to Hollywood, Cham-pion faced two challenges in leaving his mark on the film musical: the genre was suffering a slow death when he showed up in the early 1950s, and he never earned the genuine movie-star credentials that translated into power on the lot. Champion tried to (and did) create innovative cinematic numbers, but he never enjoyed a major hit film. His stature within the system, despite national fame on television, was never secure. Champion never got control of the admittedly tottering system in Hollywood in the 1950s. Control was exactly what he did secure in the 1960s on Broadway, where Champion flourished as a powerful director-choreographer, creating such landmark shows as *Bye Bye Birdie* (1960), *Hello, Dolly!* (1964), and *42nd Street* (1980).

When seen against Champion's on-again, off-again Hollywood career, the felicity of Astaire's timing is apparent. When Astaire first arrived in Hollywood, the studios were in the business of making stars for the still-new sound film format. When Champion showed up, the remaining musical stars were competing for increasingly limited opportunities in a genre and industry fighting for survival. With no competition from any other audiovisual medium and as the primary asset of RKO, a small major studio with money troubles, Astaire was able to leverage early box office success into enduring control over his dances and films. Champion was without patron or position at Metro, a studio confronting the paired problems of excess capacity and a shrinking market for its signature expensive product. And Astaire was a more charismatic and well-rounded performer than Champion, whose singing voice had to be dubbed (which was extremely unusual for a male musical film star). Champion's truncated Hollywood career leaves him as more a potential than an actual dancing leading man.

Astaire and Champion also differed fundamentally in their approach to dancing and dance making. Champion combined partner work and passable light acting with a Kelly-like athleticism. He almost never tapped; it wasn't part of his toolkit. Champion had no connection to jazz music or musicians. His dances were conceived as stories, with narratives complex enough to require spoken monologues in some cases. Champion favored film dances that exploited complicated sets in complex, story-related ways. See the dance on the street from *Everything I Have Is Yours* or the apartment sequence from *Three for the Show* (1955). Both engage with their respective sets in a manner unlike anything Astaire or Kelly, who favored big empty spaces, ever attempted.

Gene Kelly is the only Hollywood dancing leading man besides Astaire to assemble a body of musical films on which he was also a primary creative force. But Kelly is Astaire's peer in a limited sense only, as an overview of Kelly's career makes plain.[11] If Champion's timing was off, Kelly's was spot on, at least for his first decade in Hollywood. He arrived just before the historic mid-1940s peak in American movie attendance, a time when the studios were still in the business of making stars, color was becoming standard for musicals, and MGM was expanding its production of musicals, risking the future viability of the studio on the genre. These conditions did not last and, as a result, historical circumstances did much to curtail Kelly's Hollywood career.

Kelly's Broadway and Hollywood careers alike were characterized by brilliant bursts of energy, fundamentally different from Astaire's sustained success in both realms. On Broadway, Kelly progressed from chorus boy (*Leave It to Me,* 1938) to leading man (*Pal Joey,* 1940) in two short years. He went directly to MGM in 1942 under the sponsorship of Judy Garland, an established star. Within two years Kelly had used a loan-out to Columbia for *Cover Girl* to demonstrate his ability to create innovative cinematic dances that were entertaining on their own merits and integrated in dramatic terms to a remarkable degree. (Loanouts permitted a star under contract at one studio to appear in films at another.) Columbia gave Kelly his first chance to direct, and the success of his special effects–driven alter ego number helped convince Metro to give Kelly ever greater control, up to and including codirector credit on his films—almost unprecedented for a studio-era star. Kelly's shared director credits with Stanley Donen mark the reticence of the system to give any performer complete control over a film.[12] Astaire never asked for more screen credit than star billing: his name above the title. Kelly's unusual opportunity to direct himself was also due to his close connection to Arthur Freed (one of three musical producers at Metro), the special skills required by the musical as a genre, and Kelly's own passionate advocacy of his ideas (such as shooting the opening sequence of *On the Town* on location). Giving Kelly so much creative control proved a mixed blessing for MGM. He brought critical acclaim to the studio with multiple Oscars for *An American in Paris,* but recurring expensive flops— *The Pirate* (1948) and *Invitation to the Dance* (released in 1956)—suggest Kelly's creative instincts and agenda were not particularly commercial. Astaire always thought in commercial terms when making his dances, and popular music and dance trends served as a consistent reference point for his creative work entertaining his movie audience.

Kelly's early connection with Garland and the missed profits from his hit film on loan-out to Columbia installed the big new talent at MGM for the remainder of his studio career. His work is intimately tied to the specific creative environment at Metro and must be understood as the product of this particular Hollywood hothouse. Metro gave him a lot of work to do, and not just in musicals. MGM turned out as much

Kelly product as possible. Like Ginger Rogers at RKO in the 1930s, Kelly, after completing a musical, was dispatched to play leading roles in nonmusical films. Freed's pull was never used to exempt Kelly from dramatic assignments, and the studio developed Kelly's star persona in a continuous fashion across musical and nonmusical genres. His first two films for Metro—the musical *For Me and My Gal* (1942) and the war film *Pilot #5* (1943)—cast Kelly in remarkably similar roles: cocksure, ambitious, ultimately sympathetic men who learn the hard way that honor requires sacrifice to a higher good. Kelly's natural intensity made him a good fit for the moralistic stories of the war years. On either side of wartime service as a filmmaker for the Naval Air Forces, Kelly played a sailor in *Anchors Aweigh* (1945) and a returning soldier in *Living in a Big Way* (1947), a topical drama about hasty wartime marriages and the national housing shortage. Three musical sequences were added to *Living in a Big Way* after the dramatic scenes had been completed, making the film a revealing hybrid joining the generic ground Kelly occupied at MGM. Kelly closed out the 1940s with two period pieces: the troubled *The Pirate* and the successful adventure flick *The Three Musketeers* (both 1948). These patterns of work continued into the 1950s: successful musicals (*On the Town*, 1949; *Singin' in the Rain*, 1952), unsuccessful musicals (*It's Always Fair Weather*, 1955; *Invitation to the Dance*), and topical action dramas (*Black Hand*, 1950; *The Devil Makes Three*, 1952).

Kelly was a tremendously valuable commodity for Metro: a hard worker, flexible generically, a creative figure with stature (but perhaps lacking commercial judgment), and that rarest of Hollywood figures, a dancing leading man able to stand beside Astaire, who was regathered into the Metro fold in the late 1940s (ironically as a result of Kelly's pulling out of *Easter Parade* due to an injury sustained playing volleyball on his day off). But Kelly's interests and time were divided many times over. It's hard to imagine Kelly ever saying, "I just dance," as Astaire did at the end of his autobiography. Kelly wanted to do a lot more than dance: Astaire never really did (except perhaps for his lingering desire to write hit songs). In dramas, Kelly's physical presence was tremendously expressive; his minimalist acting in dramatic roles, restrained line readings, and almost boyish physical beauty fit into Hollywood trends producing a new sort of leading man of the Marlon Brando, Montgomery Clift, James Dean variety. It isn't hard to imagine Kelly succeeding as a movie star without dancing a step. Looked at in its totality, Kelly's screen career bears little resemblance to Astaire's focused work in a single genre done at many different studios.

Indeed, no dancing leading man matched Astaire's longevity, singular connection to the musical, consistent box office appeal, and variety of studio working environments. Astaire was able to do his thing—as a creator of dances and as a performer—in many different creative contexts. He worked all over town, at virtually all the musical-making studios, large and small. This, in itself, was unusual in the studio era, when star personas and bodies of work were typically attached to a particular studio's house style. After leaving RKO in 1939, Astaire was never again technically a contract star. Virtually all his subsequent films were made under one or two film contracts. This gave Astaire maximum flexibility and also made him a viable option for casting at most any studio. He could go from a lavish Metro musical teamed with dancer Eleanor Powell to a low-budget, independently produced film that allowed him to work with bandleader Artie Shaw. He could make chronologically overlapping pairs of films with Rita Hayworth at Columbia and Bing Crosby at Paramount without the complication of being loaned out from a home studio. And at a time when stars like Cagney, Bette Davis, and Olivia de Havilland were struggling for greater say over the parts they played, Astaire was allowed by MGM to walk out of a three-film contract in 1946 only to be welcomed back on his own terms two years later (when the studio needed him for *Easter Parade*).

This is not to suggest that Astaire was the only freelancer in the early 1940s: other leading stars moved from studio to studio (such as Cary Grant and Barbara Stanwyck, who both managed to sign nonexclusive contracts with more than one studio). But Astaire was the only *musical* star to move so freely from studio to studio in this period. After the war, independent production and freelance status was an increasingly common choice for several major stars. None worked in the musical, a genre whose production processes worked against independent production. The musical was an intensely studio-bound genre. Astaire gained unprecedented control at RKO in the 1930s and enjoyed great freedom to move from studio to studio in the 1940s and '50s. The studios all recognized that Astaire's dances were the product of his own creative energies. If he was uninterested in a project, there was no way to force him to make it. No one just handed him a script: Astaire had to make the musical numbers, the scenes that counted. In this concrete creative sense, as a dancing leading man Astaire brought more to the filmmaking process than the average movie star. And what he brought, again and again, was a connection to popular music and jazz. None of the six dancing leading men profiled above shared Astaire's animating interest in jazz music and dance. In that, too, he was incomparable.

SINGING LEADING MEN

Unlike Murphy, Cagney, Raft, Montalban, Champion, and Kelly, Astaire was also a popular singer who worked in the medium of popular records across his career. For this reason, Astaire can be fruitfully compared to other popular singers active in film and, later, television. Setting aside the dancing that was always central to Astaire's film persona, were there any singing leading men whose careers paralleled Astaire's?

Al Jolson was the breakthrough figure in musical film, and like Astaire, Jolson made the transition from Broadway to Hollywood star. But Jolson failed to hold the screen after the novelty of synchronized sound wore off. His film career was essentially over by the time Astaire arrived in Hollywood. And Jolson's film career didn't survive in popular memory either. The earliest sound films—Jolson's prominent among them—did not get replayed on television. Astaire's did. Just before his death in 1950, Jolson enjoyed a final burst of popularity. The twin biopics *The Jolson Story* (1946) and *Jolson Sings Again* (1949) initiated a late-career surge of interest in Jolson and were pillars of the postwar color film nostalgia cycle in which Astaire participated to a limited extent. Unlike Jolson, Astaire never tried to re-create his past and resisted the idea of any film telling his life story. Looking back was foreign to his sensibilities, which were always focused squarely on the present. Astaire continually adjusted his performance style to music and dance trends while Jolson rigidly sold the same personality-driven product.

Astaire never worked with Jolson, but he collaborated repeatedly on film, radio, and records with Bing Crosby, a close peer in the singing leading man category. Crosby and Astaire were remarkably similar contemporaries in several respects: unlikely leading men in the looks department, both introduced new songs and always got the girl. When they worked together Crosby got the girl, a home studio advantage. But Crosby was always a much bigger star than Astaire. Indeed, it is hard to overestimate Crosby's screen presence from the early 1930s to the late 1950s, exactly the period Astaire was active. Crosby helped define the Paramount musical as a comedy with songs, films with modest production values that could be made quickly with a minimum of rehearsal and a short shooting schedule for the very busy Bing.[13] Crosby's career strategy prefigured that of a later popular music star: Elvis Presley. Crosby's forty-seven studio-era feature films made from 1932 to 1956 are in every way comparable to the thirty-one movies Presley made between 1956 and 1969. Crosby's *Waikiki Wedding* (1937), with its hit song "Sweet Leilani," and Presley's *Blue Hawaii* (1961), with its title tune, mark pop culture journeys to the same destination for similarly short stays. Both personality and song-driven cycles were consistently successful (or broke even) at the box office in their time, even if most of the individual films come off as forgettable today. (Crosby successfully explored a vastly greater range of film roles and genres than Presley was ever allowed to attempt.) Crosby and Elvis's constant, even excessive output moderated the importance of any single project. With so much product going out, no single film could sink either series. Both singers used their feature films to bolster a larger public presence. Crosby and Presley's films were by definition intertextual, with radio appearances or radio play intended to move the viewer into the movie theater and the new songs heard in the film segueing into purchases at the music shop or record store.

Astaire, by contrast, viewed his films (and the routines within them) as the primary locus of his creative work. Recordings were a sideline. Astaire even cut short his successful weekly radio program in its second season when the show began to interfere with the preparation of dances for his films (see figure 1). Such a move would have been inimical to Crosby's entire career strategy, an absurd curtailing of the singer's audience-reaching potential. But dropping his national radio audience never fazed Astaire, who chose instead to focus his intense work ethic on special moments, creating a limited output of high-quality musical numbers hosted by feature films in which he also played the leading man. In an era when the only place moving pictures could be seen was in a movie theater, scarcity was the keynote of Astaire's career. By contrast, Crosby flooded the market, leveraging his aversion to rehearsal and easygoing style into a tremendous volume of product disseminated on screen, radio, and records. And Crosby's efforts bore fruit. He was, for close to two decades, among the top stars of popular music, radio, and film.[14] Astaire never achieved Crosby's level of fame, but key to both men's enduring success was constant labor in the entertainment marketplace: they took few if any breaks, establishing a rhythm of new work that could be relied upon by the public and the large corporate entities presenting them to the public. Taking different tacks toward sustaining their careers, Astaire and Crosby alike enjoyed extraordinary

FIGURE I. Astaire danced on the radio—and on the cover of this radio listings guide from 1937—before dropping his high-rated variety show in favor of time spent working on his films.

longevity, sharing recording sessions and television specials into the 1970s.

Frank Sinatra may seem an unlikely peer of Astaire's. The two men never worked together, although Sinatra turned several songs written for Astaire into signature tunes of his own, "Night and Day" and "One for My Baby (and One More for the Road)" chief among them. Nor were the two men peers in terms of age: Sinatra was sixteen years younger than Astaire. Like Crosby, Sinatra's Hollywood career spanned the generic spectrum, from musicals to adult-oriented comedies to dramas, and Sinatra's masculine musical persona was easily dropped into almost any generic context (again, similar to Crosby).[15] Astaire, by contrast, was bound to the musical—no other genre permitted dancing—and when the genre disappeared, so did Astaire's place as a singing leading man.

In the 1960s, Astaire repeatedly said he esteemed Sinatra above all others on the current entertainment scene. Astaire likely recognized an affinity with Sinatra that had less to do with the movies and more to do with Sinatra's similar approach to creativity, rootedness in a musical style identifiable as swing, and impatience with revisiting the past. Pianist Lou Levy said of Sinatra, "He's a swing era guy."[16] Astaire was too. And although they entered the story at different points—Astaire in the 1920s, Sinatra in the late 1930s—both remained rooted in a swing-derived rhythmic sensibility even after popular music changed around them. Shared values that both brought to the art of singing popular songs include intelligible delivery of lyrics, commitment to the melody as written, and understated, personal approaches to phrasing. These aesthetic priorities didn't preclude some tentative forays into rock and roll, and both tested the waters in the mid-1950s in remarkably similar ways. Compare Sinatra's "Two Hearts, Two Kisses (Make One Love)" (1955) to Astaire's "The Ritz Roll and Rock" (1957). Like Astaire, Sinatra continually revised his approach and had little interest in re-creating past work. Sinatra biographer Will Friedwald noted, "It's quite beyond Sinatra to fathom why anybody would be sentimentally attached or even interested in his old recordings."[17] Astaire expressed similar sentiments many times. He, too, was mystified that anyone still watched or discussed his past work. The nostalgic impulse was foreign to both men.

Like Astaire, Sinatra took a hands-on approach to creating his own signature products: in Sinatra's case, recordings. From the mid-1950s forward, Sinatra took particular care shaping his recorded work, assembling a group of collaborators—songwriters, arrangers, and musicians—to make a series of concept albums that topped the charts, garnered critical acclaim, and brought swing-era songs, musicianship, and entertainment values into a contemporary idiom.[18] As purveyors of both old and new popular songs in a personal style, Sinatra and Astaire alike recognized the impact arrangers and orchestrators could have on an audience's immediate understanding of a given number's intentions. Both combined this awareness with control over the means of production, the power to choose who would arrange for them and to accept or reject individual arrangements. In Astaire's case, the resources and reach of the studio system were put entirely in his hands. In Sinatra's case, the desire for full creative control led to the actual ownership of a record label (Reprise in the 1960s), although he usually worked for well-capitalized major labels that, like the film studios in Astaire's case, got out of Sinatra's way creatively because of his consistently good return on investment. Unlike Astaire, who was in charge of his creative work from almost the very start of his film career, the early phases of Sinatra's career—his years with Tommy Dorsey and while at Columbia Records—involved some struggle against creative limitations put in place by corporate powers who wanted to shape Sinatra's output. The analogy between Sinatra and Astaire's working conditions and level of control is most fully realized in Sinatra's early 1950s comeback at Capitol Records and after, yet another example of how unusual Astaire's consistent control across his entire career was.

HOLLYWOOD TAP DANCERS

Astaire's talents were so broad that he can be put within yet a third category of peers: Hollywood tap dancers. The list is short and almost impossibly diverse: Eleanor Powell, Bill "Bojangles" Robinson, Harold and Fayard Nicholas (the Nicholas Brothers), and Astaire all tap danced enough times on film in the studio era to build up meaningful bodies of work. Each can also be heard tapping on record. The roughly simultaneous Hollywood careers of Powell, Robinson, and the Nicholas Brothers speak for the importance of tap in the 1930s and early 1940s. Only Astaire retained a solid place tapping in film and on television beyond the war (Robinson died in 1950). But it would be a category mistake to compare this group by any measure beyond the taps on their shoes. Taken together, the varied careers of the Hollywood tappers highlight several general aspects of the studio musical. First, there was room within the genre for singular talents to find a place despite race or gender. Second, finding a lasting place in the musical demanded a well-roundedness not all specialty performers had. And third, race severely limited the sphere of the possible in Hollywood, preventing talented performers from showing their full potential and opening up an unrecoverable lack in the historical record film provides.

Astaire's brand of tap was inherently masculine, and he used gendered terms to praise Eleanor Powell: "She 'put 'em down' like a man, no ricky-ticky-sissy stuff with Ellie."[19] For a time, Metro convincingly platformed Powell as a unique female musical star who stood on her own two tapping feet rather than leaning on a romantic partner.[20] Powell's optimistic energy and the physical vitality of her dancing presence resonated with mid- and late-1930s audiences, who often favored strong female characters. But Powell's time in the spotlight was held in check by her limited abilities as an actress and singer. She was not a triple threat. Unlike Astaire, who developed his acting chops on Broadway and enjoyed a second career as an actor in nonmusical roles in his later years, Powell never showed a desire to be more than MGM made her: a specialty dancer given the grandest of frames. (Hollywood's double standard for male and female stars as they aged played a role in shortening Powell's career as well.) For as long as her style was marketable, Powell had success (at least at the star-making Metro). In some routines Powell incorporated strong acrobatic, eccentric, and trick elements that had the capacity to become mannered. By comparison, Astaire kept it relatively simple—rhythm was his primary concern—and his ability to engage with different sorts of music by way of a tap-centered dance style stood him in good stead as a tapper who could outlive the popularity of tap, which waned considerably after the war. Powell's career as a leading player lasted about eight years, effectively ending in 1943.

Race was central to Astaire's position as the only male tapper with a Hollywood platform on which to create and perform. For the duration of Astaire's studio-era career black leading men were ruled out in Hollywood except in very rare cases (such as Paul Robeson). Hollywood had yet to invent the very notion of the African American leading man in any context, much less in a light genre such as the musical. Astaire had no need to fear competition from even the most skilled black performers.

The Nicholas Brothers, clear candidates for leading man status by the 1940s, were relegated to specialty numbers, limiting their time in any given film to an intense few minutes of song and dance.[21] It's not hard to imagine a series of romantic comedies with songs starring these two, buddy films on the model of the Crosby and Hope *Road* pictures, sprinkled throughout with knock 'em dead dance routines. The Nicholas Brothers' version of "Chattanooga Choo-Choo" from *Sun Valley Serenade* (1941), where they vie good-naturedly for Dorothy Dandridge's affection, affords a fleeting glimpse of films that could have been made had Hollywood not held the color line so rigidly. The Nicholas Brothers didn't even have complete creative control over their dancing, working with white dance director Nick Castle during their short career at Twentieth Century-Fox. No black dance director had a sustained Hollywood career (unlike black arrangers in the music department, as will be shown).[22] Relying on the spectacle of their fantastically energetic dancing bodies, the Nicholas Brothers' routines are relatively modest in production values and always too short and too few, a lack felt at the time, when black audiences were known to demand that the reel with the Nicholas Brothers' specialty on it be run a second time. The Nicholas Brothers' body of work—seven major specialties in seven films—expresses the core nature of the musical as the Hollywood genre that, above all else, served as host to singers and dancers who needed a truly national stage.[23] On that basis alone, the Nicholas Brothers were able to carve out a significant place in the history of the genre. But, as with Powell, specialties would only take them so far. Astaire was able to fill other capacities within the genre, such as playing the leading man. Race kept Harold and Fayard Nicholas from getting that chance.

Like Jolson and Astaire, Bill Robinson spent many years playing vaudeville and Broadway.[24] His hard-earned reputation entertaining American audiences live and in person earned Robinson his initial breaks in Hollywood. A successful connection with Shirley Temple sustained a short career that climaxed with the black-cast *Stormy Weather* (1943), the product of wartime lobbying for more and better roles for black performers in Hollywood. Only the rarest of film occasions permitted Robinson to dress up sharp or show interest in an adult woman. The standout example is the nonromantic routine Robinson did with black female tapper Jeni LeGon in *Hooray for Love* (1935), which also included Robinson singing and doing scat vocals with Thomas "Fats" Waller at the piano. (LeGon briefly had a contract at Metro but was released when she upstaged Eleanor Powell at a live studio promotion event.)[25] Astaire's routines were often expensive production numbers, the centerpieces of their films. Robinson's were, by comparison, very modest—usually just Robinson dancing a couple of choruses in his signature style, up on the balls of his feet. Still, Robinson's solos stand out for their vitality and musical subtlety. As a dance discipline, tap is engaging for its technical display of (largely invisible) physical control and its creation of a crackling musical line. This is one reason tap remains thrilling: the body becomes an instrument, the dance part of the music. Robinson's screen dances—no matter the context or costume—reveal the sophisticated technical mastery of a showbiz professional, a pose that, in Robinson's time, gave the lie to Hollywood's narrow range of demeaning stereotypes of African Americans.[26]

The Hollywood studios produced a vast quantity of films, musical and otherwise, larger than any viewer or scholar can hope to assimilate. But the record of Hollywood film offers a seductive illusion of completeness that must always be remembered for what it is: selective, subject to random influences, fundamentally shaped by corporate decisions made for immediate profit taking in the motion picture exhibition business. (As MGM mogul Marcus Loew said, "We sell tickets to theaters, not movies.")[27] In the area of tap dance, the priorities and limitations of the studios must be kept in mind. There were two performance spheres for solo tappers in the 1930s and '40s: the fairly expansive realm of live performance with bands in a variety of stage and nightclub contexts, and the much narrower opportunities to be found in Hollywood films, where tappers often appeared without fanfare as specialty acts seen fleetingly and then were gone. Most nightclubs and bands included tap dancers in their shows, providing a range of gigs for dancers when the vaudeville circuits petered out. When nightclub floorshows and touring bands began to disappear during and after the war, tappers lost their showbiz niche. Some swing tappers survived to teach later generations, but tap's place in popular culture and its appeal to a mass audience were gone for good. Tappers looking to connect with bebop (and later rap) took off in decidedly different directions from tap in its showbiz heyday. And so the fragmentary record in Hollywood film is all that remains of tap dancing as a popular, professional dance discipline performed to swing music.

The frustratingly truncated film career of John W. "Bubbles" Sublett— the tapper Astaire most often referred to as an inspiration—serves as a case in point. Despite a stage and nightclub career spanning five decades, including being the first Sportin' Life in *Porgy and Bess,* Bubbles only appeared in four feature films made by major Hollywood studios.[28] His numbers, all but one specialties with partner Ford L. "Buck" Washington, are short, often truncated affairs. Bubbles never had the chance to really hoof on film, a medium that has enjoyed surprising resilience on television. He did, however, enjoy a more transient resurgence of sorts in the early 1960s, when he was a semiregular presence on television. For example, Bubbles dueted with Bing Crosby on *The Hollywood Palace* the same season Astaire hosted four episodes. Unfortunately, these television performances remain largely inaccessible outside

of museum collections today. Most of Bubbles's career was live. The re-
coverable traces of his artistry are few but his impact was attested to by
several generations of tap dancers, Astaire among them. Bubbles's technical and artistic innovation was a down-on-the-heels style that certainly
had a formative impact on Astaire's own rather heavy, into-the-floor
style of rhythm tap.

Before ending this discussion of Astaire's tap dance peers, Astaire's very
status as a tap dancer must be addressed. Constance Valis Hill's recent
book *Tap Dancing America: A Cultural History* provides a fresh context for the consideration of Astaire within the history and traditions of
tap. Hill defines tap as "a percussive American dance form distinguished
by the interplay of rhythms and amplification of sound by the feet."[29]
This expansive view allows Hill to bring a broad range of dancers under the umbrella of tap, showing continuities across American show
business history, bridging black and white while always mindful of the
limits segregation and racism put on individual careers and interracial
performance. In her discussion of the 1920s Hill defines a special sort of
tap called "jazz (tap) dance."

> It was in the 1920s, as jazz rhythms reshaped new "low-down" dances, that
> jazz tap emerged as the most rhythmically complex form of jazz dancing. Set-
> ting itself apart from all earlier forms of tap dance, it matched its speed to that
> of jazz music and often doubled it. Here was an extremely rapid yet subtle
> form of drum dancing that demanded the dancer's center be lifted, the weight
> balanced between the balls and heels of both feet. While the dancer's align-
> ment was more upright and vertical (unlike that of buck dancers), there was a
> marked angularity in the line of the body that allowed for the swift downward
> drive of weight. Full bodied and rhythmically expressive, jazz tap dancing
> evolved into an endless array of individual styles and specializations.[30]

Although Hill does not put him there, Astaire belongs among her cohort of jazz (tap) dancers shaped by the "rhythmic revolution" of the
1920s. He would have learned just as much about rhythm from the
black Broadway shows of the early 1920s as he did from stride pianists
in Harlem and, as subsequent chapters will show, he wrote publicly
about the importance of watching black dancers for anyone wanting to
learn low-down styles. (In 1978, Bubbles claimed to have taught Astaire
some steps in the late 1920s, right around the time Hill's jazz tap cohort
was coalescing.)[31] Hill makes no mention of Astaire's outsized and
noisy presence on Broadway in the late 1920s, focusing instead on his

film work and generally highlighting his partner dances rather than solo routines.[32] My discussion of Astaire hopefully complements Hill on this count.

The only established term Astaire used to characterize his dancing was the word *hoofer,* a designation jazz dance historians Marshall and Jean Stearns, writing in 1968, took issue with: "[Astaire] likes to write of himself as a 'hoofer,' which he decidedly is *not,* for the word usually designates the one-spot tapping of an old-timer who works only with his feet. . . . The pose is harmless, the motive modesty. But his consistent use of tap reinforced the acute sense of rhythm on which all of his dancing is based. Astaire always dances with some sort of a beat."[33] Granted, Astaire does move around, partly because he worked in a medium that was primarily visual. But when he was in the recording studio he was happy to stay in one spot, anchored to a four-by-four-foot dance floor. Astaire tapped live on radio in the mid-1930s and on records many times. When conditions demanded it, Astaire could be a hoofer in the Stearnses' sense. But the Stearnses' definition of hoofer is too narrow and not specific to Astaire. By *hoofer* Astaire meant two things: a dancer whose most fundamental resources are rhythmic and a dancer who works tirelessly to please his audience. Gene Kelly understood this usage, calling Astaire a "hoofer" and grouping him with other historically important tappers on a 1948 LP salute titled *The Song and Dance Man.*[34] Besides his tribute to Astaire, Kelly's album included song-and-dance salutes to blackface minstrel George Primrose, George M. Cohan, and Bill "Bojangles" Robinson, all of whom made noise with their feet and entertained the broadest of audiences, all "hoofers" by the most common definition. In his liner notes, Kelly exalted Astaire as "the greatest of all, for he has done more to set America dancing than any other 'hoofer.'" By invoking the word *hoofer* Astaire declared himself an entertainer rather than an artist, a designation with which he repeatedly expressed discomfort.

As the Stearnses remark, Astaire always danced with "some sort of beat." If we look at the length and breadth of Astaire's career, he is almost always either making noise while he dances or dancing to specially arranged music that provides a syncopated musical punctuation to his moves. Sound—musical sound—lay at the heart of his sensibilities as a dancer and dancemaker. Tap is the dance discipline most closely attuned to the music, specifically jazz, that made Astaire dance. Tap and jazz drumming—Astaire did both—are extensions of the same musical practices, as the next section will suggest. Recognizing the importance of tap (and rhythm) in his dance and dance-making process helps place Astaire's creative practice within the syncopated tap and jazz traditions he gravitated to again and again. Emphasizing the privilege Astaire enjoyed as a white male—with Broadway credentials at first and Hollywood box office success early on—grounds his career as a tapper in the realities of race and gender in Hollywood and the United States at the time.

In her discussion of tap and bebop, Hill emphasizes the interplay between drummers and tappers as rhythmic innovators and the ability of some tappers, such as Baby Laurence, to add musical lines that qualify as substantial contributions to jazz music making. Hill describes Laurence's style of "jazz-tapping" as "designed less to be seen than to be heard."[35] I will make similar claims about Astaire, particularly when he, like Laurence, tapped on record. The jazz tapper's capacity to contribute musically to the jazz moment was never constrained by style or time period. Jazz tappers made musical contributions well before bebop, albeit at a time when jazz and tap were both, as Hill notes, "popular in design and commercial in intent."[36] Swing tappers, like Astaire and so many others, were also swing musicians.

MUSICIANS

Early in his film career Astaire made a point of highlighting his skills as a musician. Both *Roberta* and *Follow the Fleet* feature extended piano solos. Displaying his piano skills in his routines was nothing new. Astaire had been doing so from the very start of his vaudeville career.[37]

The biggest influence on Astaire's piano playing was George Gershwin, whose stride piano style is remarkably similar to Astaire's favored technique. Stride built upon and extended the strict division of labor between the hands established by ragtime. The left plays a leaping, widely spaced pattern of bass notes on beats one and three and mid-keyboard chords on two and four. The right solos on the tune, often in the flashiest of manners. As a piano idiom, stride is marked by fast tempos, full voicings in both hands, very loud dynamics, and a visual, competitive sort of virtuosity. Pianist Jack Gibbons, who has reconstructed and recorded both Astaire and Gershwin's stride recordings, finds a palpable similarity in approach between the two.[38] Stride was a product of black Manhattan, a transformation of ragtime into a modern sound matching the post–World War I emergence of Harlem as a Jazz Age black metropolis. Astaire and Gershwin's midtown careers on Broadway in the 1920s were fueled in part by periodic trips uptown to hear stride players like Eubie Blake, James P. Johnson, Thomas "Fats" Waller, and Willie "The Lion" Smith.[39] Stride was closely tied to simultaneous dance innovations, and Astaire absorbed music just as he did dancing: by watching others and listening. With the added resource of very large hands—a physical trait he tried to minimize while dancing but a real boon when playing stride—Astaire's keyboard skills were formidable, and he wasn't shy about claiming a spot as a musician when among musicians. At a 1952 recording session produced by jazz entrepreneur and activist Norman Granz, Astaire played a stride solo (on a song he had written) before handing off the keyboard responsibilities to jazz pianist Oscar Peterson, surely the act of a confident player. To his credit, Astaire introduced the cut by saying Peterson would step in to "save him," but Astaire was, in this challenging jazz context, a fully equipped musician.

Although Astaire did not do so on the Granz-produced set, Peterson remembered the dancer being cajoled into demonstrating his skill playing drums during the same sessions.[40] Playing drums at home with jazz records was a lifelong hobby of Astaire's and a recurrent motif in his films and interviews. Hollywood columnist Sidney Skolsky's 1955 "tin-type" of Astaire noted, "He says his favorite relaxation is to play the drums ('I'm a "beat" man.') He would rather listen to beat music, play it on his drums ('I play with the best recorded bands'), or dance to it than do most anything else."[41] A major profile of Astaire in *Look Magazine* from 1959 described his home practice sessions.

> In his big, sprawling house in Beverly Hills, Calif. . . . Astaire has a room which contains many mementos of the 31 films he has made since 1933. In the corner of the room are a set of drums and a record player. At almost any time of the day or night, Astaire might put on jazz records and play the drums along with the music. I watched him do this one afternoon. He sat there with an unlighted cigarette dangling from his lips and beat the drums with dedicated frenzy—to the music of the Buddy De Franco Quartet. His shoulders bunched forward, his face dripped perspiration, his shirt was rumpled. After about 45 minutes, he suddenly stopped and resumed his normal, well-groomed composure.[42]

Astaire demonstrated his home drum kit on television during a visit by Edward R. Murrow for a 1957 episode of *Person to Person* and was quoted in 1973 with regard to the habit: "I've played the drums with a lot of very famous bands—in my room."[43] Four prominent film solos—from 1937, 1944, 1948, and 1955—feature Astaire's skill with the sticks. He made three additional drum-related dances opposite jazz drummers on his television specials. The modern drum kit was still being solidified in the 1930s, and Astaire's awareness of these developments is on display in the drum dance finale to *A Damsel in Distress*.

The visual element was important to swing drumming, whether live or on film, and drummers, including Astaire, knew that showmanship and keeping the beat went hand in hand. As jazz pianist Billy Taylor remembered of three major black drummers of the swing era:

> Chick [Webb] and Sid Catlett and Jo Jones had something important in common. They all were great showmen. These guys came up when the drummer and everybody, for that matter, had to hold his own spot. If you had a spot in a show in a theater or club and you didn't get as much applause as the juggler, singer, or shake dancer, then you lost that feature. Somebody else got it. It was a fight for survival. That's why drummers threw sticks and did all kinds of show biz things, while they tried to play in a marvelous musical manner.[44]

Given this need to stand out visually, the stick-throwing drummer was a natural cinematic subject. Drummers Gene Krupa and Buddy Rich were both featured in highly stylized drum-centered routines, as were tappers Bill Robinson and Eleanor Powell.[45] Astaire's audiences understood how narrow the line was between drumming and dancing. Every time Astaire threw a drumstick or danced with a drum he exemplified the showmanship that was central to success for every swing-era jazz drummer, black or white. (The drummer as dancer and drum dance routines find an earlier source in the work of Vernon Castle, a model for Astaire in his youth.)

Astaire regularly incorporated piano and drums in his dances across his entire career. These were not faked performances: he always recorded his own piano performances and, in some instances, his drumming can also be heard. The band industry trade magazine *Down Beat*, with its constant attention to the sound/image relationship in Hollywood film, noted that MGM drummer Frankie Carlson did "a large portion of the drum sounds" in *Easter Parade*'s "Drum Crazy." But, *Down Beat* went on, "some of the drumming, such as that on the toy drums seen in the picture, actually was recorded by Astaire. You can tell by the way he handles the sticks that they were not strange to him."[46]

On occasion Astaire would learn the rudiments of an instrument for a specific routine, the results highlighting the importance he placed on musical performance as part of his act. He learned accordion for the Broadway version of *The Band Wagon*, and he gives a credible show on harp in *Yolanda and the Thief* (1945), where he was certainly not playing on the soundtrack. Publicity flacks said that, in learning the harp, "Astaire satisfies a life-long ambition. . . . Between scenes Astaire practices his harp lessons by playing his own tune 'Oh, My Achin' Back,' which he wrote in collaboration with Willie Shore following his recent U.S.O. show tour of the Western front. . . . [T]he song is to be published shortly."[47] This squib efficiently plugs the film *Yolanda*, Astaire's new topical song, and the star's recent contribution to the war effort. In the film Astaire demonstrates sufficient knowledge of the harp to integrate it accurately into a short dance. He raps out rhythms on the soundboard with his fingers, touches the strings in a credible way, and uses the harp's multiple pedals as part of the dance, employing his musical prop with the utmost integrity. Without a doubt, looking competent and comfortable around instruments was important to Astaire. He shaped his screen image carefully, making sure his audience knew he could do more than just dance and sing.

Astaire's identity as a musician had important implications during the first decade or so of his screen career, a period when improvising jazz instrumentalists were national figures. Astaire's career flourished at a time when Jewish clarinet players could rule the pop music world (Benny Goodman and Artie Shaw), black pianists could lead nationally known bands (Duke Ellington and Count Basie), and a white trumpet player could marry a movie star and appear on the covers of movie magazines (Harry James and wife Betty Grable, known as "The Horn" and "The Legs," respectively). All these musicians had movie careers, though those of the black players were of a much more circumscribed nature. During the height of the swing era—1935 to 1945—Astaire presented himself as a musician among musicians in a Hollywood context where musical virtuosity was a cinematic subject worth lingering over.

When real musicians appeared on film, they brought an authenticity that was tremendously attractive, particularly for music lovers who saw movie stars as lesser beings than their own musical heroes. As one fan from Detroit wrote to *Down Beat* in 1941, "Boy, how [the Hollywood studios] burn when the [Glenn] Miller, [Artie] Shaw and [Tommy] Dorsey guys who can do something start replacing their [Clark] Gables and [Robert] Taylors in the public eye." (The writer continued bitterly, "They lure 'em [band musicians] out to Hollywood with huge sums of money and make jackasses out of 'em in front of their followers.")[48] The emphasis on men who "do something" was a powerful mark of jazz mastery and masculinity, putting jazz players into the category of boxers and baseball players as active men to be emulated. Astaire's alignment with musicians did much to reinforce his image as an unassailably masculine dancer. Hollywood product, made under the playback technique, was always suspect in the eyes of musically minded viewers, and *Down Beat* regularly took up the mantle of custodian of authentic film performance, parsing the sound/image relationship for its (mostly male) readership of professionals and devoted fans. Astaire's total package on film—singer, dancer, leading man, and musician—carried an authenticity that *Down Beat* frequently recognized. At a time when instrumental performance was central to popular music culture, Astaire alone among Hollywood stars was understood to be a genuine player.

As the above examples show, Astaire made a conscious effort to cement this view in the public imagination. Putting Astaire among white jazz figures who had film careers—such as Goodman, Shaw, and Krupa—sheds new light not only on Astaire but also on the swing bands and the film musical as similarly embedded in the larger entertainment industry, in the process demonstrating one way that jazz history can be illuminated by Astaire's career and creative loyalties.

Astaire's engagement with jazz extended far beyond the end of World War II. For this reason, beyond an examination of Astaire's creative work, the story told here supports a revision of jazz periodization. I will argue throughout for an expanded view of the swing era that reaches to the end of the 1960s. The narrow definition of swing as lasting from the mid-1930s to the early '40s serves a particular line of jazz historiography, as Sherrie Tucker argues with regard to all-girl bands of the war years.[49] Allowing for a "late swing era" extends the swing period to the end of World War II, when—so the story goes—with the rise of bebop and the disappearance of the dance bands, jazz dropped off the popular music radar. At this point, a historiographically privileged branch of the music began its rapid transformation into an art music for listening rather than a popular music for dancing. Along an alternate branch, committed swing players went on doing what swing had done originally with such success: staking a claim for genuine jazz musicianship in the popular (read mainstream white) arena. Astaire's postwar jazz collaborators all had a common aesthetic and professional strategy: they sought out the largest possible audience, never losing faith in the belief that the disciplines and energies of jazz could find a sizable popular following. The jazz musicians Astaire worked with after 1945 include Oscar Peterson and other Jazz at the Philharmonic regulars, trumpeter Jonah Jones, bandleaders Count Basie (after his 1955 resurgence) and Ray Anthony, singer Joe Williams, composer, arranger, and pianist André Previn, organist Jimmy Smith, the Young-Holt Unlimited trio, and arranger Neal Hefti. All had major national careers—they sold records—and all have been marginalized in jazz scholarship. They do not exemplify the innovation and art music–oriented values of most jazz historians. They do, however, typify the swing era's belief in jazz as a song-based art that showcased virtuosity and artistry in popular music packaging. They never lost touch with the commercial roots of jazz in the realm of show business. All sought ways to make relevant, contemporary music from the basic materials of swing in the decades beyond the decline of the big bands; all remained engaged with popular music and culture; all tried to attract multigenerational audiences in a spirit of showmanship. Their work with Astaire traces one journey across what I call the "long swing era," reaching into the late 1960s, when social and musical changes and the simple passage of time finally closed the door on musical styles and performers who first flourished in the formative years of the 1930s. The long swing era can be viewed most clearly in the careers of jazz musicians—black and white, players and arrangers—who were raised on swing and never converted entirely to modern, noncommercial jazz idioms. Their careers after World War II were a dividend of musical technique and show business savvy paid out over several decades.

With the collapse of the swing bands, many of these players—whites mostly—found steady work on the Hollywood studio scene, which encompassed film, pop records, and television. Astaire encountered them there. Television proved to be an important platform for both old swing survivors and new popular-oriented jazzmen. Black swing veterans were particularly well served by this new media, but younger players working in "soul-ful" idioms could also find a place on television. A swinging beat was still chasing a popular audience even after the onslaught of rock and roll, and Astaire used his television work to connect with exactly these players and these sounds. While chatting with Astaire, who was hosting the *Hollywood Palace* television variety show in 1966, trumpeter Herb Alpert described this beat as "sort of an American jazz pulsation." That particular changing-but-always-swinging beat underlies most everything Astaire did, and for as long as this "jazz pulsation" had a place near the center of popular music, Astaire was close by. Tracing out the line of popular jazz proves another important way the study of Astaire's career brings a new perspective to the story of jazz.

Astaire never worked with drummer Buddy Rich, but their careers have a discernible symmetry worth noting here as a sort of map of the entertainment territory explored in the chapters that follow.[50] Astaire and Rich traversed this same show business landscape without ever crossing paths. Eighteen years younger than Astaire, Rich also grew up on a vaudeville stage. The child of vaudeville performers, he was billed as "Traps the Drum Wonder" from a very early age, and by age fourteen Rich was among the highest paid child stars of the day. His specialty act involved tap dancing and playing drums, a combination that was central to Astaire's persona as well. Rich hung on to the bitter end of vaudeville, eking out a living into the mid-1930s. With the writing on the wall, Rich decided to abandon the variety stage, join the musician's union, and become a drummer. He fell in love with jazz and learned the craft of big band drumming by playing along to records and radio broadcasts (as Astaire did for fun). Rich's timing and talents were right and he very quickly became a major swing star in the Shaw and Tommy Dorsey bands, narrowly missing Astaire on several occasions during the height of the swing era. After service in the war, Rich pulled together his own band. His much-praised group tried and failed to find a formula for success in the late 1940s, a period when there was no workable model for being both a commercial dance band and a serious jazz band. The effort collapsed, despite help from Rich's friend Frank Sinatra, and in 1949 Rich entered into a long-term connection with Norman Granz's Jazz at the Philharmonic, making many LPs with small groups. Astaire allied himself with Granz around the same time and for similar reasons, seeking a jazz connection in changing times.

Television extended Astaire's song-and-dance career beyond the shuttering of the studio musical production units. In similar fashion, television revived Rich's career in the 1960s, in particular through ongoing guest appearances on *The Tonight Show* with Johnny Carson (himself an amateur drummer often seen playing along with his house big band with two pencils at his desk). Rich bucked the trends and established a long-lasting name band in 1966. His group never cracked the charts but they did keep working, playing Las Vegas and staying on the road in the old 1930s way. Rich's band had a swinging beat and consistently tried to find popular venues, playing pop tunes, Broadway scores, and movie themes of the moment in arrangements that made room for improvisation (the old swing formula of playing all the current tunes and saving some space for jazz soloing). As a 1970 album titled after a

Paul Simon song declared, Rich wanted to "Keep the Customer Satisfied." Astaire shared this sentiment. Still an active player and leader, Rich died just eighty-one days before Astaire did in 1987.

Rich's career suggests an alternative biography for Astaire, a more narrowly musical road not traveled. Their lives in music were made of remarkably similar stuff. Both started out as tappers and drummers on the variety stage in the formative post–World War I jazz era: the rhythmic connection between dance and music was there from the beginning, as was the centrality of routines, arrangements, big solos, and pleasing the audience. Both took their rhythmic sensibilities from black models, journeying to Harlem for indoctrination into swing from its African American sources. Rich, a generation younger than Astaire, was influenced by swing drummers like Chick Webb, whom he sometimes sat in for at the Savoy Ballroom. Astaire and Rich embraced different career strategies in their common effort to transcend vaudeville. Astaire diversified: he learned to do comedy, crafted a useable singing style, and played romantic leads despite his lack of leading man looks, setting his routines within musical narratives that demanded these extra skills. Rich specialized: he moved behind the drums (although he relished novelty solos, such as his no-hands act with two bass drums) and stuck with the music business (although he did make some film dances, in particular a drum routine with Eleanor Powell in the 1942 band pic *Ship Ahoy*). When the big bands folded and the studios closed up shop, Astaire and Rich both found new opportunities with Jazz at the Philharmonic, a modern jazz context that retained swing values, and new venues on television, where their skills at rhythm and routine making could still find an audience.

Age marks one final similarity between Rich and Astaire. Astaire stopped dancing in public in 1976, his brief routine with Gene Kelly in *That's Entertainment, Part II* closing out his dancing days. An inner-ear imbalance compromised his equilibrium. Barrie Chase, Astaire's television dance partner, remembered him saying, sadly, "Barrie, it's one thing to give up dancing because you choose to. It's another if you have to."[51] Rich was able to keep performing almost to the day he died despite the physical challenges of his instrument. Both Astaire and Rich were still active at age seventy, a not-uncommon trait among swing veterans. The longevity of many of Astaire's swing peers shows the staying power of swing as a style that never aged. Among dancers, the extreme length of Astaire's career is especially stunning. His creative commitment to making musical routines for film and television made this possible. In any other context Astaire could never have danced on his own terms so well for such a large audience for so long.

Placing Astaire among perhaps unlikely musical peers in this first chapter is intentional. My central tenet—encapsulated in my title and laid out in brief in the introduction—is that music triggered Astaire's dancing, both in the crafting of dances on his own body and the subsequent performance of these creations on film using his own body. He was his own instrument, and the music he liked to play most was jazz, a contentious word that requires and receives unpacking throughout the book.

To lay it out here in preliminary fashion, by jazz I mean American popular music generally characterized as swing or swing-inspired. Jazz of the swing variety is a song-driven mode of music making that allows creative performers—musicians, dancers, and singers working in groups or alone—to build their own creative personas on the work of songwriters who, in turn, build their songs on a limited set of readily heard structural options (such as the thirty-two-bar song or the twelve-bar blues). Creative mastery and manipulation of musical materials are central to swing, an approach to music making that revels in equal measure in the inspiration of improvising soloists and the control, skill, and surprise of ensembles playing carefully crafted and rehearsed arrangements. The makers of this kind of jazz all sought a large popular audience—this sort of jazz is, by definition, a realm of show business—and they did so by making a welcoming, accessible, entertaining art that has never entirely lost its appeal. The music is intimately bound up with dancing, whether as performance, social interaction, or a combination of both. Songs are fundamental: listeners and players follow the tune and keep the words in mind while they listen, dance, or play. This sort of jazz brought black and white performers together around a set of music and dance practices understood by everyone involved to be derived from African American sources. The founders of the style were black: Louis Armstrong, Duke Ellington, Thomas "Fats" Waller, and Fletcher Henderson—all active in New York in the late 1920s, when Astaire was a Broadway star—are foremost among them. Individual black Americans reached a national audience by way of this kind of jazz, and some white Americans—Astaire among them—privileged in every way within the realm of entertainment and American society at large, invited these black jazz masters into collaborative work that only whites could initiate. In a harshly segregated, racist nation, whites and whites alone controlled the commerce of swing. From his unique position within the

Hollywood studio system, Astaire was among the most empowered of these jazz-making whites. This large category of swing jazz overlaps with much of American popular music between 1930 and 1955. It's the music of a quarter century of American life, the golden age of radio and the Hollywood studios. But it survived to the end of the 1960s (and even beyond), continuing to flourish for as long as a section of horn players could not be replaced by a synthesizer or a sampler. Several of the original makers of the music remained active into extreme old age. Most, Astaire among them, were silenced by age or death by the close of the 1980s. The above definition of jazz is the one evoked in my subtitle. This is the music that made Astaire dance.

But a solely musical analysis of Astaire's work would be insufficient. His primary medium was moving pictures, a realm that demands its own sort of analysis, parsing both the moves he made and the way those moves were framed and assembled within specific production contexts. Behind the music, the dance and the films themselves lay the intertwined creative process of making all three. This was collaborative work, and Astaire certainly did not work alone. Much of what follows concerns the many individuals who added their own creative work to Astaire's labors, but he is the common denominator. Revealing the process behind Astaire's work with so many others and grounding their common achievement in both Astaire's creative sensibilities and the larger popular culture context form the overarching intent of *Music Makes Me*, which is both a study of Astaire's work in recorded media and a creative biography of Astaire himself. Process and product, together with the contexts informing both, are of equal interest.

My reading of Astaire's creative process frames him from a particular point of view: an American born in 1899—he's always one year older than his century—whose long career marks seminal transitions in popular culture; a performer in love with syncopated music—what he called "the beat"—from his youth, eager to make good, both critically and financially, in the competitive, expanding, changing world of popular entertainment; a popular music polymath—singer, pianist, drummer—as eager to write his own tunes as he was to get inside songs written by others for his use; a hoofer who always wanted to make noise with his body and saw the world around him as a drum to be played in broken rhythms; a white dancer who created interracial contexts where he might dance to the music of black musicians; and a song-and-dance man animated his whole life long by the singular desire to make socko routines that left his audience on its "ass in the aisles."

CHAPTER 2

"I am a *creator*"

Astaire wrote out his own autobiography in longhand at the end of the 1950s. Published in 1959, *Steps in Time* is a bland recitation of one success after another. Always an admittedly uninteresting interview subject, Astaire, when telling his own tale, was polite and distant. But the published book bears almost no resemblance to Astaire's first draft, which was cantankerous, colloquial, and often technical about the process of movie making. In one lengthy chapter that was cut entirely from the book, Astaire took on the major film critics one by one, revisiting a quarter century of reviews (mostly positive, but that didn't prevent Astaire from harboring some hard feelings).

In a revealing passage preserved among other rejected draft chapters, Astaire articulated in direct language his professional goals, working methods, internal relationship to work in progress, and how he thought about his creative labors relative to other Hollywood stars. Astaire frequently underlined words for emphasis when writing. In the draft he staked a claim to a particular artistic identity in succinct terms: "I am a *creator*," he wrote.[1] Astaire believed a creative imperative hung over his stardom, separating him from most other Hollywood stars. He had to work longer on a picture than did his screen peers, a group he called "dramatic actors." While three or four months might be a long schedule for others, Astaire noted for the record, "I don't think I've ever been less than 7 months on one of my 'epics.'" Mocking the supposed lightness of his generic home—musicals, unlike epics, have never been high-status pictures—Astaire challenged the reader to take seriously the time he spent making, rehearsing, and filming his routines. Dramatic actors, Astaire pointed out, showed up on the set and played roles that were "written" by others. Making a film wasn't so simple for him.

Astaire went on to explain the priorities that drove his creative work, agonizing about his "constant fear and cognizance of the fact that the public, although it may have a great and devoted interest in you, can drop you like a hot plate if you don't come through and hold your spot. My type of work is, as I have said, the kind that can deteriorate by slowing up—running out of ideas or gas—going stale, in short—'slipping.'" Every Hollywood star ran the risk of losing the public's interest: sustaining a career was a chancy undertaking for even the most successful screen personalities. But Astaire framed his need to hold on to his audience in concrete terms that were completely in his control. *He* was the one who had to come up with something new on every picture, "dig[ging] for ideas," trying "never to repeat anything I've done before and also never appropriate from others." In his view, it was his own work, primarily that done in the rehearsal hall, that made the difference. He would, he thought, succeed or fail on his musical numbers alone. These short song-and-dance films set within the longer narrative film product were what counted most, and, in any event, they were the pieces of the finished film in his hands. In his draft autobiography, much more than in the published version, Astaire revealed himself as a self-starter, his successes built on his own creative labors, defined in isolating, even romantic terms: he describes the "sweat and fury and wonderment" attending his creative process, falling just shy of the more formulaic "blood, sweat, and tears." Crucially, Astaire's goal was not self-expression. He consistently resisted any notion he was out to say something. In the 1970s, when his life's work was first being hailed as enduring popular art, Astaire delighted in puncturing that particular bubble. He told one reporter, "I was trying to make a buck. . . . I just did it for entertainment. I had no idea about saying anything. . . . I'm a rat if you want to get to know me."[2]

Astaire's lifelong task was to entertain, to keep his public interested and engaged, pleased and applauding. "I am a *creator*," he stated unequivocally, a maker. This chapter introduces the aim of Astaire's creative labor (making musical numbers), the materials he used (popular songs, old and new), and select creative individuals who assisted him in the collaborative art and craft of musical filmmaking (songwriters, rehearsal pianists, dance directors). Along the way, Astaire's approach to music and dance making emerges in general terms. A pendant to chapter 1, this chapter presents a portrait of Astaire in his creative element before diving back into history and putting his work in the larger contexts of Hollywood, popular music, and jazz. Several Astaire numbers discussed at length in later chapters are previewed in brief below. Pointers in the text direct the reader to these more exhaustive analyses.

SONGWRITERS

Al Jolson once said, "I am a salesman of songs and jokes. . . . Just as any other man sells merchandise, I have to sell my goods to the audience. I got selling experience in small stores; these stores were called vaudeville."[3] Astaire, a salesman of songs and dances, also began in vaudeville, and his career followed the growth of the popular culture industry, moving smoothly from vaudeville to Broadway revues and book shows, to Hollywood narrative musical films and occasional work on radio. Then, when the studios disappeared, he moved on to television variety shows. Each of these contexts welcomed Astaire's song-and-dance routines, which were consistent in form and content across his career. The creative task before him remained basically the same no matter what format or venue he worked in. Lasting on average from three to five minutes, Astaire's routines followed one of two predictable larger structures: most began with Astaire singing followed by Astaire dancing; some involved only dancing. The music was always squarely in a popular vein and usually built on a popular song. Songs were the basic currency of popular music and culture for almost the entire length of Astaire's life in show business, and almost all of his films were popular culture events as much for introducing new songs as for offering a cinematic song-and-dance experience. For example, *Top Hat*'s original audience could make the film part of their daily lives by learning the five new songs by Irving Berlin featured on-screen, lyrics for which were marketed for popular consumption on newsstands (see figure 2). At the most basic level, Astaire's creative work rested on a foundation of songs, and songwriters were his most important collaborators.

Astaire was fortunate in many things, but as a seller of songs and dances he was most fortunate in the quality of the new merchandise he introduced. An extraordinary number of lasting songs were written for Astaire. With the exception of Ethel Merman, no performer enjoyed a similar connection to so many of the great songwriters of the pre–rock and roll era. Astaire's musical and choreographic choices flowed from

FIGURE 2. Lyrics for all the new songs in *Top Hat* could be had for just a nickel.

the songs he was offered, so his relationships with each of the top "clef-fers" is of vital importance. Below, I introduce the major songwriters Astaire worked with in quantifiable terms—both in the number of films and the number of songs sung by Astaire and/or used by him in the creation of dance routines. Astaire never had a bad word to say about any of his songwriters, yet how he used their songs tells much about the musical inspiration he needed, expected, and received from each. This overview begins the process of parsing Astaire's musical relationships with songwriters, a matter of interest that runs throughout the book.

Astaire forged a deep connection with George and Ira Gershwin in the 1920s, long before he ever went to Hollywood. The Gershwins wrote two Broadway book shows for Fred and his sister Adele (*Lady, Be Good!* 1924, and *Funny Face,* 1927), penning ten songs introduced by Astaire alone or with Adele.[4] Astaire used one of these, "The Babbitt and the Bromide," for his duet with Gene Kelly in *Ziegfeld Follies.* When the Gershwins came to Hollywood in 1936, their primary purpose was to work for Astaire, contributing twelve numbers to two Astaire films before George's unexpected death from a brain tumor. Eleven years later Ira provided lyrics to five Harry Warren tunes for *The Barkleys of Broadway.* For the same film Astaire and Rogers reprised "They Can't Take That Away" from *Shall We Dance,* this time as a partner dance. At the close of his studio-era career Astaire returned to the Gershwin brothers' catalog, using five Gershwin tunes in *Funny Face,* including two originally written for him on Broadway.

Astaire and George Gershwin's parallel rhythmic sensibilities are generally understood to come from black jazz players and dancers. The specific experiences and sources each drew upon remain somewhat vague, but anecdotal accounts of both men journeying to Harlem in the 1920s to learn from African American musicians and tap dancers have entered the historical record.[5] As Samuel A. Floyd Jr. has noted, "social interaction between black and white musicians was intense," and for "white musicians, including Gershwin, the process of learning black music was osmotic."[6] The same can be said for Astaire. Astaire's rhythmic sensibilities, which burst upon the screen fully formed in 1933, were developed in his collaborations with Gershwin on Broadway, a context that welcomed sustained interplay between performers and songwriters. Having absorbed a basic approach to syncopated music and stride piano from their black Harlem contacts, Gershwin and Astaire nurtured this shared love in the crucible of Broadway productions made for white audiences. They learned together and were natural friends (at least on a professional level). Given the segregated nature of Broadway in the 1920s, neither Gershwin nor Astaire could have collaborated directly with black jazz players at the time. Making a Broadway musical involved weeks spent living together in theaters and hotels, hammering out the show, and experimenting on out-of-town tryout audiences. Gershwin missed this sustained interaction between songwriter and performers in the more segmented Hollywood production process, where songs were typically handed over by songwriters and either accepted or rejected for use on the film. No songwriters appear to have entered Astaire's rehearsal hall sanctum when he was making his film dances.

Astaire described his and George Gershwin's creative interaction during their Broadway years in a 1973 interview.

> He used to sit and play piano for my rehearsals. I'd be dancing, and he'd get up and say, "Why don't you try *this* step?" And he'd do a little dance. I'd say, "Oh, that again; I can use that!" Then he used to like having me play the piano for him. He'd run up to the keyboard and ask, "Now, what was it you just did there?" I could play pretty good jazz piano, while he, of course, was the great concert man. But little things I did amused him like that. And the little things he did in *my* racket amused *me*. So we had a good little game going with each other.[7]

George Gershwin was among Astaire's first rehearsal pianists, and Astaire's earliest records were made with Gershwin at the piano. Their ebullient duet on the song "My One and Only," recorded during the West End run of *Funny Face* in 1928, reveals something of the "little game" they had going.[8] Pianist and dancer trade solos, sharing the recording equally. In places Astaire taps the stems rather than singing the tune and lyrics, transforming the Gershwins' song into pure rhythm. Abundant hot breaks occur throughout, which Astaire fills with tapping and clapping. The tempo is fast, indeed furious, at the close. On an earlier record, "The Half of It, Dearie, Blues" from 1926, Astaire and Gershwin shout asides to each other, revealing a warm friendship and shared musical sensibility grounded in jerky syncopated rhythms.[9] Gershwin confidante and musical assistant Kay Swift described the link between Gershwin and Astaire, music and dance, in a 1975 interview.

> [Gershwin] danced well at social dancing, and I went dancing with him a lot of times. He used to tap-dance waiting for elevators. And it was at that time, he did sometimes carry a stick. I think Fred Astaire must have done it, too. He would do a tap dance using the stick. It made a most interesting, percussive rhythm. He improvised tap steps. I think Fred Astaire is a very good example of one phase of Gershwin's music, and it was evidenced in a case which Fred himself mentions. He had a step, which I always think of as the Astaire step. It was a sort of walk around with a great leap. Just a series of strides, forward strides. And Gershwin said, "Why don't you continue that and make it your exit?" And he did—and that was it—a combination of Astaire and Gershwin, really. I thought that Astaire and Gershwin were particularly one in music and dance. The dance expressed the music so well.[10]

Astaire's rhythmic sensibilities were aligned closely with this "one phase" of Gershwin's music, which found its most direct expression in popular songs like "Fascinatin' Rhythm" and "I Got Rhythm," syncopated tunes that consistently stay off the beat in the sort of broken rhythmic patterns Astaire favored.

In his thirty studio-era films Astaire performed more songs by Irving Berlin than any other single songwriter. Astaire introduced twenty-six original Berlin tunes in six films dating from 1935 to 1948. Six of these were sung by others in the film (Rogers, Crosby, or a chorus), with Astaire using the tunes for dance making only (a significant choice, as will be shown below). The three principal new songs Astaire introduced in *Easter Parade* were written with Kelly in mind. The opening "Happy Easter" sequence seems to have been added after Astaire came on the film. In addition, Astaire used four older Berlin songs, including "Puttin' on the Ritz," for prominent film routines. Astaire was already a movie star when Berlin first wrote for him, and, as will be shown, Berlin sometimes had difficulty writing to Astaire's rhythmic tastes. But Berlin always kept trying, pushing himself to create tunes that met Astaire's desires. Berlin's personal papers prove revealing on the question of how songwriters worked with Astaire to make exactly the tune the dancer wanted. (See the discussion of "The Yam" in chapter 6.)

Second only to Berlin in the number of Astaire films he worked on, Johnny Mercer wrote the words or both words and music for nineteen original songs heard in five Astaire pictures dating from 1941 to 1954. In addition, Astaire requested Mercer's song "Dream" for use in *Daddy Long Legs,* the only Astaire film—indeed, the only musical film—for which Mercer wrote both words and music. Mercer also composed some original tunes used for dance sequences in the film. On his other four Astaire films, Mercer wrote words to the music of six composers. In numerical, chronological, and creative terms, Mercer was the single most important songwriter in the post-RKO phase of Astaire's film career. Besides Astaire's dance collaborator Hermes Pan, Mercer is the sole continuing presence in Astaire's work across the dancer's peripatetic 1940s and 1950s. Furthermore, Mercer was the only songwriter whose active connection with Astaire extended into the dancer's decade on television. In 1959 Astaire and Mercer collaborated for a final time on the song "The Afterbeat" for the one-hour variety special *Another Evening with Fred Astaire.* The Mercer-Astaire songwriting team had enjoyed a modest hit more than two decades earlier. In 1935 Mercer wrote the words and Astaire the tune for "I'm Building Up to an Awful

Letdown," among the earliest times these two men worked together.[11] The song briefly put Astaire on the Hit Parade as a songwriter. When Mercer died in 1976, Astaire acknowledged the songwriter's consistent contribution to his career in a condolence note to Mercer's widow.[12]

Born in 1909, Mercer was writing songs for "B" musicals at RKO in the 1930s when the Gershwins, Berlin, and Jerome Kern—all a generation older that he—were on the lot writing for Astaire and Rogers. Unlike Astaire's other major lyricists, Mercer was not a Broadway writer: his voice was more attuned to popular music and jazz and his career centered on radio and records. Mercer was positioned at the heart of emerging trends in popular music from the founding of Capitol Records in 1942 through the mid-1950s, about the same period he worked with Astaire. Like Astaire, Mercer had an unassuming vocal style. Unlike Astaire, Mercer frequently crossed over into racial mimicry in his singing, and his slangy lyrics invite such performance choices. Many radio listeners assumed Mercer was black.[13] Astaire virtually never affected black dialect in his vocals, but Mercer's songs take him as close as he ever came to striking explicitly hep poses.

Jerome Kern and Cole Porter each wrote eleven tunes for Astaire's use. In addition, Astaire sang or danced three Kern and four Porter tunes introduced by others on Broadway. Kern's work on three Astaire pictures was mediated by two strong lyricists—Dorothy Fields (*Roberta* and *Swing Time*) and Mercer *(You Were Never Lovelier)*—who played important roles guiding their respective projects. Porter penned his own lyrics, and his four film collaborations with Astaire stretched from the beginning to the end of the dancer's screen career. Astaire's stage career ended with Porter's *Gay Divorce*. When the show was adapted for Astaire's first leading film role, Porter's entire score was eliminated except for the song "Night and Day" (which was, astonishingly, omitted from early drafts of the script). Porter's songs for *Broadway Melody of 1940* were few in number—Astaire only sang two—and the film's big finale was danced to "Begin the Beguine," a song not written for Astaire but used in the film because it was a colossal swing band hit. Like Kern's *Roberta,* Porter's *Silk Stockings* began as a Broadway show created for someone other than Astaire. Porter wrote two new songs for Astaire's use in the film version (both discussed in later chapters). Porter was never involved in the filmmaking process. Astaire remembered Porter was seldom seen at the studios beyond the initial meeting on a film (unlike Berlin, who was deeply invested in the development and production process).[14] Astaire's use of Kern and Porter songs intended for dance numbers suggests an ambiguous relationship between both song-writers and the syncopated rhythmic sensibility Astaire drew upon most directly. And Astaire was not shy about simply dismissing Kern and Porter's efforts and going his own way musically, a strategy he rarely used when working with Gershwin or Berlin.

Hollywood composer Harry Warren wrote sixteen songs introduced by Astaire in four films produced at MGM between 1944 and 1951. These four—*Ziegfeld Follies, Yolanda and the Thief, The Barkleys of Broadway,* and *The Belle of New York*—were among Astaire's less successful projects, and the weakness of Warren's songs undoubtedly hurt these films both in their time and subsequently. Astaire's most distinctive dance number to a credited Warren tune—"Bouncin' the Blues" from *Barkleys*—turns out to be only distantly related to anything coming from Warren's pen (see chapter 8).

Important singleton collaborations include Vincent Youmans (with a signature Astaire score for *Flying Down to Rio*), Harold Arlen (three tunes for *The Sky's the Limit* with lyrics by Mercer) and Frank Loesser (words and music for *Let's Dance*).[15] Youmans and Arlen inspired Astaire's dance-making creativity. Loesser, for the most part, did not.

Astaire made two films of mostly recycled songs by well-known song-writing teams. In *Three Little Words,* the old-fashioned Tin Pan Alley tunes of Bert Kalmar and Harry Ruby were avoided by Astaire for the purposes of dance making. Instead, Astaire turned to music director André Previn, a composer and budding jazz pianist of great stylistic flexibility, for the musical underpinnings to his major dance routines in this songwriter biopic. For *The Band Wagon,* Howard Dietz and Arthur Schwartz retro-fitted "A Shine on Your Shoes," one of their old tunes, for Astaire's use, customizing it to his precise specifications and writing a new verse.

To a person, Astaire's songwriters valued the opportunity to write for Hollywood's preeminent singing and dancing star. They appreciated his straightforward singing style and solid track record as a hitmaker. Mercer called Astaire "hit insurance" for songwriters.[16] In the 1930s, RKO hired elite Broadway songwriters for the Astaire-Rogers series. Astaire credited producer Pandro S. Berman with the creative initiative to get the best songwriters—Astaire's Broadway credentials certainly helped—who provided Astaire with excellent raw material to be translated into signature work. Most of the songs that came to be identified with Astaire in later decades were written for these films, which were among the first group of studio-era classics to be broadcast on television. (The entire RKO library was licensed for television in December

1955, at which point all the Astaire-Rogers RKO pictures, except for *Roberta,* reentered the popular culture mainstream as late-night and prime time features.) Even though Astaire continued to work with all his RKO collaborators (excluding George Gershwin) after leaving the studio in 1939, none of their post-1930s scores had the staying power of those early Astaire-Rogers hits, many songs from which entered the jazz canon as well.

In the 1940s Berlin loomed large in Astaire's identity as a song-and-dance man, a function of Berlin's increased presence in Hollywood from the late 1930s on. Astaire renewed his stardom after parting company with RKO and Rogers by participating in high-profile Berlin projects that originated around others. *Holiday Inn* and *Blue Skies,* both produced by Paramount, were Crosby films first: Astaire was a coequal guest star on Crosby's home lot (see figure 3). Both films were huge hits. In a useful table, Mueller uses gross receipts to estimate the rank achieved by each of Astaire's films in its year of release. By this reckoning, both Berlin-Crosby-Astaire films broke the top five worldwide on their initial releases and were exceeded in Astaire's film musical career only by *The Gay Divorcee, Top Hat,* and *Easter Parade* (the latter two, of course, also Berlin films).[17] Always aware of the mechanics of the entertainment business, Astaire reiterated as late as 1976 the benefits to his own career of teaming with Crosby at the height of the crooner's fame.[18] Berlin's first MGM film, *Easter Parade,* was intended for Judy Garland and Gene Kelly. In taking over for Kelly, Astaire enjoyed a major midcareer success that set the table for his 1950s films at MGM and elsewhere. The continuing viability of Astaire's career benefited immensely from these very successful films, which were not, in essence, Astaire-centered projects, this triptych of 1940s successes forming yet another example of Astaire's sustained good luck. When seen within the development of the popular song and jazz repertory, Berlin's strategy of mixing old and new songs in the scores for all three films put Astaire at the point of origin for the evolving category of songs called standards. As *Variety* noted of *Holiday Inn,* "The titular 'Holiday Inn' idea is a natural, and Berlin has fashioned some peach songs to fit the highlight holidays. A couple are a cinch to take their place as American popular song standards, along with his now classic 'Easter Parade.'"[19] The notion of "popular song standards" was just taking shape in commercial terms in the early 1940s: Hollywood musicals, seen in movie houses and later on television, would play a large role in this process. Astaire, often by association with Berlin, was always close by.

FIGURE 3. Paramount's promotional priorities are graphically expressed in this magazine advertisement for *Holiday Inn*.

"MOMENTS"

Astaire did much more than simply sing the songs written for him. (He did, of course, also sing them simply, and Astaire's songwriters valued his faithfulness to words and music, his plugging their songs in a professional manner and teaching the vast popular audience lyrics and tunes that would come to form the fabric of popular culture.) But as a dancer who crafted his own dances on his own body, Astaire reshaped the musical material of songs for his own purposes. This is a venerable, solidly American approach to musical creation, an approach Richard Crawford defines as "performer's music . . . ruled by performers who shape composers' scores to fit the occasion, . . . a realm where works aspire to accessibility: to acceptance by the target audience."[20] The realm of performer's music was shared by popular performers and jazz artists alike. Astaire was both.

Astaire used songs as raw materials from which to create completely planned routines. *Routine* is an important word here. The practice has its roots in vaudeville, where performers were responsible for their own acts, either doing their own creative work or hiring a routine-making specialist to design an act for them. During Astaire's time on Broadway, similar practices prevailed in both revues and book shows. Astaire had acknowledged ability as a routinemaker before heading to Hollywood. He doctored some dances for Ginger Rogers in the Gershwin musical *Girl Crazy* (1930) and routined most of his and his sister Adele's numbers. Making a song into a routine was the basic creative task confronting Astaire across his entire career.

Astaire's creative emphasis on routine making comes into further focus when we distinguish between making musical films and making musical numbers. Acting was part of his work, and he played light romantic comedy with a skill honed by years on the musical comedy stage, where he was required to read lines clearly, deliver jokes with the right timing, and play conventional characters. But acting was always a sideline, never the main event, and his nonmusical work on film and television remains a nonessential footnote to his creative career. Astaire was never seriously interested in creative control over the plotlines of his musical films. There is some evidence of dialogue altered on the spot—often when the subject of music came up—but Astaire did not get involved with plot questions beyond a desire to avoid kissing his leading ladies.[21] His primary creative interest lay in the making of self-contained musical numbers, an expressive unit that remained consistent across his vaudeville, Broadway, Hollywood, and television work. All these venues required of Astaire was the stunning smash number. A tendency toward music- and dance-centered rather than dramatically integrated musical numbers is evident across Astaire's output. This is not to undercut those instances when Astaire did create an integrated dance number or when a particular number can be read as furthering the plot. But I find little evidence in the archival record that Astaire saw integration of song and dance with plot or storytelling as in any way central to the task of making routines, which were instead principally designed to have internal coherence and stand out from their film contexts.[22]

In the final pages of *The Whole Equation: A History of Hollywood*, film critic and historian David Thomson aptly summarizes Astaire's accomplishment and sets it within the larger context of the studio era. Thomson's single sentence on Astaire speaks to the challenge of routine making, a creative task that demands the making of memorable moments.

> There was once an ease and good nature and a lyrical expression of behavior in American films that shrugged off all the stupid orthodoxies about "happy endings." It knew not to wait for endings, but to trust to the moment. And maybe no moments are so fine, as beautiful and as free from "meaning" as the way Astaire moves, over the course of thirty years in American pictures, doing "Pick Yourself Up" with Ginger Rogers in *Swing Time;* "Begin the Beguine" with Eleanor Powell in *Broadway Melody of 1940;* or "All of You" with Cyd Charisse in *Silk Stockings*. Or pick your moments.[23]

Astaire was a maker of moments. His goal wasn't so much integration as exhilaration. And so Astaire's career is best understood as a body of musical numbers (or routines, or moments) hosted by the feature-length narrative films that were (and remain) the stock in trade of the movie business, the product the Hollywood system was best equipped to sell at a profit. For a time—a relatively long time—the movie public bought musicals, and during almost the full length of that time Astaire was in a position to make musical routines on himself using popular songs as raw material. The "moments" Astaire made, to use Thomson's term, are satisfying in themselves, and making them was enough for Astaire. Many of the routines discussed in this book are available in the form of independent clips on YouTube, an expression of Astaire's Internet fans recognizing that the essence of his work is found in musical numbers that can be profitably extracted from the films that originally hosted them.

Astaire understood the importance of musical numbers and the risk that good work on his part might not find an audience because of poor work on someone else's part. His draft autobiography includes this lament: "My my—it is always regrettable to waste good numbers in a mediocre picture. . . . You can dance your head off and perhaps it could be one of the best things you've ever done but if it's smothered in a 'nuthin' [sic] opera you are just dead—that's all." Astaire's frustration betrays a lack of interest in integrating the content of his musical numbers into the fabric of the films hosting them. He worked alone making a specific and defined part of the film under the constant risk that his best work might be "smothered" by someone else's failure. Of course, Astaire did work with others, specifically screenwriters, to place his numbers in narrative contexts. This wasn't all that difficult given the conventional nature of musical plots and Astaire's power (especially at RKO) to demand a spot for a number he was interested in making. If he wanted to do a golf dance, the studio simply wrote one into the film. Still, tension between the content of musical numbers and plot and dialogue proves important again and again in extant archival documents. Writers thought in narratives, Astaire in musical numbers. Consistent evidence, mainly from treatments and script files, reveals how Astaire frequently transformed a screenwriter's idea for a dramatically integrated number into a stand-alone song-and-dance routine. Astaire tended to resist (or just ignore) writers' attempts to integrate a number they imagined him doing or dictate the internal narrative of a routine. He preferred instead to make numbers that were about music and dance and kept his audience from dropping him "like a hot plate." Examples stretch from the beginning to the end of Astaire's career. Three are described below.

Early scenarios for "Let's Face the Music and Dance," the final number in *Follow the Fleet,* brought the story enacted in the pantomime opening into the dance itself. In this stage-bound number presented as a self-contained narrative within the film, Astaire and Rogers appear as sophisticated Monte Carlo gamblers, both contemplating suicide. Playing more serious versions of character types they had portrayed in earlier films, "Let's Face the Music and Dance" can be read as a miniature Astaire and Rogers's film—the melodrama they never made—complete with dramatic underscoring by Max Steiner for the pantomime sequence at the opening.[24] Screenwriters Dwight Taylor and Allan Scott certainly understood the number as a short dramatic film. After losing his money at the gambling tables and blithely contemplating suicide, Astaire spots Rogers about to kill herself by leaping into the sea. He stops her, pulls her from the parapet, and sings the tune. Then they dance. In Taylor and Scott's imagination, the threat of suicide was to hang over the first section of the dance: "They both dance with a frenzy because both expect to die at the end of it."[25] The shooting script, broken down into specific shots, called for Astaire to toss Rogers's gun into the sea at the midpoint of the dance. A quick cutaway was to show "the gun fall out into the water," then cut back to Astaire and Rogers dancing: "There is a triumphant reprise of the number. They are both in love with each other." The internal narrative is here imagined to both motivate the dance and cue changes within it. In the film version, under Astaire's control, the gun is tossed into the sea before the vocal even begins, facilitating a dance that is focused more on movement and gesture than story. Rogers's distinctive beaded dress becomes the visual keynote to the sequence, which offers a maximum of contrast with the rest of the film. The dance of poses and patterns Astaire made from Berlin's "Let's Face the Music and Dance" lacks any dramatic through line.

Early scripts for *Let's Dance* envisioned a nightclub set with large windows opening onto a New York street.[26] Playing a character initially imagined as an unmotivated former child star more interested in playing the horses than dancing, Astaire, while rehearsing a nightclub solo, was to see his bookie through the windows and exit the club during the dance to place a bet. After reentering the club, while still dancing, Astaire was to see Betty Hutton's character Kitty, his long-lost love, on the street and exit again in pursuit of her, this time with coat and hat, to close out the number. A nightclub set with windows onto a busy street was impractical for many reasons, expense being uppermost. Studio sets were usually either interior or exterior—seldom both. The indoor-outdoor element was among the first to go as the scene was revised. Don, Astaire's character, was framed as both lazy and uninterested in show business, and later draft scripts, by experienced Astaire screenwriter Allan Scott, tried to hang on to the notion of Don being distracted from dancing while dancing. The 4 April 1949 script has Don shuffling through papers in his briefcase during the dance.[27] The nightclub manager watches, regretfully thinking Don is just throwing away his talent. In this draft, Astaire's exit from the club at the end of the number was still motivated by him seeing Hutton, this time through the nightclub doorway.

In the final filmed version, all references to the plot are removed from the "Ad Lib Dance." Hutton has nothing to do with the number: Astaire runs into her by chance in the next scene instead. Astaire's Don goes into his dance for strictly musical reasons, motivated by the contrast between a waltz and a bluesy groove at first, then carried away by the music as the number progresses. Scott revised his description of the number in the final version of the script: "This is the AD LIB NUMBER, and it ends with Don dancing with unbelievable brilliance, astonishing the on-lookers by dancing right out of the supper club, indicating that this is enough rehearsal for him for the day."[28] Scott hangs on to a shred of character motivation for the exit, but viewers are hardly thinking in plot terms at the end of the "Ad Lib Dance," one of Astaire's most spectacular and surprising routines. The concept of a tossed-off, disinterested rehearsal routine came from a screenwriter. Astaire, making the number in collaboration with his veteran aide Hermes Pan, removed any and all connections between the plot of *Let's Dance* and the number, except for his character's initial reluctance to rehearse. For any viewer who had read an Astaire profile in a newspaper or fan magazine over the previous two decades, there was delicious irony in Astaire's line, "Rehearse! Oh, that horrible, horrible word." This line first appears in a script dated just a week before the number and the short scene leading into it was shot, suggesting Astaire, having finished making the dance, had turned his attention to the dialogue setup. (Other examples of dialogue revisions made just before an Astaire solo was shot are discussed below.) Astaire loved rehearsing: it calmed the perfectionist in him. In *Let's Dance,* Astaire visibly relishes saying a line so at odds with his known star persona. Once the dance gets going, and crucially once the music changes to a bluesy stride piano idiom, Astaire dives completely into the number. The notion that he would stop to go through a briefcase is laughable. He does, however, stop and play a few boogie-woogie blues choruses at a conveniently placed piano. Astaire exits with coat and hat before astonished onlookers, but there is nothing casual or offhand about his dance. He's fully into the routine once it gets going, and music motivates the dance from start to finish. (In chapter 8, I analyze the musical content of the "Ad Lib Dance.")

In his final studio-era musical, Astaire bucked the efforts of director Rouben Mamoulian to integrate dance more closely into *Silk Stockings*. A champion of musical-dramatic integration, Mamoulian was returning to pictures after an eight-year absence.[29] He brought with him strong ideas for integrating dance in the film, flooding producer Freed's office with memos outlining in detail his concept of *Silk Stockings* as a dance movie where the dancing was more than "mere ornamentation." Mamoulian wrote, "We should make it serve some important dramatic purpose. So let us think of Astaire's and Charisse's dancing as one of the most vital and emotional factors in advancing the story." Mamoulian envisioned two moments when Astaire and Charisse could bring dramatically integrated dance into the film: when they initially fell in love and at the end of the picture, when Charisse's Communist character Ninotchka finally embraces the West in the person of Astaire. Mamoulian hoped that "the Dance here becomes the climactic factor which resolves the whole story."[30] In the end, a short dialogue scene—neither song nor dance—resolved the story, and Astaire and Charisse danced in fairly standard places. The flirtatious dance to "All of You" is clearly an integrated number, as Mueller points out.[31] The musical-dramatic potential of casting Charisse, a dancing star, as a buttoned-down Communist serves as an authentic source of dramatically integrated dance throughout the film. Her dances, all made by Eugene Loring, are integrated to a high degree. Screen credit for the choreography pointedly divides the film into Astaire's dances (created by Astaire and Dave Robel) and everything else (created by Loring). Astaire and Charisse's only dance duet besides "All of You"—to the added film song "Fated to Be Mated"—was a quickly assembled partner routine with little plot meaning. The dance doesn't suggest any change in their relationship, makes little sense given Charisse's character's background, and was created in a hurry by Hermes Pan as a replacement for a bicycle-riding idea that proved too time-consuming to shoot.[32] The highlight of the final reel—that spot "next to closing"—is taken up by Astaire's completely unmotivated nightclub solo "The Ritz Roll and Rock," another added song and an obvious nod toward changing popular music trends (see chapter 7).

In all three of the above cases—drawn from films made in 1935, 1949, and 1956–57—differences between draft and shooting scripts and the finished films highlight the control Astaire had over his numbers and, more to the point, show how he felt free to ignore scriptwriters' and directors' suggestions to create narrative dances or integrate the content of his numbers with the plot of the film. Instead, Astaire made the dances he wanted to make, expecting his own musical and choreographic work, rather than the screenwriter's logic, to carry the number and, in the end, the film. This focus on the striking song-and-dance moment was his consistent (and consistently achieved) goal.

Looking at the breadth of Astaire's work on camera from the perspective of artistic choices and archival evidence, four larger priorities are consistently evident in his approach to routining music and dance "moments." The first three are matters of content and style; the fourth involves process. First, Astaire explored a broad range of popular music forms and styles. The music and his dancing change with the times while remaining faithful to his signature persona, already in place when he arrived in Hollywood. Astaire was typically more attentive to the popular music environment surrounding American movie theaters than to details of plot or character within a particular movie.

Second, Astaire liked variety within his dances. Shifts of tone and style occur consistently within his routines. There is virtually always a change of tempo (or speed) in the music. Contrasting dynamic (or volume) levels, often extreme, are common as well. Variety, whether musical or choreographic, serves a basic function: it keeps audiences interested, unsure of what feats of dancing or rhythmic prowess lay just around the corner. Variety as an internal principal of routining a song can, of course, stand in the way of dramatic integration, which demands a through line. Astaire's shifts of tone and style seldom have a linear effect. Instead they follow the logic of a kaleidoscope, eliciting delight and wonder at every turn.

Third, Astaire cared about the sound content of his dances. On a musical level, he carefully selected arrangers and orchestrators (see chapter 5). On a choreographic level, his sensitivity to sound manifested itself most directly in his consistent use of tap, which gave audible presence and added musical content to his dances. But the importance of sound is also evident in his meticulous application of dubbed foot sounds throughout his film work, even when tap is not the central style of a given dance. The sound of his body—like all Hollywood sound effects, a meticulously constructed illusion—added heft and presence to Astaire's dancing image. Foot sounds were nearly always recorded in the postproduction phase, after music and image had been edited together. Astaire was always up for this final step in the process. He went on at length about foot sounds in his draft autobiography, describing the difficulty of remembering a long series of dance steps and matching them back to the edited picture as "hard labor plus," particularly when weeks or months elapsed between shooting and dubbing. While a dance could fill a large space during filming, dubbing was done in a contained area, similar to the four-foot-square wood pad on which Astaire tapped during his radio shows. In effect, the moves of the dance had to be altered to add the sounds to the sound/image whole. Astaire even noted the welcome technical advantage of doing the dubbing while wearing headphones without wires, a further example of how practical he initially intended his autobiography to be. Dubbing foot sounds was "a laborious chore," something the audience may not directly notice but necessary even in "less important numbers," which, Astaire emphasized, "have to be thoroughly and completely presented."

Beyond the necessary dubbing of foot sounds in tap-centric routines, foot sounds inserted into any routine enhanced the on-screen illusion that Astaire's dancing body had weight and substance, more than just two dimensions. Foot sounds were not the norm across musical pictures, and many musical numbers were presented to the public in a playback vacuum, where bodies make no sounds at all. Busby

Berkeley and Gene Kelly both favored dances in a playback vacuum, typically adding foot sounds, usually brief tap combinations, in an abrupt on-and-off fashion. Kelly often tapped in loafers: Astaire always wore proper shoes and often his taps are visible. In Astaire's films, foot sounds are the norm. His careful application of an added layer of sound reveals his creative process as one that reached beyond simply making moving pictures of dancing to music: he wanted something close to real presence, a goal that made his routines all that more immediate. The added element of foot sounds also underlines how important the dimension of sound was to Astaire's creative sensibilities. Without adding in the sound of his body, his dances and the music accompanying them would be incomplete. (See the discussion of the "Jukebox Dance" below.)

Fourth, Astaire demanded an absolute meticulousness of preparation. Filmed routines were made in layers, and successful planning and execution were part of doing the job right. His creative process yielded an efficiently made, seemingly spontaneous film artifact of a thoroughly synthetic nature. Astaire was not only a musician and choreographer but also a studio technician who knew how to use the expensive production apparatus of the Hollywood studio to make extraordinary and innovative routines at a minimal cost of time and labor. He worked well with the technicians on the set. Astaire's ability to do this should not be underrated: it was highly valued by producers and the front office. Astaire's careful process had aesthetic ramifications, particularly if we are to attach the word *jazz*, commonly associated with spontaneity and improvisation, to this most careful of planners. The push and pull between spontaneous invention in the rehearsal hall, complete planning on the set, and the appearance of spontaneity in the finished product form a constant theme in Astaire's creative labors.

ROUTINING AND BESPOKE TAILORING

A lost Astaire routine to the song "Got a Bran' New Suit" from *The Band Wagon,* described in detail by associate producer Roger Edens in a production document, lays out Astaire's typical process creating a routine (albeit in the context of a stage production within a film). Edens's rundown of the multipart routine reflects production priorities specific to the music department, enumerating usages of the song for practical rather than dramatic purposes. The distinction between production and nonproduction usages is revealing.

There are five usages:

a. Miss Fabray sings one chorus of the song for Mr. Astaire. She is merely auditioning the song. There is no attempt at production.

b. Mr. Astaire, with a rehearsal pianist, is rehearsing the number—trying to find an "idea" for its use in the show. He sings the song, abstractedly, for a few bars only. This usage is very brief.

c. Again, Mr. Astaire is rehearsing the number. This time he discovers a device with his cane—that gives him an inspiration for the staging of the number. This usage is also very brief.

d. Mr. Astaire working with his cane. Although we assume that it is based on the song "Got a Bran' New Suit" because we have established that song in this brief montage effect. However, no use of the song is made in this spot. He dances only with drums.

e. Mr. Astaire has now perfected the number, and he sings and dances two full choruses of it for Mr. Levant and Miss Fabray. This is done in rehearsal clothes and is on the stage of the theatre. It is not a performance. There is no scenic production. There is no audience. At the finish of his dance he is told by Mr. Levant and Miss Fabray that the number has been cut out of the show.

Usage: The entire usage in the five scenes consist[s] of approximately five choruses.

Status: Has been recorded. Has been shot.[33]

This entire sequence was itself cut from *The Band Wagon* by early March 1953. The soundtrack for usages "a" and "e" survives (without the tap breaks).[34]

As suggested by "Got a Bran' New Suit," Astaire began with a song and then proceeded, through intense rehearsal with a pianist (and sometimes a drummer), to shape the song to his own ends, often by the addition of an unrelated physical element or conceit (such as a cane) or unrelated musical materials (such as rhythms provided by drums alone). The entire process can be compared to ordering, making, and fitting a bespoke tailored suit. The work is done in private and the customer, in this case highly informed, has the final call on all decisions. The goal is absolute consonance between the clothes and the man. Continuing with the theme of "Got a Bran' New Suit," I use the metaphor of bespoke tailoring in this overview of the collaborative relationships between Astaire and his songwriters, rehearsal pianists, dance directors, and cameramen. A song provided for Astaire's purposes is roughly comparable to material chosen or offered for a suit: songs have qualities of their own that might be described using tailors' technical terms such as hand, drape, or pattern. After the material is selected, bespoke tailors and their customers discuss the intended cut, style, and function of the garment before it can be cut out and stitched together. Fittings and adjustments continue until the suit and the man are ready to step outside the secluded realm of the tailor shop, a space in every way similar to Astaire's relentlessly private rehearsal studio. Cutting, fitting, and stitching together prove felicitous terms for the purposes of this bespoke tailoring metaphor.

In the process of routining a song, Astaire cut, fit, and stitched his musical materials in two ways: musically and cinematically. First, he arranged the component parts of the song to suit his needs, selecting, cutting, and arranging the song text in whatever order worked best. Sometimes this required adding to the material provided by the songwriter, or in effect padding or patching the song with other musical materials. Several of Astaire's solos are motley garments, with most of the materials borrowed from elsewhere. Astaire's grasp of popular music and jazz practices allowed him to take full control over the musical content of his dances. Second, Astaire routined his numbers with the camera always in mind, building the dance with camera angles and shot lengths already set. This was normally the director's job. But Astaire's directors were virtually never around while the dance was being made in the rehearsal studio. Instead, once the creative work was completed—once the dance was made—they were confronted with a fully worked-out routine, ready for filming. There was really only one way to shoot it, and often the director supervising the shooting of dance numbers was the dance director on the film, who likely spent time with Astaire in the rehearsal hall, and not the credited director, whose time was spent on the dialogue scenes. (Assistant director, or AD, reports reveal who was in charge on any given set on any given day.) In Hollywood lingo, Astaire's meticulous planning of shots in advance was known as editing in the camera, a strategy associated with directors who were both efficient on the set and good at exerting control over the final product. Editing in the camera creates a situation where there is no extra footage or coverage. The editor, or cutter, is left with few choices: the shots work together only one way. Astaire certainly participated to some extent in the editing process as well.[35]

Astaire was a picky customer when selecting tunes for routining. He could demand exactly the song he wanted, and on occasion he ignored what he was given. For example, Astaire's big solo in *Swing Time* posed a challenge for composer Jerome Kern. Astaire wanted a rhythm number, but Kern was not known for syncopated tunes. Lyricist Dorothy Fields remembered, "This was a tough one for Kern." Astaire, Fields said, tried to help by dancing around her house for a few afternoons, tapping out broken rhythms to get Kern into a syncopated mood.[36] Kern and Fields responded with "Bojangles of Harlem," a two-beat tune not quite in line with Astaire's desires. When he first played the song for Astaire, rehearsal pianist Hal Borne recalled Astaire "had a kind of strange look on his face."[37] In routining the number, Astaire handed off the vocal to an unseen chorus, and his assistant Hermes Pan created ensemble routines to Kern's melody for the large female dance chorus and Astaire. (Astaire apparently never routined an ensemble dance.) For his own heavily syncopated solo segments in "Bojangles," Astaire danced to original material, an instrumental chorus using a jazzed-up descending minor tetrachord, most of it vamps created and played by Borne. The arranging staff didn't even bother to notate Borne's piano sections. He played it directly onto the soundtrack, which is pieced together like the separate shots on the image track. In similar fashion, Astaire rejected Porter's try at a bugle call-based dance tune for the guardhouse routine in *You'll Never Get Rich*. Porter's "A-Stairable Rag," a series of twenty-bar instrumental strains, was set aside. Instead, Astaire built his solo on a usage of the twelve-bar blues known to all popular music listeners under the title "Bugle Call Rag" (see chapter 7).

But most of the time Astaire was pleased with the musical material his songwriters provided. His most direct method of routining a song fell within the logic of live performance: sing the verse (if there is one), then sing the chorus, then dance one or more instrumental choruses. (Astaire avoided singing after having danced.) Some songs written for Astaire arrived with a musical structure that could be quite easily routined in just this way. Irving Berlin's "Cheek to Cheek" from *Top Hat* affords an exemplary case of a song that routined itself. After Astaire sings the chorus—Berlin provided no verse—while dancing with Rogers casually on a crowded floor, the couple moves across an elaborate bridge to an empty pavilion set aside for this moment. Crossing the bridge takes six bars: it's the only passage in the number that does not use Berlin's melody in a straightforward fashion. Once in the pavilion, Astaire and Rogers dance a chorus and a half of a song with built-in shifts of mood and scale. Berlin's tune fell right in line with Astaire's priority of variety as an essential quality of the successful routine.

"Cheek to Cheek" is a long song—seventy-two bars—in an unorthodox AABBCA structure. The double-length sixteen-bar A phrases are delicate and emotional, beginning with a repeated sigh figure—sung twice to the word "heaven." Four more sighs carry the phrase to its melodic height, after which Berlin closes with a cunningly syncopated line—"when we're out together dancing Cheek to Cheek"—that includes the title phrase and leavens the perhaps too ardent opening. The yearning, somewhat tentative quality of Berlin's A phrase yields a restrained dance when Astaire and Rogers begin. They initially turn past each other, as if not yet ready to get too close. A distinctive backward dip, restrained in both expression and extension, occurs three times in the first two A phrases, unifying this opening, which is further tied together in movement and music terms by a repetition of the same steps for the final four bars of the phrase, where the couple steps along with Berlin's syncopated melody.

The B phrase takes up only eight bars. But instead of being heard only once, it's heard twice, the resulting BB (like each A phrase) taking up sixteen bars. (Berlin built "Cheek to Cheek" on an especially generous scale, one reason Astaire could shape the dance so directly on the song.) The mood of the song changes in the B phrases. The melody takes on a jaunty syncopated style and the lyric, about active, manly pursuits like mountain climbing and fishing, acquires a less elevated diction. Astaire and Rogers match the B phrase's change of tone with two contrasting dance moods. A bit of side-by-side soft shoe and a noticeably lighter, witty sort of movement are used for the first B. Foot sounds come to the fore here, heard clearly above the dynamically restrained arrangement that trades in the violins for the sound of a swing band. For the second iteration of the B phrase, Astaire and Rogers go into closed partner position for a combination (done twice) involving a quick turn and a slow-motion dip. In both danced versions of the B, the rhythmic patterns of the dance, both as heard and seen, play against Berlin's melody.

The C phrase marks a dramatic shift in tone harmonically, melodically, and lyrically. The imperative sentence "Dance with me" begins a phrase full of heretofore unheard dotted rhythms and utilizing large melodic leaps over surprisingly distant harmonies, lending a more extroverted, broadly romantic quality to the song. It's the only moment open to parody—there's something sort of grand about it—but this bit of high-toned romance passes after only eight bars. The dance matches the C phrase's elevation of tone with side-by-side moves incorporating rapid large gestures and unpredictable holds and poses that highlight Rogers's feather dress. When the A phrase returns to close the first pass through the chorus, Astaire and Rogers return to the more tentative nature of the opening. After they have danced the tune in its entirety once through, the music skips back to the C phrase for a closing half chorus. The grand style of the C phrase returns and is sustained almost to the end of the tune, with the most dramatic poses, leaps, lifts, and dips yet seen done to an arrangement that pulls out all the stops.

But at the syncopated close to the final A phrase, the final four bars of the song, Berlin's jaunty little melody reasserts itself for a quiet ending. "Cheek to Cheek" has to end softly. Molded to Astaire's vocal frame, which favors stylish understatement over the big vocal finish, Berlin's tune dictates a dynamically soft close in the music and a gradual coming to rest in the dance. The style of the dance and the orchestration mirrors the tone of Berlin's melody and lyric phrase by phrase. By this musically sensitive method, Astaire makes a varied dance on the patterns of Berlin's wonderfully varied tune. "Cheek to Cheek" suits Astaire and Rogers's eclectic style particularly well: its inherent mix of volume, motion, rhythmic style, and expressive levels matches the stylistic range of their dancing, from casual soft shoe to romantic partnering to theatrical leaps and dips just on the edge of parody. With so much musical variety built into the song—both words and music—it worked to simply sing it, then dance it one and a half times. In the case of "Cheek to Cheek," Berlin's cloth could easily be made to suit Astaire and Rogers's danced romancing.

Astaire's straightforward building of a dance routine on song structure in "Cheek to Cheek" proves the exception. More often, Astaire reshaped songs to his own ends in a more intrusive manner. This recutting often involved a selective use of the materials provided. He used mostly the chorus of "No Strings," also from *Top Hat*, cycling through the song five times at various tempos while singing, dancing, and then playing a dramatic scene opposite Rogers. When some variety was needed in the underscoring, Astaire brought in the verse, which goes unsung in the film (but is heard on Astaire's contemporary pop recording of the tune). Sometimes additional musical material was needed to fill out a routine. Robert Emmett Dolan, musical director at Paramount, composed vamps for both the "Firecracker Dance" *(Holiday Inn)* and "Puttin' on the Ritz" *(Blue Skies)*, and Arthur Schwartz provided a vamp for his own tune, "A Shine on Your Shoes" *(The Band Wagon)*, among other revisions to the song.

Astaire's more invasive approaches frequently prove the most revealing. For example, he sometimes added measures, distorting the conventional shape of a song. The motivation for added measures may be musical. In the initial vocal chorus of Porter's "I've Got My Eyes on You," sung and played by Astaire at the piano in *Broadway Melody of 1940,* he inserts extra measures between phrases to lengthen the breaks. Into these longer breaks Astaire inserts rhythm pounded out by his feet on the floor and the piano itself. Similar lengthened breaks occur in the jazz concert solo at the end of *Second Chorus* and in "I'm Old Fashioned," a partner dance with Rita Hayworth in *You Were Never Lovelier.* In the latter, the added measures facilitate Astaire and Hayworth's repetition of Spanish-style foot rhythms that lead into a rumba-flavored section when the tune returns. Stephen Banfield laments this moment as a "meaningless Hispanic break of a few bars," but variety such as this was central to Astaire's routine-making aesthetic, and all the creative players on the film followed Astaire's music and dance-making lead.[38] Perhaps the bit of stylized Latin rhythm was inspired by Hayworth's background or the setting of the film in South America. Within the routine, the added measures serve the goal of introducing rhythmic and stylistic variety into the otherwise conventional shape of the song, withholding the return of Kern's tune in a pleasurable way. When it comes back, with a rumba beat, the melody is all the more refreshing for having been put off for a few bars.[39]

Inserted measures could also be filled with quotations from other songs, a core practice among improvising jazz musicians. Astaire's use of quotation in a film was, of course, preplanned and sometimes entailed paying a fee to the owners of the quoted song. In the whiskbroom dance with George Burns and Gracie Allen from *A Damsel in Distress,* the Gershwin tune "Put Me to the Test" is interrupted by a quote from "Organ Grinder Swing," during which Allen pretends to be a dancing monkey and Burns and Astaire wait for a coin to drop. Once it does, Gershwin's tune resumes. Quotation of this hit 1937 tune necessitated a licensing fee, an added expense for the film.[40] In a similar novelty vein, measures of Scottish drone were inserted into "My One and Only Highland Fling," and the strains of the hoochie coochie dance are heard during the carnival shooting gallery portion of "Shoes with Wings On" (both Warren songs in *Barkleys*). In all the above instances, when Astaire recuts a given song to his own specifications, the song remains recognizable. Such additions are understated, often comic, and respect the musical structure handed to Astaire by the songwriter.

In the most extreme cases, Astaire completely redesigned the materials handed to him by his songwriters. Here the metaphor of Astaire as a tailor's customer begins to break down. Astaire is not only supervising the details of the cut but fundamentally reweaving the fabric. Often only the most basic structural elements remain unchanged. At times the song is effectively rewritten, to the extent that the original songwriter does not receive composition credit on the film's cue sheet, which goes instead to the arrangers and sometimes Astaire himself. These examples reveal Astaire's competence to serve as his own musical tailor and further emphasize just how difficult it is to sort out or set limits on the creative roles he played. In these dances Astaire is at once dancer, dance-maker, arranger, and even composer.

Using an old song for new purposes, Astaire refashioned the patter from "A Shine on Your Shoes," excising some measures, adding others, and regularizing the whole into a balanced trade-off between sung measures and measures of rhythm (provided by Astaire's shoe shiner dancing partner, LeRoy Daniels). The effect becomes one of singer and dancer trading fours, a familiar jazz practice. The melody and harmonic structure of Schwartz's tune is utterly changed, so much so that the new patter is not a variant so much as a new composition using basic materials from the song. This wasn't the first time Astaire made so bold a move. For the "Drunk Dance" in *Holiday Inn*, Astaire sampled a riff from Berlin's song "You're Easy to Dance With" and otherwise restructured the song so completely it necessitated a composer credit for the arrangers (see chapter 5). For "Drum Crazy" in *Easter Parade*, Astaire sang Berlin's verse and chorus and then proceeded to dance to a different set of chords entirely. "Drum Crazy" is in ABAC form: the first instrumental dance chorus of the "Drum Crazy" routine is AABA. Berlin's song disappears in favor of an original thirty-two-bar strain in stop time, leaving plenty of room for Astaire to pound out rhythmic licks on any and all drums in the toy shop. For the casual listener, the stop-time AABA dance chorus is seamlessly integrated with Berlin's tune. Beneath the surface of this routine, Astaire's control of his musical materials is evident. "Bouncin' the Blues" from *Barkleys* was never issued as sheet music. The surviving lead sheet contains nothing but the barest hint of the music heard in the film. Composer Warren provided a snatch of tune: Astaire built his own musical structure in collaboration with jazz musicians drawn from the MGM staff orchestra (see chapter 8).

In other cases Astaire didn't limit himself to a single song but instead assembled music for a routine from preexisting materials arranged in a montage or medley. The final partner dance in *Swing Time* combines a new song, "Never Gonna Dance," with reminiscences of several other tunes heard earlier in the film. The "Audition Solo" in *You Were Never*

FIGURE 4. Astaire and a pull-out group from Xavier Cugat's band (with Cugat in the light suit) are ejected from Adolph Menjou's office in this lobby photo from *You Were Never Lovelier.*

Lovelier is danced to a medley of excerpts from Xavier Cugat's hits. Seven members of Cugat's band accompany the number on-screen (see figure 4). How the number came to be made is not known—production documents for Columbia Pictures are almost entirely lacking—but clearly Astaire saw the chance to collaborate with the country's premiere Latin big band as more compelling than making a solo to a new song by the film's composer Jerome Kern. For his *You'll Never Get Rich* version of "Bugle Call Rag," Astaire assembled excerpts from the best-known jazz versions of the tune, creating an anthology of jazz practices (see chapter 7).

While music was the source of Astaire's dancing, he always made the music do what he wanted it to do. He exercised firm control over the musical structures he danced to, and songwriters were expected to give him free rein. His approach to routining songs reveals a level of control over musical materials possible only for a musician literate in the structures and possibilities of popular music and jazz. Astaire's unusual status as informed customer—he knew enough to recut the material himself, to talk in technical terms, perhaps even to step to the piano and demonstrate what he wanted (as Astaire's memory of working with Gershwin records)—brings his individuality into play yet again. And just as Astaire's actual tailor remembered him trying out a new suit by putting it on and dancing around the shop, when Astaire routined a number, he took over the musical tailor shop completely.

Astaire, an aspiring songwriter his whole life long, deeply respected the logic of popular music. While engaged in the process of routining a song, any alterations he made to the song's structure were invariably subtle, at times opening the door for Astaire's collaborators to do extraordinary work in their own right. No example of this delicacy with a song, and the musical rewards it could yield, exceeds the single measure Astaire added to Dietz and Schwartz's song "Dancing in the Dark" for the partner dance with Cyd Charisse in *The Band Wagon*. Astaire worked with choreographer Michael Kidd on this number. Here, a single additional bar opened the door to an artfully designed musical arrangement of this much-played jazz and pop standard. Astaire did not perform "Dancing in the Dark" in its original Broadway context, and it had remained a jazz and dance band standard during the two decades separating the stage and film versions of *The Band Wagon*. Astaire's choices in making the dance for the film yielded musical dividends that set this version of "Dancing in the Dark" apart from all others on musical grounds alone.

In the film there is no vocal, and the verse goes unheard. Dietz and Schwartz's chorus is in ABAC form. Astaire adds a single measure at the halfway point—between the B and second A—creating a thirty-three-bar tune in the process. Astaire and Charisse dance the altered chorus twice in succession. This addition redesigns the shape of the song as published in the 1931 sheet music and allows for a beautiful timbral crescendo in Robert Franklyn's orchestration. (Mueller and Levinson credit this arrangement anecdotally to Conrad Salinger. MGM music department records, which detail Salinger's work on various other numbers in *The Band Wagon*, list Franklyn as the sole orchestrator on "Dancing in the Dark." Songwriters Dietz and Schwartz receive composer-arranger credit.)[41] The extra measure was added by Astaire and Kidd while making the dance. It was an existing element Franklyn had to deal with. His arrangement is outlined below, with an analysis following.

FIRST CHORUS

A	8 bars	melody in cellos; oboe breaks from sheet music
B	8 bars	melody continues in cellos; flute and horn breaks from sheet music
1 added bar		*ascending scale* taking melody upward an octave in range
A	8 bars	melody in midrange violins; oboe and horn breaks from sheet music
C	8 bars	melody continues in midrange violins; three offbeat brass chords (original to this version) in break, followed by *ascending scale* taking melody upward an octave in range

SECOND CHORUS

A	8 bars	melody in upper-range violins; rhythm of brass breaks derived from sheet music, more assertive gestures begin
B	8 bars	melody continues in upper-range violins; two offbeat brass chords
1 added bar		third offbeat brass chord; followed by *ascending scale*
A	8 bars	melody in brass; strings play the breaks
C	8 bars	melody continues in brass and strings; horn breaks from sheet music return
Coda		repetition of title phrase twice more, with countermelody in horns

The A phrases of "Dancing in the Dark" begin with a rhythmically distinctive intonation of the title phrase on a single note. Franklyn uses this structural marker to advantage in his arrangement. Every half chorus Franklyn raises the pitch level of the melody by an octave. This occurs twice. Beginning at a low octave in the cellos, the melody is passed into the tenor range midway through the first chorus. The extra measure is filled with an ascending scale, smoothly carrying the tune up to the next octave. A similar stepwise rising melodic line ushers the melody into the upper register of the violins at the start of the second chorus. By this point the violins are already at the top of their comfortable range, and so Franklyn does not have the option of transposing the melody up an octave yet a third time at the halfway point of the second chorus. Instead, he moves the tune into the brass, led by the shiny sound of Metro's crack trumpet section. The effect is one of the arrangement suddenly opening up, beautifully expanding outward in both volume and timbre, with orchestral color taking over from the upward octave shifts in the strings, just as the choreographic content of the dance also reaches a climax. It's one of the great musical moments in musical film. Franklyn's strategy of raising the pitch level of the melody by an octave at each half chorus may find its origin in Schwartz's tune, which itself traces a rising melodic gesture, and it's not clear if Franklyn was handed the idea of an ever-rising octave for the melody or not. It is not a common approach to arranging the song for singers.[42] Whatever its origins, the extra measure at the halfway point opened the door to Franklyn's patient treatment of "Dancing in the Dark."

The melodic content of the breaks in "Dancing in the Dark" show the relation of musical arrangement to choreography in routines that lack foot sounds, while also pointing toward the ways Astaire and his collaborators might find inspiration in both the published sheet music and their own work with the tune in the rehearsal hall.[43] In the first chorus the breaks at the end of each phrase are derived from an inner voice found in the original sheet music and played by a solo oboe. Astaire and Charisse dance in time to these breaks, dancing the stems in a gestural if not audible way. One can imagine the dance being made right off the sheet music, perhaps inspired by the rehearsal pianist bringing out this particular musical detail. The extra bar at the halfway point of the second chorus extends a pattern of offbeat brass accents, each matching (or matched by) a pose from the dancing couple. First heard at the end of the first chorus, these brass punctuations are original to this arrangement, catching Astaire and Charisse's increasingly assertive moves in the latter stages of the dance. Here the pianist may be following the dancemakers, who needed strong musical gestures to match large physical gestures. Alternately, the offbeat chords could have come from something the pianist was trying out. Astaire could have played either role—that of dancemaker, or that of pianist. Undoubtedly, he liked the result.

The origin of the extra measure in "Dancing in the Dark" shows the subtlety of Astaire's approach to musical form and its grounding in the dance-making process, the extra bar facilitating choreographic choices integral to the routine. Astaire was able to make the structure of a given song bend without breaking; Franklyn, in turn, could make the orchestration progress upward in register, beautifully preparing the vibrant burst of brass at the end.

COLLABORATORS IN CAMERAWORK, MUSIC, AND DANCE

Given Astaire's consistent strategy of editing in the camera—conceiving his dances in a shot-by-shot manner—directors largely got out of his way. With the exception of his first starring vehicle and the three films Astaire made with director Vincente Minnelli, we can assume the sensibility behind the camera when Astaire is dancing belongs to the dancer. This awareness of and power over camera angles—something typically noted with regard to the likes of Greta Garbo, Marlene Dietrich, and Joan Crawford—was the ultimate in star control. Cameramen and directors were largely following Astaire's planned angles and shots. They came in after the dance was done and served as technical advisors. This does not mean Astaire took for granted the contribution that cameramen made to his work. In his draft autobiography, he recognized several individual cameramen. They were essential collaborators, but they were also always under his direction. As Astaire's closest dance collaborator Hermes Pan explained to *Cineaste:*

> Fred and I had complete artistic control. We more or less told the directors what to do. A lot of directors didn't know very much about music so there wasn't much choice. We even told them the angles we wanted, where it should be shot, what had to be cut. We explained how a step looked better from here, not so good from there. The cinematographers were very crucial in all this. They might have a suggestion that we try something different. Or they would explain why what we wanted couldn't be done. I would always consult them. I'd ask about the lens and if they could pull away, all sorts of technical details.[44]

Before turning to the important figure of Hermes Pan and the handful of other choreographers Astaire worked with, I want to introduce Astaire's rehearsal pianists. (Astaire's collaborations with arrangers and orchestrators are treated fully in chapter 5.) Astaire's rehearsal pianists never received screen credit. They were too low on the studio totem pole to warrant such recognition. But, as has already been suggested, they were essential to Astaire's process from the start. The most important was Hal Borne, who began work with Astaire on *Flying Down to Rio* and remained a stalwart partner through the end of the 1930s and into the very early 1940s. Astaire first heard Borne messing around at the piano in the sideline band suspended in a hot air balloon basket for the Aviator's Club scene in *Flying Down to Rio*. Astaire requested Borne for his pianist because, as Borne remembered in 1972, "He was looking for someone who could do what I do, and what I do is, I guess, a little special, because not only am I a composer but I'm an arranger, and I'd had a complete classical training back in Chicago. . . . I played some of my own things for Fred and some of Gershwin's and Kern's—things I'd known—and he said, 'Yeah, I think we got a piano.' "[45] Borne did substantial arranging work. For example, he worked out the introduction to "Top Hat, White Tie and Tails," an eighteen-measure modulating compilation of the most syncopated elements of Berlin's tune.[46] At RKO Borne was Astaire's closest musical collaborator, able to answer specific questions about Astaire's musical desires. After almost a decade with Astaire, Borne shifted to work outside film. Among his first projects after leaving the studios was Duke Ellington's 1941 *Jump for Joy,* a stage musical presented in Los Angeles. Borne was credited as a songwriter, although it's unclear how the connection with Ellington was made. In later years Borne became a music director for pop singers such as Tony Martin.

Among Astaire's other rehearsal pianists, Tommy Chambers stands out. Chambers regularly played for Astaire throughout the 1940s, working on *You'll Never Get Rich, The Sky's the Limit,* and *Let's Dance,* each made at a different studio, and each containing important routines discussed below. He was twice referenced by name in dialogue, and he once appeared on-screen as (unsurprisingly) Astaire's rehearsal pianist. Astaire and Chambers were even pictured together playing piano four hands in an article for *Life* magazine.[47] Walter Ruick worked with Astaire on *Broadway Melody of 1940* and also on *Funny Face* some seventeen years later. Occasionally evidence will pop up in production files naming Astaire's pianists—such as Harry Lojewski in *The Band Wagon*—but often the identity of these key collaborators can only be determined by inference. Rehearsal pianists sometimes received credit for their work on music department documents, where composition credits were noted separately from pay for time spent rehearsing. The composing and arranging contributions of Astaire's pianists were often substantial, and reference to these concealed collaborators will occur often in the following pages.

Across his forty years in Hollywood, Astaire worked with a surprisingly small group of dance directors. (The word *choreographer* came into use only in the 1950s.) Chief among them was Hermes Pan, who started out with Astaire on *Flying Down to Rio* and proved a lifelong collaborator, their work together extending to 1968. Already in 1937 reviewers were calling Pan Astaire's "vet terp aide."[48] The exact contribution each made to their collaborative work is difficult to determine. As screen-writer Leonard Gershe noted in 1988, "No one must ever minimize the contribution of Hermes Pan to the legend that is Fred Astaire. His contribution was not only in the choreography but also in the humor. . . . Both of them were very modest, shy people, so nobody ever said who did what. To my knowledge, they never argued; they just did their work. They were professional, and they set about it every day."[49] But Astaire and Pan's bond went beyond temperament and a strong rehearsal ethic. A rhythmic affinity, a matter of the musical content of the dance, also underlay their long creative partnership, as Pan explained to Astaire biographer Bob Thomas.

> I always loved after-beats and broken rhythm. And he was the master of the broken rhythm. The first thing I showed him was a broken-rhythm thing, and that appealed to him. It's a black tradition, and I learned it from the blacks in Tennessee. There was such a difference between that kind of tap and the kind I learned from dancers in New York. I used to dance on my flat foot and heel, which Fred does. Most tap dancers do it on their toes; it's the orthodox style: tip-tap. It's more mechanical, but very intricate. . . . Fred and I used to call [our style] "gutbucket." He and I would work up terms so we could understand each other. Like, "a whip" or "right-now beat." He'd do something and say, "What do you think?" I'd say, "Great." He'd say, "I don't like the way you say 'Great.' If you said, 'Knocked-out,' I'd believe you."[50]

Pan and Astaire's work together sounds experimental, immediate, and unscripted, never a matter of stringing together set steps from standard dance practice, whether ballet, ballroom, or tap. Pan's reminiscence echoes Astaire's description of the "little games" he and Gershwin indulged in while making Broadway shows. Astaire, Gershwin, and Pan were all grounded in a style they understood to originate among African Americans, whom they admired greatly but were unable (or unwilling) to bring directly into the creative process. The need to "work up terms" for the steps Pan and Astaire were inventing suggests a restless search for new figures, new effects, new sounds, the more "broken" the better. Separating Pan from Astaire proves exceedingly difficult. And Pan added to the complexity in a 1989 interview: "Yes, [Fred and I] were quite the team. However, there was one more to this team than just Astaire and Pan—someone who was perhaps just as instrumental in the shaping of these dances as either of us—a gentleman by the name of Hal Borne. . . . [Hal] could take a thing, play certain breaks and rhythms that would inspire steps."[51] The musical origin of Astaire's dancing is again underlined. Astaire, Pan, and Borne evidently egged each other on, and their sustained collaboration at RKO from 1933 to 1939 certainly helped forge Astaire's broken-rhythm style. (The threesome worked together a final time away from RKO on *Second Chorus,* for which Borne finally got composer credit for a song in an Astaire picture.) But whatever elements of Astaire's dances originated with Pan, in the end they were embraced by Astaire and executed by him on-screen, and he was able to make similar dances without Pan's assistance.

Astaire's work at MGM in the 1940s and 1950s brought him into contact with strong creative players who had a hand in making his numbers. At Metro he was not in complete control, as he had been at RKO and everywhere else. Of course, Astaire didn't need MGM to make him a star, and, unlike most Metro types, he never expressed undue appreciation for the chance to have worked there. Astaire brought his own homemade chicken soup for his lunch breaks and elected not to eat in the Metro commissary, where Louis B. Mayer's family recipe for chicken soup was always on the menu.[52] Unlike many at Metro, Astaire had done good work all over town, and in a move unthinkable for most Hollywood stars, Astaire simply walked away from a Metro contract in 1946 with the studio's blessing. Consistent with his rather distant personality, Astaire was never part of the chummy Arthur Freed Unit so fondly remembered by many associated with the group.[53] Astaire was temperamentally unsuited to the Freed group, which favored a stylized, theatrical mode and was largely unconnected to popular music and jazz trends. However, younger players in the Freed Unit, such as Stanley Donen, Charles Walters, Betty Comden, Adolph Green, and Michael Kidd, showed Astaire creative deference at Metro, always mindful that they were working with a living legend who had defined their own idea of what was possible in musical film. So while there was room for him to create signature numbers at Metro, Astaire's routines for Freed—nominally choreographed by or in collaboration with Robert Alton, Eugene Loring, and Michael Kidd—are a mixed bag in terms of creative control. (Pan was brought in to Metro in a limited extent as well.)

Robert Alton proved a flexible and willing collaborator, if one discounts "This Heart of Mine" and "Limehouse Blues," the two "panto-ballets" in *Ziegfeld Follies* that were directed by Minnelli. These two high-concept routines show almost no evidence of Astaire's creative input. One giveaway is the complete lack of foot sounds in both, creating playback vacuums matching their stylized, soundstage-bound settings. On-the-beat choreography, gimmicky use of treadmills, mannered hand motions and poses, and the complete lack of tap also suggest Astaire was being told rather than telling. Minnelli's swooping crane shots and discontinuous editing show that Astaire relinquished control over the camera. But in later years Alton proved able to assist Astaire on his own terms, making more rhythm-centered routines for *Easter Parade, The Barkleys of Broadway,* and *The Belle of New York,* all three directed by Charles Walters, who revered Astaire and had an unassuming but skillful way with direction. These films marked a return to form for Alton, who had worked as an able Astaire assistant on the Columbia film *You'll Never Get Rich* before the Minnelli "panto-ballets."

Choreographer Eugene Loring and Minnelli crafted the most pretentious musical sequence Astaire ever appeared in: the nearly sixteen-minute dream ballet in *Yolanda and the Thief.* Astaire yielded complete choreographic control to Loring, and the outcome was not successful.[54] Astaire avoided Loring thereafter. They worked together only once more, on *Funny Face* some eleven years later, and it's unclear how much input Loring had on Astaire's solo in that film. As noted earlier, the screen credits for *Silk Stockings* explicitly make the point that Loring and Astaire did not collaborate. The production process on the *Yolanda* ballet was extremely inefficient. Scenarios in the extant scripts and treatments don't match the film version at all. AD reports tell a tale of on-set improvisation of the sort Astaire himself never would have countenanced. The number took eleven days to shoot. Some days yielded no usable footage, an absurd situation in the studios, where production was measured daily in scenes completed and feet of film shot. In a number with no foot sounds and no syncopated jazz content, Astaire was, for the first time, surrounded by trained dancers, particularly the men playing jockeys. Loring found little for Astaire to do with these men and, as a result, Astaire at times disappears from his own dream. It is perhaps no coincidence that, after making three high-concept, non-rhythm-based routines under Minnelli's direction in *Ziegfeld* and *Yolanda,* Astaire chose to terminate his Metro contract prematurely and go into retirement in 1946.[55]

In stark contrast, about seven years after *Yolanda* Minnelli and choreographer Michael Kidd worked with Astaire to create a signature ballet in *The Band Wagon:* the twelve-minute "Girl Hunt Ballet: A Murder Mystery in Jazz." By his own admission, Kidd took the lead in making the dances for this number, and "Girl Hunt" rewards close viewing for this reason: Astaire dances without foot sounds but with a rightness and conviction that had a lasting impact on his work. Astaire was enthusiastic about working with Kidd but reticent at times about trying new ideas. Kidd remembered working feverishly during off-hours to create finished combinations to present to Astaire during the nine-to-five rehearsals.[56] Their collaboration was not reciprocal (or rhythm-centered) but more closely resembled the common practice of a choreographer shaping a dance for a specific dancer—although, of course, the ultimate say belonged to Astaire, who had approval over any and all moves he made. Convincing a sometimes-reluctant Astaire was evidently part of Kidd's task.

Kidd found a way to use Astaire's persona and abilities to great effect opposite Cyd Charisse, a new partner with a physical style that contrasted strongly with Astaire's. Kidd's approach to the couple centered on dramatic poses. The subway dance—with Charisse in a blonde wig—is all poses, held then released, sometimes with twitchy readjustments of arms or feet during the holds. In one instance Charisse faces Astaire with her back to the camera. They are in a modified partner position with their bodies in close if not full contact. Astaire's right hand begins at the small of her back and he slowly moves it upward toward her neck, caressing her as she moves her free hand along his outstretched arm. The erotic nature of the gesture has no precedent in Astaire's work. The moves that follow stay within this pose-centered partner style, growing more and more explicitly sexual as the dance goes on. Charisse's flexibility—she easily slides in and out of the splits—proves an important new element unseen in Astaire's more refined sensual dances with Rogers, which never depart from the physically restrained language of social dance. Effectively solving the challenge of pairing Astaire with a ballet-trained partner, Kidd turns Astaire's history dancing with women on film to new erotic account in the subway sequence.

In the dance with the brunette Charisse in the "Dem Bones Cafe," called a "bop joint" in the script, Kidd favors a style driven by Astaire's jazz sensibilities. There are still no tap or foot sounds, but the strong correspondence between the dance and the music provides a sense of broken rhythms seen on the body if not heard. Kidd creates an entirely different mood for Charisse and Astaire—all sharp angles, asymmetrical patterns, and speed—in a style that can be found nowhere else in the work of either dancer. Drawing on the basic modes of Astaire's partner work—side-by-side mirroring and a variety of closed positions—Kidd invented a movement vocabulary that works for both dancers. Kidd recalled Astaire early on expressing a desire to do some of the choreographer's "jerky movements." Kidd responded, "*Jerky,* I always thought of them as being syncopated."[57] And while the mode may fit Charisse's younger body better, Astaire does more than keep up. His facial engagement with the dance is complete. He seems to be relishing the opportunity to dance hard, mad, and tough. Charisse's face is blank. Neither plays it for laughs. The dance is cold and expressionless, a dance of release under great pressure, exactly the qualities Kidd associated with bebop (see chapter 4).

Working without the net provided by standard song forms, both these partner dances are just the right length: Kidd had a firm grasp of how long a given choreographic conceit might be sustained. Kidd had to imagine himself into Astaire's body rather than experiment on him. That he could view decades of Astaire on film must have helped Kidd create moves that would be both possible and pleasing to the dancer, who Kidd manages to serve well while still serving his own vision of cinematic dance. Astaire revisited the *mise-en-scène* and movement vocabulary of "Girl Hunt" several times in his television shows. Kidd's solutions to the challenge of creating a number for Astaire and a much younger partner, in a new jazz idiom not incorporating tap rhythms, must have seemed solid to Astaire himself.

Astaire's approach to routining a song with a dancing peer can be considered in comparative fashion by looking at his work with Gene Kelly, with whom he made one duo number for *Ziegfeld Follies,* and Eleanor Powell, with whom he costarred and danced three major duets in *Broadway Melody of 1940.* Astaire, Powell, and Kelly worked in similar ways, making their own dances and exercising considerable control over the filmmaking process. The anecdotal evidence for Astaire's collaborations with Kelly and Powell suggests an overly polite creative environment in both cases: a fear among all involved of figuratively stepping on each other's toes. Archival evidence adds some subtlety to the received view, along the way providing a bit more perspective on Astaire's approach to making routines. The grounding of Astaire's work in rhythm making is brought into further focus as well.

"The Babbitt and the Bromide," Astaire and Kelly's only duet during the studio era, is a special case. They were not anywhere close to peers in 1944 when "Babbitt" was made. Astaire had been at the top of the film musical genre for a decade and was already a legend; Kelly had been around Hollywood for only a few years and was still just a precocious talent. In a 1981 interview Kelly claimed the choice of song was Freed's and that no other choreographer worked with them.[58] The MGM archives suggest otherwise.

An obscure Gershwin song, "The Babbitt and the Bromide" first appears in *Ziegfeld Follies* production files in a series of lists of proposed numbers from early 1944.[59] The song was initially assigned to Astaire and Garland, one of several duets floated for the team. Perhaps Freed was thinking along the lines of Fred and Adele Astaire, as "Babbitt" was originally written for the siblings on Broadway in *Funny Face* (1927). Robert Alton came up with a different scenario, using "Babbitt" to team Astaire and Kelly. Alton's 31 March 1944 scenario, "Idea Suggested for *Ziegfeld Follies*," describes how "Babbitt" could be routined for Astaire and Kelly in great detail: where it would be set, the characters the two would play, the nature of each dance section, their costumes (with attention to the Technicolor aspect), and even necessary musical adjustments to the song (the insertion of four bars between verse and chorus to cover the lap dissolves during which Astaire and Kelly age and change costumes). Alton's text—filled with "shoulds"—proposes a number not yet routined. Astaire and Kelly followed Alton's scenario very closely. Only the opening exchange of star persona–driven dialogue was added. Alton's description of the pair as a "couple of young smart elecs *[sic]*" suggests the horseplay early in the number is not a matter of professional rivalry between the two, but rather a function of youth at the start of a number about aging. The final section—which features the two men dancing as partners—is described by Alton as "an elderly gentleman's conception of swing, with jive and jitterbug movements in it." It's unlikely this scenario was Astaire or Kelly's idea put on paper by Alton. Alton wrote many detailed "ideas" for *Ziegfeld*, trying, no doubt, to be the key dancemaker on the film. There is no evidence Astaire ever committed plans for any song-and-dance routine to paper. He never needed to submit his ideas for approval by others.[60] But when Kelly and Astaire faced the idea of making a dance together, Alton's detailed scenario for "Babbitt" served as a template that smoothed the way forward. Alton presented them with a little play—all they needed to do was work out the steps.

Broadway Melody of 1940 was a one-film deal at MGM pairing Astaire with his only dancing peer at the time, Eleanor Powell. Powell's creative and technical process in making her dances ran exactly parallel to Astaire's. There was little for either to adjust to in working together beyond the fact that they wouldn't be alone in the rehearsal hall. Dance-loving audiences adored both Astaire and Powell, recognizing they offered similar movie dance experiences. The Hollywood and national dance media correctly understood *Broadway Melody* as a dance summit. Even decades later Powell compared their teaming to the meeting of two champion prize fighters: "It was a great big curiosity in the dance world. . . . We were very serious. . . . So many people expected something wonderful out of us."⁶¹ In the same interview Powell remembered very long rehearsals, claiming they set an alarm clock to be sure they would stop and give the pianist a lunch break.

The public knew that both dancers made their own dances. Their similarly polite personas led one member of the Hollywood press to compare the two to "Alphonse and Gaston," cartoon characters who were constantly deferring to each other, saying, "After you," "No, after you," and never getting anywhere. The nonsexual quality of their collaboration is underlined by this comparison of Astaire and Powell to two men. Powell remembered the slow start of their work making dances together. She very much wanted Astaire to feel comfortable working off his regular lot, and she hoped Metro would bring in Borne to play for rehearsals. Union rules prevented this, so they had to work with Powell's pianist, Walter Ruick. Soon they were sitting in Powell's practice bungalow listening to Ruick play "Begin the Beguine" over and over for half an hour, nobody moving. Finally, they decided to split up and work on ideas for the first eight bars.

> It was like two interior decorators. One likes pink and one likes blue, so you make it a pinkish blue. You know, we got together on it. You would think that we were developing a cure for cancer, the way that we were with every beat. . . . But what we were doing, actually, what all tap dancers do, if we can bowl over the musician, if we can get the musicians to say "wow wee," you know, like an offbeat, and the counterrhythms against one another.

In the end, rhythm broke the ice. Experimenting separately, they arrived at different steps yielding the same rhythm. Enthusiasm about the discovery of a fundamental rhythmic compatibility led to a fruitful exchange of ideas.

No single number demonstrates their most comfortable shared ground like the so-called "Jukebox Dance" or "Italian Café Dance." Astaire and Powell did not use a Porter tune, instead dancing to an original thirty-two-bar strain that lacks both lyric and melody. The music features a rippling riff played over a rhythmic groove that, in places, employs a boogie-woogie bass. Composer credit on the number went to Ruick. The musical text was, in all likelihood, generated alongside the dance as these three professionals worked out ideas in relation to each other. Music and dance emerged together. Powell described the dance as, first and foremost, a musical challenge.

The thing about the "Jukebox" nobody realizes—I don't think anybody, even dancers—nobody realizes how hard that number was, technically speaking. That's my favorite number in the whole picture. . . . And he loved that, because it was real hoofing, what you call real down slapping the boards. Hoofers like Bubbles, and people like that, just go wild. Because it was grooving. It grooves. And Fred just loved that, he said, "Oh Ellie, I'm having a ball." . . . I think he was very proud of the work we did. Because he sent me a letter after, but he said, "Ellie, wasn't it great to hear the applause, wasn't it great how hard we worked." I think he was very proud of the work we did. The counterrhythms were so different, you know. The musicians just fell out, you know, it was like [pianist George] Shearing. When Shearing came out on the piano with these fabulous counterrhythms, which to the ear, the average ear, would be discordant. But to anyone who understood it was way ahead of its time. And that's what we were doing.

Some of the soundtrack recordings of Astaire films released on CD in recent years provide an accessible illustration of just how essential the musical contribution of tappers like Powell and Astaire could be, as well as evidence for how even sympathetic audiences might misunder- stand the musical nature of tap. The series of soundtrack recordings of classic film musical scores produced by George Feltenstein for Rhino Records (and, later, Turner Classic Movies) in the mid-1990s and early 2000s returned to original studio masters for maximum sound quality. These are the playback recordings Astaire filmed his dances to: the dubbed tap sounds are, of course, missing, and embarrassingly empty breaks can result. The most egregious example is the "Jukebox Dance." Without the tap line, this collaboration in rhythm between Astaire, Powell, and Ruick lacks all musical sense. Select tap fills redeem some of the holes in "Begin the Beguine," but without the continuous tap line accompanying the band on the soundtrack the recording becomes little more than an incomplete artifact of the production process. The dance numbers on these discs are best listened to as a means to appreciate—in its disturbing absence—the crucial musical element Astaire and Powell added with their feet.[62]

Astaire's musical engagement with Powell the dancer and Ruick at the piano as fellow rhythmmakers generated innovative work that characterized both dancers equally well. As Powell said of their collabo- ration in her remarks at the AFI salute to Astaire in 1981, "We're just two hoofers." Both were grounded in tap rhythms and musical motiva- tions. Neither had an "average ear." Kelly could not engage with Astaire on that level: he did not approach dance making from a musical angle. He was a character dancer, not a hoofer. Alton provided a narrative frame for their number: that Astaire and Kelly followed it so closely hints at the creative distance between the two men. Faced with a younger peer who was not motivated by music or rhythm making, Astaire deferred to Alton and Kelly, yielding a number that fails to capture Astaire's distinctive creative vision in either form or content.

When free to work on his own terms—the vast majority of the time—Astaire suffered few constraints on his creative work routining popular songs into film musical moments. This almost ideal situation was underwritten by Astaire's interests, temperament, and record of success. Astaire's routines were typically quite modest—he never asked a studio to bankroll a fifteen-minute ballet (like Kelly routinely did)—and he preferred dancing alone or with one other dancer, which simplified the rehearsal process considerably. In group numbers Astaire delegated the task of creating and teaching the ensemble portion to his dance assistants. These matters of preference played well with producers and others interested in the bottom line. Astaire was an efficient worker who did not waste time on set or off. Paid a flat fee (and sometimes a percentage of the profits), he could rehearse as many weeks as he pleased without incurring much added expense in the process—just the cost of his rehearsal pianist, dance assistants, and dance-ins (stand-ins for his partners during the creative phase), who were typically hired on per-film contracts. On *Holiday Inn*, Astaire worked beyond the contracted period without extra pay to get things right. Paramount officially thanked him.[63] On *Royal Wedding*, Astaire paid for a one-day reshoot of a musical number out of his own pocket.[64] In short, Astaire was a good employee and a good manager of his own and the studio's time. Certain studios favored simpler numbers in terms of production scale, but this hardly seems to have affected Astaire's creativity. If need be, he would rehearse in a nearby funeral parlor, as he did on a Hayworth film for Columbia, and the essence of his style was easily captured in the settings most commonly found in studio era films: moderately scaled interiors. Astaire was happy to make a simple dance on a floor of almost any size. For bigger ideas Astaire was content to carry around an expensive special effects concept—such as dancing on the walls and ceiling, or dancing in slow motion—until he found himself in a production context that made realizing the idea technically possible and economically feasible. Most of his dance ideas could have been effectively placed into the plot of almost any of his films, further evidence of his number-oriented approach. In the final analysis, Astaire was satisfied to make straightforward dances on his own body in a defined space. This contentment in simplicity was one reason Astaire's transition to television proved so successful.

Each of Astaire's routines—bespoke popular culture products crafted by a team of experts with Astaire virtually always in charge—must be understood in historical context. I strive below to support readings of these routines by way of their archival backstories, while also situating the numbers within the larger realm of popular culture. Like all Hollywood stars, Astaire's stardom constantly changed relative to the ever-shifting nature of the movie business. Astaire made each of his routines within a particular business context, which dictated the nature of the work at the level of production values and creative personalities involved. Because Astaire was a musical star, connecting with popular music and social dance formed an important element of his continuing viability as well. This aspect of Astaire's work has not been studied enough. Accounting for these shifts becomes important if we are to understand Astaire's creative freedom across his career. Central to this creative practice was the most fungible currency ever created in American popular culture: the popular song. Astaire lived his creative life in a singular position: routining songs with the full support of the greatest dream factories of his time, production companies that had a limited lifespan that just happened to match Astaire's. How he used this power is the subject of this book. No one else had his opportunities. No one else had his array of talents and interests. And timing was on his side again and again. Astaire put this power to personal ends in a business where letting him have his way was a successful business plan. Astaire met the real test of Hollywood stardom on almost every occasion: his movies made money.

Astaire did not perform in any normal sense of the word in his movie musical routines, and I avoid the verb *to perform* for that reason. (Television is a slightly different matter.) Rather, Astaire's numbers are synthetic sequences employing a variety of always-changing technologies of recorded sound and moving pictures to create the illusion of actual performance. His film numbers were intended for projection on large screens for (hopefully) crowded theaters, and Astaire was almost always committed to making them appear to be "real," despite the huge size his dancing image assumed in the movie palaces of the past. Even special effects—dancing on the ceiling, on the air, in slow motion—are rendered in the service of an illusion of enhanced reality. Only rarely does he defy the realist codes of classical Hollywood, a surprising artistic choice, perhaps, given that Astaire worked in the one Hollywood genre that regularly threw the conceit of realism to the wind and created elaborate fantasy worlds set to music. Still, making Astaire's songs and dances involved physical work. Frequently, AD reports note intense perspiration and the need for rest breaks during shooting. Like the labor of a tailor fashioning a bespoke suit, there was nothing virtual about the recording of sound or image in the studio era. Moviemaking was work, what Daniel Goldmark has called the "performer's physical toil."[65] Production files help document the "physical toil" of Astaire and his collaborators in rehearsal halls, recording studios, and soundstages. Only by getting into these spaces can we begin to understand the musical impulses shaping Astaire's creative life. Astaire's creative output, almost always turning on the routining of a song, sits at a particular historical junction between a creator and performer's physical work, the technologies of sound and moving image production, and the large business enterprises with the capital to invest in so risky, so ephemeral—and so surprisingly lasting—a pop culture product as a song and a dance on film.

PART TWO

Astaire at the Studios

CHAPTER 3

"I play with the very best bands"

But when we come to the subject of music in the musicals, we
come to the first consistent expression of popular songs and
rhythm that this medium has seen, namely Fred Astaire. . . .
whatever he may do in a picture he is in, has the beat, the
swing, the debonair and damn-your-eyes violence of rhythm,
all the gay contradiction and irresponsibility, of the best thing
this country can contribute to musical history, which is the
best American jazz.

—Film critic Otis Ferguson (1935)

BACKGROUNDS

The *New York Times* reviewer for *Broadway Melody of 1940* excused
himself from the task of dealing with the plot. That wasn't why he or
Astaire's audiences were there in the first place. "It is always the sincerest
form of sabotage to analyze the plot of a musical production, and in this
case it might be doing an active disfavor to the reader himself, if thereby
he might be deprived of the sheer, unmental pleasure of following the intricate arabesques of sophisticated rhythm which the startling Astaire still
manages to tap out with his not yet superannuated toes."[1] Few historians
of the film musical have elected the "unmental pleasure" of focusing on
musical numbers over the "sabotage" of analyzing plots. Integration has
been the watchword, and analyzing the genre in narrative terms has
dominated scholarship on musical film.[2] And yet, with Astaire, different
priorities prove more useful. As Jeanine Basinger wrote of Eleanor Powell, "Her movie career was mostly one long specialty number, with her
plots and co-stars thrown in around her as an excuse for her dancing."[3]
While this may overstate matters a bit in Astaire's case—unlike Powell,
he was a credible romantic lead—Basinger's view of the balance between

plots and specialties is apt for Astaire. With Astaire as dance creator at the center of my story, I will not be cataloging plot types or considering how individual numbers forward the narrative. Rather, in this chapter—the first of three forming a triptych depicting production methods in the Hollywood studios—I survey Astaire's films through the lens of what industry types called the background, the general setting of a film that plays host to the story, characters, and, most crucially, song-and-dance routines. Selecting the background was the job of producers, the men who decided what films would be made under the studio system. This chapter concerns the big decisions producers made: many reflect straightforward attempts to leverage popular music groups—dance bands—for the benefit of a given film product, and often Astaire's tastes seem to be driving the choices. Chapter 4 travels to the writing department, where screenwriters grappled with Astaire's musical proclivities. Chapter 5 journeys to the music department, where the arrangers who worked with Astaire receive in-depth attention. All three chapters place specific creative types working beside Astaire in the Hollywood studio system in direct relation to the popular music industry, where jazz was a marketable style.

Producers had real power in Hollywood. They made the key casting and story decisions, whether it was conceiving a film for Astaire or adjusting an existing script to his persona. Certain backgrounds allowed Astaire to move more freely, and the range of backgrounds within which he could comfortably dance was, unsurprisingly, somewhat limited. Astaire functioned best against a popular entertainment background. Quite often these backgrounds included jazz or dance bands and popular music contexts. Below I divide Astaire's films into three more or less discrete categories based on their backgrounds. As will be evident, jazz-friendly contexts dominate. (The following discussion omits Astaire's 1933 cameo debut as himself in *Dancing Lady,* the plotless revue film *Ziegfeld Follies,* and his post-1957 films.)

Theatrical Backgrounds

In nine films Astaire plays a musical comedy star in a vaudeville, Broadway, or West End background. In musical terms, these films usually echo the sound of Broadway shows, with the Hollywood studio orchestra deployed like a theater pit orchestra.

- In *You'll Never Get Rich,* Astaire portrays a Broadway dance director and performer. The film moves from a Broadway stage to a highly professional troop show, and both dress rehearsal and performance numbers are presented.

- *The Barkleys of Broadway, Royal Wedding,* and *The Band Wagon* all center on stage performers and theatrical productions. The success or failure of a stage musical is only germane to the plot in *The Band Wagon,* the only genuine backstager Astaire ever made. In *Barkleys* and *Royal Wedding,* the stage musical within the film provides a context for musical routines but remains unrelated to the unfolding of the plot.
- Two of Astaire's four period films place him against a vaudeville background. *Easter Parade* and *Three Little Words* both tell tales of stage professionals who move from vaudeville to Broadway, a standard trajectory of American show business success.

Theatrical backgrounds in Astaire's films are sometimes quite thin, as flimsy as a line or two of dialogue labeling him a musical comedy star. In three instances Astaire plays a stage performer whose professional life is entirely peripheral to the action of the film, which itself takes place against a non–show business background.

- In *Top Hat,* Astaire's character Jerry Travers appears in action on stage for the title number only. Except for a short dialogue scene in a dressing room, the theatrical milieu is absent from the film.
- In *The Gay Divorcee* and *A Damsel in Distress,* the connection between Astaire's character and the musical stage remains nominal at best. In the former, Astaire's character never performs on a stage. The only dance contextualized as a performance in *The Gay Divorcee* is the nightclub solo from the opening scene, an impromptu dance in a nontheatrical venue. In *A Damsel in Distress,* Astaire's character is famous enough to be recognized on the street—where he taps out a brief solo—but his big solo is done in collaboration with a dance band and a drum set at a party. The background in these two films leans heavily toward the realm of nightclubs and jazz bands.

Nightclub Backgrounds

In ten films, Astaire is placed against a background of nightclubs, supper clubs, ballrooms, and floor shows. These more dispersed live performance contexts are perhaps difficult to identify with today. Unlike

Broadway's constellation of legitimate theaters, which continue to illuminate midtown Manhattan, the starry night of smaller venues featuring live entertainment, food and drink, and social dancing that were scattered across America in the first half of the twentieth century sputtered out long ago.[4] But any perusal of *Variety* prior to 1950 will demonstrate the dense network of such establishments that once covered the nation, providing employment for performers and bands and diversion for paying customers in every city in the nation. Many Hollywood musicals are set against a nightclub background, and this lively milieu regularly pops up in studio-era comedies and dramas as well. And while the Hollywood dream factory may have idealized these spaces, for the audiences of the 1930s and '40s, mixed-purpose venues—where you could dine, dance, and see a show while anchored to the same table—were a delightful fact of life. Table seating around a dance floor with a prominent bandstand provides a visual key to these venues. Musically speaking, jazz and dance bands provided the music for this nighttime realm, which nurtured swing bands and swing music. Live radio hookups, sometimes heard nationwide, promoted bands and venues alike. The ten Astaire films set against nightclub backgrounds tend to use the milieu in meaningful ways.

Seven of the ten situate Astaire as a singer and dancer appearing (within the film, at least) only in nightclubs.

- *Follow the Fleet.* Although it is never completely clear where Astaire and Rogers's characters did their act described as "genteel dancing and high-class patter," the film inhabits a nightclub milieu. The early scene at the Paradise Ballroom, a taxi-dance hall, dips into the lower end of the nightclub world.
- *Swing Time.* Astaire and Rogers play exhibition ballroom partners in a story that turns several times on the ownership of a nightclub or a band.
- *Shall We Dance.* Astaire plays a ballet dancer who is never seen dancing on a concert stage. The only performed numbers are done in a nightclub roof garden—a typical New York, but not a legit Broadway, venue.
- *The Story of Vernon and Irene Castle.* Exhibition dancing in nightclubs was the Castles' means to success. The film highlights this aspect of their careers by having Astaire and Rogers move, as

exhibition couples did, from a table to the dance floor to perform their specialties. The Castles' Broadway appearances are not re-created, although Astaire appears briefly in a troop show in a theater.

- *Holiday Inn.* Crosby's country inn is a classic nightclub where performers mingle freely with patrons in an intimate, convivial setting.
- *You Were Never Lovelier.* Astaire pitches himself to hotel owner Adolph Menjou as a solo specialty act to be featured alongside Xavier Cugat's band in the hotel's rooftop nightclub.
- *Let's Dance.* Similar to *Holiday Inn,* this film is anchored in the supper club milieu, constructing a nurturing family atmosphere behind the scenes.

In three of his ten films set in nightclub backgrounds, Astaire portrays a member of a jazz or dance band, working on the bandstand playing swing music for dancing customers.

- *Flying Down to Rio.* Astaire plays accordion and is second-in-command of the band that flies down to Rio for a hotel nightclub job.
- *Roberta.* Astaire plays piano, sings, and dances with an American band that travels to Paris for a nightclub gig.
- *Second Chorus.* Astaire plays trumpet, fronts a traveling college band, and auditions for and ends up conducting Artie Shaw's outfit.

Two Astaire films combine theatrical and nightclub backgrounds, suggesting how easily the same performance style might find a spot in both realms. (Fred and Adele briefly doubled on Broadway and at the Trocadero nightclub in 1925.)

- In *Broadway Melody of 1940,* Astaire and George Murphy progress from the floor show of a down-market nightclub to the Broadway stage. Astaire and Powell's "Jukebox Dance" confirms their compatibility as dancers—all that really counts, in the end—in the context of a little café with jukeboxes on the tables and a tiny dance floor. This intimate venue—site of a serious dance number—typifies the ubiquity of the nightclub format in these decades.

- The background of *Blue Skies* is neatly divided between Astaire and Crosby. Astaire does several numbers in a theatrical setting with the audience shown or suggested, while Crosby traverses a string of nightclubs that provide diverse, colorful backgrounds for Berlin's songs. A radio broadcast—part of the nightclub milieu—frames the entire film.

Non–Show Business Backgrounds

In the seven films in which Astaire does not play a performer, the live performance milieu included in the film invariably evokes a nightclub rather than a theatrical background. Dances in a public context in these films tend to feature a visible band in a recognizable social space: a nightclub or something like it.

- *Carefree.* Astaire plays a psychiatrist who used to be a dancer. He dances socially with Rogers, who plays a radio singer, at a country club.
- *The Sky's the Limit.* Astaire's fighter pilot character dances at a servicemen's canteen, an important wartime nightclub venue, and spends most of his time in various nightspots.
- *Yolanda and the Thief.* Astaire as a con man dances at a Latin American fiesta that looks and sounds like a North American nightclub.
- *The Belle of New York.* Astaire's wealthy gentleman character takes a job as a singing waiter at a turn-of-the-century New York restaurant, exactly the sort of establishment that initiated nightclub-based nightlife.
- *Daddy Long Legs.* Astaire's wealthy businessman character plays the drums at home to jazz records and joins in with a crowd of college kids at a dance played by Ray Anthony's famous band.
- *Funny Face.* All the dances for Astaire's fashion photographer character are book dances, although he does visit a Left Bank dive where Audrey Hepburn does an impromptu dance to a hip jazz combo. Astaire and Kay Thompson's "Clap Yo' Hands" combines hipster lingo and old-time vaudeville patter in a parody of a floor show specialty. Thompson had a long career as a cabaret performer prior to the film, and the number is an extension of her nightclub work.[5]

- *Silk Stockings.* For no apparent reason, Astaire's character, ostensibly a film producer, leads a major production number at a Russian-themed Parisian nightclub in the final reel.

As this overview shows, the most common background for an Astaire routine observed by an on-screen audience is a nightclub or supper club. Performances situated in theaters are the exception. Jazz and dance bands, rather than pit orchestras, are the norm. Bands of several types play major roles in Astaire films.

BANDS

Bands with fictional names were often written into the cast of characters for Astaire's nightclub-based films. *Flying Down to Rio,* a film with four elaborate nightclub settings, features three invented bands: Roger Bond and his Yankee Clippers, the Carioca-playing Turuna Band, and the tango band at the Aviators Club. Astaire dances with all three. Astaire's character fronts Huck Haines and his Indianians at the Café Russe in *Roberta* (see figure 5) and Bake Baker and his Navy Blue Blowers on a Navy ship in *Follow the Fleet. Let's Dance* includes two briefly seen sideline bands: an army outfit accompanying the troop show in the wartime prologue and a nightclub house band for the "Ad Lib Dance." Neither is particularly convincing or even visible, but they are there, reflecting an investment in extras. Bands were an essential part of the scene. Ray Noble, the best-known British dance-band leader in the States during the 1930s, plays a supporting role as a swing-obsessed lad with his own little band in *A Damsel in Distress,* and Astaire and Burgess Meredith's college band, Danny O'Neill's University Perennials, shares *Second Chorus* with the real Artie Shaw and His Orchestra.

Bands and nightclub backgrounds were fairly common prior to the swing explosion of the mid-1930s—the first synchronized song in *The Jazz Singer* takes place in a nightclub—and more than a few early sound films center on the lives of band musicians and other nightclub denizens. The films of George Raft typify the pre-Code, pre-swing, pre-Astaire Hollywood nightclub, a darkly conceived night realm, seedy and full of danger, leading, more often than not, to death or disappointment at the close (see, for example, Raft's *Dancers in the Dark* from 1932 or *Stolen Harmony* from 1935). In these serious, even desperate worlds, jazz carried the mark of menace or sexual laxity. Astaire's nightclubs were different. His was a cleaned-up night world, bright rather

FIGURE 5. Astaire and the invented band in *Roberta* strike a pose just like real dance bands often did for promotional photos.

than dark and generally without a trace of underworld influence, re-flecting the mid-1930s revival of a legitimate café society. (The club- and band-owning gangsters in *Swing Time* threaten with smiles and never pull a gun on anyone.) The emergence of a wholesome and legal Hollywood nightclub realm had many sources: the lifting of Prohibition in 1933, the enforcement of the Production Code beginning in 1934, and the Hollywood strategy of meeting the Depression with escapist fantasies of glamour and wealth.

The explosion onto the popular music scene of name bands playing hot jazz in the mid-1930s fostered yet another shift in the depiction of nightclubs and band culture. Real name bands became movie stars and a new musical subgenre was born: what *Variety* and *Down Beat* dubbed the band pic (band pix in the plural). *Down Beat* regularly covered the suddenly abundant opportunities for jazz and dance bands—primarily white ones—to find national exposure in Hollywood films. By Septem-ber 1940, *Down Beat* was reporting, "The use of name bands in current movies seems to be developing into what approaches a major film trend."[6] Among the projects listed in this article was *Second Chorus,* a film Astaire did, he said, solely for the chance to work with clarinetist and top bandleader Artie Shaw. This was the first of several Astaire films to include a real name band playing themselves.

Second Chorus was an independent production headed by Boris Morros (formerly of the Paramount music department), and the bandleader originally signed for the picture was Paul Whiteman. By 1940 Whiteman was a venerable old name in popular music, more associated with 1920s symphonic jazz than modern swing. But Whiteman went into Metro's *Strike Up the Band* instead, and, in his place, Morros engaged Artie Shaw, an immensely popular but controversial leader making a comeback. Shaw had made one film at Metro *(Dancing Co-ed)* and was slated for Astaire's *Broadway Melody of 1940* when he promptly disbanded his group and took off for Mexico, one of several attempts to flee the business.[7] Shaw's signature hit "Begin the Beguine" stayed in *Broadway Melody* in a Shaw-esque arrangement. But Astaire still wanted to work with Shaw and went from Metro's deep pockets to producer Morros's upstart independent to do it. The script for *Second Chorus* was rewritten several times. The original version, by Shaw's friend Frank Cavett, dramatized a middle-class Midwesterner's struggle to realize his true calling as a jazz trumpeter. As Shaw remembered it, the goal was to offer a revealing take on the tough choices faced by jazz musicians. "It was meant to be a kind of sad story and comment on what jazz was as a growing, evolving art form. In those days, people thought if you were playing jazz, you were stepping down. And in the film, we had the intention of showing that if you wanted to play jazz, you had to step way up."[8] With John Garfield penciled in for the lead, *Second Chorus* was originally a downer, a dark view of the competitive jazz scene, an early 1940s *Young Man with a Horn.*

When Astaire came onto the film, the script was utterly transformed. *Second Chorus* became the most direct expression of the band pic strategy in Astaire's filmography. With no need to explain swing to the movie audience any longer, the film could instead comment on the popular music regime ushered in by the rise of hot bands and players. As part of the plot, lyricist Johnny Mercer wrote two sets of lyrics to the same Bernie Hanighen tune. One set, titled "Hoe Down the Bayou," is sung to convince Charles Butterworth, playing a tone-deaf but rich music lover who dreams of playing mandolin (!) in Artie Shaw's band, to back the band in a concert where they can do the music "their way." Mercer mercilessly parodies the Swanee song tradition and tells a botched version of jazz history, with the story ending in Cincinnati (Butterworth's character's hometown). Later in the film Astaire sings a second set of lyrics, retitling the tune "Poor Mr. Chisholm," as an audition for an arranging job with Shaw. It's a jazz insider's mocking tribute to Butterworth, a fellow who clearly cannot dig the jive. When he tries to swing, he breaks a string. Both Mercer lyrics take the measure of current popular music and jazz mentalities: marking "the poles of hipster and square" was a Mercer specialty.[9] Hanighen's tune for "Hoe Down the Bayou/Poor Mr. Chisholm" returns for use by Astaire in his solo dance conducting the Shaw orchestra at the concert that ends the film. Astaire dances to an instrumental version—with a few twelve-bar blues choruses thrown in along the way—and bobby-soxers in the balcony scream their approval. Shaw, who used the film to launch a new band, plays himself in a supporting speaking role and is credited with the film's music at the opening. Every aspect of *Second Chorus* was keyed to the ongoing swing craze, and all of distributor Paramount's publicity emphasized the film's musical content. Prepared reviews in the press kit identified the film's genre as "swing-comedy" and "swing film," both serviceable stand-ins for the industry term *band pic*.[10] Swing music was dance music, and the band tie-in was inextricable from a social dance tie-in with a new category of teenager: the jitterbug. As chapter 6 shows, *Second Chorus* came complete with a new named-dance song, instructions for which were printed on magazine ads for the film.

Appearances by popular name bands continued in Astaire's films of the early 1940s, regardless of which studio made them. *You Were Never Lovelier* featured Xavier Cugat and His Orchestra, who were heard nationally on the radio from the Starlight Roof, their elite perch atop New York's Waldorf Astoria. In the film they play the house band for a similar rooftop nightclub at a Buenos Aires hotel. The first musical number in the film is the Cugat specialty "Chiu, Chiu," which Astaire observes approvingly from a little table, his fingers beating a counter-rhythm to Cugat's signature Latin sound. One reviewer complained the nightclub set in the picture was too small, perhaps overly similar to the real places a band like this might play (see figure 6).[11] The genial Cugat was a more than passable actor, and he and his always visually stimulating group went on from this, their cinematic debut, to become a major film band, surviving to the very end of the band pix era in the early 1950s. Boogie-woogie pianist Freddie Slack was just launching his new band when RKO picked him up for a prominent place in *The Sky's the Limit*. Slack's "Cow Cow Boogie" had recently emerged as Capitol Records' first real hit, and Slack's girl singer Ella Mae Morse was set to

Xavier Cugat and his Orchestra play Jerome Kern's magnificent melodies!

FRED RITA
ASTAIRE * HAYWORTH
in
"YOU WERE
NEVER LOVELIER"
A COLUMBIA PICTURE

FIGURE 6. Despite the caption at the bottom this lobby card, Cugat's band does not play Kern's music in this scene from *You Were Never Lovelier,* but instead offers "Chiu, Chiu," a Latin specialty by Nicanor Molinare.

appear in the film. She was cut when she got pregnant. Music files for *The Sky's the Limit* suggest the extent to which the sound of the Slack band fills the soundtrack. Several of their signature numbers, including "Cuban Sugar Mill," were included, although Slack's boogie-woogie piano style goes unheard in the final cut. His eight-bar solo in "My Shining Hour" stays on the cocktail piano side. Candid stills from the shoot show a gleeful Astaire at the piano, jamming with Slack's men. During his months entertaining troops in the United States and Europe during the war, Astaire danced live with Kay Kyser's band and members of Glenn Miller's Army Air Force Band.

As name bands began to lose both their economic niche and pop music market share in the immediate aftermath of the war, the band pic genre faded away. The brief inclusion of Phil Regan and His Orchestra in *Three Little Words,* a Jack Cummings production at MGM, was part of the plot and not an attempt to leverage a popular band to the film's benefit. Regan's sweet sound bears no relation to the film's background, which remains amusingly vague in relation to actual time period.[12] No

name bands are seen or heard in any postwar Freed Unit film, one reason these films seem disconnected from postwar popular music. *The
Band Wagon* features a syrupy hotel band at the lavish party after the
disastrous out-of-town premiere of the show within the film. Astaire,
the only person to show up for the misbegotten celebration, beats a hasty
retreat. The sticky music might be one motivation for his quick exit. The
lack of name bands in Astaire's films at Metro is brought into relief by
his first project away from the studio after *The Band Wagon*.

Twentieth Century-Fox's *Daddy Long Legs* prominently features
Ray Anthony and His Orchestra, among the last of the national name
bands to reach a white teenage audience before rock and roll crashed
over the musical landscape. The abundant source trail for *Daddy Long
Legs* offers evidence that it was Astaire who brought dance band and
jazz content into the film. When Astaire was signed, *Daddy Long Legs*
became a band pic.

Fox chief Darryl Zanuck had been tossing around the idea of remaking *Daddy Long Legs* since 1951. It was a tried-and-true property for
the studio, with two earlier Fox versions: a Mary Pickford silent (1919)
and a Janet Gaynor talkie (1931). The first set of screenwriters Zanuck
tapped for the 1950s remake wanted to update the old chestnut by modeling the title character on Raymond Loewy, a modernist designer who
had recently appeared on the cover of *Life*.[13] The look of the film would
coalesce around modern architecture filmed on location. Mature, sophisticated leading men like David Niven and Cary Grant were under
consideration for the title role. The project was passed around for two
years, revised each time Zanuck changed his mind about who the stars
would be. Then, in the middle of dictating a memo to producer Sol Sie-
gel in July 1953, Zanuck saw two names in lights: Leslie Caron and Fred
Astaire. Zanuck's memo reads like a scene in a movie. The all-powerful
mogul imagines a film around two stars, then makes that vision a reality
on movie marquees everywhere. Caron, on loan from Metro, had already been chosen as the girl. Her foreign accent and the cachet of ballet would define the feminine side of the film. "It might have the same
charm as LILI," wrote Zanuck. "LILI is not a hit in the regular theatres
but it does good business and in the small art houses it does outstand-
ing business."[14] The changing landscape of Hollywood is evident in
Zanuck's thinking. Following the success of *The Red Shoes* (1948),
small theaters had remained a profitable niche market for musicals. But
Daddy Long Legs was to be a CinemaScope release, the kind of grand
musical picture Fox was still making in the mid-1950s. The male lead

would need to carry the film in the large downtown movie palaces. Danny Kaye was Zanuck's first idea opposite Caron, and he envisioned the film by analogy to Kaye's most recent success: *Daddy Long Legs* "has a tremendous title and the title is just as good if not better than HANS CHRISTIAN ANDERSEN. Made as a musical comedy it might very well be one of those great attractions that reach the type of audience that Walt Disney reaches." Zanuck also wanted a new score with hit songs (just like Disney was getting). At this point, with one movie in mind, a different cinematic vision suddenly appears as Zanuck thinks aloud.

> I have just thought of another casting idea that I think would be sensational and that would be Leslie Caron and Fred Astaire. During your absence I am going to ask Lew Schreiber to get the material and have a talk with Fred Astaire and tell him the type of musical we see and also to tell him about the wonderful success of the English musical version. From the standpoint of age, class and distinction Fred Astaire is ideal for this role. If necessary I will see Astaire and give him my views on it.

In 1953 Astaire still had the clout to rate a sit-down with a mogul of Zanuck's stature: producers were still seeking Astaire, whose star seems not to have diminished one bit in their eyes. (*The Band Wagon* had just opened when Zanuck dictated this memo.)

Having signed Astaire, Zanuck handed the script to Phoebe and Henry Ephron. Like so many of his postwar collaborators, the Ephrons were in awe of Astaire and thrilled at the chance to write for him.[15] From the earliest of the Ephrons' scripts, Astaire's persona and tastes invade the world of *Daddy Long Legs*. The modernized story now rests on modern dance music. Astaire's character is introduced this way: "JERVIS PENDLETON, III, the head of the Pendleton Corporation, is seated at a magnificent set of drums, ecstatically playing an accompaniment to a Les Brown recording which plays beside him. He is completely absorbed and appears to be absolutely gone."[16] Astaire enters the film in the throes of a (for Astaire) authentic musical passion, and with him came jazz and contemporary dance-band leaders as important elements in the film's background. With the addition of Ray Anthony's group, *Daddy Long Legs* became a latter-day band pic, one of the last to be made before rock and roll entered the scene.

In addition to the name bands that appear in Astaire's pictures, a short list of bands that might have been can be assembled from studio archives. The most dramatic example is *Swing Time*, the Astaire-Rogers picture most invested in the world of bands and nightclubs. The band-centered story of *Swing Time* was to turn on a love triangle, with Rogers caught between Astaire and real-life piano-playing bandleader Eddy Duchin. Duchin was certainly handsome enough to be a Hollywood leading man: Tyrone Power offered a visually convincing portrait of the pianist in a 1956 biopic. Astaire and Rogers knew Duchin from their Broadway days. In her autobiography, Rogers lingers tellingly over a date she and Astaire had in 1930. They went dancing at the Central Park Casino, Duchin's regular spot.[17] In the Duchin version of *Swing Time,* the setup for Astaire's solo has him responding to the sound of Duchin's group in typical fashion. At this point Astaire's character, Lucky Garnett, owns a nightclub and has engaged Duchin's band to play.

> *Lucky:* I suppose you can play—that is, well enough to get by?
>
> *Duchin (turning to this orchestra):* Let's toss him a tune, boys.
>
> He lifts his baton, and the boys go into action. Lucky listens with slowly mounting enthusiasm. They have got rhythm—yes, sir, they've got rhythm—His shoulders feel it, his hips start swaying, his feet begin tapping—and finally—he just lets himself go—into his dance. . . .
>
> Lucky finishes his dance and the orchestra finishes the music. McCloskey and Garnett applaud vigorously.
>
> *Lucky (smiling):* Nice, huh?
>
> *Ed [McCloskey] (happily):* The boys are okay, if I do say so myself. (then, to Lucky) What's your opinion?
>
> *Lucky (glaringly):* Well, I have danced better—but I can't remember where.[18]

Duchin was an odd choice as Astaire's romantic rival and musical collaborator. First, Duchin had movie-star good looks. It would have made visual sense for Ginger to prefer him over Astaire. John Clum has noted how Astaire's status as a romantic lead was enhanced in the RKO films by surrounding him with an array of eccentric, effeminate males. By comparison, Astaire comes off as both acceptably masculine and the only viable option for Rogers.[19] Duchin would have upset this strategy. Second, Astaire could have whipped Duchin in a piano duel without even trying. Indeed, he already had. Compare Astaire's stride solo (with Borne comping along) on "I Won't Dance" in *Roberta* (which, by the standards of 1935, was definitely hot, especially for a white band) to Duchin's fey 1935 version of the same tune, which relies on licks taken from the sheet music and is the opposite of hot.[20]

Duchin's participation evidently was never secured and the plan was scrapped—but only after a complete script had been prepared. *Swing Time* was rewritten with fictional Latin bandleader Ricardo Romero in the role of Astaire's rival for Rogers's affection, and any outside threat to the Astaire and Rogers's relationship was dialed down considerably. The slick but ineffectual Romero leads a fictional band with a distinctly sweet, even Duchin-esque sound. Astaire ostensibly dances to Romero's band on two occasions in the film—"Waltz in Swing Time" and "Bojangles of Harlem"—but their musical style is never put into words or commented upon, and no music-centered scene about their sound occurs. One point of musical contrast that is made comes with the song "The Way You Look Tonight." After Astaire sings it in his intimate half-voice style at the piano, the film cuts to Romero singing the ballad in a pompous full-voiced manner backed up by syrupy strings. Musical style works to separate the two men vying for Rogers's affection, and, as always, there's really no contest. After all, Ginger likes jazz too.

Duchin was a nationally known popular music figure, and the aborted plan to put him in *Swing Time* was doubtless a matter of his perceived marquee value. But there were other, more directly musical reasons to bring a name band into an Astaire film. *Shall We Dance* provides a telling example. Audiences for *Shall We Dance* heard a distinctly hot sound during Astaire and Rogers's dance numbers, and some might have thought they recognized a nationally famous band somewhere in the mix. The Jimmy Dorsey Orchestra was in Hollywood backing up Bing Crosby on his weekly radio variety show, the Kraft Music Hall, when *Shall We Dance* was in production. Fifteen members of the band, including drummer Ray McKinley and pianist Freddie Slack, were hired under the table to play on all the dance numbers in the film, including the fragmentary dances Astaire does to a phonograph record in the early scenes. Using Dorsey's group was risky for the studio and the band. As bandleader Charlie Barnet recalled, "union rules denied traveling musicians a steady engagement until they had waited out six months and become 'local' members. The union was quite strong in L.A."[21] Musicians with staff positions at the studios did not travel, and the union protected their lucrative jobs in the film industry. But someone at RKO wanted (and got) the Dorsey players, figuring their sound alone would add an important element to the *Shall We Dance* soundtrack.

The principle of hearing but not seeing a name band continued in a slightly visible manner with the inclusion of Bob Crosby's name band on the soundtrack of *Holiday Inn*. By the early 1940s there were enough high-profile bands working in Hollywood for *Down Beat* to run a regular column detailing the goings-on at the studios, a powerful entertainment sector suddenly making regular alliances with the dance band business. *Down Beat*'s Hal Holly described *Holiday Inn* as a "super-super musical," and the participation of the Crosby band was news to the band industry for a variety of reasons.

> Strings may be added to the combination for some numbers, according to [Paramount] musical director Bobby Dolan. The Crosby band will not be seen in the picture at any time. The musicians seen in the picture will be Hollywood "sideline" musicians who go through the motions of playing to a recording when the scenes are photographed for the purpose of synchronization.[22]

Holly's next column, a week later, included a correction.

> Our report that the Bob Crosby band would record the entire score for Paramount's *Holiday Inn* was not quite correct. The Bob Cat bunch will do at least seven musical numbers of the picture's 12 or 13, including all the Fred Astaire dance routines and most of Bing's vocals. The band will do all its numbers using its own original combination exclusively, though strings will be cut into a couple of sequences. . . . Although not seen in the picture the Crosby band will be given "screen credit" (mention on the listing of actors, director, technicians, etc. that follows the title). The Paramount studio is footing the bill for the 100% stand-by union fee, required in most cases when non-local bands record for pictures, plus all incidental expenses such as arranging, copying, etc.,—and forking over a nice hefty price for the band in addition. . . . A very nice little deal for the Dixielanders, who have been doing right well for themselves at the Trianon in the meantime.[23]

Holly's columns provided useful information designed to put jazz musicians at ease should they buy a ticket to *Holiday Inn*. His advice can be summarized as follows: Don't look for Crosby's men in the picture, but do take note of the outfit's screen credit, a studio term helpfully translated for music types. When you see Astaire dance, you're hearing the Crosby guys play. If you hear strings in the band's numbers—the inclusion of a string section in dance bands was a point of debate around this time—don't blame Crosby; it's the studio's call (or fault). Beyond this viewer's guide to the sound/image relationship, Holly explains in detail where the money is going, arguing, without emphasizing the point too much, that this kind of invisible work was a good thing, "a nice little deal" for Crosby's group, an adjunct to what they were really in town to do, which was playing live music at the Trianon Ballroom in Southgate, a short drive south of downtown Los Angeles. That was a gig *Down Beat*'s readers could understand.

CHAPTER 4

"Tell them to let it swing"

The production of musical films brought together two, normally separate studio departments: writers in the writing department conceived of the story and wrote the dialogue; composers, lyricists, dance directors, arrangers, and orchestrators loosely allied in an expanded music department created the musical numbers. The archival traces left by these two departments offer different, often complementary perspectives on the filmmaking process. Scripts were the blueprints for the studio system production process. These story-centered documents were essential to the system's rational approach to making an expensive, inherently risky product like the feature film. Beyond the final shooting script, draft scripts, outlines, and treatments afford glimpses of the writing and filmmaking process. Script files put words to pictures, offering clues to how producers, directors, writers, and others were thinking about a film as it was being conceived and prepared for production. Music departments largely worked without descriptive, story-based documents. Archival evidence from the music departments comes in two types: a variety of lists (such as rundowns of musical numbers made for budgeting purposes, recording session schedules, and lists of musical cues and songs used) and musical scores (mostly arrangers' full scores and conductors' short scores). Music department matters are taken up in the next chapter. This chapter stays close to the writers, showing how the musical content of Astaire's routines was understood by the creative figures charged with describing films in words before the cameras started rolling. Along the way, the word choices of several of Astaire's lyricists come into play as well.

Astaire's postwar screenwriters were a relatively young bunch: most had grown up watching Astaire in his prewar films. For several, Astaire defined what Hollywood and the musical meant, and they approached writing for him with a combined sense of thrill and humility. Leonard Gershe reflected on the experience of writing *Funny Face:* "Never once did he ask me to define the character, or what the motivation was. I knew how to write a line for Fred Astaire—economical, simple, easy. . . . It was fun to write for that image that you'd grown up seeing, and I knew how he should talk. He dictated to me, in other words."[1] The first generation of Astaire screenwriters didn't have the advantage of this history. The writers working for Berman at RKO in the 1930s had to invent backgrounds and scenarios into which Astaire's developing persona would fit. The Duchin version of *Swing Time* suggests they didn't always get it right. Astaire's identification with music and dance of a particular kind shows up regularly in the RKO script files, and there is plenty of evidence that Astaire himself had a role in revising dialogue that got too close to matters that were important to him. At issue in most of these cases are words about music: specifically, the words *hot, swing,* and *jazz.*

Hot, swing, and *jazz* were 1930s code words for improvised, highly syncopated music and music making. All carried connotations of black music making, and all turn up regularly in the script materials for Astaire's films in the 1930s and early 1940s, in both dialogue and descriptive text. The word *blues,* with a long history in the popular music lexicon, also appears from time to time. When invoked by screenwriters, these key words point toward musical contrasts that might not be heard so easily today. Below is a digest of uses of *hot, jazz,* and *blues* in RKO scripts written between 1933 and 1937.

> *Flying Down to Rio:* Early descriptions of the dance portion of "The Carioca" show how an American blues sound was to be used as both contrast and complement to the exotic Turuna band.
>
> Three Clippers at near-by tables leap to the band-stand[,] seize cornets, and blow "blue" notes, which makes Fred change to a jazz step and then go back into the Carioka [sic]. He waves the crowd back into action. fred: Come on—everybody Carioka [sic]!
>
> The music is so arranged that as the Turunas stop, the boys play a hot break on their instruments and the ensemble resume[s].[2]

Follow the Fleet: Allan Scott and Dwight Taylor's final shooting script uses the word *hot* in descriptive passages from start to finish. Astaire's star entrance in the first number, "We Saw the Sea," is imagined this way. "In a moment, Bat Baker (Fred Astaire) appears. He is jauntily playing away on his tin whistle. In the middle of the tune, he breaks into a hot lick step, continues to play his whistle and joins his band who are already playing and singing along with a couple of other sailors."[3] The description of Astaire's piano solo employs similar language. "MED. CLOSE SHOT—of Bat and his little orchestra gathered on the afterdeck with their instruments. . . . As we come to them, Bat is playing a hot chorus on the piano." The lead-in to Astaire's major solo again builds a dramatic moment on contrasting musical styles.

As the Captain and his party pass along the deck inspecting the ship and men, we hear the ship's band playing the solemn "Pomp and Circumstance" music and against it, we hear as a kind of counter melody, the rhythmic red-hot music of obviously Bat's orchestra playing.

Captain (calling to the Ensign who is accompanying the party): "Have that jazz band stop playing at once!"

After a British member of the captain's party says, "I have a fancy for American music," Astaire performs "I'd Rather Lead a Band." Berlin's lyric refers to a "hot trumpet," and this song is among a handful of tunes in which Berlin used the word *hot* in this way. (Another is "Let Yourself Go" from the same film.)

A Damsel in Distress. Just before his drum dance finale, Astaire exhorts the band with the cry, "Come on you Totleigh Wild Cats. Give!" The screenwriter describing the number, which he likely hadn't seen, added laconically, "They start playing hot number as Jerry [Astaire] moves to drums."[4]

Hot was the word of choice for RKO writers tasked with describing an Astaire solo, whether it was danced, played (on piano or drums), or a combination of both. In popular music lingo, *hot* meant fast tempos and improvised virtuoso solos; it was the opposite of sweet arranged music of a more sedate kind, slower in tempo, lower in volume, and without standout soloists. In the 1930s, bands' styles and listeners' tastes were roughly divided into the hot and the sweet. *Down Beat*'s annual polls sorted the entire world of popular music into these two large categories. Sweet music was associated with respectability, hotel ballrooms, and older listeners, hot music with jazz clubs, jam sessions, the young, and

African Americans. (In *Follow the Fleet* Astaire comes upon his sailor buddies sitting around with their instruments and says, "Say, how 'bout breaking up this sewing circle and getting into a jam session." This line never shows up in any script; it could have been added, or improvised, on the set.) The final time the word *hot* appeared in an Astaire script was RKO veteran Allan Scott's 1949 draft for *Let's Dance*. Scott referred back to what must have been RKO writers' code for the kind of music Astaire liked: "As the music becomes hotter, Don [Astaire] continues dancing with the easiest kind of brilliance—dancing all over the place."[5]

Astaire himself defined the word *hot* in an unsigned text that only could have originated with him. Astaire and Rogers were hugely popular in Britain, and in 1936 a British publisher released two lavishly printed "albums" of photos from the couple's film dance numbers along with basic ballroom dance instructions. For one of these albums Astaire contributed an extended text titled "Hot Dance," which defines the word in precise if stereotypical terms.

> We've come to the "Hot Dance"; the maddest, fastest, dizziest combination of them all.
>
> "Hot Dance" is not a very attractive term, but it is the only one I can use to describe dances like the "Lindy Hop," and the "Shim Sham Shimmy," which were originated by the coloured people. And incidentally, how I do love to watch coloured people dance.
>
> The "Hot Dance" is the Fox-trot gone mad. It's an expression of bubbling-over spirits and exuberant vitality. It's a combination of the primitive and the ultra-modern. Savages did their "hot dances" to the beat of the tom-tom. Jungle rhythm still strikes a responsive chord in our beings after many hundreds of years of civilization.
>
> To be a good "hot dancer," one must catch the spirit of Harlem and tingle to the peculiar spell of "low down" music . . . moaning blues and torrid rhythms. The effect of all this is a sort of inner combustion which breaks out in whirlwind action.
>
> There are few rules and fewer regulations about "hot dancing." It's a case of evolve your own steps and put 'em over.
>
> This red-hot style of dancing is developing into the most intricate forms of broken rhythm and taps. You'll see some examples in the "I'll Be Hard to Handle" number which Ginger Rogers and I do in RADIO'S "Roberta," and in the "I Won't Dance" number which I do alone.

It's the type of thing I like best to do. With the right kind of music there's nothing I enjoy more.

Which brings up an important point. The music has to be "right" for this type of dance. The sort of music that makes your feet do impossible tricks of speed and dexterity fairly smokes![6]

Astaire echoes many of the standard white readings of hot music as linked to both primitive urges and the ultramodern spirit, as something blacks had direct access to but that struck "a responsive chord" in anyone. Astaire does not suggest that hot dancing is somehow natural to African Americans, only that the best examples can be seen by watching "coloured people" dance. They are the models to follow. And while he hints at a development toward more "intricate forms of broken rhythms and taps," refinements are not necessary to make hot dancing acceptable. In fact, there's no sense that hot dancing needs refinement at all: it's meant to be a dance of release, of "inner combustion" driven by the music. Astaire's use of the phrase "broken rhythm," a code phrase he shared with Pan, links this approach to rhythm to the category of hotness and supports the contention that Astaire (and not a ghostwriter) was indeed the author of the text. Astaire's definition of "hot dance" may also hint at how the word *hot* entered screenwriters' usage at RKO. Astaire attended some story meetings, and, as we will see, he had much to say about the songs submitted by his songwriters. The word *hot* was likely introduced into RKO's studio vocabulary by Astaire's own use of it to describe the kind of dances he had in mind to make. These dances or musical solos then had to be fit into the scripts in order to meet Astaire's creative demands. *Hot*—a word Astaire calls "not very attractive"—was a practical term and, as the above suggests, a code word for Astaire's link to black dancers and music.

Swing entered the popular music vocabulary in a big way with the explosion of interest in hot bands and hot music usually marked by the 1935 breakthrough of Benny Goodman's band. A shift in popular music taste initiated by white teenagers listening to network radio, swing, like rock and roll and rap after it, was a musical marker that quickly became a marketing tool.[7] *Swing* was a new word for *hot,* and Hollywood swiftly embraced the term and the musicians associated with it. For example, Goodman's ascent to Hollywood fame was rapid. Warner's wrote him into an existing project, *Hollywood Hotel* (1938), which provides one prototype for the band pic as an excuse to point the movie camera at famous musicians and just let them play. Although the movie was originally conceived as a film version of gossip columnist Louella Parsons's radio show, Goodman's role in it was expanded with each subsequent draft, to the point where Parsons herself disappeared in one version, replaced by a fictional columnist. A détente between the Hollywood establishment and the swing invaders was eventually arranged, so that Parsons and Goodman could share the story, but the writing was on the wall.[8] Swing would be a powerful force in Hollywood, as the studios sought to refashion the musical genre around the emergence of swing music and musicians.

Hot was a descriptive word, and seldom spoken aloud in an Astaire film. The word *swing,* however, was so prominent and so connected to the marketing of hot music that writers repeatedly tried to get it into dialogue. Often these attempts were blocked along the way. Ironically, *swing* first emerges as a problematic word in the scripts for *Swing Time,* the original title of which was *Never Gonna Dance.* Typical of a film directed by George Stevens, the final shooting script differs markedly from the film. All uses of the word *swing* in the script were cut in the film. For example, Astaire was to shout, "Tell them to let it swing," to the stage manager as he called him to the stage for "Bojangles of Harlem." Instead, he sings the start of the "Bojangles" chorus, breaking off just before Fields's lyric uses the phrase "hot stuff."

The best example of the care with which Astaire approached the words *swing* and *jazz* in a dialogue scene can be found in *Shall We Dance,* a film sold to audiences on the notion that ballet and jazz would engage in some creative mixing. ("Jazz—Ballet Merge" says one magazine article pictured in the film.) The film begins in a ballet company's rehearsal hall. Astaire is first seen in a life-size painting as the "Great Petrov," a Russian ballet dancer. The director of the company, played by Edward Everett Horton, enters, goes looking for Astaire, and is directed to a side room. The earliest treatment describes the moment when Astaire's ballet-dancing character is introduced: "As [Horton] expectantly opens the door he stops in horror as he sees Fred, the great Petroff, going to town in a hot tap routine to the accompaniment of a low-down swing record."[9] Although the action remained the same, a subsequent script revised the description, using even more musical code words: "He opens the door: then recoils as he is greeted by a blast of hot swing MUSIC. As [Horton] enters and stands petrified with astonishment. A portable talking machine is blaring out a hot tune. Petroff is tap dancing!"[10] From the first scene, *Shall We Dance* assures its viewers that Astaire is still the hot hoofer they know him to be. The ballet background of the film is immediately compromised. The viewer's first glimpse of Astaire, revealed in the middle of a "hot" routine to a "lowdown" "blast of hot swing," doubles down on Astaire's true identity, denying at the outset the advertised premise that Astaire will play a ballet dancer (read effeminate puff). Clearly, the makers of *Shall We Dance* never intended to take the ballet side of the story seriously. The first draft of the dialogue for this scene differs from the film. After spicing up a ballet leap with a tap break, Astaire defends himself against Horton's accusation "That's not art."

> *Pete:* Maybe not. But it means dancing to 100,000,000 American hearts. I have a marvelous idea, Jeffrey. Suppose we could combine the technique of the ballet with the warmth and passion of jazz!
>
> *Jeffrey (shocked):* Jazz! You're not thinking of being a jazzer!!
>
> *Pete:* Why not!—Dancing to jazz has so much more meaning. Why—it's the skyline of New York, and the dust bowl of the Middle West—and the roar of the Mississippi—and the sun of California.
>
> He bursts into a newer and bigger enthusiasm.
>
> *Pete (cont.):* It's Broadway, Jeffrey—and Main Street—all at once and together—It's—why, it's tap dancing.[11]

Astaire was always loath to talk about "meaning" in his work, and it isn't difficult to imagine him nixing these stilted lines about the meaning of jazz or any kind of dancing. The scene was reworked again and again. In one draft Astaire defends his character's full name, Pete P. Peters, as "a good old American name—it's got rhythm."[12] This weak joke on the Gershwins' "I Got Rhythm" was cut. The Gershwins' own melodic and lyrical reference to "I Got Rhythm" in the bridge of "Slap That Bass" was left in and Astaire tapped the stems to exactly those bars. A final set of revisions was typed out and distributed on blue sheets to be inserted into the cast and crew's scripts on the same day the scene was shot. By this point, well into production, the screenwriters were likely at work on other projects.[13] Director Mark Sandrich usually deferred to Astaire, and there's no reason to think Astaire wasn't behind this last round of changes, for once again, musical code words were at issue. The revised blue sheet reads:

> *Pete:* Jeff, I wish we could combine the technique of the ballet with the warmth and passion of . . . this other mood.
>
> *Jeffrey:* Mood!—What other mood? You mean jazz?

Pete: Jazz went out with the flapper, Jeff.

Jeffrey: Look here—you're not thinking of becoming one of those hoofer persons, are you?

Pete: Oh, this is different. It's got swing, rhythm . . . It's the skyline of New York . . . the roar of the Mississippi . . . and the sun of California. It's the short cut to a hundred million American hearts.[14]

But even this revision doesn't match the film as released. All the geographical talk about where swing and rhythm came from was cut, along with the code words themselves. The word *hoofer,* the only dance word Astaire regularly used to describe himself, was also excised. The line "Jazz went out with the flapper" became "Oh, jazz went out with the flapper. That isn't jazz." If Astaire is the author of this revision, he may be drawing a distinction between 1920s flapper jazz, the music of his youth, and 1930s swing, the modern music he was enjoying in this particular scene, music recorded especially for the scene by the moonlighting Jimmy Dorsey players. (Astaire's 1951 piece on 1920s jazz for *Esquire* demonstrates his awareness of ongoing shifts in jazz styles and terminology.)[15]

The *Shall We Dance* script files show that nailing down this bit of dialogue, innocuous as it may appear, caused a great deal of difficulty. The writers wanted to make a point: Astaire's Petrov was American and, at heart, the jazz tapper or hoofer audiences already knew. Code words were bandied about and, at the last moment—on the set perhaps—Astaire and his collaborators revised the dialogue, sweeping away most of the code words—in particular the trendy word *swing.* This struggle over jazz code words behind the scenes reveals the film version to be a negotiation of sorts. Astaire likely had the final word, and *swing* was one word not to be uttered. The music and his dancing to it could speak for themselves. Similar reticence around music and dance categories runs across Astaire's career.

This first scene of *Shall We Dance* raised sensitive issues, defining Astaire's relationship to ballet as distant even as he was being introduced as a character who was a ballet dancer. *Variety*'s reviewer read what was at stake with a clear eye: "That early terpsichorean kidding [the phonograph rehearsal bit], incidentally, may have an ulterior motive. Apparent idea is to immediately take the curse off those dainty ballet gestures so that no hard-boiled balcony can construe Astaire as having a rose in his teeth."[16] Throughout the film Astaire studiously avoids "dainty ballet gestures," shrugging them off like a bad idea in "Slap That Bass" and lampooning them at the start of "They All Laughed." The unquestioned masculinity of the jazz tap dancer, however, is taken for granted.[17]

Variety's concern for Astaire's masculinity raises an issue in Astaire scholarship worth addressing here. In a widely reprinted and referenced article on Astaire, film scholar Steven Cohan argues that song-and-dance men in the Hollywood musical inevitably take on a feminized position as "an object of vision" to be gazed upon during their routines.[18] Using this frame, Cohan reduces Astaire's persona to three terms: "*narcissism* . . . , which defines his body in terms of boundless energy and joyful motion; *exhibitionism* . . . , which defines his performance in terms of self-conscious spectacle and display of style; and *masquerade* . . . , which defines his identity in terms of theatrical play and social manners."[19] All three categories owe more to the schematic patterns of film theory than the practical terms of film history, and Cohan (like Feuer) misses the key to Astaire's song-and-dance persona: technical mastery of a known song-and-dance idiom. Astaire's routines, however theorized by later viewers, exhibited specific musical and choreographic content to their original audiences. Most of this content was directly connected to popular music and jazz of the hot and swinging kind, as the pervasive use of hot and swing in Astaire scripts demonstrates. Astaire's identity as a song-and-dance man who also plays a hot piano and dances with drums locates him in a specific, historically defined, inherently masculine show business realm. Audiences watched him dance in the same way they watched Goodman, Shaw, or Krupa play. All displayed the masculine power of jazz. Cohan's overly theoretical concept of show business—limited, as it is, to the visual—cannot account for the musical content of Astaire's work and, in the process, misreads the gender coding of Astaire's persona.

Swing as a jazz code word passed out of fashion after the war, and traces of post-swing jazz lingo, often with racial overtones, crop up in the script materials for Astaire's postwar films. The musical arrangement of "Bouncin' the Blues" in *The Barkleys of Broadway* is described as "very modern, very jivey" in a music department memo (see chapter 7 for an analysis of this number).[20] At the party scene early in the same film, Oscar Levant pulls Astaire and Rogers aside, saying, "Just thought I'd rescue you from that jungle of squares." Levant plays the hipster here, but his credentials collapse when he launches into his "Sabre Dance" piano solo. While greeting the French playwright Jacques Bardou in a forced, overly friendly fashion, Astaire's Josh shouts out "Hiya Jackson. Dig ya later, boy." In popular lingo, a name like Jackson implies a black individual. This line is not in the script, and it's an odd moment, among Astaire's only lapses into hipster talk.[21] It works because of the animosity already established between Astaire and Bardou and the aural similarity between Jacques and Jackson. Even Ira Gershwin gets into the act, using the word *bebop* in the patter to the tune "Manhattan Downbeat." This was the only time Gershwin ever put the word *bebop* into a lyric, and his use of unexpected jazz lingo in *Barkleys* reflects the practice of many of Astaire's lyricists, who identified Astaire with music, dance, rhythm, and jazz words that did not normally appear in their work.

Allan Scott tried, without success, to insert a reference to bebop into the dialogue cue for the "Ad Lib Dance" in *Let's Dance*. When Astaire's character, Don, is asked what kind of music he wants the band to play, Scott has him say, "Just tell them to play anything—a little bee-boppy."[22] The spelling alone raises suspicions; the *–y* at the end falls in line with Hollywood's practice of offering the jazzy rather than jazz, the bluesy rather than the blues. The line was rewritten in the final shooting script, on pages dated just a week before the scene was shot. By then, Astaire would have known that the music used in the number was solid swing with no bebop elements. (It also may have been the first time he really looked at the dialogue.) In the rewritten scene, Scott's line is changed to "Oh, anything. Anything inspiring. Something that'll send me." Astaire frequently used the verb *send* to describe his personal reaction to music in the late 1940s and after. Removal of Scott's "bee-boppy" and the insertion of Astaire's "send" suggest yet again that Astaire took a hand in rewriting dialogue referencing musical style.

Bebop was on Michael Kidd's mind when he was creating *The Band Wagon*'s "Girl Hunt" ballet. Kidd described his thinking at a special Academy-sponsored screening for industry professionals, after which key technical players on the film participated in a panel discussion. Kidd revealed his conception of "Girl Hunt," in particular his desire to capture the shift in popular music fandom he had observed in the transition from swing to bebop.

> The very last sequence [in Dem Bones Café] was something that I'd always hoped to do somewhere because at the time bop was popular, I went around to many of the bop joints in New York City and I was always impressed with the fact that there were no visible joys. There was no visible joy in the ordinary sense of the word, no external joy visible as we found with Bobby Soxers going to a Benny Goodman. People are quiet and listen quietly, it is a very odd feeling, very odd air, almost of concentration hanging over the

place. And I felt it was the type of thing that could be translated to movement and from that would lend itself to the feeling of tension. And though they dance in the bop joint, which is contrary to the attitude of bop, nevertheless, I tried to keep the dancing and the type of movement down to a stylized form which reflected no joy—had a feeling of unfulfilled tension and would lead to the watchful, tense atmosphere of the fight that evolved as a result of it.[23]

Script materials for "Girl Hunt" bear out Kidd's claims. The "Dem Bones Café" is described as a "Bop joint" and the dancers inside are called "bebop characters."[24] Once again, contemporary jazz terminology turns up as a means for creative figures in the studio system to get down on paper the effect they were looking to generate in the nonverbal realms of music, dance, and film. Without the evidence of production archives, these intentions might not be caught by later viewers.[25]

The Ephrons' attempt to insert a jazz sensibility into *Daddy Long Legs* shows writers struggling to define jazz in a mid-1950s film, only to have someone—likely Astaire—cut the words so the music could speak for itself. When Pendleton is interrupted at his drums by his assistant Griggs, the earliest script contains the line "But I was right in the middle of a riff!"[26] In the film, Astaire says, "I was right in the middle of a . . . thing . . ." and trails off, letting the music make the point. (Drummers lay down the beat; they don't play riffs.) The Ephrons also wanted to list some name bands as part of a joke. After defending his drum playing to the uninterested Griggs, Pendleton was to ask his assistant to have a "letter written to Benny Goodman asking how much he'd charge me for a recording made without any drum accompaniment whatever. Send the same letter to Artie Shaw, Les Brown, Tommy Dorsey, Gene Kru . . . no, no, not Gene Krupa . . . and Harry James." A later version of the script changes the list of bands, removing Shaw (who didn't have a band any more) and inserting Ray Anthony (now signed for the picture).[27] The Krupa joke is lame: a drummer's band recording without drums? But the idea of any dance band recording without a drummer is absurd. Just about any part could be left out *except* the drummer. Astaire, who played along with jazz records on his home drum kit, just like his character does in the scene, would have seen the weak logic informing the Ephrons' attempt to capture a jazz sensibility. He would not have wanted his character to be as ignorant as his writers apparently were in jazz matters. The line was cut entirely in the final script. A similar fate befell all but the first few lines of Mercer's lyric for "History of the Beat," the stick-throwing dance solo that follows (see figure 7).

FIGURE 7. Dancing with drumsticks, a central trope for Astaire across his career, gets a final turn in "History of the Beat" from *Daddy Long Legs*.

Mercer wrote a long, tedious history of jazz from ragtime to bop, five verses in all, a veritable lexicon of jazz lingo. Astaire recorded and filmed this portion of the song, but it was summarily (and rather bluntly) cut out of the print, leaving only a very short vocal intro addressed to Griggs and a brief dance around the room. Mueller wonders if the number was reduced because "it may have been particularly affected by [Astaire's] grief" over the very recent death of his wife from cancer at age forty-six.[28] An alternate reason may be that Astaire came to dislike the obvious nature of Mercer's lyric, which violated his practice of avoiding jazz code words.

As in so many previous scripts, where his screenwriters wanted to use jazz-related words to describe the music Astaire makes, in *Daddy Long Legs* the music is allowed to speak for itself. This seems to have been Astaire's approach throughout his career. Just as he was reticent to say more than "I just dance," he wanted to let the music play, unqualified by trendy categories. Zanuck well understood this economical approach to musical storytelling. In a set of notes on the final script for *Daddy Long Legs*, Zanuck called for a page of introductory dialogue to be eliminated. In its place he asked for "an amusing direct cut" from a cubist portrait of Astaire to Astaire himself at the drum set.[29] Musically, the cut was accompanied by an abrupt shift from a string quartet to a blaring big band midphrase. Music and image, modern jazz and a Picasso-esque portrait of Astaire, could do the work of character introduction just fine, and the 1950s audience could be relied upon to infer the jazz credentials that had defined Astaire's screen persona for the previous twenty years.

CHAPTER 5

"Fixing up" tunes

Writing and music department staffs at the Hollywood studios did not normally mix. Astaire worked closely with the musicians, and it is to their specialized task of making musical numbers that we now turn.

Synchronized sound films confronted studio music departments with a diverse set of creative and technical tasks demanding a division of responsibilities, with one man—and these were all male preserves[1]—doing the composing in a sketched-out fashion, others orchestrating and laying out the details, teams of copyists turning out parts, and conductors (sometimes the composer) leading the staff musicians in the studio's own recording studios, where custom-made musical cues were recorded to match edited film sequences. All these tasks were typically done in a short period of time—a matter of weeks or even days—during the postproduction period, after the film had been shot and edited. Scoring films—adding original composed cues to an image track that had already been edited together—was specialized work demanding a mastery of classical music techniques (writing for symphony orchestra), a technical knowledge of specific production practices (such as the use of a click track), a sense for what sounded good when mixed with dialogue and sound effects, and the ability (and willingness) to serve the priorities of the film story rather than purely musical values. The music department's collective task was as distant from the live context of the concert hall as Astaire's routines were from the concert dance stage. But for all their collective skills, studio music departments were not necessarily equipped to meet the needs of the musical as a genre.

Musicals, the most expensive of studio genres, made extra demands on the music department and brought added players into the process. Songwriters—seldom professional musicians competent in the ways of the music departments—took the place of the composer for the musical numbers and required extra care (as we shall see). Under the playback system, the score for a musical film was recorded in two phases: prerecording of musical numbers to which singers lip-synched during filming, and the standard postproduction scoring of all other music in the film. Some musicals have a lot of scoring *(Follow the Fleet);* others almost none *(Top Hat).* The music for musical numbers was almost always recorded before the images were shot. The creative process driving this music originated in the dance rehearsal hall or the vocalist's coaching sessions. Preparing numbers for filming to playback drew more on the practices of live entertainment than film scoring. This aspect of musical numbers, the unique element of the genre, ended up bringing studio outsiders into the process. In the band pix phase of the genre, nonstudio personnel from the world of jazz and dance band arranging increasingly found their way into the music departments, among them some of the very same arrangers who transformed popular music and brought in the swing era.

Arrangers and orchestrators are key creative figures in popular music history. (The two terms—arranging and orchestrating—cannot be entirely separated from each other and are used interchangeably here except where sources allow for separation.) The importance of these musicians who worked with pen and paper has been consistently underestimated by the improvising soloist-oriented thrust of most jazz historiography. This situation has begun to be addressed in recent years by Walter Van de Leur, Jeffrey Magee, and Eddy Determeyer.[2] Songwriter-centered popular music historiography has also frequently left out the important role played by arrangers on Broadway and in Hollywood. Again, recent work by George Ferencz and Steven Suskin has sought to remedy the omission.[3] If jazz is only about improvisation, then arrangers are side characters engaged in nonjazz activities. (It is not so easy to eliminate the songwriters who provided the scaffolding for jazz artists to improvise upon, although this has largely been the case as well.)[4] But separating the improvisers from the arrangers forces a false choice: for most of jazz history, and certainly in the swing era, the music was fueled by both. And in the case of the Hollywood studios, there was little room for improvisers but plenty of space for arrangers to inject the sounds of jazz into film scores. To get the sound they wanted, studio music departments opened their doors to jazz and dance band arrangers. Some were African American. In this way, the imperative to swing forced open the all-white world of the studio music departments, at least a little bit and for a short time. The best way to track how jazz arrangers found their way past the studio gates is to follow the careers of dance band arrangers who crossed over into film work.

Given the pen-to-paper nature of arrangers' work, their contributions are relatively easy to spot. For Astaire films with surviving complete conductor's scores—*Blue Skies* and *Funny Face*—the task of separating out who did what is straightforward.[5] Arrangers and orchestrators usually signed their work. Since they were paid by the page, keeping track of who did what was a payroll necessity. When scores are lacking, other department files often provide the needed information. Complete breakdowns of prerecording and scoring sessions for all of Astaire's MGM films, with arranger/orchestrator credits for each cue, survived the general destruction of the studio's archives. In the case of RKO, where scores and production documents were haphazardly preserved, the arranger credits for Astaire's films can only be reconstructed in a piecemeal fashion. Astaire's two films opposite Rita Hayworth at Columbia are especially difficult to study, given what one scholar calls the studio's status as an "archival blank spot."[6] Lacking any production documents or even a single surviving script, *You Were Never Lovelier* offers an interesting case.

Screen credits for music typically list only the composer, the director of the department, and, sometimes, an arranger. (In the 1950s more specific orchestrator credits became more common.) But *You Were Never Lovelier* was excessively specific in its music credits, which take up two title cards. The first has but one credit:

MUSIC BY
JEROME KERN

The second card is laid out as follows.

LYRICS BY
JOHNNY MERCER
Musical Director . . . . . LEIGH HARLINE
Assistant . . . . . PAUL MERTZ

Musical Arrangements by CONRAD SALINGER
Musical Arrangement of "THE SHORTY GEORGE"
by LYLE [SPUD] MURPHY
Xavier Cugat Specialty "CHIU CHIU"
by NICANOR MOLINARE

The division of tasks on *You Were Never Lovelier* is expressed graphically. Everything began with Kern's music, to which Mercer added lyrics. The relative size and position of the two names privileges Kern's contribution, reflecting the composer's name recognition for the public, professional status among songwriters, and industry clout. Kern was a star, musically speaking, and his separate card showed it. Kern's standard contract language normally stipulated that authorship for all music in the film would be assigned to him, even if he hadn't, in fact, written all of it (for more on this, see below). Columbia music department chief Leigh Harline comes next—he likely conducted most of the recording sessions—with his assistant Paul Mertz listed below. Harline would have organized the distribution of tasks within the department, a division that is detailed a bit in the final three names on the second card.

Conrad Salinger apparently did the bulk of the arranging and orchestrating on this film, which has a wonderfully excessive amount of scoring. Salinger was a studio specialist, master of all film music tasks but particularly suited to the demands of the musical. He worked effectively on both sides of the musical production process, prerecording and scoring. Salinger worked on Astaire's *Carefree* at RKO and joined the staff at Metro in 1940, remaining there until the musical production units closed down in 1958. *You Were Never Lovelier* is one of very few films Salinger did off the Metro lot. Salinger's best-known orchestrations are for Freed and Kelly pictures, including much of *Singin' in the Rain*. Astaire worked with Salinger relatively little at MGM. A creator of lush yet transparent studio orchestra textures, Salinger was Gene Kelly's man at Metro. (Astaire favored Skip Martin, a swing-based arranger with a different approach.) Salinger's scoring for *You Were Never Lovelier* adopts a light romantic style. Astaire is introduced with a Gershwinesque muted trumpet theme heralding his character throughout much of the score. Salinger very well may have composed this particular melodic idea. Without archival materials it is impossible to tell. Scoring dramatic scenes like the music department professional he was, Salinger weaved Kern's orchid theme into the film from start to finish. The lyric is only heard in the final reel, when a group of delivery boys sing

Mercer's slangy lyric to playback: "Oh, si-si-si-si, Mama,/See how I love you!/Oh, si-si-si-si/Comma,/Say you love me, too!" The revelation that a tune used throughout the film has such a cheeky text recalls the craftsmanship of director Ernst Lubitsch, whose light touch and way with details hover over *You Were Never Lovelier*. Salinger's scoring adds this musical element to an already finely crafted romantic musical comedy.

Salinger's arrangement of the partner song and dance to "I'm Old-Fashioned"—which would have been prerecorded—picks up the mention of rain in Mercer's lyric with strings and xylophone. The dance portion is fluid and smooth, matching Hayworth's supple body and freely expressed (but not ballet-derived) arms. There's no rhythm section here: it's the sound of a pit orchestra, Hollywood style, a Salinger specialty. At one point Astaire uses a partner move that recurs throughout his work, and Salinger's arrangement gives the move a particular character appropriate to this film, this partner, and this number. In closed position, Hayworth travels in a circle around Astaire, turning him in the process. Astaire is standing on one bent leg with the other leg (also bent) extended to the side. Mueller calls this a tap pivot/promenade.[7] In "Pick Yourself Up" with Rogers and the "Jukebox Dance" with Powell, Astaire interprets the move rhythmically. Rogers's steps are matched by the orchestra; Powell makes furious sounds with her feet, to which Astaire stamps his own syncopated line with the extended foot. With Hayworth, the move is executed without foot sounds, and Salinger meets the moment with soaring strings. It's all motion.[8] (Astaire did dub in foot sounds at key moments in "I'm Old-Fashioned" when the accompaniment drops below a certain level.)

When it came to a genuine jive number for *You Were Never Lovelier*, the arranger's baton was passed to Lyle "Spud" Murphy, who received screen credit for "The Shorty George." Screen credit for a jazz band arranger's work on a single named number is very unusual; I know of no analogous case. Murphy was there when swing went national, but it's unlikely his name was well known outside professional circles. He was among Goodman's principal arrangers in the mid-1930s, when Goodman kicked off the swing revolution in popular music. At their mammoth 6 June 1935 recording session, Goodman's band recorded fifty selections, fifteen arranged by Fletcher Henderson (often credited with being the formative voice behind Goodman's sound), seventeen by Murphy. The 1937 textbook *Spud Murphy's Swing Arranging Method* remains a useful guide to the style. Chapter 1 deals with instrumentation. Murphy notes, "The violins should be used sparingly in swing arrangements, unless they are of the melodic type and slow or moderate tempo."[9] This rule of thumb describes Astaire's practice entirely. As will be shown, the choice of instrumentation, often a matter of including or excluding violins, proves important. Arrangements lacking violins tend to be made by professionals hailing from the dance and jazz band world rather than the studio music departments.

Murphy and his work on *You Were Never Lovelier* offers a prototype of the kinds of swing arrangers and arrangements Astaire favored to the end of his career. Murphy's arrangement of "The Shorty George" stays squarely in the groove while also selling the tune, which remains clearly heard, although at times it's adjusted rhythmically to match and emphasize the dancers' moves. Like all Astaire's arrangers, Murphy must have worked from a score detailing the various accents Astaire and Hayworth would hit in the dance. In that sense, Astaire and his (unknown) rehearsal pianist on the film did the arranging, with Murphy contributing his expertise in jazz orchestration by adding dance band textures and figures. While there are no hot solos beyond a touch of boogie-woogie piano, Murphy uses a sectional approach typical of his work for Goodman and others. A mixed vocal group à la Tommy Dorsey's Pied Pipers sings part of the time. The number concludes with a riff-based pass through the chorus. For all intents and purposes, Astaire and Hayworth are dancing to a swing record, albeit in an arrangement finely tuned to their spontaneous (and carefully rehearsed) dance. Murphy was a well-regarded jazz arranger but not a big figure around the studios. He has only one other known screen credit, also at Columbia. How Murphy managed his very public nod on the *You Were Never Lovelier* title cards is unknown, but it provided a clue to the sound/image relationship that knowledgeable swing fans could catch and appreciate, waiting for the genuine swing number promised by name in the opening credits.

One unanswerable question surrounding "The Shorty George" is who is playing on the soundtrack. The number is situated as a nightclub rehearsal: Astaire is running through his numbers with Cugat's band. Cugat counts off the start of "The Shorty George," and his band is periodically visible during the dance, but the sound of Murphy's arrangement is foreign to everything Cugat's band stood for. That's not to say Cugat's outfit couldn't or didn't play non-Latin numbers, but swing wasn't their bread and butter, and elsewhere throughout *You Were Never Lovelier* the contemporary Latin sounds of Cugat's band dominate. The Cugat sound was familiar to national audiences from the band's weekly radio program sponsored by the Reynolds Tobacco Company in the early 1940s.[10] The title card highlights "Chiu, Chiu," one of Cugat's hit records, and the song's composer, Nicanor Molinare, gets a mention on the crowded musical screen credit. Sheet music for the number was published together with the film's Kern and Mercer songs. Beyond "Chiu, Chiu," a small pullout group accompanies Astaire on his solo dance to a medley of Cugat hits. The music was pieced together from Cugat's existing book and transitions specific to the routine created in the rehearsal studio. Astaire and Cugat must have collaborated on this, and the players seen on-screen are almost certainly heard on the soundtrack. Perhaps working together on the specialty led to Astaire's giving Cugat his enduring nickname, Coogie.[11]

Attentive listening to the score for *You Were Never Lovelier* might hint at the division of labor outlined on the title cards: a mix of romantic prerecorded musical numbers and scoring, a swing band feature, and the signature Cugat sound. Instrumentation offers a key: the work of Salinger, Murphy, and Cugat's band could be inferred based on the size and makeup of the ensembles heard and seen in the film. Salinger's scoring uses a full studio orchestra; "The Shorty George," big band forces (reeds, brass, and rhythm); "Chiu, Chiu" and Astaire's specialty, the Cugat group with its characteristic Latin hand percussion. But aural analysis and stylistic comparison only go so far. Musicals are highly technical assemblages, and getting beyond the film surface to the actual credits remains crucial for any solid interpretation of a specific film and its relation to popular music and jazz. The aural and visual cues alone would not reveal the extent to which Columbia went outside its own institutional structures to get the desired sound. In particular, Murphy's screen credit reveals that there were musical effects the studios did not feel the need to simulate: they could hire actual popular arrangers who did this sort of work in the world of popular music. That this happened at Columbia on an Astaire partner routine—on a dance embedded in the swing moment, as the next chapter will show—forges yet another direct link between Astaire and professional structures of popular music and jazz.

You Were Never Lovelier, a film with almost no paper trail, manages to clue the viewer in to the process behind the music, pointing toward the range of professional competencies heard in the contrasting styles of music in the film. More typically, screen credits do not reveal the division of labor within the music departments, so internal sources must be relied upon. When these documents exist, they pull back the curtain on how the music that made Astaire dance was itself made. Some representative examples follow.

Broadway and Hollywood arranger Robert Russell Bennett made a first try at scoring Astaire's golf solo "Since They Turned Loch Lomond into Swing" for *Carefree*. Bennett's version—which used a full complement of strings and orchestral winds—was rejected in favor of a second try by Gene Rose, who nixed the strings and used a smaller ensemble of nine reeds, eight brass, and four rhythm. A swing band on steroids, it was too big to be profitable in the real world circa 1938, but the group was easily assembled for a single recording session at RKO.[12]

Studio professionals were normally expected to create acceptable facsimiles of any musical style. For example, Bennett and Salinger split the task of orchestrating "The Yam," an important dance band number from *Carefree:* Bennett did the vocal, Salinger the dance.[13] Their work here highlights the necessity of arrangers being conversant with a wide range of musical styles. Bennett and Salinger were never known for jazz band arrangements: they favored studio orchestras and did not work outside dramatic contexts, whether stage or screen. On "The Yam," both work out of character stylistically but in character professionally, exhibiting their chameleon-like ability to produce whatever it was that a given film required. (In a 1940 program note for the Carnegie Hall premiere of one of his concert works, Bennett enthused, "and Fred Astaire likes my saxophone parts.")[14]

But studio music departments preferred to work to individual strengths, allowing specific arrangers and orchestrators to contribute sounds and styles marked by their unique voices. In such a situation, arrangers were empowered to insert their own sensibilities into a film score in creative, clearly audible ways. Two examples from *The Band Wagon* are instructive. A novel duet for Astaire and Charisse was created, recorded, and shot to an instrumental version of the Dietz and Schwartz song "You Have Everything." (The entire routine was cut from the film. Only the soundtrack survives.)[15] The gimmick of the number was spatial: Astaire and Charisse each danced alone, in separate but adjacent rehearsal halls, with the screen image cutting from one to the other and sometimes showing both. The contrast between their dancing styles—ballet and jazz—was made visible and, in the collaborative musical arrangement, audible. Salinger arranged Charisse's portions, while Skip Martin, a jazz player and arranger active in Hollywood in the 1950s and profiled at length below, was responsible for Astaire's. It was not a collaboration so much as a division of labor, echoing the themes of the number and the film itself. The conceit—studio strings contrasted with jazzy brass—was likely inspired by Salinger and Martin's earlier work on "The Portland Fancy" in *Summer Stock* (1950), in which a sedate string group playing for a genteel barn dance (Salinger's part) is displaced by a swing combo that grows into a roaring big band (Martin's bit).

The musical accompaniment for *The Band Wagon*'s "Girl Hunt" ballet was assembled like a collage from prerecorded and scored cues utilizing every method in the studio arsenal, as Adolph Deutsch, music director on the film, explained at the Academy screening: "In the recording of the ballet we used a greater variety of techniques available to us than I've ever seen used in any one number. Sections of it were prerecorded orchestrally, other sections were prerecorded on a piano, other sections were done through counting steps and other sections were scored like a dramatic sequence. So practically every technique known to motion picture scoring was involved in that ballet."[16] Music department records sort out the facts behind Deutsch's description.[17] Composer credit was divided between Schwartz (the songwriter whose old songs were the basis for the score and who was around while filming was going on), Salinger, and Edens. The continuously sounding music for the ten-and-a-half-minute "Girl Hunt" combines sixteen different cues, each recorded separately and then edited together like so many shots. Most of the ballet was scored like a dramatic film, after the editing had been completed. Fourteen separate cues were recorded during two postproduction recording sessions in March 1953. The longest runs to one minute and thirty-three seconds; the briefest lasts a mere sixteen seconds. The two danced sections—the only ones with sustained choreographic content—were filmed to playback. These were the dances for Astaire and Charisse described earlier in connection with Kidd's choreography. Franklyn, a longtime Metro staffer whose work on "Dancing in the Dark" was discussed above, orchestrated Astaire's lyrical dance with the blonde Charisse in the subway (1'18' long). Franklyn is also credited with all fourteen of the scored postproduction cues. Skip Martin orchestrated the "Bop Joint Sequence" (2'27"), including Astaire's nervous dance with the brunette Charisse, the only section of the ballet that uses a prominent jazz rhythm section. "Girl Hunt" is an ideal example of studio collaboration understood as a division of creative tasks among members of a group, with individuals assigned to do their most characteristic work.[18]

Sometimes only part of a musical number would be prerecorded, with the rest left to be scored after the edit was done. For example, Martin arranged *The Band Wagon*'s "A Shine on Your Shoes" from Astaire's vocal entrance onward. Alexander Courage arranged the two-minute cue accompanying Astaire's walk around the arcade before the song and dance proper begin. Both segments inflect the jazz character of the number.

Sometimes rescoring a prerecorded arrangement was deemed necessary, replacing the soundtrack used for filming to playback with a new arrangement recorded to synchronize with the already edited image track. This rarely used practice expresses in practical terms the synthetic, layered nature of musical film as a carefully assembled simulacra of actual performance. For example, the third section of "Fated to Be Mated" from *Silk Stockings* was rerecorded in a jazz combo version with André Previn at the piano. Around this time Previn, together with drummer Shelly Manne and bassist Leroy Vinnegar, scored a big success with an LP of tunes from *My Fair Lady* that became a top seller. Previn's rescored section of "Fated to Be Mated" tapped directly into this surprise hit record, using what studio records called a "jazz orchestra" built around Previn at the piano. "Fated to Be Mated," the last studio routine Astaire made, closed out his studio-era career with a fresh, contemporary sound that was a scoring phase afterthought.

SEVEN ASTAIRE ARRANGERS

In 1988, Liza Minnelli recalled dancing with Astaire in the mid-1960s: "When I was about seventeen, I danced with him at a party. It was a rock 'n' roll song, with heavy drums, and he was dancing away, and then he looked at me and said, 'I always tried to get this sound on the drums at Metro.' He wanted the best really laid down."[19] How might Astaire have gone about trying "to get this sound on the drums at Metro"? An obvious way was to be present at recording sessions, even when he wasn't required to sing. Consistent evidence in production files from across his career shows that Astaire attended all recording sessions relating to his numbers. Presumably he had input, even final say, on matters of tempo and style. Another strategy was to bring in select players who could deliver the sound Astaire was looking for. As the use of players from Jimmy Dorsey's band in *Shall We Dance* demonstrates, this was impractical and unusual. Union rules dictated that, except under special circumstances, staff musicians played on all studio soundtracks.

But by the 1950s, with most big band jobs now history, there were a good number of swing professionals with jazz credentials in the ranks at MGM. Astaire's "Bouncin' the Blues" would draw on these talents concealed in the studio's staff orchestra. One consistently flexible element in music department structures was the choice of arrangers and orchestrators. This was work for hire at set union rates, open to selection of creative staff on a film-by-film, number-by-number basis, a singular moving piece in the music department. The choice of arranger was one way Astaire could "get the sound" he wanted. Considering select Astaire arrangers here helps further locate the Hollywood genre of the musical squarely in the middle of the popular music industry from the 1930s to the '50s, reinforcing the direct links between jazz, the musical, and Astaire. Profiles of seven representative Astaire arrangers follow. Fud Livingston, George Bassman, Lennie Hayton, Paul Wetstein, Phil Moore, Calvin Jackson, and Skip Martin each traveled between jazz and musical film arranging. Their individual connections to Astaire shed light on the variety of ways the skill set of the jazz arranger could enhance the already expansive capabilities of studio music departments. The length of each profile reflects available archival sources. Beyond their point of contact with Astaire, the careers of these musicians illuminate the opportunities and limitations for jazz professionals, black and white, in the studio system.

Fud Livingston was a reed player and arranger employed by Jimmy Dorsey. When the Dorsey band was brought onto *Shall We Dance*, RKO also hired Livingston to do the arrangements. It made sense to do so. Without the right arrangements the Dorsey band wouldn't sound like the Dorsey band (even though there was no public admission that the band played on the soundtrack). Livingston arranged every number Astaire and Rogers danced in the film. For "Let's Call the Whole Thing Off," he created the first riff-based arrangement in an Astaire film, replacing Gershwin's melody with a rhythmically oriented texture built on the song's harmonic changes. Livingston also made arrangements for the band's own book of all four dance tunes he scored for the film. Dorsey recorded these charts at a single session in March 1937, just before their soundtrack sessions for *Shall We Dance*. Though not formally linked in business terms, the band and the studio were seeking a kind of synergy fueled by the release of a clutch of new Gershwin tunes.

The musical numbers for *A Damsel in Distress* were all arranged by Robert Russell Bennett, with the notable exception of Astaire's extended drum dance finale, which was handed off to George Bassman.

Bassman had composed and arranged Benny Goodman's theme song "Let's Dance," heard at the start and finish of every Goodman radio appearance. (He also composed Tommy Dorsey's theme song, "I'm Getting Sentimental Over You.") Trained at a conservatory, Bassman spent most of the 1930s in the dance and radio band business before moving primarily into film work around the time that he arranged Astaire's complicated solo, which uses six reeds, eight brass, and rhythm, and bears more than a little resemblance to Goodman's contemporary sound. Astaire even quotes the opening of "Sing, Sing, Sing" on a tom-tom.

Lennie Hayton arranged several numbers for Artie Shaw's band in *Second Chorus*. Hayton's career ran a well-worn path from jazz and dance band arranging to permanent studio work. Hayton started out with Paul Whiteman in the late 1920s, led and arranged for Bing Crosby's radio shows in the early 1930s, and ended the decade with his own touring name band. After the brief stint arranging for Shaw, Hayton joined the music staff at Metro in 1940, and he remained until 1953 as a conductor, composer, and arranger (also meeting and marrying black MGM contract star Lena Horne in 1947). He worked in a variety of capacities on three Astaire films.

Using an outside arranger could cause trouble, as the brouhaha over Paul Wetstein's arranging work for *Holiday Inn* demonstrates. Wetstein was an arranger with the Bob Crosby band, which, as noted earlier, played for most of the score and all of Astaire's numbers. Wetstein's hiring apparently bruised no egos in the Paramount music department, but he inadvertently brushed up against a big musical ego belonging to someone who really mattered: Irving Berlin.

The 30 January 1942 issue of the *Hollywood Reporter* reported the following about *Holiday Inn*, a production that was already much anticipated.

"WETSTEIN TUNES 'INN'"
Paramount has gone outside the studio and has tabbed Paul Wetstein, Bob Crosby's band arranger, to fix up the Irving Berlin tunes to be sung by Bing Crosby and Fred Astaire in "Holiday Inn."[20]

This one sentence initiated a daily bicoastal exchange that went on for a week and sounds close to panic on the West Coast end. Berlin started the correspondence, writing to Robert Emmett Dolan, his main contact in the Paramount music department. Berlin mentioned the article and added that he had already called Harry Ginsberg, a front office man at Paramount, about the matter. Berlin was intent on addressing what he viewed as a public slight. "Almost all the best men, in Hollywood, have made arrangements for the different pictures I have done, and this is the first time anything like this has happened. The little colored boy story stopped bothering me many years ago, but I think this is deliberate and something must be done about it. From my short acquaintance with Wetstein, he seems a nice guy and I don't think he would want anything like this." Berlin sent a similar letter, with the offending article included, to his good friend Mark Sandrich, director of the film.[21] It's unlikely Paramount needed Berlin to point out an item in the industry's daily trade sheet—Berlin's wife Ellin brought it to his attention—but when Berlin, a valuable creative asset who sold his songs all over town, raised the issue it became something to be dealt with both publicly and privately.[22] Paramount needed to defend the songwriter as if he were a star. Accordingly, and likely under direction from above, Paramount's music chief Louis Lipstone planted a text with the columnist for the *Hollywood Reporter,* forwarding a copy to Berlin.[23]

> The article stated in effect that Mr. Wettstein [sic] had been engaged to "fix up" the Irving Berlin songs in HOLIDAY INN. This is a gross injustice to Mr. Berlin and not in accordance with the facts.
>
> It is customary when engaging bands or important musical organizations for pictures, such as Bob Crosby's band, that the orchestrators of these particular groups arrange the compositions to be played, because of their familiarity with the style and instrumentation of their units. In engaging the Bob Crosby band for HOLIDAY INN, this procedure was followed and Paul Wettstein [sic] of the band, was assigned to do the orchestrations for several of the Irving Berlin numbers.
>
> Mr. Berlin has an assured place in America as the outstanding composer of popular tunes of our times and no letter of mine can add laurels to the permanent ones he has already acquired. It is only to keep the records straight and the facts six-two-and-even, that I write this letter and kindly request you to publish it in your estimable publication.[23]

The *Reporter* never bothered to print Paramount's protest. It remained for the studio to sniff out the rat who dared utter foul words against the man who, in Jerome Kern's memorable formulation, "*is* American music." Ginsberg reported on the results to Berlin, blaming, of course, someone from outside the studio: "After a thorough investigation George Brown of our Publicity Department, found that the story which appeared in the *Hollywood Reporter* was concocted by the publicity man handling Bob Crosby's band, of which Wettstein [sic] is a member."[24]

Poor Paul Wetstein. Everyone spelled his name wrong. Even the *Holiday Inn* cue sheets misspell his name. Perhaps confusion of this sort encouraged Wetstein to change his name to Paul Weston, which he did soon after. (The change to a less Teutonic moniker may also have been motivated by the onset of war with Germany.) Under the name of Weston this young arranger would go on to define the sound of Capitol Records, a major label founded by Paramount studio head Buddy De-Sylva and Johnny Mercer in 1942. DeSylva and Mercer hired Weston as Capitol's first music director shortly after *Holiday Inn* wrapped, and Capitol's first six 78s were released just weeks before the film hit the nation's theaters.

Three days into the crisis Dolan tried to salvage Wetstein's reputation with Berlin. Dolan wrote in support of this talented young professional and even spelled his name right.

> I just want to add one more piece of information that might be of interest to you: Yesterday I showed the item to Paul Wetstein and it was immediately obvious that he was completely surprised and flabbergasted to read it. He, himself traced it down and later called to tell me that the Bob Crosby press agent had a carbon copy of the release he gave the REPORTER and it, in no way even suggested slightly any such things as "fixing up" tunes. It merely said that Paul Wetstein had done orchestrations for the picture. I, myself haven't seen this release, but I told Paul to send a copy of it to you.
>
> I am sure you agree with me when I say that Paul is a highly intelligent and sincere boy and would never in a million years cook up this sort of thing.[25]

Berlin's sensitivity circled around where the creativity for the score originated. Was it his own genius for crafting tunes or the arranger's skill in arranging them? No one was going to sell *Holiday Inn* as a Wetstein score—even the Crosby group wasn't that big—but Wetstein did, after all, do something Berlin could not: he created fully realized musical scores. The whole affair emphasized the need for arrangers to remain invisible. And yet, because popular music is, in essence, a business matter, credit must be given where it is due. An extremely useful postproduction document produced for legal reasons comes into play here, allowing us to dig deeper into exactly what Wetstein did on *Holiday Inn*.

"Cue Sheet #4129"—*Holiday Inn*'s production number—details every music cue in the film, assigning authorship (a matter of royalties) for every second of the score.[26] The list also distinguishes between borrowed material (tunes by Berlin on which a given cue is "based") and composition (which, in this case, is the act of arrangers doing sufficiently original work), a common studio music department way of distinguishing between different kinds of creative labor for the purposes of compensation. Berlin retained the rights and royalties for his tunes; studio staff did not. Almost all of *Holiday Inn*'s score involves straightforward arrangements of Berlin tunes, and, unsurprisingly, the vast majority of the cue sheet assigns authorship to Berlin. However, the cue sheet also reveals the specific niche Wetstein found on *Holiday Inn*. Five of Wetstein's six composer credits had something to do with a danced routine by Astaire.[27] Astaire and Wetstein must have worked together closely. Wetstein was behind the finale of *Holiday Inn,* which slides seamlessly across three Berlin tunes, from "I'll Capture Your Heart" to "You're Easy to Dance With" to "Let's Start the New Year Right," a well-routined segue that summarized the film in musical terms in a popular idiom that did not evoke old-fashioned musical theater finalettos, which reprised snippets from anticipated hits in the score just before the curtain fell. Anchored in popular arranging for radio and records, Wetstein was expert at selling tunes. Wetstein also received composer credit on the "Jitterbug" and "Firecracker" dances—easily the most prominent dance moments in early viewers' minds. Given these credits, Wetstein may have served as Astaire's rehearsal accompanist. Assuming he did makes sense from a practical standpoint. If it was understood at the outset that Wetstein would be doing the arrangements for the band and that the band would be playing for Astaire's specialties, then putting Wetstein at the piano in the rehearsal hall jibes with analogous cases discussed earlier in which Hal Borne and Walter Ruick were given arranger or composer credits for similar numbers.

The most interesting revelation of the cue sheet is the cocredit on the "Jitterbug Dance"—Astaire's drunk dance during the New Year's Eve scene—for Wetstein and Bob Haggart, which puts Astaire next to one of the hottest bass players of the time. Teamed with drummer Ray Bauduc, Haggart scored one of the major novelty hits of the swing era in "Big Noise from Winnetka" (1938). The novelty "Jitterbug Dance" is a two-and-a-half-minute riff-heavy jazz record loosely based on Berlin's tune "You're Easy to Dance With" (introduced vocally by Astaire earlier in the film). Wetstein and Haggart—working with Astaire— completely refashioned Berlin's tune using techniques direct from the world of jazz.

"You're Easy to Dance With" is long—fifty-eight bars—and oddly shaped.

A	*16 bars*	a6 + a6 (step higher) + b4
A	*16 bars*	a6 + a6 (step higher) + b4
B	*8 bars*	c4 + c4
B1	*8 bars*	c4 + d4
A1	*10 bars*	a6 + e4

The A sections are split into three subphrases: a6 + a6 (a step higher) + b4. The b4 subphrase sets the title words in a tossed-off patter style that reinforces the casual diction of the song as a whole. The double-length B section divides into two balanced eight-bar phrases, matching the longer A phrases in scale. The final A1, only ten measures long, recasts the opening and sets a variant of the title phrase to a new melodic figure (e4) that demands a more sustained singing style. While unusual, Berlin's phrase lengths are expertly molded to the moment and the lyric. "You're Easy to Dance With" works brilliantly as a song-and-dance number for Astaire and partner Virginia Dale, who perform in a high-class New York nightclub. In the very different context of the drunken "Jitterbug Dance," Wetstein and Haggart (and Astaire) abandon Berlin's odd phrase lengths—regularizing the tune to forty-eight bars (six eight-bar phrases)—and select the most distinctive elements of Berlin's melody as material for riffs.

AA	*8 bars*	first two notes of "a6" used as riff
AA	*8 bars*	
BB	*8 bars*	first four notes of "a6" used as bass line
BB	*8 bars*	
CC	*8 bars*	"c4" adapted for melody line
DD	*8 bars*	first four notes of "a6" used as bass line

Wetstein and Haggart's AA phrase uses the first two notes of Berlin's tune—a rising major third—as a riff in the saxes. Their BB phrase builds a repeated rising bass line on the first four notes of Berlin's melody. The CC phrase draws on Berlin's descending c4 idea, and the closing DD phrase brings back the rising bass line in a slightly different form. Fragments from Berlin's original are everywhere, but it's impossible to sing Berlin's tune along with Wetstein and Haggart's recomposed version. If you try, you might be forgiven for thinking you're drunk. The drunk dance affords a prime example of Astaire collaborating with skilled jazz musicians, drastically altering the structure of material he's been given and making the song fit his needs rather than slavishly following Berlin's tune.

The music modulates up a step for the second dance chorus, which unexpectedly states Berlin's tune exactly. Berlin's a6 subphrase ends with a two-bar break. Wetstein and Haggart's arrangement leaves three of these breaks empty of sound. Astaire is the obvious candidate to fill these empty breaks—in "Music Makes Me," the joke was that he couldn't stop himself from doing so—but here he just wanders about, too drunk to put rhythm where he normally would. Berlin's unusual structure is turned to a comic effect any swing fan would have gotten on first hearing.

The brief "Jitterbug Dance" structurally disfigures Berlin's song to a greater extent than usual even for Astaire's more invasive numbers. Wetstein and Haggart must have been close to Astaire's creative process when the drunk dance was being made. The number was recorded by the Bob Crosby band, including Haggart, without "augmentation" by Paramount staff musicians. Astaire and his dance partner, Marjorie Reynolds, were called to the session, even though neither sings in the number.[28] The complexity of the arrangement for the drunk dance strongly argues for Wetstein being Astaire's rehearsal pianist on the film.

Wetstein's other arrangements for Astaire's dances utilize swing approaches as well. For his "Firecracker Dance," Astaire combined instrumental versions of two songs sung in a prior scene. The first dance chorus, using the chord changes from "Let's Say It with Firecrackers," is totally riff-based: the tune goes unheard. Played by the Crosby band in a tight, spare style, Wetstein's arrangement matches the explosive idea of the number, which includes firecracker pops and special effects mixed effectively with Astaire's explosive tapping. For the most part, the arrangement stays well out of the way of Astaire's taps and the explosions. In one passage the band matches Astaire tap for tap, further suggesting Wetstein was in the room when the dance was put together. *Holiday Inn* shows how conversant Astaire was with jazz music and music making of the early 1940s: he was able to work with swing professionals, crafting arrangements of popular songs that worked for his purposes as well as the band's.

Wetstein also arranged the Crosby-Astaire-Dale trio "I'll Capture Your Heart Singing," which opens the film. Built on the contrast between Crosby's crooning and Astaire's hot rhythms, the number called for side-by-side sweet and hot arranging. Crosby even works in a bit of scat singing, harkening back to his earliest records with the Whiteman band. Wetstein's flexibility is on display, with hot swing rhythms giving way to sweet strings in thirds. The arrangement is a microcosm of the Capitol Records sound, which was being born around this time. Wetstein's versatility—he could do swing charts and string scores; he was always looking for the big middle of the market—made him an excellent match for an upstart label. The first major record company to set up shop in Hollywood rather than in New York, Capitol Records would capitalize on a transitional moment in the music industry, situating its catalog squarely on the divide between jazz in a popular idiom and popular music for sophisticated listeners. Fueled by the considerable musical instincts and energy of its founders, Wetstein (now Weston) and Mercer chief among them, Capitol rapidly emerged as a central player in the reinvention of popular music in the postwar period, when the label would lead the way in creating high-quality pop and exploiting the new LP format. And while Weston would never arrange for Astaire again, the classic pop aesthetic he helped pioneer at Capitol can be heard in several later Astaire films. For example, Franklyn's masterful arrangement of "Dancing in the Dark" for *The Band Wagon* finds a popular music twin on the Columbia Records album *Jo Stafford Sings Broadway's Best with Paul Weston and his Orchestra*.[29] (Weston and Stafford briefly decamped to Columbia in the 1950s.) Weston surrounds Stafford's close-miked voice with dramatic brass, swirling strings, and mixed backup singers. Unlike in Franklyn's dance version for Astaire, there is no audible rhythm section driving Stafford's vocal, but it's no stretch to imagine Astaire and Charisse dancing to Weston and Stafford's record. The tempos are about the same, as is the overall character: leisurely, lushly romantic, swooning in a mid-1950s "dream dancing" manner. The flexibility to stay in the game is evident in Astaire and Weston's contemporary versions of "Dancing in the Dark." Just ten years on from *Holiday Inn*, both men had reinvented themselves, adjusting the sound of their music to fit (and also shape) changing tastes, along the way staying at the top of their respective yet connected popular music and film musical spheres.

Black arrangers working for white dance bands were common enough to be unsurprising in the swing era. In the early 1940s, at the wartime height of Hollywood's interest in swing bands, Astaire worked with Phil Moore and Calvin Jackson, two African American arrangers who briefly found regular employment on studio music staffs. Both used swing band connections to get a foot in the door.

Occasional arranging for the studios made up only one aspect of Phil Moore's Hollywood career. Born in 1918 in Portland, Oregon, into "a unique, rather privileged background," Moore was something of a child prodigy on piano.[30] He soloed with a local youth orchestra at age twelve, and, in a career move suggestive of the limits put on black musicians, Moore was playing in speakeasies at thirteen. He moved to Los Angeles in the 1930s, where he worked on the black-cast musical film *The Duke Is Tops,* Lena Horne's feature film debut. Soon Moore became a studio liaison for black musicians. For example, MGM hired him to arrange music for the black chorus number "All God's Chillun' Got Rhythm" in the Marx Brothers' *A Day at the Races* (1937). (Ellington vocalist Ivie Anderson was the featured soloist—a rare spotlight for a black female singer. Shortly after the film was released Judy Garland recorded a cover of "All God's Chillun" for Decca, copying Anderson's scat vocals syllable for syllable.[31] Moore was hired by Metro as a rehearsal accompanist in 1941, becoming, as Donald Bogle notes, "what is believed to have been the first Black musician in a Hollywood studio music department."[32] Moore was never permitted to work with a white female singer without supervision, but access to major stars brought opportunities for work and friendship off the lot. He coached Ava Gardner personally, in intimate contexts, for the role of Julie in *Show Boat.*[33] Moore simultaneously worked as a freelance arranger all around the movie capital—at RKO, Columbia, and Paramount—usually without credit. His arrangement of Astaire's solo "One for My Baby (and One More for the Road)" in *The Sky's the Limit* falls into this category.

Moore left Metro and the movie business in 1945 to do arranging and vocal coaching for live acts. This was not unusual. All the black arrangers who gained footholds in the studio music departments had short tenures. In a business where white individuals routinely held secure studio posts for decades there was no such continuity for African Americans. And Moore was more than just a vocal coach: he was also a jazz pianist and a visible leader of small swing combos in New York and Los Angeles. After leaving Metro he took the first all-black outfit into New York's Copacabana. The *California Eagle,* the movie capital's black newspaper, celebrated the breakthrough: "The opening of Phil's five was also the opening of the Copacabana to colored entertainment and perhaps the cracking of the color line on the East Side. And, just as important, maybe jazz has come to stay on the tony side of Fifth Avenue."[34] In a parallel move on the West Coast, Moore coached and accompanied African American entertainer and actress Dorothy Dandridge when she opened at Hollywood's elite supper club, the Mocambo. Bogle, who interviewed Moore at length for his biography of Dandridge, sums up Moore's professional life in entertainment this way: "During a career which spanned some six decades, Moore coached or did special arrangements for a gallery of stars, including Mae West, Ethel Waters, Ava Gardner, Frank Sinatra, Louis Armstrong, Marilyn Monroe, Lucille Ball, Ann Sothern, Count Basie, Dinah Washington, Charlie Mingus, Bobby Short, and later Diahann Carroll, The Supremes, Leslie Uggams, Goldie Hawn, and Johnny Mathis."[35] This well-integrated list, combined with his dance band and jazz combo credits, locates Moore's career firmly in the long swing era. Like so many musicians whose careers intersected with Astaire, Moore worked in a song-based popular music economy, doing a range of things to songs, whether arranging them for vocalists to sing (live or on record) or improvising to them himself in a variety of jazz styles (live and on record). Moore's race did not prevent him from having an active career both behind the scenes, onstage and on records, but his exit from a formal position at Metro suggests that he saw little future in coaching female singing movie stars with a chaperone in the room.

The only archival evidence for Moore's contribution to *The Sky's the Limit* is his name on the extant arranger's score for the number.[36] No records or anecdotes tell how Moore got the gig arranging Astaire's solo for the film. Someone at RKO must have asked for him specifically. It could have been Astaire himself, or perhaps someone recommended Moore to Astaire as a flexible and inventive jazz arranger working around town. Moore may also have come onto the film by way of the Freddie Slack band, for which he had occasionally arranged.

"One for My Baby" is a traveling solo, moving from the "Flamingo Bar" to "Kiefer's Hamburgery" to the "Colonial Club," three locales seen earlier in the film. Using them in the number efficiently recycled sets that had already been built, at the same time tracing the length of Astaire's character's all-night bender as he revisits important nightspots where the film's romantic plot had played out. Moore's arrangement is among the most extraordinary ever done for Astaire in its variety of colors, instrumentation, and range of musical styles. Moore musically shadows Astaire's progression from bar to bar while simultaneously signaling his changing emotions with musical idioms that drew on different aspects of popular music at the time. "Kiefer's Hamburgery" features a distinctive jangly piano effect. Moore scored the sequence for two "mechanical pianos" (one of which he could have played himself), bass, guitar, and drums, a slightly expanded version of his own quartet. A frenetic riff chorus for a large dance band accompanies Astaire's destructive rage as he destroys glassware and mirrors behind the Colonial Club bar. Empty breaks are filled with the destructive sounds of glass breaking, a disturbing effect distant from the comically empty breaks in Astaire's drunk "Jitterbug Dance." Moore's work came in for some postproduction tinkering, with some sweetening at the four-bar reference to "My Shining Hour" heard just before the dance on the bar.[37] Sweetening was a standard strategy, adding a complement of strings playing a unison line—usually the tune—to an existing track.

Charles Emge of *Down Beat* reviewed *The Sky's the Limit* favorably—for a paper that didn't like movies to begin with—and celebrated Moore's role in particular.

> SLACK PICTURE (?) RELEASED
>
> *The Sky's the Limit* (RKO), which stars Fred Astaire and Joan Leslie, and purports to feature Freddie Slack's orchestra, is less a filmusical *[sic]* than a comedy-drama in which the principal performer happens to be a dancer. . . .
>
> Probably more notable from the spectacular standpoint is the rhythm routine Astaire does to "One for My Baby and One for the Road," *[sic]* in which he kicks over stacks of glasses while dancing on and around a gleaming cocktail bar. Note the high quality of the music that accompanies this sequence. It was arranged (much of it is original) by Phil Moore and recorded by a 40-piece ork [orchestra] containing Lee Young, Barney Bigard and other excellent Negro musicians.[38]

The large size of the group, its interracial makeup, and the inclusion of non-RKO staffers suggests that "One for My Baby," especially the music, was treated as a big deal on the production end. New Orleans–born reed player Barney Bigard was just coming off more than a decade with Ellington's band. After moving to Hollywood in 1942, he was briefly a member of Slack's band, which is likely the reason he made the session. Drummer Lee Young was highly visible around Los Angeles in the 1940s and '50s. Spotting a guest drummer, much less an African American one, in a high-profile studio context as was done here puts this recording session even further outside Hollywood norms, likely one reason *Down Beat* noted it in the first place. Young was one of the only African American musicians to obtain a playing position on a studio staff orchestra. Moore's varied application of jazz band arranging styles to a shifting narrative context makes this among the most musically varied of all Astaire's solo turns. The mixed racial makeup of the orchestra puts the number among Astaire's interracial numbers (a category discussed in more detail in chapter 9).

Calvin Jackson was born in Philadelphia in 1919 and attended the Julliard Graduate School—where all students had fellowships—as a pianist from 1937 to 1941. One of a small number of black students at the elite conservatory, Jackson studied piano with James Friskin and composition with Bernard Wagenaar, and took courses in philosophy at NYU. While still a student Jackson played professionally in a variety of styles.[39] Jazz critic Leonard Feather enthused about Jackson in *Down Beat* as early as 1940, writing, "He's quiet and modest about his ability on piano and organ, but plays anything from Brahms to the blues with a style and technique which more professionals would find hard to beat."[40] Just after graduating Jackson began accompanying tap dancer Paul Draper in concert and club performances, including at the Copacabana in Rio de Janeiro. Draper tapped to classical and swinging popular music, and Jackson's stylistic flexibility and ability to improvise must have been a good match. Jackson worked with Draper for about a year.

Despite his classical background and varied skills as a pianist, Jackson ended up working as a professional musician in the world of jazz and dance bands and, briefly, in the Hollywood studios. The story of an African American musician with classical training going into popular music to make a living was not uncommon in those decades. The tale simultaneously underscores the openness of the popular music field to black talent and indicts the American musical establishment for limiting the directions black musical artists could go. Jackson's arranging career began with white trumpeter Harry James's band, a connection that quickly took him to Hollywood and a studio contract at MGM.

James's band was perfect for band pix. James was a melodically oriented trumpeter capable of virtuoso turns (like his show piece "Flight of the Bumble Bee") and a competent actor who could even participate in staged musical numbers. In addition, he was among the most generically handsome of the big-name bandleaders. Married to iconic pinup Betty Grable in 1943, James was surely among the most envied of American men during World War II. With band in tow, James played a series of supporting roles in band pix between 1942 and 1946. James's band made two films simultaneously for Metro in mid-1943: the Esther Williams–Red Skelton musical *Bathing Beauty* and the soldiers' canteen film *Two Girls and a Sailor* (which included a star-making number called "The Young Man with a Horn," sung by June Allyson about and to James in the boldest studio attempt to generate real movie star heat around a bandleader). Jackson contributed arrangements to both films, doing everything from swing numbers and boogie bits for James to Latin specialties for the Cugat band to separate vocal features for James's singer Helen Forrest and Metro's new starlet Lena Horne (accompanied by the MGM orchestra). Jackson remained at Metro after these two James projects were over, earning a staff position in the music department.

An alternate route to the Metro position for Jackson may have come through his work on composer Dimitri Tiomkin's staff for *The Negro Soldier* (1944), one in a series of War Department propaganda films produced by Frank Capra. Warren Sherk attributes about one-fifth of the film's score, both composition and arrangement, to Jackson.[41] Phil Moore also worked on *The Negro Soldier,* as did black composer William Grant Still. The three men formed something of a fragile African American studio arrangers' fraternity during the war years, when inclusion of black Americans in all parts of the movie business was being encouraged strongly by the federal government and by civil rights groups such as the NAACP

Jackson began as an assistant to Georgie Stoll, head of Metro's large music department, in November 1943.[42] According to André Previn, who came to MGM as a Stoll assistant himself around the time Jackson departed, Stoll played piano with one thumb and could only read treble clef.[43] With a weekly guarantee of $150, Jackson's contract called for him to play piano "if and when required, at the union scale," and set rates of $40 per minute of music composed and $5 per page for orchestrating. Most of Jackson's work involved the adaptation or paraphrasing of popular songs.[44] His duties generally matched those of Phil Moore. Jackson's contract was noted regularly in the black press, which referred to him even in short articles as a "Negro piano player under contract to MGM studios," a one-line résumé marking considerable accomplishment in Hollywood's black community.[45]

Jackson's first known assignment after signing with MGM brought him briefly into Astaire's orbit, and he was well prepared for the task by both his arranging work for James and his accompanying experience with Draper. These items on Jackson's résumé proved a good fit for a particular music department problem that could have cost MGM both time and money.

Astaire's solo to his own song "If Swing Goes, I Go Too," from *Ziegfeld Follies,* affords an example of a shift from a studio orchestra to a jazz band aesthetic in an Astaire routine. A first version was orchestrated by an unknown hand and rehearsed on 16 March 1944. Hayton conducted the thirty-six-piece orchestra, which included twelve violins, oboe, clarinet, six saxophones, four trumpets, four trombones, three horns, and a rhythm section.[46] The arrangement was deemed unsatisfactory, for two days later Jackson submitted a revised version. Jackson used a tighter ensemble of twenty players sans strings: oboe, clarinet, seven saxophones, four trumpets, four trombones, and a rhythm section. Hayton recorded Jackson's version on 20 March. (The soundtrack survives, although the image track was lost.)[47] The smaller, jazz-oriented group bucked the trend toward grandiosity manifest in every other musical number in *Ziegfeld Follies*. Astaire's two "panto-ballets" were lavishly orchestrated by Salinger and Franklyn, using a huge (by studio standards) fifty-piece orchestra. "The Babbitt and the Bromide" called for thirty pieces, with strings and harps necessary for the number's final sequence in heaven. Had "If Swing Goes" not been cut from the film, Jackson's arrangement would have sounded lean and tight, qualities that cannot otherwise be attributed to the Metro-sized grandeur of Freed's *Ziegfeld Follies*.

With a dance chorus of twenty-four men, "If Swing Goes" took more than a week to film. Astaire essentially ran the shoot. The AD on the set described the action of the number as "Astaire throwing drum sticks to dancers" and "Astaire attack on drums."[48] (Figure 8 affords the only surviving glimpse of the routine.) Jackson's arrangement is jazz oriented through and through. In one section Jackson employs a rhythmic idea from his own arrangement of "Paper Doll" for Horne in *Two Girls and a Sailor*, work from just months earlier. Jackson uses a sectional approach throughout, pitting the brasses against the saxes in tight figures that play back and forth. In the driving final section, surprisingly dissonant chords are jumped on fortissimo by the whole group, and brilliant juxtapositions of overlapping rhythmic patterns fill the air. Jackson and Astaire didn't have a "real" swing band, but they did have the skilled professionals on the Metro staff. The recording is sharp and swinging, capturing the smooth values of the larger wartime swing bands, yet sparing the syrupy finish often associated with the Glenn Miller sound of the period. From full-band fanfare opening to screaming conclusion, Jackson's arrangement as played by Hayton's MGM outfit captures the ultimate in deluxe swing custom-made for Astaire's flashy dancing.

Yet, for all its drive and size, the most notable part of Jackson's arrangement comes just after the opening, when the band drops out and a series of soloists enters over the rhythm section: piano first, then clarinet, trumpet, and trombone. Each is added onto the other until the texture resembles a collective improvisation aesthetic associated with New Orleans, Chicago, traditional, or Dixieland jazz. At this spot in the

FIGURE 8. Dancing with drumsticks atop a set of Latin drums in the lost routine "If Swing Goes, I Go Too" from *Ziegfeld Follies*.

surviving piano-conductor's score, two words not normally associated with the Hollywood studios turn up: "ad lib."[49] The piano, clarinet, trumpet, and trombone jam is exactly that, a genuine jam session. Jackson would have known the players at Metro and known their abilities to pull off an unscored, improvised section: Hayton as conductor and Astaire as star and de facto director would have gone along readily with the idea. The rippling, elegant piano that starts it all off must be

Jackson himself. He recorded similar solo piano features on an album of 78s titled *Hollywood Melodies* with Georgie Stoll and His Orchestra in 1947, an early release on MGM's still-new record label.[50]

Jackson's jam session opening to "If Swing Goes" shows that on occasion studio musicians were allowed to improvise on a soundtrack just as they might on the bandstand or in any other jazz context. Doing so on a film soundtrack may have required special permission. Arranging an Astaire dance routine for the Slack band in *The Sky's the Limit*, Gil Grau advised on one sax part, "SOLO—SWING LEAD (AD LIB. IF CONDUCTOR OKAYS)."[51] The written record is too patchy to conclude exactly where a genuine ad lib passage occurs in Astaire's soundtracks, and we are cast back on our ears to find spots where the music sounds improvised. Other possibilities include the Shaw-esque clarinet and vibraphone solos in the swing band section of "Begin the Beguine" *(Broadway Melody of 1940)* and the collective improvisation aesthetic heard in the section before "A Shine on Your Shoes" gets started in *The Band Wagon*. The latter item, a scored track called "Penny Arcade," was credited to Alexander Courage, but close listening reveals a free musical texture played by clarinet, trumpet, trombone, piano, and drums. It would have been a waste of time to notate. This is Dixieland jazz played over Courage's AABA-structured rewriting of the song's original verse. Astaire hadn't used the verse in his solo, so it was musical material already paid for and waiting to be turned to use by the system.

After "If Swing Goes, I Go Too," Jackson contributed arrangements for musical numbers in at least ten more films before leaving Metro on his own initiative. Jackson never broke into the scoring end: his assignments were limited to prerecording work on musicals. With the exception of the number for Astaire, Jackson remained outside the closed, even snobby circle of Freed Unit arrangers.[52] Jackson worked mainly for Metro's two other musical-producing units, led by Joe Pasternak and Jack Cummings. MGM renewed Jackson's contract regularly as late as February 1947, but studio files suggest that at a certain point the arranger simply stopped showing up.[53] Jazz critic Leonard Feather, writing notes for a 1961 Jackson LP, said he left the studios "frustrated by a persistent lack of credit and recognition for his writing."[54] Given a warning, then what looks like a negotiated leave (with a payoff of $1,500), Jackson went back to New York, accompanying white jazz singer Mildred Bailey at Café Society and starting a new career as a small group leader. He spent many years in Toronto, was frequently heard on CBC radio, and recorded several albums with his combo in the 1950s and '60s. During his short stay in Hollywood Jackson's work remained limited in scope and variety. With solid musical training at a top conservatory, Jackson was treated as if all he could do was vocal arrangements, band numbers, and contrived jam sessions. The contrast with André Previn, who began at the same level as Jackson but quickly rose in the ranks of the music department, is marked. Like Lena Horne, who similarly bowed out of her prestigious Metro contract in 1950, Jackson left behind the limited opportunities coming his way at MGM, seeking and finding other creative work in the wider popular music world beyond the Hollywood studios.[55]

Phil Moore and Calvin Jackson had similar disappointing experiences in the Hollywood music departments. While both achieved formal employment within the system, neither remained for long, choosing instead to return to live entertainment and recordings, where both demonstrated skill sets the studios were unprepared to explore or develop in the mid-1940s. Both men asserted their compositional abilities on records. Jackson recorded and played the solo part on a 1958 disc titled *Jazz Variations on Gershwin's Rhapsody in Blue,* with jazz players interpreting a lightly revised score in a contemporary jazz idiom.[56] Leonard Feather's liner notes from 1961 praised Jackson as "a soloist willing and eager to explore the worlds of concert music, popular songs and jazz, and unusually well equipped to instill into a performance an inventiveness and technical finesse that reflect his broad experience in these disparate but reconcilable worlds."[57] Moore composed a trombone concerto for jazz player Will Bradley that was premiered by the CBS Symphony Orchestra and a made-for-records "Fantasy for Girl and Orchestra," which combined a voice-over monologue, solo violin, and a shifting orchestral fabric to maximum hi-fi effect. In 1947, Moore and Jackson made some recordings together on Clef (a precursor to Norman Granz's Verve label). Among these was Moore's short "Fugue for Barroom Piano" for jangly piano—Jackson on an instrument with just the sound heard on "One for My Baby"—and orchestra. The outer parts of this three-part work are a breathless baroque *perpetuum mobile* for piano and pizzicato strings. This display of musical erudition frames a haunting adagio, a jazzy mood piece with icy string chords, lonely fragments of melody in the piano, and several long silences. Moore and Jackson had abundant technical skills and ample musical vision to do much more than the studios let them.[58]

Skip Martin was the most important arranger on Astaire's films from *Royal Wedding* onward. Table 2 summarizes Martin's work for Astaire, as well as select other films Martin worked on during his ten years in Hollywood. A signature arranger for the decade, Martin contributed an instantly recognizable sound (once you know to listen for it), a postwar big band aesthetic that emphasized sheer size, tightness of ensemble, and brightness of timbre. Martin's work marks a direct connection between the film musical and popular music arranging in the period after the decade of swing ascendancy. The specificity of the link—its location in a behind-the-scenes figure like Martin—is important here because the swing, jazz, dance band sound was not completely silenced after the rapid collapse of the name band–based popular music economy. Many of the men who made this music in the 1930s and '40s continued to create popular music in the 1950s and beyond, and Astaire drew on this well of talent and experience to the very end of the long swing era. Among the sustainers of the swing aesthetic, Lloyd "Skip" (or "Skippy") Martin holds an important, if forgotten, place.

Born in Indiana in 1916, Martin was playing clarinet in the Indianapolis Symphony by age seventeen. His first band job was with the Gus Arnheim Orchestra, and his first big break as an arranger came with Count Basie, who was never reticent about hiring white arrangers. In his 1985 autobiography Basie recalled Martin's work and how he slipped away.

> While we were around Indianapolis, we picked up a few arrangements from a young fellow named Skip Martin. Somebody recommended him because we needed some numbers to level the book off and cool us down a bit. . . . Skip was a very young cat at that time, but he did some nice little things for us, and a lot of other bands used his arrangements. He also played sax in bands like Jan Savitt, Gus Arnheim, Glenn Miller, and Benny Goodman. Charlie Barnet stole him, so he worked as Charlie's staff arranger for a while. Then he went with Les Brown. The big hit recording that Les made of "I've Got My Love to Keep Me Warm" is one of Skip's things.[59]

Charlie Barnet added some mystique to the story in his 1984 autobiography: "Nobody knew much about Skippy—he was what we called a misterioso. . . . After he left me, he went back to California, where Johnny Mercer befriended him. Unfortunately, he had become an alcoholic and he died shortly after Johnny."[60] Martin also worked briefly on the staffs of NBC and CBS in New York, putting in some time with commercial studio orchestras. A pilot during the war, he went to work as an arranger for Les Brown in 1946—when Brown was based in Los Angeles as music director for Bob Hope's television and radio shows—before shifting to Hollywood studio work, mostly at Metro, beginning

TABLE 2   SELECTED MUSICAL NUMBERS ARRANGED BY SKIP MARTIN, 1949–1957

Date	Film	Title	Notes
1949	*The Duchess of Idaho* (MGM Pasternak)	"Choo Choo Choo to Idaho," "Of All Things," "You Can't Do Wrong Doin' Right," boogie-woogie solo for Eleanor Powell	Shares screen credit with Al Sendrey
	Summer Stock (MGM Pasternak)	"Dig-Dig-Dig for Your Dinner"	Arr. and orch. w/ George Siravo
		"The Portland Fancy"	Arr. and orch. w/ Conrad Salinger
1950	*Royal Wedding*[1] (MGM Freed)	"Get Happy"	
		"Sunday Jumps,"[1] "How Could You Believe Me . . ."[1] *Fred Astaire's Music for Tap Dancing*[1] (LP for Capitol L341)	
1951	*Excuse My Dust* (MGM Cummings)	Dream ballet (created by Hermes Pan)	Shares screen credit with Leo Arnaud
1952	*Singin' in the Rain* (MGM Freed)	"Moses"	
1953	*The Band Wagon*[1] (MGM Freed)	"Gotta' Bran' New Suit,"[1] "I Love Louisa,"[1] A Shine on Your Shoes,"[1] "You Have Everything"[1] (with Salinger), "Bop Joint"[1] in "Girl Hunt Ballet"	
	Kiss Me, Kate (MGM Cummings)	"Too Darn Hot,"[2] dance interlude for Bob Fosse and Carol Haney in "From This Moment On"[2]	Shares orch. credit with Salinger

Year	Film	Song(s)	Notes
1954	A Star Is Born (Transcona Enterprises, producer; Warner Bros., distributor)	"Thanks a Lot But No Thanks"	
	It's Always Fair Weather (MGM Freed)		
	Daddy Long Legs[1] (Twentieth Century-Fox)	Astaire's drum solo before "History of the Beat" (received composer credit),[1] "History of the Beat,"[1,2] "Sluefoot,"[1,2] "Something's Gotta Give"[1,2]	Jazz arranger Billy May also listed in screen credits
1955	Guys and Dolls (Sam Goldwyn)	"Crap Shooter's Ballet,"[2] "Luck Be A Lady"[2]	Shares orch. credit with Alexander Courage, Nelson Riddle, and Sendrey
	It's Always Fair Weather (MGM Freed)	"Baby, You Knock Me Out"	Shares arr. credit with Previn, orch. by Al Woodbury
1956	Funny Face (Paramount)	"Clap Yo' Hands"[1]	
1957	April Love (Twentieth Century-Fox)	"Do It Yourself," sung by Pat Boone and Shirley Jones[2]	
	Silk Stockings[1] (Arthur Freed Productions, producer; MGM, distributor)	"Fated to Be Mated,"[1] "Red Blues," "The Ritz Roll and Rock"[1]	

[1]Created for Astaire.

[2]Credited to Martin based on style analysis. Martin is listed in arranger and orchestrator screen credits for these films.

in 1949. Martin continued doing occasional arranging for Brown into the mid-1950s, keeping his hand in both the film and jazz band realms. Martin worked all around the movie capital to the end of the 1950s, and his arranging and orchestrating talents can be heard in MGM, Fox, and Goldwyn musicals. He's the sole arranger and orchestrator credited on Judy Garland's independently produced 1954 comeback vehicle *A Star Is Born*. Martin apparently never crossed over from prerecording to scoring: he was a musical number specialist, bringing a powerful big band sound into the fading genre of the studio musical. In 1958, when Astaire shifted to television, Martin began arranging and conducting jazz LPs, a lucrative new popular music market dominated by Sinatra's concept albums on Capitol and Norman Granz's songbook series with Ella Fitzgerald on Verve.[61] Martin's contributions to the jazz pop concept album market include discs of standards for big band, jazz arrangements of themes from television crime dramas—he composed the *Mike Hammer* theme—and symphonic jazz discs that slipped a little solo improvising into Wagner's *Tannhäuser* and Rimsky-Korsakov's *Scheherazade* (this last with the catchy title *Skip Martin's Scheherajazz*).[62]

Close friend Johnny Mercer profiled Martin on the back of the 1958 MGM Records album *8 Brass 5 Sax 4 Rhythm,* which featured Skip Martin and His Orchestra (a studio pickup band).

> Lloyd "Skip" Martin, whose friends think of him as a roly-poly Santa Claus type and whose enemies may describe him as having the shape of a cello, was born in Indianapolis, Indiana. He immediately began arranging for big bands. Seriously, according to his mother, at the age of one and a half he toddled over to the piano and sounded middle C. After spending the required amount of years getting an education, he headed for his objective.* (*girls and booze). . . . He is most interesting to talk to; alert, fun, and a tenacious questioner. He wants to know exactly what you mean, and has no hesitancy in telling you what he means. . . . His personality is sort of a cross between Rabelais and Tom, the fun loving Rover. Being a real family sized gourmet, he insists on the best food and plenty of it—not only for himself but for everyone present.[63]

Martin was clearly a member of the band. Mercer's character study locates him squarely within jazz tropes of masculinity ("girls and booze"), native talent, early and long experience on the road, and a big appetite for good times. Martin reportedly took his own life in 1976.

Martin favored a melodically oriented arranging style, with close-voiced homophonic chords for brass or reed sections, often in unpredictable broken rhythms that called for a maximum of ensemble tightness:

hence his fit with Basie, Barnet, and Brown, all three bands known for virtuoso ensemble playing. Martin's charts are filled with sharp articulations—sometimes just a single spiked chord. The brash surprise was his favorite effect: see the very end of the Esther Williams vehicle *Dangerous When Wet* (1953), where Martin provides four vicious chords to punctuate four points of action and reaction that assure us Williams has married Fernando Lamas before spending the night in his hotel room. Mueller spots this tendency in Martin's arranging for Astaire, criticizing such "slamming into position . . . underlined by percussive effects in the orchestra" and the "raucous quality" of Martin's "blaring jazz arrangement."[64] These aspects of Martin's sound were derived directly from the swing bands where he served his apprenticeship, and their prominent use in Astaire's films marks the music-motivated dancer's ongoing engagement with jazz-centered popular music in the 1950s.

Martin's swing band background informed his approach to film musical arranging. From Basie, Martin absorbed the importance of a prominent rhythm section as the engine of the band. Basie's 1939 recording of Martin's "Miss Thing" has all the driving four-beat energy of Martin's later film work. Martin was Barnet's brassy flag-waver specialist, providing charts for "The Right Idea" and "Clap Hands, Here Comes Charlie" (both 1939), and "Flying Home" (1940), the earliest recorded Martin chart to feature the spiked brass chords that became his Hollywood signature. And Martin found himself in the right place after the war, working with Brown's band, which kept the flame of dancer-friendly swing alive into the 1950s. Martin's arranging is featured prominently on Brown's live two-disc set *Concert at the Palladium*, recorded in September 1953, shortly after Martin had scored *The Band Wagon*'s "bop joint."[65] Indeed, the Brown sound proves a benchmark against which musical film scores of the 1950s can be measured, a way to ground the musical in an ongoing popular music scene. Recall that the Ephrons wanted to name Les Brown in the scene from *Daddy Long Legs* where Astaire's character is introduced at the drums, playing along with a wild Skip Martin chart blasting out of the nearby hi-fi.[66]

Before Martin arrived on the studio scene, the big band aesthetic at Metro was the work of staffers like Leo Arnaud ("Shoes with Wings On"), Robert Franklyn ("Ev'ry Night at Seven"), and Wally Heglin ("The Babbitt and the Bromide," "Swing Trot"). None of these arrangers had the solid jazz credentials Martin possessed: after all, he had been a member of Goodman's sax section just before Pearl Harbor and was at the Palomar Ballroom with Barnet's band on the October 1939 night when the Los Angeles swing landmark literally went up in flames. Arnaud, Franklyn, and Heglin did passable swing-style arranging—saxes to the fore—usually with a conventional use of sectional interplay, big string sections, and invisible close-harmony vocals (disembodied voices being an MGM favorite). For all the trappings of big band music in their arrangements, these numbers are not played in the idiom; they don't swing. This would change with the arrival of Martin, who was able to bring out a more powerful sound from the studio orchestras he arranged for and, on occasion, conducted.

Martin's first Metro film was *Duchess of Idaho,* an Esther Williams film produced by Joe Pasternak and a latter-day band pic centering on a fictional band—Dick Layne and His Music—led by Van Johnson and featuring jazz pop singer Connie Haines. Thanks to Martin's arranging, this made-up group sounds like a convincing Les Brown knockoff. Martin continued to bring aggressive big band energy to MGM in his next assignment, Pasternak's *Summer Stock,* where Martin's brash sound could bounce off Salinger's more refined aesthetic. For this film, Martin arranged Kelly's tap solo "Dig-Dig-Dig for Your Dinner" and Garland's iconic rendition of "Get Happy." Kelly used Martin rarely after *Summer Stock,* most notably for the tap-centered "Moses" in *Singin' in the Rain.* Garland called on Martin regularly in subsequent films and concerts. Both *Duchess of Idaho* and *Summer Stock* exploited the newly enhanced range and fidelity of postwar sound recording, which gives all of Hollywood's films of the 1950s greater sonic richness. The vibrancy Martin gets from the studio bands is, in part, a function of the superior recording technologies he enjoyed. Astaire, working on the same lot as Martin, would have heard all these numbers. And in Astaire's next musical, *Royal Wedding,* Martin made a strong showing.

Astaire employed Martin on two big numbers in *Royal Wedding,* "Sunday Jumps" and "How Could You Believe Me When I Said I Love You When You Know I've Been a Liar All My Life." The former opens on a bass figure, melodically and rhythmically surprising and not derived from Burton Lane's tune. Martin gives this leaping line to the virtuoso MGM trombone section. Lane's tune is stated in close harmony by muted trumpets or midrange tenor saxes. The rhythm section stays cool or heats up at will, moving from the front to the back of the mix and keeping the whole thing cooking along. The presence of a rhythm section is a crucial swing-referencing element. Martin's super-tight chords are heard at the end of the number as well. It's a catalog of Martin's signature tropes, all matched to Astaire's virtuoso prop dance. "How

Could You Believe Me" shows Martin's flexibility in novelty numbers. In this number, scored for big band—there are no strings, even though a pit orchestra is supposedly playing—Martin finds the edge between show-biz razzle-dazzle and a bright, jazzy sound that would come to mark Metro in the 1950s. This exaggerated comic turn makes full use of Martin's ability to bring out the quality of a particular routine while still catching the falls—and there are a lot of them—along the way.

Martin's two numbers for *Royal Wedding* are virtuoso examples of what the experienced arranger had to offer, and Astaire kept him close by. With the exception of Astaire's next project, the ill-fated *The Belle of New York,* the dancer used Martin on every remaining film he made over the next seven years—no matter the studio—usually calling Martin in to do the big jazzy numbers designed to really send the audience. These include the colorful sound of "A Shine on Your Shoes," the nervous energy of "Bop Joint" in "Girl Hunt," the craziness of "Clap Yo' Hands" (another comic turn for Martin), the adult jazz mood of the vocals and first dance chorus of "Fated to Be Mated" (a rare Martin chart with strings), and the rhythm-and-bluesy but always swinging sound of "The Ritz Roll and Rock." Martin is listed among the arrangers on *Daddy Long Legs* along with up-and-coming jazz arranger Billy May, whose work bears a strong resemblance to Martin's. Either could have done "History of the Beat," "Sluefoot," and "Something's Gotta Give," the three Astaire dance specials with big band content. No studio records survive in this case, but "Sluefoot" seems especially close to Martin's earlier work with Astaire.

Martin's numbers demanded great variety on the arranger's part, but a continuity of approach ties them together. The Skip Martin sound is marked by:

- A rhythm section well to the front and always audible, reminding the listener that a dance band (and not a pit orchestra) is playing.
- A melody almost never disguised or fragmented beyond recognition. The tune can always be found and followed. Asymmetrical rhythmic fills by an entire section, sometimes abstracted from the tune, are more common than riff choruses.
- A generally massive, brass-dominated sound. Strings, gone from dance-oriented big bands by this time, are almost always absent.
- Extreme dynamic contrasts, often dropping from screaming brass down to restrained saxes or muted trumpets in close harmony.

- A rhythmically sharp aesthetic with nothing sweet about it.
- A clear "Technicolor" sound, with "shiny" voicing in all sections.
- An extreme tightness in the playing (similar to Basie's bands in the 1950s and '60s).
- A glitzy quality that does not invoke Broadway but rather comes from swing sources. Indeed, Martin's approach could hardly be more different from Broadway at the time, dominated as it was by the sweeping orchestral effects of Robert Russell Bennett's orchestrations for Rodgers and Hammerstein and others.

Beyond their film work together, in 1952 Astaire called on Martin to arrange and conduct a novel project, the Capitol Records ten-inch LP *Fred Astaire's Music for Tap Dancing*.[67] Astaire chose eight tunes from his films, and his friendly liner notes explain that the album "is specially arranged by 'Skip' Martin for tap dancing—music that gives you a real 'lift'; yet leaves the 'breaks' for *you* to fill in with your own tap rhythm." (Again, Astaire underlined for emphasis when writing.) A short bio lists Martin's swing band credits and then notes he "is now arranger-conductor for a major film studio in Hollywood where he directs the musical sequences of important pictures," a quite strongly worded description of Martin's role at the unnamed MGM. Aimed at the tap dance instruction market, the album is a jazzy little product that runs the gamut of tap styles, from buck-and-wing to soft shoe to tango, samba, and swing tap. Likely composed of Capitol session musicians, the band shifts easily between straight time and swing time, typifying both the flexibility required of studio players in the 1950s and the professionalized jazz pop aesthetic of the decade.

BIG BAND CODA: JAZZ POP TV

Swing arrangers like Martin lost what had been a consistent Hollywood niche when the musical production units shut down in the late 1950s. And by the time of Astaire's final studio musical, it would seem that the swing, dance, jazz, or big bands—pick your adjective—informing his work had passed from the scene at last. Beyond the concert works of Duke Ellington, big bands and arranging as a jazz discipline disappear from most innovation-oriented jazz histories with the wartime rise of bebop, which has been presented consistently as a small-group improvisation-centered music. But the world of jazz and the "jazzy" has always been broader than that. In the postwar, post-swing landscape, only Basie and Ellington among the major black bandleaders kept their outfits going. Neither leader showed any sign of lapsing in their continued creative and economic commitment to the swing band format. Basie and Ellington were, in essence, bandleaders: arrangements were part and parcel of the music for both, as was a sustained engagement with popular music. Both played Beatles covers in the 1960s.[68] White big bands of the postwar period have been marginalized in jazz historiography: groups led by Stan Kenton, Les Brown, and Woody Herman were famous in their time, primarily with white audiences, but they faded quickly in the estimation of the critics who wrote jazz history. But swing-derived, big band–arranged jazz was blaring all over the place from the postwar years through the late 1960s, when the sonically thrilling but manpower-intensive combination of reeds, brass, and rhythm finally ended its long run at or near the center of American popular music. This quarter-century addendum to the canonical swing era can be thought of as a swing dividend, a period when jazz players still had outlets in the commercial world and the word *band* could still mean something besides three or four guys with guitars and a drum set doing original material. Astaire's television shows—described in musical terms for the first time here (and in later chapters)—were one place where the long swing era played its final out chorus.

Television, a new audiovisual medium doing its part to transform popular music, was an important postwar venue for swing-derived, popular-oriented jazz bands (and, by extension, jazz arrangers). On variety shows, a vibrant television genre in the 1950s and '60s, big bands survived as house bands, swinging pit bands for a revived vaudeville culture of personality performers simultaneously selling songs and jokes to live studio audiences and a nation watching in their living rooms. The house band was a quickly established television institution that survives to the present in reduced form (for example, Paul Shaffer's outfit on various incarnations of David Letterman's late-night show). Among the best-remembered house bands was the NBC Orchestra on *The Tonight Show*, led by Doc Severinsen for most of its existence. Severinsen joined the group when it was first established by host Steve Allen in 1952. He became leader in 1967 and retired with host Johnny Carson in 1992. For Severinsen, a stratospheric trumpeter in the tradition of Harry James and Ray Anthony, late-night television provided a secure spot to lead a big-time big band and survive the tumultuous changes in popular music. Carson insisted the expensive sixteen-piece band remain through the end of his tenure. With Carson's hand-off to Jay Leno, the *Tonight Show* house band was reduced to eight players under the leadership of guitarist Kevin Eubanks, effectively disbanding the last big-time commercial swing band.[69] Tommy Dorsey's television stint in the mid-1950s, at times accompanying the young Elvis Presley, was a similar if less long-lived gig for a swing band on television variety. Fulfilling all the functions of a vaudeville pit orchestra, house bands played for any and all musical guests who did not have their own accompaniment and contributed a consistent brand of musical energy to every telecast.

Astaire worked with three house bands in his television years. For his self-produced television specials in 1958, 1959, and 1960, Astaire hired Hollywood veteran David Rose and His Orchestra. A good fit for network television, Rose aimed squarely at the biggest target out there: the middle-of-the-road viewer with common pop music tastes. Rose's lush studio orchestra set off the leaner sounds of Astaire's jazz guests: Jonah Jones's combo and Basie's band are sources of musical variety and a declaration of the host's musical taste. More often than not, Astaire did his own dances to the music of his jazz guests on these specials.

During the seven-year gap between his third and fourth television specials, Astaire hosted four episodes of the long-running ABC variety series *The Hollywood Palace,* a re-creation of vaudeville that combined popular music stars of the moment, older Hollywood and Broadway stars of the pre-rock era, stand-up comics, comedy skits, specialty dance numbers, and circus acts from around the globe, all presented in color before an appreciative live audience at a Los Angeles theater. The house band for the series was Mitchell Ayres and the Hollywood Palace Orchestra. Led by a swing band veteran, Ayres's group of Hollywood studio regulars—which included strings and orchestral winds—could accompany any sort of singer or dancer and simulate any showbiz or concert music style from vaudeville corn to 1960s hipster. *Hollywood Palace* telecasts always featured a circus act, and Ayres's troupe was expert at catching the falls, playing in a tradition that went back to vaudeville itself. Resting on a jazz rhythm section, Ayres's relentlessly colorful and restlessly changing sound fits in the tradition of symphonic jazz reaching back to Paul Whiteman's overactive arrangements from the 1920s.[70] Jazz guest stars such as Louis Armstrong, Lionel Hampton, and jazz organist Jimmy Smith (who appeared on an Astaire-hosted episode) brought a musical focus to the proceedings, and Ayres could sustain a straight-ahead swinging sound when called for.

For his final special in 1968, Astaire hired Neal Hefti and His Orchestra as the house band. The swing-era tradition of arrangers as important creative players remained alive in Hefti's prolific output: he was a recognizable name in the 1950s and '60s, working in particular with Basie, who recorded several albums of Hefti originals. Born in 1922, Hefti came up as a trumpeter in the big bands, establishing his composing and arranging credentials with the Woody Herman and Charlie Barnet bands. In the 1960s, Hefti successfully carved out musical identities in adjacent jazz and pop worlds, writing for Basie's traditional instrumentation and producing pop-oriented, guitar-centered music for records, film, and television. Hefti's exploration of new sounds—fuzzed-out guitars and funky little electric organs—shows his embrace of rock and pop production techniques, his colorful approach to instrumentation, and his desire to define the moment in sonic terms. His *Batman* television theme has a permanent place in 1960s pop culture.

Hefti coined a useful phrase in the title of his 1962 album *Jazz Pops: Neal Hefti and His Jazz Pops Orchestra*.[71] This album, like Astaire's specials, was a musical mix of old (swing) and new (post-rock pop) in contemporary, self-consciously jazz packaging. Scored for a sizable swing band plus French horns, a flute, and some Latin percussion, Hefti mixed original tunes (like "Lil' Darlin'"), a modern jazz standard ("Take Five"), the theme from Ernest Gold's 1960 score for *Exodus* (among the first orchestral soundtrack LPs to top the charts), and several selections rooted in jazz history. "Petit Fleur" is a Sidney Bechet composition: the legendary New Orleans clarinetist had just died in 1959. A cut called "One & Two O'Clock Jump" slyly combines Basie's 1936 blues-based hit ("One O'Clock Jump") and Harry James's 1939 salute to it ("Two O'Clock Jump"). James's version was a swing-era admission—at the level of the title—as to where swing originated: Basie (a black bandleader) started the tune; James (a white bandleader) picked it up from there. Hefti's arrangement recalled this shared history while proclaiming the continuing relevance of swing music and players, putting some solid swing in the middle of an LP that explicitly argued for a continuing connection between jazz, pops, and the orchestra (meaning big band). In his note on the back of the dust jacket, Hefti anticipated skeptical responses to the vision behind the disc: "People are going to challenge certain tunes. 'You call that jazz?' they'll say." To Hefti, it was all jazz, and Astaire would have agreed. *Jazz Pops* exemplifies the long swing era in its 1960s phase: rooted in the past yet with a contemporary sound, popular in feel and professional in execution, committed to tunes and the swinging, thrilling sound of a big band aggregation.

Hefti and Astaire shared the goal of staying hip without abandoning their roots in swing. The opening music Hefti composed for the special—an instrumental titled "Fred"—sits completely in the 1968 groove. (It's heard again at the close.) Astaire, wearing a light turtleneck, dark double-breasted blazer, light pants, black socks, and white shoes, dances alone in a spotlight to Hefti's tune on an otherwise dark stage. A perky electric keyboard, straight out of Hefti's 1967 film score for *Barefoot in the Park,* dominates the arrangement. The sixteen-bar instrumental uses a smooth Brazilian beat—very much of the bossa nova moment—and each strain ends with a big, empty break. During the first break Astaire looks at the camera and says, "Good evening," the only words uttered until the very end of the special. In the other breaks the screen cuts abruptly, one by one, to the lineup of guest stars, posed and standing perfectly still. The guests, in order, are: Barrie Chase (Astaire's television dance partner), Sergio Mendes and Brasil '66, Young-Holt Unlimited, The Gordian Knot, The Herb Ross Dancers, and "Special Guest Stars Simon and Garfunkel." Astaire, holding a cane throughout the dance, makes reference to each guest star in dance terms after their images are flashed on the screen. After Chase, he uses the cane as a partner. After The Gordian Knot, he breaks his normal body carriage and indulges in some funky moves. After Simon and Garfunkel, he mimes using his cane as a guitar, one of the only times Astaire made reference to the quintessential rock instrument in a dance. (In "Clap Yo' Hands" from *Funny Face,* he danced while holding a guitar, writhing on the floor in mock beatnik agony.) Unlike the house bands on Astaire's earlier television appearances, Hefti brought a hip tone to the show, and Astaire matched the new groove nicely, particularly in the opening and closing dances to "Fred," both of which have a strong improvised quality. Hefti worked across the jazz pop spectrum: on records, film, and television; with jazz and pop performers; and with new and old instrumental combinations. The continuing importance of the arranger as a central creative player keeping jazz current and connected to popular music endures in Hefti's career, which, like the careers of so many jazz arrangers before him, came into fruitful contact with Astaire's similar priorities.

PART THREE

Astaire in Jazz and Popular Music

CHAPTER 6

"Keep time with the time and with the times"

I've always observed that Arthur Murray's pupils do two important things—keep time with the time and with the times. . . . A drummer notices something like that.

—Gene Krupa's dust jacket blurb for Arthur Murray's *How to Become a Good Dancer* (1942)

Popular music has almost always been dance music.[1] The dance bands' primary economic role was playing for dancing, and the film musical—especially during the era of the band pix—reached out to dancers in particular. This chapter considers how Astaire's films bridged the gap between dancing couples on-screen and real social dancers moving to the changing beat of popular music. This connection is easiest to see and hear in the named partner dances Astaire created and introduced across his career.

Named dances embody a specific marketing strategy: create a buzz around a new dance that generates interest in a new film. In this light, named-dance songs fit into the patterns of Hollywood's standard promotional efforts. If stars like Greta Garbo or Joan Crawford could drive women's fashion trends by way of direct promotion of film fashion knockoffs in the franchised Cinema Fashion Shops, then Astaire was the ideal salesman for new partner dances to a nation full of social dancers.[2] Importantly, Garbo and Crawford's fashions were created by others. Astaire, who made his own named dances, participated directly in studio promotion efforts. From a reverse angle, Astaire well understood how a new named dance might help his own interests beyond the successful marketing of a new film. As historical texts, named-dance routines are denser than regular partner routines. Beyond the filmed dance number, originally accessible to audiences only from its embedded position within the film narrative, other texts and discourses surround the named dance. All were intentional products of the Hollywood publicity machine—which was, in essence, the Hollywood production and distribution system itself. The specific strategies behind named dances include:

- A new song with a one- or two-word title naming both dance and song.
- Lyrics referring to the dance directly, sometimes describing its movements and often locating it relative to other named dances.
- Published sheet music, sometimes including dance directions in the form of pictures, diagrams, descriptive text, or all three.
- A step, move, or pose that instantly identifies the dance, serving as a way for dancers to know when they are doing it.
- Still photographs of Astaire and partner engaged in a signature step or steps, a frozen moment capturing the dance in reproducible visual form.
- Directions on how to do the dance, in written and pictorial form, created for use by newspapers, magazines, and publications targeting dancers.
- Recordings of the song by dance bands, sometimes with Astaire on the vocal, for use at home or on jukeboxes.
- Specialized instruction from professional teachers at social dance schools such as the Arthur Murray or Fred Astaire Dance Studios.

On the grandest scale, several of these strategies were combined in media campaigns managed by studio publicity departments. In reciprocal fashion, on a few occasions Astaire used a named-dance routine to put in a tacit plug for his dancing schools.

New named dances appear in eight of Astaire's films, almost a third of his output. No other musical film star made so many. Indeed, the named dance followed Astaire as he moved from studio to studio. It was closely tied to Astaire's persona and career strategy. Created under specific production contexts, each of Astaire's named dances serves as a barometer of sorts for 1) the changing relationship between social dancing in actual ballrooms and depictions of social dancing in the film musical, 2) the changing style of social dance and the sound and beat of popular music, 3) the persistent emulation by white dancers of black social dance innovators, and 4) Astaire's creative negotiation of the ever-widening age gap between both himself and his partners and himself and the youth audience driving popular culture. This chapter illuminates the above issues by way of musical and visual analysis and information gleaned from archival and media sources. Named-dance song lyrics are almost invariably self-reflexive, frequently defining the world of social dance within which the new dance was seeking a place. Johnny Mercer wrote the lyrics for four of Astaire's eight named-dance songs, and so this chapter also provides a window on Astaire and Mercer's collaboration. A short final section—another TV coda—looks at Astaire's television partner dances in the nontouch social dance styles of the 1960s. Astaire took to the post-Twist dance floor with characteristic aplomb. Having been among the Charleston set during his own youth in the 1920s, he was unafraid to do the Freak and the Jerk in the 1960s.

One of the most important routines of Astaire's career, "The Carioca" launched Astaire and Rogers as a couple. It was not only their first named dance but their first dance together on film, and the social dance element of the routine formed a key ingredient of its success. The named-dance identity of "The Carioca" tied the new couple to a new social dance phenomenon, the one reinforcing the other to good, even historic, effect.

The *New York Times* reviewer did the work of named-dance promotion quite efficiently. "An impressive series of scenes are devoted to a dance known as the Carioca. During this interlude that nimble-toed Fred Astaire and the charming Ginger Rogers give a performance of this Carioca. The music is delightful, and besides Mr. Astaire and Miss Rogers many other persons dance the extraordinarily rhythmic Carioca, one feature of which happens to be that of the couples pressing their foreheads together as they glide around the floor."[3] Those "many other persons" are segregated by skin color. "The Carioca" is the only production number in an Astaire film to include an ensemble of African American dancers. The racial content of the routine proves a defining feature, offering an early example of how Astaire's screen dances often defied—in subtle fashion—classical Hollywood's standard practices in the representation of racial characteristics and differences. The Brazilian background of *Flying Down to Rio* plays an important enabling role as well.

Set at the elaborate Carioca Casino, the number begins with light-skinned, high-class Rio couples who take the floor to the sounds of the resident Turuna Band. Each couple dances in their own way—their moves are not coordinated—as Astaire and Rogers, together with other members of the Yankee Clippers band, look on. The gimmick of "The Carioca" is that partners dance in closed position with their foreheads pressed together, a physical intimacy framed as shocking, sexual, and irresistible. Watching a particularly intense pair on the dance floor below, Rogers says, "I can tell what they're thinking about from here," after which the film cuts back to the couple as the woman pulls away, slaps her partner full across the face, and then falls back into his arms to dance on. (The script called for the man to slap the woman as well.) It's the perfect example of a named dance coalescing around a step or pose that can be identified instantly by dancers and watchers alike and easily captured in a photograph. Among Astaire and Rogers's first publicity photos is a shot of the pair with foreheads pressed together and slightly guilty grins on their faces. The lyric begins with a visual cue, asking the listener if they have "seen" the Carioca—identification is visual, not aural. The lyric immediately goes on to distinguish the new dance from the fox trot and the polka. The tendency of named-dance lyrics to reference other dances forms a recurring trope in most of Astaire's named dances.

What Astaire and Rogers do that none of their fellow *Norteamericanos* do is grab hands and boldly venture onto the floor—not the nightclub dance floor, but a raised revolving platform supported by seven pianos. With everyone watching Astaire and Rogers begin their first dance, modeling a social bravery and personal confidence mere mortals went to Arthur Murray to obtain. They are also displaying a desire and willingness to copy the dance moves of a group of racial others—here, high-class Latins, a group with a definite exotic chic in the Hollywood racial imaginary of the 1930s.[4] The conceit, of course, is that they are just dancing, when, in fact, they always perform a highly planned routine. A comic lightness leavens their style from the start. The head touching is used as a novelty element, with Astaire and Rogers putting on a show of awkwardness at first, even bumping heads and then staggering about a bit dazed. Their head bump is "caught" in the music with a hollow percussion beat—a coconut shell sound—that makes it even funnier. The first part of "The Carioca" is entirely instrumental and all about social dancing as sexual innuendo. The musical arrangement draws on actual Brazilian dance band sounds. RKO even acquired sample arrangements from a São Paulo dance band to get the desired effect, a typical example of studio research methods.[5] Part one closes with a round of applause for Astaire and Rogers's dance, marking them as special and clearing the way for the floorshow.

During part two, the high-class couples resume their position as patrons seated at tables around the dance floor, which shifts from a space for social dancers to a stage for professionals. Three light-skinned female singers introduce the lyric from positions above the dance floor, which quickly fills with thirty light-skinned (white) couples costumed identically. They perform a coordinated dance, mostly group formations and arm motions shot from novel perspectives. Staged by dance director Dave Gould, part two is a nod toward Busby Berkeley's aesthetics, still current in 1933. But even here the male-female couple remains the basic unit of "The Carioca," sustaining a relational tone absent in Berkeley's frequently all-female fantasies.

No pause for applause marks the end of part two. Instead, the transition to part three is racially defined, as the light-skinned singing trio and dancers give way to black singer Etta Moten, costumed as a *baiana*, and a group of nine dark-skinned couples. (*Baianas* were lower-class, usually dark-skinned women from the Brazilian state of Bahia, often depicted wearing large jewelry and a turban or basket on their head. Carmen Miranda would bring an over-the-top *baiana* to Hollywood in 1940. It's not clear who decided to costume Moten, an African American blues singer, as a *baiana*. Her costuming, like the sound of the Turuna band, provides evidence for the effort to give *Flying Down to Rio* some authentic Brazilian touches.)[6] Figure 9, a behind-the-scenes production still including the camera crane, captures the light-skinned dancers, arrayed on the steps and bandstand, and the dark-skinned dancers, seated on the dance floor below. Astaire and Rogers stand between the two groups on the raised circular platform where they perform their combinations. The music gets suitably hot when Moten and the black couples appear, with a clarinet likely improvising its line above the driving arrangement by Eddie Sharpe (the saxophonist in the small group heard on "Music Makes Me"). The darker-skinned dancers present unrestrained versions of the smoldering light-skinned couples who started the number and are now, no doubt, picking up ideas from their positions seated at tables around the dance floor. The modeling of social dance on black models is a directly expressed theme of "The Carioca," and an extended feature for one black couple comes close to upstaging Astaire and Rogers's second combination, done in response to the black couples and introduced by Astaire with the line "Um, kinda hot, let's try a little of that, babe."

FIGURE 9. All eyes, including the crane-mounted camera, are focused on Astaire and Rogers in this production still of "The Carioca" from *Flying Down to Rio.*

The black couples bring two kinds of hotness to "The Carioca." In physical terms, their hot dancing exhibits greater speed, strong pelvis and hip articulations, shimmying hands and heads, much closer partner holds, and generally bolder, more explicitly sexual postures. A separate hot element introduced by the black couples is tap breaks in broken rhythms done as a group. Mary-Kathryn Harrison has called attention to the way Astaire and Rogers's combinations in "The Carioca" tend to lower the sexual heat projected by the other couples.[7] This is due to Astaire's bias toward flashy technical steps and tap. He was never comfortable doing Latin motion with his hips (except as comedy) or moves with directly sexual undertones. So while the black couples both shimmy and shake and execute hot tap breaks, Astaire and Rogers pick up only on the latter, limiting themselves to a hotness defined by the rapid execution of broken rhythms. Avoiding the extreme physicality of the black couples, Astaire selects out the hot rhythmic element that is, at its core, musical rather than physical. It is crucial to remember that both sorts of hotness carried racial connotations at the time.

The editing of "The Carioca" utilizes discontinuous, rapid-fire shots of the dancers' bodies and faces, often from extreme angles, that create a sense of wildness and abandon. Corin Willis has described this approach to montage with the term "racial cut . . . an edit sequence timed to frame and freeze the character in a stereotypical 'racial' pose or gesture."[8] Without a doubt, racial cuts were used regularly in the 1930s to frame black dancers caught up in rhythmically charged music. A prime example not mentioned by Willis is the levee dance in *Show Boat* (1936). Willis argues that racial cuts leave "African Americans themselves grounded in the racial signification of the instinctive and rhythmic black body." But in "The Carioca," racial cuts are used in both parts one and three: upper and lower class, light and dark skinned, white and black dancers are all pictured in thrall to the music. Both groups find a frenetic release of sexual energy in "The Carioca," although the black group is more physically unrestrained. The overriding ideology of "south equals hot" applies to everyone in this Rio nightclub, and Astaire and Rogers are eager to be part of the scene (although their dances are not subjected to the technique of racial cuts).

All the crucial ingredients of the successful named dance are in place in "The Carioca," which constructs a web of connections between a memorable film routine, a song (sheet music available!), a beat (in this case, a little bit Latin and fast), and an instantly recognizable step, move, or posture (the greatest asset of "The Carioca"). In bringing these elements together around the teaming of Astaire and Rogers, "The Carioca" succeeded brilliantly in translating the pleasures of hot social dancing to the screen. This named dance did vital work establishing the viability of Astaire and Rogers as screen partners by showing just how fun it could be to spend time with them on the dance floor.

"The Carioca" did not have a long life in American ballrooms—although jazz players like Dizzy Gillespie kept playing the Latin-tinged tune into the 1950s—and there were no real follow-ups to this fun social dance scene in Astaire-Rogers's films for many years. "The Continental" *(The Gay Divorcee)* and "The Piccolino" *(Top Hat)* were not presented as new social dances so much as new danceable songs. Instead, the couple offered ever more refined and technical routines, frustrating the early link between Astaire and Rogers as dancing film icons and the world of social dancing. Subsequent dances might echo the physical intimacy of foreheads pressed together—"Cheek to Cheek" adjusts the pose a bit—but Astaire and Rogers's routines were way too complex to inspire real-world emulation. For example, Astaire and

Rogers's characters are happily reunited in a taxi-dance ballroom early in *Follow the Fleet*, easily the most common ground on which the couple met. They start dancing—surrounded by couples doing a stiff fox trot—and find themselves in the middle of the nightly dance contest. The song has the suggestive social dance title "Let Yourself Go." Sung earlier by Rogers, Berlin's bridge lyric advises the listener, "The night is cold/but the music's hot." The other couples in the dance contest, recruited from the Palomar Ballroom by Pan, are pretty bad.[9] Once Astaire and Rogers kick into high gear, the pair abandons social decorum entirely, executing a side-by-side tap routine with virtually no social dance content. The floor clears and they perform. With Rogers in a tailored sailor suit, there's little in the dance Astaire couldn't have done with a male partner. The routine is aggressively professional, fitting their characters but not the context. The dance to "Let Yourself Go" is presentational, so much so that the magazine *American Dancer* published a version of the routine for use by tap teachers, described in the technical language of tap dance instruction.[10]

Social dance teachers, eager to translate public interest in a pair of dancing movie stars into new students, were often frustrated by the disconnect between Astaire's creative choices and the claims of studio promotional materials. As Harrison has noted, in 1937, "two years after Thomas Parsons [in his *American Dancer* column] had first written about the absurdity of ballroom teachers trying to pass down Astaire's dance style to the general public, [Parsons] continued to feel it necessary to condemn movie studio advertisements which claimed their films contained new social dances. . . . The press, the movie studios, the ballroom professionals, all wanted to make Astaire into a ballroom spokesman."[11] But Astaire persisted in making only the most technical of dances with Rogers, a partner who could handle anything Astaire (and Pan) dreamed up. The couple's films were immensely profitable through 1936, and explicit attempts to tap into the social dance market were, perhaps, unnecessary to attract their audience. The fantasy world on offer in the Astaire-Rogers films was distant from reality in so many of its dimensions that connections to actual social dance might have been jarring. As Julie Malnig notes, "Although the Thirties public certainly admired the dancing of Astaire and Rogers (and may even have fantasized dancing like them) it did not have the same sense of identification with them [as Vernon and Irene Castle engendered], since [Astaire and Rogers's] dancing ability was well beyond what the public would realistically expect from itself."[12] This changed with the advent of swing music and swing dancing, or the lindy hop and the jitterbug. Social dancing took a technical leap upward, Astaire and Rogers's popularity began to lag, and RKO responded with a strategically placed named dance.

Shall We Dance saw Astaire and Rogers's box office slip for the second successive film, and the music and dance content of their next film, *Carefree,* showed a change of strategy for the couple's thus far bankable series. The compositional history and context of "The Yam," *Carefree's* named dance, suggests an effort by RKO to position Astaire and Rogers within the emerging phenomenon of the lindy hop, the exhibition and social dance component of the rise of hot swing music. The gap between *Shall We Dance* and *Carefree* was the longest between any two Astaire-Rogers films. Production on *Shall We Dance* ended in mid-March 1937; *Carefree* began rehearsals about a year later. During that year Goodman's band had captured the attention of the film industry, which was newly attentive to the swing phenomenon. Production documents and publicity materials for *Carefree* show how RKO sought to promote the film by way of "The Yam" and give a startling specific example of how Astaire worked with Berlin to craft a song that might excite the next big dance craze and tie *Carefree* to the phenomenon of swing.

Rogers introduces "The Yam" vocally at a country club dance with an on-screen band. Rogers plays a radio singer, and she uses "The Yam" as a means to get Astaire onto the dance floor. Together they introduce the "Yam" step. On the sustained note ending each phrase of Berlin's chorus, the dancer strikes a pose with arms up, elbows bent, fingers spread "like you hold a tray," as the lyric advises. The body remains stiff, leaning slightly back, and the feet are apart. A shuffle step—dubbed in with a soft-shoe sound—adds a bit of rhythmic interest to the "long note," which Berlin's lyric names as such. Having demonstrated the move, Astaire and Rogers literally pull couples onto the floor. Young and old, everyone enthusiastically falls in, striking the Yam pose with varying degrees of competence. The crowd then follows Astaire and Rogers as they dance and run from room to room, onto the patio, and then back to the ballroom. The couple plays Pied Piper, and everyone is having a grand time.

The Yam pose recurs again and again, always with the same rhythmic idea. Only once does Astaire break out in a complex tap combination. Rather than intricate rhythms, this Astaire-Rogers routine highlights a new full-out physicality drawing on social dance innovations originating among lindy hoppers. During their progress through the

country club, Astaire flings Rogers into a series of low-slung uphol-
stered chairs, only to pull her back to her feet with a force and energy
that is new to their dancing: as they retain a grip on each other's hands,
it's their first true swing out, where energy is passed between them in a
palpable, elastic way. References to the new lindy hop dance style continue in the finale, when Astaire catapults Rogers over his extended
right leg eight times as they circle the dance floor.[13] The athleticism of
the finale stands in stark contrast to the routines the couple had done to
this point. These are tentative air steps, toying with a new virtuoso style
of social dance originating from young black dancers at the Savoy Ballroom in Harlem and elsewhere. The air steps from the end of "The Yam"
would become a signature image used by RKO's publicity department in
their promotion of *Carefree*. Both moves differ fundamentally from the
couple's earlier use of furniture, which treated tables and couches as
obstacles to be negotiated rather than supports for physical stunts.

Astaire expressed his desire for a cutting-edge swing number early
on in the planning for *Carefree*, and his use of keywords discussed in
chapter 4 shows up in a letter he wrote to director Sandrich in late
1937.[14] Berlin had completed the first batch of songs for *Carefree*, still
titled *Change Partners*, by mid-November 1937. Having completed
production on *A Damsel in Distress* in mid-October, Astaire was set to
take his standard six-week vacation between films. (Rogers seldom had
such rest.) Before Astaire departed by train for New York, Berlin played
and sang for him the score in progress for *Change Partners*. Astaire, in
turn, reported his thoughts on the songs to Sandrich by letter while en
route on the California Limited. The letter is among the only documents in Astaire's handwriting that discusses professional creative matters relating to musical style and creative control. Astaire begins by
painting a picture of Berlin's "nervous and excited" demeanor during
the session, reporting that the songwriter fell off the piano stool twice
while demonstrating the songs. Sandrich knew of Berlin's fierce desire
to please when presenting new work, and Astaire gently pokes fun at
his songwriter for his director's benefit. However, Astaire notes that no
matter what he might write about the tunes in the letter, Sandrich
should communicate to Berlin only that he was "crazy about the stuff,"
revealing in the process some of the personality dynamics of the Astaire-
Berlin-Sandrich collaboration. Astaire next gets down to business, eval-
uating each song he heard, assessing its suitability for his own purposes
as a routinemaker and Sandrich's purposes as director of the film.

Berlin previewed five tunes for Astaire: only two made it into the film unchanged. The songs Astaire liked—"Change Partners" and "I Used to Be Color Blind"—were immediately approved. His endorsement moved these numbers into the "yes" column and, Astaire noted, "they are the hard ones to write." The songs Astaire did not care for were, to his ear, derivative. A fashion-oriented tune called "Well Dressed Man"—the plot for *Carefree* originally turned on a men's fashion magazine—reminded Astaire of "Slumming on Park Avenue," a Berlin song used prominently in the recent Fox film *On the Avenue*. Berlin's lyric for "Slumming" evokes the themes of "Puttin' on the Ritz" and "Top Hat, White Tie and Tails" in a satirical vein. Gleefully tacky and full of low humor, "Slumming" is the opposite of everything Astaire and RKO had come to represent. Astaire dismissed the song "Care-Free" as too slight and compared it to both Berlin's "No Strings" and what he called "those easy going ideas I've had so often." Astaire judges Berlin's work from the position of a songwriter, a stance of remarkable confidence, perhaps even hubris, given Berlin's stature. In the letter, Astaire gives the impression that there wasn't enough musical material in "Care-Free" to stimulate his creative energies. While he couldn't imagine dancing to it in its initial form, distinctive components of "Care-Free" would prove important in "The Yam." A fifth tune, "Let's Make the Most of Our Dream," was unenthusiastically described by Astaire as "useful": in the end, it went unused in the film.

On the cusp of a new film project—at the stage when the key creative decision was selecting songs for routine making—Astaire knew what he wanted, and it wasn't to be found in this first batch of tunes. At the close of the letter he stated his desire for something that was missing, articulating exactly what he wanted to Sandrich, who would be running interference with Berlin. With the clout to demand whatever he wished, Astaire set the aesthetic agenda for the *Carefree* score in rhythmic terms: he wanted "one *sock dance tune* from Irv. One that rides in good swing time." After several months of work, two numbers in *Carefree* would meet this test: the golf solo to "Since They Turned Loch Lomond into Swing" and the named-dance song "The Yam." In late 1937 Astaire was on a quest for a specific kind of song, one that would send him musically in a particular direction, a direction that sprang from the most contemporary rhythmic matrix of the day: "good swing time."

Around the same time he was assessing Berlin's songs for *Carefree*, Astaire met a group of young African American couples bringing an exhibition version of the lindy hop to Hollywood direct from the source, Harlem's Savoy Ballroom. Whitey's Lindy Hoppers had landed a specialty spot in the RKO film *Radio City Revels,* and Pan was working with them. Frankie Manning, a member of the Lindy Hoppers, remembered Astaire visiting rehearsals and remarking, "I wish I could dance like that."[15]

By early March 1938 at the latest, Berlin had written "The Yam," which had the following verse and chorus.

VERSE

Come on and hear the Yam man cry
"Any yam today?"
The sweet potatoes that he'll fry
Will be Yam today.
The little step that you'll see him do
With ev'ry Yam that he sells to you,
It's something that you ought to try—
Come and Yam today.

CHORUS

Come get what I've got—
It will hit the spot—
Get your sweet and hot
Yam.

Raise your hand and sway
Like you hold a tray
When you're on your way—
Yam.

Come on and shake your depression
And let's have a Yam session:
There's that long note—
One, two, three, Yam—

Ev'ry orchestra
In America
Will be doing the
Yam.

"Care-Free," the song Astaire "frankly did not like at all," was mined for musical materials when it came to making "The Yam." "Care-Free" was never published, but a piano-vocal score survives in the Berlin papers. The most striking common point between the two thirty-two bar, AABA songs is the rising seventh-chord figure used in both at the end of the bridge (see example 2). Astaire may have pointed to the syncopated rising figure and said, "That's what I'm looking for." The transfer of so

EXAMPLE 2. Berlin borrows from himself for the bridge on "The Yam" *(Carefree)*.

prominent a melodic and harmonic figure from one song to another consigned "Care-Free" to the trunk forever. The two songs' melodies share a common rhythmic profile as well: a Charleston opening, followed by the kind of syncopated rhythm Berlin knew Astaire favored. In "Care-Free," the offbeat rhythms continue in a discursive way, echoing the bridge of "Top Hat, White Tie and Tails," a song Berlin knew fit Astaire's sensibilities. But in "The Yam," Berlin opts for simplicity, taking the rhythm of the first two bars—Charleston plus offbeat figure—and repeating it above a streamlined walking bass. Berlin effectively turned the first two bars of "Care-Free" into a riff, heard three times before that "long note" on the word *Yam* rounds out the eight-bar phrase. Again, Astaire may have pointed to those first two measures and said, "That has the quality I'm after." Berlin reduced his complicated, rather rangy original melody to a catchy, compact melodic-rhythmic idea—one definition of a riff—played over and over, nine times in all. Providing contrast, the bass was smoothed out, no longer aligned with the old jerky tune but now working its own groove, positively demanding four-beat rhythmic treatment—the mark of modern

EXAMPLE 3. "The Yam" compared to "Care-Free" and "Posin'" *(Carefree)*; "A" phrases only.

swing. The harmonies were rendered bluesier—more seven chords and flat thirds—and change less often. Downbeat chord changes in "The Yam" take on the elemental quality of blues changes. The entire song has a stripped-down swing sensibility. There's little in the way of melody: it's mostly rhythm and changes.

The most significant new element in "The Yam" is the long held note to which the characteristic pose and step are performed. No such holds can be found in "Care-Free." Their source lies elsewhere. Indeed, the origins of "that long note" and the mundane word *Yam* take this tune even closer to swing and lindy hop. Songs with long held notes are unusual, but there is a precedent for Berlin's tune: "Posin'," written by Saul Chaplin and Sammy Kahn in 1937 for the *Grand Terrace Revue,* an all-black nightclub show. "Posin'" was recorded in 1937 by several top bands, both black and white, including Tommy Dorsey, Fletcher Henderson, Red Norvo (with Mildred Bailey on vocal), and Jimmie Lunceford (in an arrangement by Sy Oliver). Like Berlin's "Yam," "Posin'" is a thirty-two-bar AABA song. Every eight-bar A phrase ends with a sustained note across bars seven and eight (see example 3).

Berlin's long notes have a syncopated touch, starting on the final beat of bar six, a beat earlier than the analogous spot in "Posin'." Still, dancers could do the Yam step to "Posin'" (although "Posin'" lacks the "long note" at the end of the bridge). The musical connection between the two songs is reinforced at the level of the lyrics. Note the chorus to "Posin'," itself a named dance:

Here's a dance you ought to do
Let me introduce to you
Posin'
Everybody pose.

Get a partner then begin
Hold whatever pose you're in
Posin'
Everybody pose.

It's a dance that you can dance with your girl or wife
Find a pose then stop.
Position's everything in life.

You'll find there's no tellin' when
Bands will stop and start again.
Posin'
Everybody pose.

The word *pose* falls on held notes in the melody, just as *yam* does. Writing "The Yam" seems to have been a struggle for Berlin, and an abandoned lyric for which no tune survives makes the final connection between "Posin'" and "The Yam," a link that illuminates further the popular music and jazz basis for the *Carefree* songs. The verse—shown below and not used in "The Yam"—was adapted from an unpublished song dating to 1931. Berlin was digging around in the trunk on this one. The chorus lyric does not fit the eventual "Yam" tune, except for the bridge— the rising seventh figure from "Care-Free" is already in place—and the long notes ending each phrase.

VERSE

I'm not the feller who used to say
"Any rags any bones any bottles to day"
But I'm a salesman and here I am
Crying out "Any Jam?"
Yah, man, I'm the Jam Man
And I'm right down from the stars,
But the jam I'm talking about
Don't come in jars.[16]

CHORUS

It isn't strawberry jam,
It isn't raspberry jam,
But it's a step that I call
Jam.

I've really got something new,
And it is not hard to do,
The little step that I call
Jam.

You better shake off your depression
We're going in to a jam session:
One two three—
Follow me
Jam.

You know the band is compelled
To play a long note that's held
And when they do,
Everybody Jam.

So, before it was "Yam," it was "Jam," a word with specific musical meaning at the time. That "little step" leads to a jam session, in 1938 the prime spot for hot music making, the place where real jazz was to be found. Shaking your "depression" at a "jam session" makes sense, but what exactly is a "yam session"? Berlin was evidently satisfied the bridge lyric still worked, even with the change from "jam" to "yam." The threshold for lyrical sense and nonsense is lower in a dance tune. The final line—"Everybody Jam"—is taken wholesale from "Posin'." Indeed, that Berlin cut this bit suggests strongly that "Posin'" was a likely source for "The Yam." It's the point where the two songs are the most alike.

"Posin'" played a significant role in the development of the lindy hop from a competitive social dance at the Savoy to a routined, professionalized dance that could tour the world, a shift from social to exhibition contexts that opened the way for live and film performances (and, for Whitey's Lindy Hoppers, paying jobs as dancers). Manning recalled how the music for "Posin'" made him stop, and in those holds he realized the lindy hop could be an effective theatrical dance form.

I was at the Savoy dancing to Jimmie Lunceford's "Posin'," either while he was rehearsing in the afternoon or during one of those battle of the bands. As I've said, I used to like to catch breaks in the music, and "Posin'," which he had just come out with, had a nice stop rhythm to it. Each time Willie Smith said "Evvv-ry-bod-y *pose!*" and the music stopped, I would freeze my body, then begin dancing again when the band started up after holding for eight counts. Nobody else was doing that, but I did it with my partner because I was so in tune with the music. . . . I began wondering why we couldn't stop during *any* song. That's when I realized that I could gauge other music as it was playing in order to catch those emphatic moments and stop right on the beat.[17]

The interplay between band and dancers is primary here: music made the lindy hoppers dance, and in turn the lindy hoppers influenced how bands played. The Lunceford band was particularly known for its connection with dancers, and it was no accident their theme song was "For Dancers Only." Interaction between dancer and band lay at the core of the swing/lindy movement. The two are not separate but one, and Astaire—in his own way, within the limits of the RKO musical— tried in *Carefree* to catch this energy. He wanted a "*sock dance tune . . . in good swing time*" and apparently worked with Berlin until he got it.

Berlin's verse introduces the "yam man" in the minor mode. References to "the sweet potato that he'll fry" present this figure as a street vendor who does a little step called the Yam. The chorus—"Come get what I've got"—begins in the voice of the yam man, but his role ·as a seller of food quickly disappears. Soon he's singing about dancing and predicting that "ev'ry orchestra in America will be doin' the Yam." The patter confirms that the actual product on offer is a dance. The lyric, sung mostly by Rogers, runs through a list of six named dances or steps the singer doesn't want to do. Three hail from the 1920s: the Charleston, Balling the Jack, and the Black Bottom were each introduced by hit songs. Berlin would have known all three—each was first heard in a Broadway show—and "The Yam" was a bid to start a similar song-centered dance craze. The other three dances named in the patter—the Suzie Q, the Big Apple, and the Shag—were of more recent origin. The Suzie Q and the Shag were specific steps; the Big Apple was a group dance. In the 1938 edition of his perennially updated *How to Become a Good Dancer,* social dance guru Arthur Murray added a chapter on swing dancing for the first time. The very swing dance steps Berlin names in "The Yam" were taught by Murray in his added chapter. Berlin's patter nicely positions "The Yam" in both the past and present. It's a dance of exuberant fun that both remembers earlier dance crazes and evokes current ones. When Rogers sings the patter, she and Astaire perform characteristic moves from each dance named: their choreography follows Berlin's lyric closely. The couple effectively reenacts the historical pattern of white dancers learning new moves from black dancers.

All six dances named were derived from black social dances. But this string of allusions to white dancers' collective debt to black dancers likely was not intentional: it would be difficult to put together any list of named dances that weren't taken by the white mainstream from African American dancers. What is noteworthy here is the intensity of the field of allusions being made, all within a song introduced as being adapted from the moves of a street vendor who, by now, can be understood as black himself.

RKO used "The Yam" as the primary publicity tool for *Carefree*, a film with the future of the studio's most successful stars riding on it. The film's poster showed Astaire and Rogers dancing "The Yam" and named the dance itself. "The Yam" even made it onto the cover of *Life*, with a photo of Astaire and Rogers dancing in a free and easy style.[18] They don't strike the Yam pose but instead appear as a normal couple having a ball on the dance floor doing what looks like the Suzie Q. In-house RKO promotional booklets assured exhibitors that the Yam had been "predicted by dance experts to take the world by storm" because it was "simple enough for anyone with ballroom experience." The dance was billed elsewhere in the press materials as "a sensational new swing successor to 'The Carioca' and 'The Continental' . . . Destined to sweep a rhythm-minded nation off its feet—onto its feet! . . . Sure-fire to become the new dance craze from ballroom to porch and living room."[19] Another layout suggested hopefully, "The jitterbugs are swinging it;/Everybody's singing it./Fred and Ginger started it—/Now all you hear is YAM, YAM, YAM!" (see figure 10). Further poetic salutes to the new dance were concocted by the RKO publicity team, including a quatrain that captured the named-dance strategy in the spirit of Berlin's list-oriented patter.

> Truck and shag and Suzie Q;
> Tap and stomp and swing-a-roo!
> Wrap 'em up and holler "WHAM!"
> Here's the heat wave called THE YAM!

Astaire's regular practice of recording pop versions of the new songs in each RKO film continued with *Carefree*. His recording of "The Yam" with Ray Noble and His Orchestra is unique within Astaire's 1930s discography. Recorded in late March 1938, three months before the number was filmed, "The Yam" was specially arranged to take up both sides of a 78.[20] On side A is "The Yam" in a straightforward danceable arrangement, with short solos from around the band and Astaire filling

FIGURE 10. The RKO publicity department sells *Carefree* to exhibitors by touting "The Yam."

in the "long notes" with the same rhythm heard in the film. On side B is "The Yam Explained," a comedy dance record with Astaire and Noble bantering back and forth about "this latest dance called the Yam." Berlin composed a special set of lyrics for the chorus that purport to teach the dance (they don't really; dance instruction songs almost never do). Astaire speaks the words—rapping with the beat—while a riff reduction

of the tune plays in the background. The patter ends with an inter-
change between Noble and Astaire, real friends who had just made *A
Damsel in Distress* together.

> *Noble:* Fred, old boy, what's it all about?
>
> *Astaire:* It's about driving me crazy; you figure it out. Yam.

Perhaps truer words were never spoken: *Carefree* seems to have gone
Yam crazy. Further efforts to "make the country Yam-conscious" included yam-shaped ocarinas handed out with the film's press packets and
a Yam contest at the elite Rainbow Room atop Rockefeller Center.[21]

Seen in context by audiences familiar with the couple's earlier films,
"The Yam" would have been altogether surprising, and either thrilling
or disappointing. In their prior dances in any public context, Astaire
and Rogers had normally cleared the floor. By contrast, early on in "The
Yam" they invite everyone, good and bad dancers alike, to join them.
The action of "The Yam" travels from room to room and even outside,
with the crowd of dancers following enthusiastically. There was another such following dance also making a hit with social dancers in the
late 1930s: the Conga. This Latin dance usually called for dancers to
form a line, but the principle of a dance that moved through a building is
there in "The Yam" and nowhere to be seen in any other Astaire-Rogers
film. (The Lambeth Walk, a less structured British following dance from
late 1937, did not reach America until after "The Yam" was shot. But
when *Carefree* was released, some audiences may have registered coin-
cidental similarities with the strutting international dance craze in both
the following aspect of "The Yam" and the pose with hands up and
fingers spread, which resembles the Cockney salute on "Oi" that punc-
tuates the Lambeth Walk.)[22] In unusual fashion, Astaire and Rogers are
watched by an active (standing, dancing) rather than passive (seated,
watching) audience. In the context of the Big Apple, an energetic group
dance at its height in 1938, Astaire and Rogers's combinations can be
understood as examples of shining, when one couple steps forward to do
a fancy step or combination while others watch, ready to join in at any
time. Astaire and Rogers weren't the only screen couple doing some shining in the late 1930s. James Ellison leads Rogers and Beulah Bondi in an
impromptu Big Apple—including some Suzie Qs—in *Vivacious Lady*
(1937), and Jimmy Stewart and Jean Arthur join a group of kids doing
the Big Apple in *You Can't Take It with You* (1938).

All these social dance practices were current in 1938, when *Carefree*
was made and released. Murray's *How to Become a Good Dancer* can

serve as a sort of field guide to "The Yam" as routined in the film. His
description of "La Conga" locates the dance in exactly the social set
seen in *Carefree:* "Palm Beach society, and the best dancers in New
York's smart set, have gone wild about La Conga. . . . With a little practice, you may expect to have an immense amount of fun dancing the
Conga. There is nothing complicated or difficult about it, once you
have mastered its simple movement. Remember—it originated with,
and for generations has been danced by, simple natives. And if they
learn it, you certainly can! Now go ahead and enjoy it!"[23] "The Yam"
encourages exactly this sort of well-regulated free-for-all around a relatively simple step, with awkward older folks kicking up their heels a bit,
their attempts to join in not meant to be funny but rather a sign of what
good sports they are. Murray's added "Swing Dances" chapter included
instructions and warnings about Truckin' and the Suzie Q.

> Here are two steps that are purely in the spirit of fun! While they are not
> adaptable to a sedate ballroom, they can add a lot of liveliness to a group
> dancing to the "jam" session of a swing orchestra. . . . Both are skylarking
> steps that add variety to a basic dance pattern. Although they are used now
> principally in the Big Apple, there's no law against breaking from a Swing
> Fox Trot routine and going into one of these steps—provided, always, that
> the occasion is a frolic, the music hot, and the crowd in the mood for more
> exaggerated dancing of this sort. By that I don't mean to belittle either of
> these perfectly good and funmaking steps. But you wouldn't wear sport
> clothes to Mrs. Astorbilt's ball, would you?[24]

After setting some ground rules for a "well-regulated Big Apple" and
shining, Murray gives some hints on posing: "Leader calls out 'Everybody Pose' and dancers stop and take any pose they wish, holding it for
about 4 beats of music. Leader may call for a series of 3 or 4 poses, or
he may call dancers to go right back in circle, after just one pose. Poses
should be exaggerated. Try to make them funny!"[25] In Murray's terms,
"The Yam" is a loose Conga crossed with a well-ordered Big Apple centered on one long shine for the lead couple. Murray's chapter on swing
was a major addition to his 1938 edition: he was trying to keep the
content of his dance instruction business current enough to engage
young people, or at least give their parents a reason to force them to
learn the established dances on the way to the trendy ones. Murray's
inclusion of the latest novelty called "swing" demonstrates an imperative, felt among all established purveyors of dancing and dance music,
to meet a new phenomenon in the marketplace—a musical generation
gap playing out in the national context of network radio, traveling

dance bands, and Hollywood films. "The Yam" addressed these new conditions in similar fashion.

Some basic ironies intrude on "The Yam." Astaire and Rogers execute a refined but still energetic swing dance in the most authentically elite space yet seen in the cycle. *Carefree* is set in a realistically mounted Connecticut country club. The fantastic size and stylization of the "Big White Sets" of their earlier films, such as *Top Hat* and *Swing Time,* are absent.[26] *Carefree* is made to human scale. Astaire and Rogers's Yam dance has few genuine lindy elements, and they support their own bodies throughout. The horizontal give-and-take and improvised breakaways of swing dancing are largely lacking. They dance, as always, in a professional style that remains in control and adult. With the end of the series in sight, and their next film, the period piece *The Story of Vernon and Irene Castle,* attempting to re-create a past social dance regime, the new direction suggested by "The Yam" was never followed up on by the team. It remained their one attempt to be completely contemporary.

In 1940, Astaire admitted in an interview for *Picture Play* that the Yam had been invented for ballroom use and had flopped. But that didn't stop him from suggesting that his and Eleanor Powell's variations on the beguine in *Broadway Melody of 1940* might find favor with social dancers.[27] The desire to connect with social dancers ran deep in Astaire, though it worked at odds with his habit of making knockout dance routines that were just too difficult for easy translation outside his films.

Johnny Mercer wrote three named-dance songs for Astaire films, in 1940, 1942, and 1954. Each of the routines built on these songs paired Astaire with a partner who projected youthful vitality. An on-screen dance band, twice of the name band variety, accompanied the routines. Mercer's lyrics all touched on stereotypical black slang, often to the point of using dialect, which was not all that unusual in Mercer's work. As a group, these three named-dance routines underline the ways Astaire brought changing social dance fads into his partner routines, as well as the directly historical bent his named dances often took. Berlin's list of outdated dances in "The Yam" proved no exception: Mercer names other named dances in two of his tunes. And as with "The Yam," Astaire does some dance moves here not found in his other partner routines. In particular, the physical relationship between partners takes on an elasticity characteristic of swing and not typical of Astaire's more upright, self-supported style. The tension and release of energy between partners in these dances assumes a horizontal feel, with Astaire moving his partner

like a lindy dancer does, through a process of pull and release that expresses the youthful energy of this athletic style of dance. These dances
all bring race into the picture as well. It seems self-evident, but it needs
to be pointed out that Astaire could never have performed a partner
dance, nor sung a romantic or novelty duet, with an African American
female partner. And so race enters these named dances by other means.

To really join the youth movement in social dance, Astaire needed
younger partners. Rogers, born in 1911, was a product of the 1920s.
Her first big break was winning a Charleston contest, and she never
played anything but a woman in her films with Astaire. To really
jitterbug—the white term for lindy hop—Astaire needed a girl for a
partner. His named dances from the height of the swing era involved
two very different partners. Paulette Goddard was Rogers's age but
projected a gamine quality on-screen. She had no dance experience.
Rita Hayworth, born in 1918 and raised in an exhibition ballroom
dance family, had tremendous range on the dance floor and did a genuine lindy with Astaire.

"(I Ain't Hep to That Step But I'll) Dig It" from *Second Chorus* begins with a rap at a band rehearsal, "one of the most beguiling transitions from dialogue to musical number in Astaire's career."[28] Astaire
and Goddard start things off, trading lines that just barely rhyme.
When the drummer starts a swinging four beat, Astaire and the boys in
the band begin trading more structured poetic lines. This sort of back-
and-forth was popular in the early 1940s: Tommy Dorsey's "Marie"
popularized the practice of band members singing or chanting counter-
melodies, often with satirical words, against the tune sung straight by
the band singer. The camaraderie of the all-male band finds expression
in these youthful numbers, which often used slang, as Mercer does
throughout the rap section.

Astaire: Do ya dig me, Jack?

Band (all): We dig you, Jack!

Astaire: Can ya think of a plan?

Band member: We solid can.

Astaire: To get me out of this mess?

Band member: Ah, yes, yes, yes!

Band (all): We'll start the music and play it back.

Astaire: Solid, Jack!

Band (all): Solid, Jack!

Both solo lines from within the band are delivered in a slight but unmistakable black accent. All Mercer's named-dance lyrics afford the opportunity for this kind of racial stylization, and the possibility of delivering the lyric this way was always taken up by someone in the number, although never by Astaire himself. The spoken patter continues as the drummer's beat grows more insistent and the swing lingo gets stronger, using phrases designed to resonate with the jitterbug crowd and coming straight from Mercer, a national authority on such matters. Heard regularly on Benny Goodman's radio show, where he often spoke in rhyming patter, Mercer disseminated the latest hip expressions to an audience that was sometimes unsure whether Mercer was white or black. A 1939 interview for the *Detroit Free Press,* titled "Meet Swing Music Master; His Middle Name Is 'Umph'," introduced the singer-songwriter this way: "If you have not yet heard of Johnny Mercer, (1) you don't go to many motion pictures; (2) you don't listen to the radio; and (3) you aren't a jitterbug."[29] Hiring Mercer to write lyrics was part and parcel of the band pic plan behind *Second Chorus.* He's the only unifying presence across a score that mixes tunes credited to three tunesmiths (as well as a handful of jazz standards like "Sweet Sue"). Working with Shaw and Mercer formed two sides of the same coin for Astaire, whose personal admiration for jazz musicians was as genuine as his bid for the youth audience was new. The *Free Press* interview ended with Mercer handing out a "New Jitterbug Expression": "Mercer says that when one jitterbug wants to know if another jitterbug is ready to swing out he asks, 'Have you got your boots laced?'" In the "Dig It" patter the band asks, "Are your boots on right?" Astaire responds, "I got 'em laced up tight." Mercer's sensibility permeates *Second Chorus.*

The tune for "Dig It" is by Hal Borne. In all likelihood, Borne plays on the soundtrack with a pickup band of Hollywood musicians—*Second Chorus* was an independent production—and the tune itself was probably improvised during rehearsals. It's a thirty-two-bar AABA song with a melody made of two-bar riff-like figures, similar in every particular (except "that long note") to "The Yam." The end of each phrase features an offbeat rhythm that plugs the title and plays a large role in the dance itself. The tune fairly begs to be tapped, and Astaire does just this in the film dance and on his pop record (see example 4). The tune evaporates into a string of riff choruses during the danced instrumental following the single vocal chorus. One section expertly places the jerky rhythm of the Charleston in a swing context.

EXAMPLE 4. Borne and Mercer's "Dig It" *(Second Chorus)*; the "A" phrase as sung and tapped by Astaire on his pop recording.

The "I" of Mercer's lyric expresses a willingness to try a new step, even though he's been unsuccessful doing the Conga, mazurka, Charleston, and polka. Mercer's having fun here: no one was dancing the mazurka in 1940. But the other three were fair game. The new step is never defined in the song. The lyric instead expresses the willingness to try a new dance move, which is exactly what Goddard had to do in the film. This is her only dance number. Created for a partner with no experience and little evident aptitude, in a low-budget production context where speed and simplicity were of the essence—Pan even plays a sideline part in the band—"Dig It" is among the easiest dances Astaire and Pan ever made. In that sense, it is doable by the public, although it would have been impossible to catch the steps from watching the film in a theater (more on this below).

The steps of the dance slavishly follow the rhythm of the riffy tune and dance arrangement. Such a sustained coordination between the dance and the top rhythmic level of the arrangement is unusual. Typically Astaire explores a complicated inner rhythm or adds a new rhythm, dancing the stems selectively. Here, Astaire and Goddard stay on the stems almost the whole time. "Dig It" includes a section where the couple hold opposite hands, lean back from each other with legs slightly bent, and travel in a circle, their free hand raised up high. "Dig It" marks the first time Astaire used such a stance in relation to his partner. Swing stances like this are seen very rarely in his work, and their appearance is limited almost entirely to the 1940s. The final use of this stance is in his dances with Betty Hutton in *Let's Dance*. (Immensely popular during World War II, Hutton was billed early in her career as "Public Jitterbug No. 1.")

FIGURE 11. The *Second Chorus* magazine advertisement offered lessons in the "Dig It." The small images of Astaire and Goddard also appeared in the *New York Times*.

Astaire and Goddard were heavily promoted as models for "with it" social dancing, and "Dig It" was plugged as the highlight of the film. Detailed instructions for the dance appeared in a multipicture spread in the *New York Times*, as well as in full-page magazine ads for the film (see figure 11). The *Times* caption explained Astaire's process in making a dance attuned to swing music: "Until Astaire adopted the expression, 'dig it' was a swing term without precise meaning. He took the words literally, pressed his toe forward and down as though digging, rocked back on his heel, and came up with a brand new dance step."[30] As is typical of named dances, the emphasis is on a specific step. The phrase "dig it" supposedly describes a physical action while nicely overlapping with swing lingo. The music and dance connection becomes a matter of shared terminology, however vague the meaning in both realms. The pictures and feet patterns do not teach the dance so much as present the couple in a series of conventional poses ripe for copying. Just as with "The Yam," Paramount's promotional materials put the dance front and center and described the style on offer in the film's press book: "In the picture, Astaire and Miss Goddard go through the routine with easy grace, but the confirmed rug-cutter will probably add the violence of movement characteristic of their gyrations."[31]

Perhaps Paramount's copywriter had seen the finished routine and felt the need to put some context around it. After all, teenagers going to *Second Chorus* to hear the hot sounds of Artie Shaw's band likely had little memory of Astaire and Rogers's glory days almost five years in the past. Moving pictures were an entirely contemporary medium, and television had not yet created the conditions for old and new films to be compared. In "Dig It," Astaire faced a new audience, the bobby-soxers screaming for Sinatra and dancing in the aisles for Goodman. Hailing from an earlier time and reserved by nature, Astaire never went in for the "gyrations" of the young, but, the press book argued, that didn't mean he couldn't continue to inspire America's social dancers. (In the 1943 film *The Sky's the Limit*, Astaire has a brief exchange with a gyrating jitterbug solider who says no one understands his dancing style. Astaire observes the soldier's demonstration without a trace of condescension.) Arthur Murray got into the "Dig It" promotion business as well, and Paramount negotiated a direct dance instruction tie-in, the first in Astaire's career. In a letter reprinted in a prepared advertisement suitable for local placement by exhibitors, Murray hailed "Dig It" as "the most adaptable dance for ball room [sic] use that has yet come out of Hollywood. I am instructing all our branches to endorse and teach the 'Dig-it' in due consideration of that Jitterbug Junior that simply wont [sic] be downed."[32] The entire effort to sell *Second Chorus* by selling "Dig It" suggests the extent to which the popular music, dance, and film establishment was trying to tap into the new youth market. The film musical as a genre is again shown to be intimately tied to popular music and dance trends, a relationship that assumes particular salience in the films of Astaire.

Mercer's second named-dance song for Astaire occurs about halfway through *You Were Never Lovelier*. In partner Rita Hayworth Astaire had a skilled dancer to work with, and the appeal of the named-dance routine here lies not in the possibility of audience emulation but rather in the thrill of seeing two talented musical movie stars acting like lindy hopping kids. In the film, Hayworth plays the pampered daughter of a wealthy Argentinean hotel owner. Despite living in Buenos Aires, she speaks perfect English and knows all the latest American songs and dances. Hayworth arrives for her tap lindy with Astaire wearing tennis clothes and lace-up two-tone oxfords, the opposite of the gowns she dances in elsewhere in the film. Astaire, looking sporty in his own two-tone shoes, is also dressed down. Lindy hoppers wore similarly casual, comfortable clothes, expressing the carefree nature of this youthful dance style (see figure 12).

The named dance Astaire and Hayworth do together is called "The Shorty George," a dance move everyone already knew and a title that had already been used by Count Basie. Astaire introduces it as "a little thing from Harlem." This named-dance song doesn't sell a new step so much as piggyback on existing swing motifs steeped in the African American roots of swing music and dance. The Shorty George dance step refers to Savoy dancer George "Shorty" Snowden, who claimed to have invented the breakaway—where the couple separates and each dancer does their own thing—and performed a lindy on film as early as 1929 in the short *After Seben*. The Shorty George is a quick walking step performed solo with knees bent throughout (shortening the dancer's height). Each stepping foot is reinforced by a pointing arm—right with right, left with left—both directing their energy toward the floor, marking the four beats of the bar. Like most swing steps, it's open to wide variation. Snowden told Marshall Stearns the step was "well known in Harlem [where] they also called it the Sabu, from that elephant-boy movie, because it can be made to look kind of Oriental."[33] (Indian child star Sabu's film debut, *Elephant Boy,* came out in 1937. His first American hit, *Rudyard Kipling's Jungle Book,* dates to 1942.) Basie recorded a blues-based instrumental called "Shorty George" in 1938, and the Harry James band was playing a version of Basie's chart as late as 1943.[34]

"The Shorty George" was Kern and Mercer's second try at a named-dance rhythm number for *You Were Never Lovelier,* echoing Kern's

FIGURE 12. Casual dress and physical exuberance mark the youth-oriented "Shorty George" in *You Were Never Lovelier*.

earlier difficulties writing a rhythm tune for *Swing Time*. Their first try bore the ungainly title "Barrelhouse Beguine." Kern's contribution features an ill-fitting combination of a Cole Porter–esque triplet-heavy melody above a Latin groove interrupted by random bars of boogie bass, all inflected by Kern's complex early 1940s harmonies. Mercer's lyric takes a geographical approach, tracing the journey of the song's rhythm from some vague spot in the Caribbean northward to Memphis and from there to jukeboxes scattered across a nation crazy for the "Barrelhouse Beguine." Beyond the forced conceit of Mercer's lyric, Kern's tune is just not danceable. And while the rejected "Barrelhouse Beguine" suggests Kern was directing the songwriting process, the second try, "Shorty George," reflects Mercer's swing savvy almost entirely. Beyond the nominal attribution of the song to Kern, there is no positive evidence he wrote it.

Did Kern write "The Shorty George"? His previous problems writing rhythm numbers to Astaire's taste suggest Kern may have handed the task to others, Mercer being the likely candidate. As noted earlier, Astaire avoided Kern's "Bojangles of Harlem" in favor of rhythmic grooves taken from Hal Borne. In 1989, Pan told an interviewer that Borne "practically wrote" Kern's "Waltz in Swing Time," claiming that Borne "made it what we wanted . . . a real *jazz* waltz."[35] Borne told Arlene Croce, "Every time I hear the 'Waltz in Swing Time' I get a little sick because my name's not on that."[36] Robert Russell Bennett also claimed authorship on the "Waltz," remembering Kern sending him to Astaire with the words, "Go over to see Fred and find out what he wants." Bennett continued, "Composers are supposed to give their arrangers a little bit more than that, but they don't always do it."[37] Behind these competing authorship claims lay the controlling sensibility and judgment of Astaire. Recall his specific demands to Berlin. In short, just because Kern's name is on a song doesn't mean the musical content originated with him. If Kern did write "The Shorty George," he was working well out of character.

As with "Dig It," the song cue for "The Shorty George" uses racialized slang and swing references. Specifically, Astaire and Hayworth trade lines from the 1942 hit song "A Zoot Suit (for My Sunday Gal)" by L. Wolfe Gilbert and Bob O'Brien. When Hayworth quotes the opening line of "Zoot Suit" as evidence she's entirely hep to the jive, Astaire fairly melts before her. The "Zoot Suit" reference passes between them like a hepcat password, and certain viewers in their audience would have picked up on it with a smile. The reference also suggests Mercer's influence on the script. He was founding Capitol Records at the time and was certainly aware of what was on the Hit Parade. But the connection proves closer than that. "Zoot Suit" lyricist Gilbert was a close friend of Mercer's. The insertion of a line from the song in the film's dialogue can be read as one lyricist's salute to a pal's current hit, an inside joke that fit right into Astaire's jive dance number.

With alternative male and female sets of lyrics, "A Zoot Suit (for My Sunday Gal)" recycles the popular music trope of black folks donning special clothes to go strutting. It's squarely in the "Puttin' on the Ritz" tradition, except the clothes the singer wants here are completely "au reet" (all right), nothing high-class but rather the "walking rainbow" effect of young urban blacks in the early 1940s. Shane and Graham White have detailed the deep roots of such public displays in African American culture.[38] "A Zoot Suit (for My Sunday Gal)" was a huge hit in 1942, the year *You Were Never Lovelier* was made. Many white groups recorded it, including the Andrews Sisters, who produced a knockout version.[39] The best version by black performers was a 1942 soundie featuring Dorothy Dandridge and Paul White.[40] Soundies were prototypical music videos, short films designed for an audiovisual jukebox. Their commercial development was interrupted by the war, and then they were rendered obsolete by television.[41] The "Zoot Suit" soundie begins at "Groove Clothiers/Our stitches are hep to the jive." White and Dandridge each sing a chorus separately, then, once they are suitably attired, they meet for a final chorus on the street and strut a bit. The youthful energy of the crudely made soundie matches the character and attitude of the much more carefully produced song and dance shared by Hayworth and Astaire: the tempos are similar, with the soundie just a touch faster. Hayworth and Dandridge, who both went on to become cinematic sex goddesses, share a free body style that combines sex appeal with youthful release in these early film appearances.

Like "The Yam," "The Shorty George" describes a black character, although Mercer's lyric uses more direct terms than Berlin's: "He dances to pay the rent/And to see that you're solid sent." The verse describes Shorty's professional and home life. He's a street performer, dancing for pennies and dimes. Astaire briefly plays the part by holding out his hat, and Hayworth obliges by pretending to toss in a coin. Hayworth (dubbed) takes the vocal, and Astaire leans appreciatively toward her, his hand on the side of his head in an attitude of adoration. He gets a look of real incredulity when Hayworth delivers the line, "I know you beat yo' feet until yo' feet is beat" in a rather heavy black accent. Suddenly they're not just singing about a black character and preparing to do a black dance, but they're indulging in a bit of racial caricature that simultaneously cements their romantic relationship. Only Hayworth does the accent: Astaire never does.

The affectionate, fun dance that follows seals a deal already closed when Hayworth affects to be Astaire's "Sunday Gal." Hayworth rises from the table and does a little hop step around Astaire. Competency in black dance idioms is at issue. She knows the lingo but does she know the moves? Of course she does, both lindy and tap. The familiar Shorty George step is sprinkled throughout the dance, often at the ends of phrases. Much of the routine is done side by side, and taps are audible almost the whole time. It's a rhythm dance, with lots of broken rhythms, hand claps, holds, and even some playful patty-cake near the end. Lindy hoppers did a lot of clapping and kicking, and those elements recur throughout this dance. The handholds frequently employ the pull and release of swing dancing as well. Astaire knew his limits, and the couple never attempts any of the complicated lifts typical of lindy dancers. Rhythmic speed stands in for the athletic power of true lindy dancers. Once again, Astaire retains the sounding element. As in "The Carioca" from a decade earlier, complex rhythms endure as Astaire's primary reference point vis-à-vis black dance. The end of the number is understated and innocently romantic. Astaire and Hayworth throw their arms around each other's necks and sway to the music, turning in circles and moving offscreen, very similar to the end of "Dig It." Astaire never exited this way with Rogers. There's no presentational applause sought here, no dramatic exit. The couple sways their way out, locked in each other's embrace in the kind of private/public moment partner dancing allowed.

"The Shorty George" offers a more sophisticated tap version of "Dig It." Hayworth's versatility and physical expressiveness make the difference. Astaire had more to work with in this instance, and Hayworth, no doubt, contributed to the dance in substantive ways. While Goddard was limited to a simple social dance vocabulary, Hayworth executes difficult lindy moves while keeping the tap line going, all at a faster pace. Her unstudied ease in keeping up with Astaire is the defining quality of their partnership, and it's on display in this number, which combines youthful energy and rhythmic virtuosity. Unlike Eleanor Powell, whose technical, presentational style always calls attention to itself as a performance, Hayworth comes off as a complete film personality, her dancing, like Astaire's, just an extension of walking and generally being in the world. It's impossible to imagine Astaire doing a dance like this with Rogers, and if the viewer is disappointed that Hayworth doesn't live up to Rogers's standard, then the point of this new partnership is entirely missed. The world of popular music had changed. With the arrival of swing and lindy, black music and dance had moved to the center in an unambiguous way. Astaire and Hayworth's looser style fits the moment to a T. *Life* magazine's cover story on *You Were Never Lovelier* emphasized "The Shorty George," describing the routine as the film's "Freshest dance duet . . . a hoofing jam session which is the most intricate dance they have done together" and claiming "the dance took more rehearsing than all the other numbers together."[42] The casual tone of the routine also marks a departure from the rest of the film's obsession with refinement, visual excess, and the life of a privileged upper class. The musical contrast with Kern's songs and Salinger's orchestrations adds to the effect.

With its dialogue setup, Mercer's lyric, Hayworth's stereotypical black accent, and the use of lindy moves identified with black dancers, "The Shorty George" references the African American roots of swing music and dance on many levels. Somewhat at odds with the film's Latin background, Astaire and Hayworth put on black vernacular music and dance styles that had swept the United States by 1942. No African American couple could hope to be presented by the Hollywood studio system as Astaire and Hayworth are here, although Dandridge perhaps could have done the dance Hayworth does. Still, the overdetermined blackness of "The Shorty George" suggests a more frank admission of the African American sources of swing than the studio system customarily allowed. A more typical example of lindy hop and swing offered to movie audiences can be found in a Pete Smith specialty short titled *Groovie Movie* (a 1944 MGM production).[43] This demonstration of the jitterbug—the word *lindy* is never used—spotlights a white champion of swing dance competitions. (Dance competitions such as New York's annual Harvest Moon Ball, which included both black and white couples, provided opportunities for black lindy hoppers to demonstrate their mastery of a style they had originated. Winners often obtained featured slots in stage shows.) *Groovie Movie* constructs a history of swing dancing that writes black dancers out of the story almost completely. The minuet and waltz are presented as jitterbug's progenitors, and the Savoy Ballroom is never mentioned, even though the narration is one long string of hepcat lingo. Reference to the Shorty George step is as close as the film gets to admitting the dance's black roots. Only white dancers appear in the film, with the exception of a pair of skillful black children who are cut into the film briefly on three occasions, as if from another movie. Ending with a furious rendition of Basie's "One O'Clock Jump," the short captures Hollywood's habitual ignorance of or complete unwillingness to feature black talent in areas of popular culture where black innovators had led the way. Astaire and Hayworth's "Shorty George" bucks this trend, albeit while safely within the limited possibilities of the film musical. All the references to the black origins of the dance notwithstanding, "The Shorty George" remains a feature for two white movie stars. In his autobiography, lindy innovator Frankie Manning remembered Astaire saying, "I wish I could dance like that" while watching Whitey's Lindy Hoppers rehearse. Manning continued, "Later, [when] I saw Astaire do a brief Lindy hop in one of his films, I thought, *Yeah, Fred I know what you mean.*"[44] "The Shorty George" may be the dance that earned Manning's approval or slyly expressed negative appraisal of Astaire and Hayworth's efforts.

Twelve years elapsed before Mercer wrote another named-dance song for an Astaire film, and during that time the age gap between Astaire and his partner widened considerably. Teamed with Leslie Caron—thirty-two years his junior—and working at Twentieth Century-Fox, away from MGM, Astaire reconnected with the named-dance strategy one last time in *Daddy Long Legs*. Ray Anthony and His Orchestra, one of the few surviving dance bands still topping the charts, were part of the plan. The dance at Walston College provided an ideal narrative excuse for Astaire's wealthy businessman Jervis Pendleton and Caron's Julie Andre, a French orphan he had secretly sponsored, to share a social dance in the real world after having shared a dream ballet in Caron's imagination earlier in the film. *Daddy Long Legs* prepares the moment of their meeting carefully. Along the way, a particular sort of mid-1950s dance music gets a sustained plug.

Dance cards had been gone for decades, but the dance at Walston College revives the practice as a means to note and then transcend the age difference between Astaire and Caron. Astaire arrives in a black tuxedo; all the college men wear white or pale blue dinner jackets. Anthony's band is heard playing their hit song "Thunderbird."[45] The very willing Astaire is handed a prepared dance card that sets the stage for a series of different partners, each bringing a different dance and music style. His first assigned partner asks Astaire if the number being played by the band is "too bluesy for you." The title of the unpublished tune Mercer provided for this moment is, indeed, "Blues Theme." Like Basie in the late 1930s, Anthony found success with dancers in the early

1950s by cultivating a danceable sort of big band blues. Astaire and partner take the floor, where he announces proudly that he can do the box step and clumsily counts off. They start to dance. Astaire's partner immediately says, "You're quite good," to which Astaire replies, "I'm glad those lessons weren't a complete waste. Last week they put me on Spanish rhythms." The scene fades out, hopefully on a laugh from the original audiences, who knew of Astaire's other job as the head of the Fred Astaire Dance Studios, a national chain of dancing schools. Astaire dances briefly with two other partners before he even meets Caron, and the entire sequence plays out against a medley of dance tunes played by Anthony's outfit: the aforementioned "Blues Theme," a slow and smooth "dreamy" tune called "Dancing Through Life" (which Mercer had written for the film but Astaire didn't otherwise use), and Mercer's upbeat instrumental "Mambo" (with Astaire tossed about by a mannish girl who leads). A medium-tempo version of the swing standard "Marie" follows, scoring the above-the-title stars' first flirtatious conversation. The shifts of tempo and style in this medley echo an early 1950s innovation in popular music marketing: the dance music LP designed for home use.

The long-playing record, introduced by Columbia Records in 1948, was still relatively new, and dance discs were an early solution to the question of how to fill the longer format in a salable fashion. Social dance instructors endorsed discs that were "Perfect for Dancing," as the Fred Astaire Dance Studios' LP series on RCA Victor was called. Typically, a single LP would feature only one dance style and tempo, emphasizing the instructional nature of the discs. Arthur Murray released a series of single dance–themed discs on Capitol, teaming with different name bands on each. Anthony's band recorded a disc for the series titled *Swing Fox Trots* just one year prior to *Daddy Long Legs*.[46] But party platters with mixed tempos were also for sale, offering home dancers two twenty-minute sets—one on each side—cueing diverse dances. In the first flush of the format, Anthony released *Houseparty Hop* on Capitol, Marge and Gower Champion compiled *Let's Dance* for Columbia, and Astaire teamed with Paul Whiteman for *Cavalcade of Dance* on Coral.[47] All exemplified the mixed-tempo format echoed in the dance at Walston College in *Daddy Long Legs*.

Having at last been introduced, Astaire and Caron head for the garden, where Hollywood couples go to escape the dance floor and be alone together. The music follows them, smoothly shifting from source to background, giving the scene in the garden a romantic, contemporary feel. After they break the ice with some casual flirtation, their conversation grows more honest and the music changes to Mercer's "Dream," a song selected by Astaire for the film. "Dream" is first heard in a vocal arrangement, the mixed voices of the Ken Darby Singers located impossibly close by. The auditory perspective of the sound mixing defies any real sense of space; the music is too present to be floating over the garden from inside the gymnasium. The upper-register violins in the second chorus are particularly romantic, evoking the "mood music" of the early 1950s. This is scoring for contemporary lovers, an adult sound innovated by Paul Weston and Jackie Gleason, among others, to exploit the superior fidelity and length of the LP and further open up the new market for LPs and hi-fi turntables. Strings returned to popular music with a vengeance in the early 1950s, but the core components of the swing band—in particular the rhythm section—remained, all of it captured with the greater sophistication of postwar recording technology. The new sound fits *Daddy Long Legs'* CinemaScope Technicolor aesthetic perfectly. Just as any hi-fi-owning, LP-buying consumer might choose to do at home, Astaire and Caron talk while they dance to the leisurely but still rhythmic music, periodically stopping to just talk, creating a casual effect that had been absent in Astaire's work for decades. They could easily be posing for an early 1950s LP cover, capturing the last moments of a pre–rock and roll nation. Capitol Records employed the dream-dancing category to market Arthur Murray and Ray Anthony discs offering exactly this sort of music and mood through 1956, the year rock and roll began to change everything.[48] In *Daddy Long Legs,* the marketing ideal comes to cinematic life. Not since he and Rogers had danced in stylized nightclubs had Astaire and his female partner talked like this while dancing in each other's arms and moving to the sounds of the moment. (It's tough to chat while doing the lindy.) Mercer's "Dream" was an old song, written in 1944 as a theme song for *The Chesterfield Supper Club* radio program. The song quickly became a big hit. The arrangement in *Daddy Long Legs* directly recalls Paul Weston's version for the Pied Pipers—recorded in May 1946 on Capitol—in both tempo and character. Indeed, the entire soundtrack for the film taps into the sophisticated pop music sound innovated by Capitol Records.

"Dream" comes to a dreamy end and Caron's young man, Jimmie McBride, enters to retrieve his date. Foolishly, Jimmie sees no threat in Caron dancing with Astaire, whom Jimmie assumes is a professor. He has come to get Caron because, Jimmie announces, "they're gonna do

FIGURE 13. Lobby cards for *Daddy Long Legs* promise the latest in social dances and party dresses.

Sluefoot." All three return to the gym, where Astaire and Caron's flirtation continues by different popular music and dance means. And so "Sluefoot," *Daddy Long Legs'* named dance, is set up by a selection of stylish tunes from Anthony's band offering a smorgasbord of sophisticated adult pop and a dialogue scene planting the named dance's name. All is ready for the big number, which in some theaters had been presold in the lobby (see figure 13).

Ray Anthony himself kicks it off, with a crossfade from Astaire in the garden to the bandleader in medium close-up that reveals why this photogenic trumpeter forms a link between popular jazz trumpeters Harry James and Herb Alpert. Sometimes known as "Cary Grant in B flat," Anthony was at the height of his fame, riding the crest of his own named-dance craze, as reported by *Time* the previous year.

> Everywhere Bandleader Ray Anthony plays these days, dance halls develop a tremor under the thud of teen-age feet. The reason: a vigorous new conga-style dance number called "The Bunny Hop," in which every verse ends with "Hop! Hop! Hop!" For Anthony, it all started last spring, when he heard

that the Coke [Coca-Cola] set of San Francisco's Balboa High School had worked up the dance. Anthony contrived a tuneless tune, recorded it (for Capitol), ordered a batch of fuzzy bunny ears to give a touch of costume and started plugging song & dance across the U.S. In cooperation with parents, who regard the dance as relatively sedate, if energetic, disk jockeys and Capitol press-agents have built "The Bunny Hop" into a minor teen-age mania.[49]

On the flip side of Anthony's "Bunny Hop" single was "The Hokey Pokey." The kids at Walston College are a little more sophisticated than either of these, but surely the hope for "Sluefoot" was that lightning would strike twice: perhaps Fox, Mercer, Anthony, Astaire, and Caron could do for "Sluefoot" what Anthony and Capitol had done for "The Bunny Hop." The film musical is, again, following the popular music industry closely here.

Mercer's lyric for "Sluefoot" includes a compendium of references to other named-dance songs, first among them "The Hokey Pokey." Instructions in "Sluefoot," like "You make your right foot point to the north" and "make your left foot point to the south," sound a lot like "The Hokey Pokey," with its directions for putting feet, arms, and other body parts "in" or "out." The final A phrase of "Sluefoot," with its command "You put your ol' posterior out / And you manipulates it about," is heard only in the film and Astaire's recording: the lyric is different in the published sheet music. The choreography for this phrase, performed by a floor full of dancing couples, matches the revised lyric exactly. Perhaps Mercer observed dance rehearsals and changed the lyric before the prerecording session to match the dance. The sheet music likely would have already gone to press by that time.

Mercer's bridge lyric goes beyond "The Hokey Pokey," reaching farther back and appealing to a different crowd.

> Don't be an oddball and don't be a fig.
> Try, why be shy?
> After all, it's even better if your feet's too big.

"Don't be a fig" refers to the late-1940s jazz debate between the modernists who embraced bebop and the so-called "moldy figs," fans of the pre-swing collective improvisation style that was now being called "traditional" or "Dixieland jazz." Mercer's lyric exhorts the fig-inclined listener to embrace the new, even if it's kid stuff. It's a long shot. The devoted fig was unlikely to be caught dead buying a ticket to *Daddy Long Legs*. "Your Feet's Too Big" refers to a 1935 novelty tune, most memorably performed and recorded by Thomas "Fats" Waller, already dead for more than a decade in 1955. Mercer remembered him: others would, too. The patter, not printed in the sheet music, makes reference to "Rockin' Chair," another novelty song of the swing era, as well as "Ballin' the Jack," a reference that was old-fashioned when Berlin made it in "The Yam." Mercer's novelty lyric is surprisingly erudite and Astaire wouldn't have missed a single reference: all the dance and music references belonged to his own popular music and dance lifetime.

Mercer smoothly combines old and new popular music references within a lazy lingo touching lightly on the black dialect characteristic of much of his output as a lyricist. As sung by Anthony's all-white five-person vocal group, the slang terms in the lyric are thrown into even sharper relief. At times their delivery recalls Hayworth's slip into a stereotypical black voice that enchanted Astaire so in "The Shorty George." The most pronounced passage comes early on, in the first A phrase: "Then dig the one I'm hippin' you to." Almost fifteen years had elapsed since Mercer wrote "Dig It" for Astaire's *Second Chorus,* but the verb still worked. "Hip" was a newer locution, soon to make "dig"—or "hep," for that matter—as antique as "groovy" is today. Just like the college students in *Second Chorus,* the rich white kids at Walston College, together with the elder statesman of popular social dance, Fred Astaire, are still dancing to the sounds of a white band playing black music.

The "Sluefoot" dance as done in the movie is anything but simple, and for all the ease that the well-rehearsed dancers demonstrate, no easy social moves are taught. In fact, just the opposite. The only possible signature step evident in "Sluefoot" is a repeated rhythmic figure performed in the breaks at the end of each phrase, suggesting an underlying formal kinship with "The Yam" and "Dig It." Mueller summarizes the move as "a step combination that includes leg jutting and arm jabbing, and finishes with a hand clap and a scooping thrust forward."[50] The rhythm is hard to catch and complicated. The only dancer who has any trouble with "Sluefoot" is Astaire, and his difficulties are comic commentary on the age difference. He's not a college student, after all. But after a few missed cues—the product of excess enthusiasm—Astaire and Caron successfully lead the dance, which ends with the crowd raising both up on their shoulders. Astaire, age fifty-five, is the big man on campus.

Named dances attempt to get people dancing. Did anyone "Sluefoot"? Although the number never became a hit—Anthony recorded but never released a pop single version—the published sheet music attempted to establish the new step as part of a new popular dance style.

FIGURE 14. The inside front cover of the "Sluefoot" sheet music included basic instructions for the dance and suggestions for ways to learn more.

The inside front cover included printed "Instructions for dancing the 'SLUEFOOT'" (see figure 14). As always, the key to the dance, according to the text provided by the Fred Astaire Dance Studios, lay in recognizing the sorts of music it fit: "The character of this dance is best done in a slow movement. . . . The Sluefoot can be done to most any jazz beat but finds its best expression in a fairly slow jazz rhythm." The layout included a floor map with descriptive text for the basic pattern of the dance and a photo of Astaire and Caron in midstep. The intent was to pique the reader's interest, as "many interesting variations" on the dance could be learned at any Fred Astaire Dance Studio, "branches of which are located in most of the principal cities of the United States." Thus, "Sluefoot" was conceived as both part of *Daddy Long Legs* and an effort to generate traffic in the Fred Astaire Dance Studios scattered around the nation. As has been shown, Astaire had a marked impact on the content of *Daddy Long Legs,* and it was certainly within his reach to insert a named-dance number that could serve several functions.

The "Sluefoot" campaign echoed an earlier bid by Astaire to leverage a named-dance routine into increased business for the Fred Astaire Dance Studios (FADS). In 1947, during his year of retirement, Astaire himself launched these social dance schools that bore his name and consistently deployed his image in advertising. For the opening of the FADS, Astaire introduced a new dance called the swing trot. Described as "a fox-trot danced in a syncopated 3 beats against 4" and "a dance that is a happy medium between the Lindy and the Fox Trot," the swing trot was initially presented to the public by way of professional instruction at the FADS.[51] A popular song called "The Astaire"—released as sheet music— also advertised the new dance.[52] More than a simple named dance, the swing trot was billed as a new way to dance to jazz music, a moderate lindy appropriate for all ages that could be performed at a variety of tempos in tight spaces or on expansive ballroom floors. The dance remained part of the FADS repertoire into the early 1960s, when Astaire severed his connection to the enterprise. The 1962 *Fred Astaire Dance Book,* a published version of the FADS instruction manual, included full instructions for the swing trot.[53] But the effort to sell the new dance as a patented FADS product faltered early on, and once he was back in the musical film business, Astaire managed to get an advertisement for the swing trot into *The Barkleys of Broadway.*

The earliest musical breakdown for *Barkleys* lists a song called "Swing Trot."[54] Songwriters Harry Warren and Ira Gershwin were handed this title by Astaire, and they probably saw "The Astaire" song as well. Gershwin's lyric on the verse is clearly modeled on the earlier tune, which promises a dance that is "travelin' thru the U.S.A." Gershwin wrote of the new dance that it was "Sweeping ev'ry section / Of My Country 'Tis of Thee." (The verse goes unheard in the film.) It may have been difficult for Gershwin to take the named-dance song seriously. In the 1930s he had written two spoofs of Astaire and Rogers's named-dance songs. "Shoein' the Mare" (1934) and "The Gazooka" (1936) were both Broadway revue numbers that poked fun at the entire named-dance tune phenomenon. The latter, from the stage show *Ziegfeld Follies of 1936* and part of a lengthy movie-musical parody called "The 1936 Broadway Gold Melody Diggers," is a perfect send-up. Vernon Duke's tune is a syncopated, stuttering version of George Gershwin's Astaire song style. Ira's lyric directs the dancer while avoiding any concrete instructions.

> First you take a step,
> And then you take another,
> And then you take another,
> And then you take,
> And then you take,
> And then you,
> And then you,
> And then you,
> And that's "The Gazooka"!

Gershwin's lyric for "Swing Trot" somehow manages to keep a straight face. The very fast bridge piles up the –*y* jokes.

> It's bill and coo-y,
> Tea for two-y;
> Just watch your partner's
> Eyes grow dewy.
> *Entre nous-y,*
> You're slightly screwy
> But—irresistible!

"Swing Trot" disappeared from the lists for *Barkleys* after Garland reported for work.[55] Immediately after her removal—she appeared for just nine days' rehearsal—"Swing Trot" was promptly reinstated.[56] It proved a stubborn survivor: it was hurriedly rehearsed and shot during the final two days of production in late October 1948 (see figure 15). *Barkleys* was already being previewed in mid-December, and during the postpreview recutting it was decided to relegate "Swing Trot" to the status of background behind the opening credits, an extremely unusual decision not repeated in any other Freed musical. Astaire may have insisted the number stay in the film, with the compromise being that it was put in a compromised spot. "Swing Trot" can be seen without the titles in *That's Entertainment! III.*

FIGURE 15. Astaire and Rogers poised to give a lesson in the "Swing Trot" from *The Barkleys of Broadway.*

With "Swing Trot" opening the film, *Barkleys* begins with a social dance lesson. Astaire and Rogers's feet are framed side by side and they go right into the seven-beat basic swing trot step taught at FADS. Astaire and Rogers follow the odd seven-beat pattern for much of the routine, working the sort of variations that were likely part of FADS instruction. There are no tap rhythms, and their steps fall squarely on the beats throughout—this is not a syncopated dance—but the asymmetrical step pattern set against four-beat swing creates enlivening patterns. While it may appear to be a simple dance—among the most consistent they ever did in its style—"Swing Trot" involves complicated rhythms that were probably beyond the counting ability of most social dancers. Astaire and Rogers toss it off easily, but they always had specialized in technically challenging dances disguised as ballroom routines.

Swing trot as a named dance for popular consumption was doomed from the start. The seven-beat pattern was too difficult, and Astaire clearly didn't anticipate that few social dance customers were looking to reconcile the lindy and the fox trot in the late 1940s. Soon enough, rock and roll would challenge the very idea of jazz as dance music. It is surprising that Astaire chose to mark his new dance with the word *swing:* perhaps he was riffing on the common designation "swing fox trot." As the next chapter will show, the late 1940s were a perilous time for makers of popular culture. Astaire's song and solo "If Swing Goes, I Go Too" had been cut from *Ziegfeld Follies* in 1946 with Astaire's approval, likely because the sound and style of the number (shot in 1944) was passé in the immediate postwar period. The two-year gap between making the number and the release of the film was deadly. (Prominent reference to wartime rationing in Astaire's lyric also spelled doom for the song. By 1946 rationing was already becoming a thing of the past for Americans.) Like the FADS enterprise in general, Astaire's sense of timing seems to be off with the swing trot.

Still, it's not clear what sort of dance Astaire and Rogers could have done in *Barkleys* that would have said "now" in 1949. There's a hint of samba in "Manhattan Downbeat," but Latin beats had always been a novelty element for him. And just a few years later FADS would be selling signature dances called "Jukin'" and "The Creep," specifically designed for teenagers. Astaire was an unlikely ambassador for either. The postwar crisis in social dance and popular music is evident in *Barkleys* for the lack of a kind of social dance that would authenticate the film as of its time and place. And Rogers was too mature to exemplify future dance trends. Astaire consistently relied on younger partners in any such effort, as we have seen, and so "Swing Trot" in *Barkleys* ran up against the same hurdle as it did in the ballroom: this overly complicated dance didn't match the "time of the times." When America did start dancing again it was to rock and roll, with the Twist initiating an epochal shift to nontouch partner dancing. By the time this happened Astaire had headed off to television, and together with a new and very young partner, he set out to learn, demonstrate, and embody the social dances of yet another generation.

In his television years, Astaire largely stopped trying to introduce new named dances and instead responded to the rapidly changing dynamics of the post-Twist dance floor. (His final named-dance tune, "The Afterbeat," is discussed in the next chapter.) The Twist, like the Charleston in the 1920s, marked a fundamental change in social dancing. Both named dances kicked off periods where couples ceased to touch, lead, or follow and individuals indulged in energetic, expressive, extreme movement.[57] Astaire confronted this changed environment on his first

Hollywood Palace appearance in 1965. At the top of the show he is introduced and the curtains part to reveal not Astaire but twelve dancing girls in short, tight dresses, long gloves, and identical blonde wigs. Caricatures of the modern girl, they begin dancing a series of solo moves—the Shake, the Pony, the Jerk, the Frug, the Monkey—while Mitchell Ayres's Hollywood Palace Orchestra plays Berlin's "Top Hat, White Tie and Tails" with a heavy backbeat. Astaire enters and the girls just keep on dancing. He tries to join in—by this time all the girls are doing the Jerk—but he finds the beat and the moves less than inspiring. Still, he's a good sport—always—and ends up by welcoming the audience to "Palace A-Go-Go." The Whiskey a Go Go nightclub on Hollywood's Sunset Strip had opened just a year earlier, introducing the 1960s icon of a girl dancing vigorously, alone and in place (sometimes in a glass box). The idea that the rate of change in social dancing was accelerating out of control was quickly made in the show's opening monologue, which has Astaire joking that he has to take a lesson in the morning to know how to dance in the evening.

But the joke was just that. In fact, Astaire adapted to the new moves quite successfully in his social dance–inspired routines with Barrie Chase, who contributed more than any previous partner to Astaire's ongoing engagement with social dancing (see figure 16). Two of Astaire and Chase's routines stand out as exemplars of Astaire's approach to social dance in the 1960s. In a one-hour episode of *Bob Hope Presents the Chrysler Theater* titled *Think Pretty* (1964), Astaire and Chase played their only dramatic roles opposite each other. Early in the story, Astaire as a small-time record producer and Chase as a hard-nosed agent take to the dance floor at the Nairobi Club. This is the only narrative social dance context Astaire appeared in on television that was analogous to his film musicals and it came a decade after "Sluefoot." The dance floor had changed in almost every way. Couples do not touch, nor do coordinated steps. The heavy rock beat inspires radically altered physical postures and moves. But Astaire, now in his mid-sixties, betrays absolutely no sense of anachronism. The age question, central to *Daddy Long Legs,* is ignored. The new dance styles are presented as something Astaire already knows, enjoys, and does well. He invites Chase onto the floor and a scene that might be played for comedy is instead a display of contemporary social dance mastery. In a surprisingly integrated routine—the dialogue continues throughout—Astaire and Chase do very little traditional partnering except for a comic dip all the way to the floor. But it's not funny for being bungled; it's amusing

FIGURE 16. Astaire and television partner Barrie Chase on the cover of *TV Guide* during a week when variety ruled the airwaves.

for being extreme, unexpected, and blithely tossed off by the pair. Astaire and Chase's technical control is always on display.

A similar duo dance, this time done outside any narrative context, closes Astaire's April 1966 episode of the *Hollywood Palace*. Danced to a series of blues choruses—including a bit of "See See Rider" (the most recent version had been a Top 40 hit by R&B singer LaVern Baker in 1963)—Astaire introduces the routine as a "studied improvisation," to which Chase wryly adds, "with plenty of rehearsal." It's a typical Astaire routine, with all the marks of complete coordination between movement and musical arrangement. Drum hits catch many of the bigger motions, such as kicks, consistent with Astaire's desire to inject a rhythmic element even when he didn't have his tap shoes on. (Chase never tapped with Astaire.) Most of the routine is done side by side, and there is nothing new in Astaire's approach either. But here Chase brings her cool body and movement style to the dance and Astaire fits in without standing out. Their dancing is complementary but not symmetrical. The partnership works because both inhabit the music so fully and because age goes unmentioned. Only briefly do they pass through a closed partner position, making only the slightest reference to pre-rock partnering. Instead, they explore the new, nontouch social dance body, loose and free, spontaneous, with no need for absolute synchronicity or a matching of movement scale. Because they were so simpatico—by this point they had danced together several times on television—Astaire and Chase could dance in a nontouch idiom that managed to convey a real connection between a man and a woman. The connection was not romantic so much as musical, grounded in a shared response to the music. The dance begins with a few undanced measures, during which Astaire and Chase feel the beat individually. Once again, music cues the dance. The contrast between the youthful, full-out elasticity of Chase and the spare, rarified calligraphy of Astaire in his sixties forms a recurring trope across the television dances.

Much of the success of the couple must be attributed to Chase. Astaire had good instincts in choosing her and sticking with her. Unlike the ballet-trained Charisse and Caron, Chase's more vernacular body naturally expressed the relaxed language of jazz dance and the new social dances. In the 1960s, she came into her own. Astaire frequently programmed solos for Chase, including one in this episode of the *Hollywood Palace* in which she danced with the Tijuana Brass in a pitch-perfect, middle-of-the-road but still hip number that replays some of the basic dancer-with-the-band tropes of Astaire's own solos. Central to the Astaire-Chase partnership was a pair of refusals: the age difference goes unmentioned and Astaire's mastery of the new social styles is always assumed. Chase is never the teacher, and their relationship is one of equals. This approach forestalled any sense of Astaire growing or even being old, allowing him to spend the 1960s the way he had spent much of the four previous decades, letting the music and social dance moves of the moment cue his dancing, which virtually always "kept time with the times."

CHAPTER 7

"Jazz means the blues"

Charles Emge spent most of the 1940s on the Hollywood beat for *Down Beat*. Emge joined the Chicago-based publication when the Los Angeles–based *Tempo* was absorbed into *Down Beat* in 1940, and he introduced himself to a national readership in a self-deprecating manner that nonetheless staked a claim to insider status as a musician. "I'm still a musician to the extent that I have a small, very lousy band at a small neighborhood ballroom. At present I am masquerading as a sax player but it's pretty general knowledge around Los Angeles that I'm a reformed banjo player who had to become a leader in order to work as a musician."[1] Emge claimed to be an insider at the studios, too, and he saw it as his calling to sort out the troublesome sound/image relationship, particularly when jazz musicians were involved. Emge watched Hollywood films with an eye for what lay behind the film's surface, often naming the musicians whose work was represented on the big screen, usually without any screen credit. His review of *The Barkleys of Broadway* is typical. "We never see a picture like this one without wanting to extend a sympathetic salute to those who have to fabricate and fit the musical settings to it. In *Barkleys,* it was Lennie Hayton (remember the arrangements he did for Artie Shaw when Artie went string crazy?) and his assistants— arrangers Conrad Salinger, Robert Tucker (vocals), and others."[2] Having commiserated with the well-paid professionals who labored under the lash of the system (in some of the best jobs in town), Emge purported to describe how dance numbers in Hollywood were made.

The scoring of pictures built around dancers presents problems found in no other type of filmusical [sic]. There is no set rule, but in general, the job goes something like this: The chief arranger (in this case Hayton, who was also general music director) makes a fairly complete musical setting for each production number. From this, a piano part is fixed up for the rehearsal pianist. From that, the dancers work out their dance. Then, after the usual changes, the complete score is recorded and the dance number photographed on the set to the playback. What makes the job interesting is that dancers frequently are inspired with some terrific new idea during the shooting. Then they say: "Hey, just add a bar or two here and take out a couple at another place so the music will fit this new thing we've just hit." That prematurely gray hair Lennie has acquired after a few years in the studios gives him a very distinguished look.

Obviously Emge was ignorant of Astaire's working methods, and it's unlikely any studio would have tolerated the inefficient scenario he describes. Plans were of the essence at the studios and Astaire made his plans in the rehearsal studio, not on the set. The music department didn't create an arrangement and then reduce it for the rehearsal pianist; the process worked in reverse, from rehearsal pianist to arranger. Only one example survives of the kind of musical instructions Astaire and his rehearsal pianists prepared for their music department collaborators. A special piano score for "Since They Turned Loch Lomond into Swing" (the golf solo from *Carefree*) was prepared for arranger Gene Rose, who was making a second try at a more swing-oriented arrangement.[3] It was a complex assignment, as the dance had been filmed to a temp (or temporary) track, and one element of that track—a harmonica solo—had to be worked into the final version, which would be recorded in the scoring phase. The score Rose was handed transcribed the harmonica part and blocked out each measure of the routine, indicating only the first few notes of Berlin's tune each time it began. Inserted measures of drone were written out, as were the specific beats where Astaire's movements had to be caught or mickey moused. Some actions needed to be accented more than others, and the copyist marked these beats with an X and also described in words what Astaire was doing at that particular moment. The score serves as a guide to physical action much like the bar sheets used by animators.[4] Midway through the number Rose was advised to "see Fred and Hal about droning also in these 2 bars." Certain details could only be communicated verbally, and Borne, Astaire's closest musical collaborator, was deputized to speak for the dancer. Astaire was also listed as a source of clarification, further evidence for the substantive, practical role he took in the technical process of making his routines. Character indications, such as "Hot Clar[inet]," gave Rose stylistic clues. An earlier piano score—this one belonging to Borne and likely used by him when recording the temp track—has many more stylistic indications, such as "Clarinet a la [Benny] Goodman," "Hotter than hell, high open brass" and "SCREAM." Ostensibly built on a sixteen-bar Berlin tune, a second melody—called "Scotch Golf" and credited to Robert Russell Bennett—was incorporated into the number as well. Once again, the music for an Astaire routine turns out to be a garment stitched together from several sources. The "Loch Lomond" scores are important evidence that Astaire was in complete control of the musical structure of his dances. The musical choices were his to make. The following inquiry into musical structure in his dances reveals much about Astaire's creative approach to both music making and dance making.

Astaire danced to popular music. The structural building blocks of popular music are straightforward: thirty-two-bar choruses built on eight-bar phrases in an AABA or ABAC arrangement, twelve-bar blues choruses, introductions, verses, vamps, and big finishes. There was nothing arcane or concealed about the musical forms Astaire deployed: they can be heard easily if we attend just to the music—sometimes hard to do with all that dancing going on. Astaire, himself a musician and songwriter, certainly knew his way around musical structures. This chapter looks closely at the question of musical form in his work, and specifically at Astaire's use of the blues progression.

The twelve-bar blues—a progression at its barest using only three chords—the tonic (I), subdominant (IV), and dominant (V)—remained a viable musical form for popular musicians from the 1910s to the 1960s. In the 1920s, the blues were given prominent hearing in the work of the blues queens, African American women who sang almost exclusively for black, working-class audiences in urban theaters and traveling shows. Successful recordings disseminated their sound and style more broadly. The blues queens sang popular tunes as well as blues choruses using the traditional AAB form for the lyric (where the initial line is repeated, with the third providing a conclusion to the thought). Astaire never sang an AAB blues lyric: for him, the blues were an instrumental form. Blues choruses were not used all that much by African American stride pianists, and the form appears rarely in Tin Pan Alley and Broadway songs at any time, although everyone knew a few blues-based tunes, such as W. C. Handy's "St. Louis Blues."[5] From at least the mid-1910s, the twelve-bar blues found a place in vaudeville, an early venue for jazz as novelty music.[6] Vaudeville blues like "Livery Stable Blues" and "Bugle Call Rag" were published as sheet music and widely heard on the variety stage and early jazz recordings. These blues emphasized energy and speed: twelve bars and a simple set of changes allowed for freer improvisation and greater momentum than a thirty-two-bar song chorus might. Count Basie's Kansas City band carried a revitalized blues-based instrumental swing onto the national scene starting in 1936, and almost all the swing bands played the blues in some form or another. The boogie-woogie piano craze, which got going at the very end of the 1930s, had a similar impact. Boogie-woogie was sometimes part of swing band books, and a few (mainly white) bands had a special connection with the style. These two rhythmic matrices for the twelve-bar blues—four-beat swing and eight-to-the-bar boogie-woogie—coexisted during the war years and can be heard side by side in Astaire's films. And as with earlier jazz uses of the blues, when repeated over and over, the short twelve-bar chorus could serve as a solid foundation for improvisatory back-and-forth between players, virtuoso displays by individuals, and the spontaneous creation of head arrangements for groups of any size. All manner of flexibly structured performances were built on the blues, from three-minute 78s to twenty-minute jam sessions. Astaire structured his swing and boogie blues solos around these very same jazz band showbiz values.

Early rhythm and blues and rock and roll relied heavily on the twelve-bar blues, inflecting the progression in new and old ways. With rhythm and blues, the sung element returned to popular applications of the blues. Reviving the AAB lyric turned out to be an important step on the way to rock and roll. Pop-oriented adaptations of boogie-woogie, like Ray Anthony's "Bunny Hop," show the twelve-bar blues had a place in the white teenage music market before Elvis Presley and rock and roll appeared on the scene to erect yet another brand of popular music, in part, on the blues progression.

And jazz players were not ready to relinquish the blues form either. In the late 1950s and 1960s, black jazz players seeking to connect with larger audiences often turned to the blues. Singer Joe Williams and Count Basie found a middle ground between the blues and refined classic pop vocals that Astaire imported wholesale into his 1960 television special. Williams was a blues singer with an astonishing bass voice and impeccable diction who put the accent on elegance, in his own way not all that different from Astaire in his mix of hot and cool. In the same years, younger jazz players like organist Jimmy Smith and the Young-Holt Unlimited trio generated funky, extended grooves on a blues base, creating eminently listenable, even danceable music that looked for a big audience and went by the name "soul jazz." Astaire brought both Smith and Young-Holt into his television appearances, correctly recognizing they carried the popular blues gene that had underlain so much of his own work. Indeed, all the major pop-oriented uses of the blues progression show up in Astaire's dances. And since he was firmly in control of the music he danced to, it was Astaire himself who reached for the blues—sometimes, as we shall see, putting aside a Berlin or Porter tune in the process.

"BUGLE CALL RAG"

Astaire made low-budget solos for his two films at Columbia, the only Poverty Row studio he worked at: there were no special effects or backup chorus, just Astaire in a room, tap dancing to a popular jazz-oriented beat. In *You Were Never Lovelier,* the setting is a small hotel manager's office with music provided by a pull-out group from Cugat's band. In *You'll Never Get Rich,* the small guardhouse of an Army training camp serves as the setting for two low-tech Astaire solos. The first guardhouse solo, a Cole Porter song sung by a quintet of black singers, is discussed in chapter 9. The music for the second solo, ostensibly accompanied by the same group of five black men, is a medley of solid swing ideas laid over ten blues choruses. As noted earlier, Porter composed an instrumental called "A-Stairable Rag" for this spot, using stylized bugle calls and an original twenty-bar strain. Having requested a dance using military signals, Astaire must have considered Porter's effort insufficient for his needs. Porter's score is incomplete and open-ended, musical ideas to be worked with rather than a finished piece.[7] In the end, Astaire chose to work with the blues instead.

Astaire's guardhouse blues solo begins with the military bugle call "assembly" (see example 5). This was far from the first time Astaire had used assembly as a musical cue initiating the dance, and swing-savvy audiences would have instantly recognized a larger musical reference being made. Assembly was, as one Astaire screenwriter put it, "the signature of Bugle Call Blues."[8] It was also an Astaire signature.

In the opening scene of *The Gay Divorcee,* a Parisian nightclub orchestra plays assembly and kicks off Astaire's first film solo as a star. The scene and short dance replaced an earlier idea from the writing

EXAMPLE 5. Bugle call to assembly (*Military Signal Corps Manual*, compiled by James Andres White [New York: Wireless Press, 1918], 34).

department—a scene not set in a nightclub and without any dancing. But RKO was banking on Astaire being a dancing leading man—a nonexistent star category at the time—and the character-centered nightclub opening defines Astaire's film persona in the contemporary language of jazz. The assembly start to the solo is lacking in the shooting script for *The Gay Divorcee*.[9] Instead, a lap dissolve was to transition from rising band music drowning out the dialogue to a medium close shot of Astaire's feet already furiously tapping.[10] The screenwriter didn't understand that Astaire wanted his audience to know when and why his feet started flying, and so his reluctant walk to the raised dance floor was added. His surprise when the band sounds assembly is disingenuous. Astaire was always heading toward a danced encounter with jazz-inflected popular music.

Assembly crops up again and again in the early Astaire-Rogers pictures. The call intrudes on the middle of Astaire and Rogers's hot tap duo to "I'll Be Hard to Handle" in *Roberta,* where the trumpet brings them back into tempo after an extended tap conversation. Both respond immediately, with salutes and a unison tap break. *Follow the Fleet* picks up the gag, in one of the very few instances that one film in the cycle refers to another. The involuntary nature of Astaire's response to assembly is included early in the shooting script in a telling fashion: "As Bat reaches the bottom of the stairs and goes to a locker, one of the boys, with a wink to another one, sings the first part of the signature of Bugle Call Blues. Bat, like a fire-horse, galloping to a fire, finishes the break with a hotlick step. The other fellows laugh when he finishes."[11] The screenwriter has been told the name of the jazz tune being referenced. It isn't assembly being sounded but rather the opening to "Bugle Call Blues," even though all that's heard in this film is the opening bugle call (which, after all, was part of military life). The joke is repeated when Astaire first sees Rogers. Here he plays the call on a tin whistle: "CLOSE SHOT—Sherry. Like a fire-horse, she responds to the signature and she finishes the break with a hot lick dancing step. She turns around and her face lights up joyfully." A third use of the gag—when Astaire and Rogers respond together—cannot be found in any script. It may have been added on set. Assembly is heard a fourth time in this film with a Navy background when a real bugle call to assembly is sounded. Astaire and his buddies in the band miss the call because their raucous jam session drowns out the bugle broadcast on the ship's loudspeakers.

Repeated use of assembly as a call to the dance in these early RKO pictures references an in-joke in the RKO rehearsal room. Mueller describes the practice: "When Astaire would arrive at the rehearsal stage and close the door behind him, Hal Borne would punch out the first two measures of the bugle call 'Assembly' on the piano, and Astaire would respond 'by tapping out the last two bars with his feet. Then they knew it was Fred arriving.'"[12] Assembly was thus at once a call to work, a signal that the creative seclusion necessary to the team was in place, and a reference to a popular jazz tune built on the blues. Because they could expect their audiences to catch the public, popular-music meaning of assembly, Astaire and his collaborators could work this private signal into the fabric of their films.

Assembly was a standard start to a jazz use of the blues that Richard Crawford and Jeffrey Magee rate as the eighth most-recorded jazz standard between 1900 and 1942.[13] It went under several names, "Bugle Call Rag" being the most common. Other names include "Bugle Call Blues" and "Bugle Blues." Astaire used both "Bugle Call Rag" and "Bugle Blues," and I use these two titles interchangeably below.

In the examples described above, assembly serves as a teaser. Not until the "Drum Dance" from *A Damsel in Distress* did Astaire follow up on the formal implications of sounding assembly in a jazz context. In this (by Astaire's standards) long solo, three blues choruses interrupt the Gershwin tune "Nice Work if You Can Get It." The interruption is unsurprising, as the routine begins with a series of riffs unconnected to the song, and at a later point the tune is put aside in favor of a tom-tom solo referencing drummer Gene Krupa's opening to Goodman's "Sing, Sing, Sing." Astaire takes a particularly flexible approach to musical form and content in the "Drum Dance," which makes no sustained attempt to plug Gershwin's tune. The music goes where Astaire, playing on and dancing with a panoply of drums, wants it to go. He drives the changes in texture by initiating new beats. The only time the band takes the lead is when assembly is sounded and Astaire gleefully responds to the call, launching into the blues for the first time on film. Once into the "Bugle Blues," Astaire deploys it for his own purposes along the lines laid down by jazz musicians, but he makes no effort to reference other versions known to his audience.

224 | Astaire in Jazz and Popular Music

Astaire's approach changes appreciably in the guardhouse solo in *You'll Never Get Rich*. Here, accompanied on-screen by a group of African American sideline musicians, Astaire finally created an extended solo dance to "Bugle Call Rag." The dance is motivated by a bit of good news on the romantic front, and Astaire expresses his joy with some spontaneous tapped rhythms. As if reading his mind, the black drummer in the corner takes up the tempo and the black trumpeter blows that familiar bugle call. Astaire points toward the musicians and gives out with an enthusiastic "Yeah," before responding with a two-bar tap break of his own. In September 1941, when *You'll Never Get Rich* was released, this cue would have been immediately recognized as the start of "Bugle Call Rag," a favorite with swing dancers and a particular hit for Goodman, who recorded three versions and often played it on the radio. After Pearl Harbor the popularity of this military-themed tune soared still higher. Astaire's "Bugle Call Rag" anticipated two other film versions: the Glenn Miller band in *Orchestra Wives* (1942) and Benny Goodman's group in *Stage Door Canteen* (1943). The latter features servicemen and hostesses dancing wildly, and dialogue links the number to virtuoso jitterbugging. By 1941, the call to assembly was an invitation to the dance, and perhaps some in the audience for *You'll Never Get Rich* were itching to get up and dance in the aisles, a natural jitterbug reaction in a movie theater, although normally acted upon when the featured band in the live show was playing, not during the movie itself.

"Bugle Call Rag" had a long, rich performance tradition among jazz musicians, black and white alike, when Astaire used it as the basis for this dance. His two-minute version makes multiple references to the jazz history of this jam tune. For example, almost all Astaire's solo dances include a change of tempo. His "Bugle Call Rag" is no exception, only here Astaire uses the formal device of a tempo change to reference jazz practice. Recorded versions of "Bugle Call Rag" from the 1920s and '30s generally settle in one of two tempo ranges: 190–205 or the 240s (measured in quarter notes per minute).[14] Astaire's first section runs at 202; the second shifts into a higher gear at 244. Thus Astaire touched on both standard tempo areas for the standard to which he was dancing.

Rather than a song with melody and lyrics, "Bugle Call Rag" is a two-part template for instrumental improvisation. John Pettis, Elmer Schoebel, and Billy Meyers published a song called "Bugle Call Rag" in 1923 with a picture of their (white) vaudeville jazz band, the Original

Memphis Five, on the cover. The earliest known recording, by Ford Dabney's (black) Syncopated Orchestra in March 1922, predates the sheet music. As a variant of the blues, the sheet music should not be taken as a composition in its own right, but rather as a print version of a specific group's use of a preexisting musical practice among improvising musicians, likely derived from African American players.[15] Thus, "Bugle Call Rag" was not a Tin Pan Alley or Broadway song, but rather a blues-based practice among jazz musicians.

"Bugle Call Rag" divides the twelve-bar blues progression asymmetrically. The first four bars, those remaining on the tonic, are given over to unaccompanied solo breaks that often, but not always, reference familiar military bugle calls. The full group, of whatever size and makeup, responds in the remaining eight bars. Because of its characteristic division of the twelve-bar blues, with a long break at the start, "Bugle Call Rag" may not sound like the blues, but the underlying musical basis for the verse is that familiar progression. In a survey of more than forty recorded versions of "Bugle Call Rag," every one included a sixteen-bar verse—the eight-bar ensemble portion of the chorus (bars 5–12) played twice through—as an alternate structure upon which to improvise. Recordings of "Bugle Call Rag" typically begin with three to four repetitions of the twelve-bar chorus—different soloists trade off the bugle calls—followed by three to four passes through the sixteen-bar verse, again featuring a succession of soloists over a continuing accompanimental texture. Often the bugle call chorus returns once along the way or at the close to provide further variety of texture and melodic content. These textural shifts, in particular the refreshing breaks where the band drops out and an unaccompanied solo takes over, are central to the characteristic sound of "Bugle Call Rag" across the 1920s, '30s, and '40s. Astaire did not use the sixteen-bar verse in his relatively short version, opting instead for a total of ten trips through the twelve-bar chorus, five at the relaxed tempo and five at the faster tempo. This provided opportunities for ten bugle call breaks. Table 3 summarizes the musical content, formal structure, and references to familiar bugle calls, tunes, and recordings in Astaire's "Bugle Call Rag."

"Bugle Call Rag" survived because it proved almost infinitely flexible: it was a killer diller of a flag-waver with plenty of room for hot improvisation that did double duty as a novelty number through the use of quotation in the chorus-opening breaks. Its vaudeville origins and swing-era use for exhibitionist social dance testify to the multiple levels on which "Bugle Call Rag" could be enjoyed. Recognizable bugle

TABLE 3   MUSICAL STRUCTURE OF ASTAIRE'S "BUGLE CALL RAG"
(You'll Never Get Rich)

Chorus[1,2]	Quotation	Break (bars 1–2)	Break (bars 3–4)	Group Response (bars 5–12)
1	Assembly	Trumpet	Astaire	Trumpet and clarinet in collective improvisation texture
2	Reveille	Trumpet, Astaire	Trumpet, Astaire	As above
3	Bugle call variant	Clarinet, Astaire	Astaire	Clarinet solo
4	First call (varied)	Trumpet, clarinet	Astaire	Trumpet and clarinet together in stop time texture, guitar rhythm underneath
5	First call	Trumpet	Astaire	Trumpet and clarinet in collective improvisation texture
6		Drum solo, initiates faster tempo	Drum solo	Swing texture, riff 1 (quotes Mundy's arrangement for Goodman)
7	Yankee Doodle	Trumpet section, Astaire	Trumpet solo, Astaire	Tailgate trombones
8		Trombone section, Astaire	Astaire	Riff 2
9	Jazzy bugle call gesture	Sax section, Astaire	Astaire	Riff 3
10	Jazzy bugle call variants	Trumpet solo, Astaire	Add drumroll, Astaire (flash turns)	Riff 4

[1] Astaire dances during measures 5–12 on each chorus.

[2] The first chorus is preceded by a four-bar introduction: a two-bar break in drums, answered by a two-bar tap break by Astaire.

calls—most often first call, assembly, and reveille—and familiar song incipits can be heard in many recorded performances.[16] Astaire's version sports the best-known bugle calls, as well as solo breaks abstracted from these calls or using bugle call–like triadic gestures. For example, chorus 4 features a slowed-down portion of first call, which is heard at regular speed in chorus 5. Chorus 9, a Glenn Miller–style sax section in close harmony, and chorus 10, a driving trumpet break, both incorporate swung bugle call gestures that echo the contemporary big band practice of swinging the classics. Chorus 7 quotes the opening notes of "Yankee Doodle Went to Town." Reference to this impudent patriotic song turns up rather rarely in the recorded tradition of "Bugle Call Rag." In the decade before Astaire used it, three black groups—the Mills Brothers, and Cab Calloway and Don Redman's bands—referenced "Yankee Doodle" in just this way.

Astaire's arrangement complicates the formal structure of "Bugle Call Rag" by dividing the opening four-bar break into two halves, creating further opportunities for solo-group contrast. In choruses 1, 4, and 5 Astaire makes no noise with his feet for the first two bars, handing those measures over to the soloing trumpet (joined by the clarinet in chorus 4). In choruses 1, 3, 4, 5, 8, and 9, the band drops out for measures 3 and 4, giving Astaire an empty break to fill on his own. This division of the opening four-bar breaks is an innovative approach to "Bugle Call Rag" and shows Astaire carving out a place for his tap contribution within the patterns and structures of jazz practice surrounding the tune. It's also the kind of structural subtlety the playback system encouraged. Astaire's "Bugle Call Rag" is not improvised in any conventional sense of the word, but he is laying out a spontaneous-sounding structure that tightly connects solo and group playing with his own tapped rhythmic contribution. In choruses 2, 7, and 10, Astaire and soloing musicians play together across all four bars. These shared breaks provide another contrast of texture and add to the unpredictability of the number as a whole on both musical and choreographic levels. Constant variety forms the underlying principle of the ten chorus-opening breaks in Astaire's "Bugle Call Rag."

In chorus 6, Astaire cedes the entire opening break to the band, specifically to a drum solo that initiates the shift to the faster tempo. During this four-bar solo the film cuts to a shot of the five black men ostensibly accompanying the number. The sideline drummer, playing an improvised jailhouse drum kit, is Chico Hamilton, a young black drummer who would go on to an illustrious jazz career. Even though he probably didn't play on the soundtrack—there's no evidence either way—at the very least Hamilton has the right instrument to hand. During the dance, Astaire regularly looks offscreen left to the black musicians who remain just out of the frame throughout. The trumpet player sits closest to Astaire, and the bell of his horn appears occasionally at the margins of the screen during the dance. The cutaway to the musicians at the start of chorus 6 reminds the viewer who it is Astaire keeps looking at while he dances, reinforcing in visual terms the connection between the dance and jazz practice. (How the black combo gets into the guardhouse is detailed in chapter 9.)

"Bugle Call Rag" thrived as a scaffold for improvisation and arrangement in two successive jazz styles: both the collective improvisation of the 1920s and the riff-based swing arrangements of the 1930s and early 1940s. Astaire drew on both. His first, more relaxed half employs polyphony throughout. This approach to the tune may have been inspired by a 1940 recording by Rex Stewart's Big Seven, a group composed primarily of Ellington sidemen performing under the direction of trumpeter Stewart.[17] Their version bears a striking resemblance to the first half of Astaire's film routine, which was filmed just months after the Stewart version was recorded. Both use similar soloists: trumpet, clarinet, drums. Additional solos for the bass and piano are heard in the Stewart version. These instruments are not heard in Astaire's version, which, in the first part at least, sticks to sounds that could be attributed to the sideline musicians on-screen (although the makeshift drum kit crosses the credibility line). A singular feature found in both the Stewart and Astaire versions is the drum solo. No earlier recorded version had given an entire four-bar break to drums alone. At 196 beats per minute, the Stewart version has a relaxed quality that, by the start of the 1940s, was uncommon in recorded "Bugle Call Rags," which were getting faster and faster, in step, perhaps, with the approaching drums of war.

After the unusual but not unprecedented drum solo initiates the faster tempo, the size of the band accompanying Astaire's routine increases noticeably and the style shifts to contemporary swing. A characteristic riff from Jimmy Mundy's arrangement, as recorded by Benny Goodman, is heard prominently at the shift to the faster tempo (chorus 6). The full band response (bars 5–12) changes in each of the last three choruses. Each offers a brief exposition of a different riff, as if the listener is being dropped into different big band versions or experiencing a particularly kaleidoscopic arrangement. The second half of Astaire's arrangement sounds identical, rather than just similar, to the popular music of the time. That he situates this music as being played by black musicians distinguishes the guardhouse as a space where Astaire could dance with black musicians to music with African American roots.

In chorus 10, the trumpet plays across the entire break and the drums come in for the last two bars with a drumroll that effectively ushers in the climactic chorus. Astaire dances across all of this. During the drum-roll he executes a flash step, a turning figure that makes no sound. Flash steps were common at this point in rhythm tap performances with a big band. As an arrangement increased in volume and taps could not be heard, rhythm tappers shifted to steps with more visual than auditory appeal. According to black tapper Pete Nugent, "You have to open and close with something that catches the eye. . . . With the music *fortissimo*, nobody can hear taps."[18] Astaire returns to these same flash turns at the very end of "Bugle Call Rag." Between the two sets of flash steps he repeats a single time-keeping move. Astaire's right foot lands in front of his left and then kicks out to the side when his weight passes to the left. He twists at the waist in the process. Astaire's upper body remains still, his arms swinging boldly in the opposite direction of his legs. This simple repeating step marks the four-beat rhythm underlying the arrangement. As a flash move it has little visual interest. While doing this step, Astaire moves out of his position as soloist and becomes a time-keeping member of the rhythm section. The step is uncharacteristically easy for Astaire, particularly in this spot at the end of a solo. Most often, his solos close with an extended spinning combination (as in "Slap That Bass" and "Sunday Jumps"). Astaire's use here of a simple repeating step between two sets of flash turns directs the viewer back toward the band, which has raised its dynamic level considerably. Astaire does the repeating step and looks offscreen left, toward where the band is understood to be, enjoying the sheer volume and accumulated energy of the music as it reaches its climax. Surprisingly, this unusually easy repeating step appears for the first time a full chorus earlier. Astaire introduces the move at the start of chorus 9. Indeed, except for two brief syncopated solo breaks totaling six out of twenty-four measures, the simple time-keeping kick step is all Astaire does for the final fifth of the solo. He hops from right to left in a danced imitation of the kicker on the bass drum, his kicks with his right foot visually reinforcing the rim shots on beats two and four. Or perhaps the rim shots are audibly reinforcing the kicks. Either way, Astaire finds a means to dance to the music without being the center of attention. He joins the band rather than fronting it. In these last two choruses, something of what jazz meant to Astaire begins to become evident. Known for playing drums with jazz records in the privacy of his home, here Astaire abdicates the right to a danced climax and hands the big finish off to the band, a band symbolically represented by the sideline group offscreen left, to whom Astaire directs big smiles through the end of the number.

Four of the five sideline players in the guardhouse were, in fact, jazz musicians: Buddy Collette on clarinet, Red Mack on trumpet, Alfred Grant on guitar, and Chico Hamilton on drums. Levinson interviewed two of these musicians more than a half century after the scene was shot. Collette recalled being "treated like we were nothing" and being tired from having to get up so early in the morning for shooting after working his regular late jazz hours. Hamilton described Astaire as "a hardworking dude. I had my sticks and played them on a table and on a little Indian drum. I must say, though, he was pleasant to work with."[19] Hamilton suggests he participated at least partly in the preparation, or at least rehearsal, of the number in Astaire's rehearsal hall. Are any of these sideline players heard on the soundtrack? Likely not. All were still quite young, just barely arrived in Hollywood. Union barriers against incursions by nonstaff musicians and black players more generally would have worked against their participation in the recording studio. Still, the possibility exists that Astaire made this routine in collaboration with some very young African American jazz players. Hamilton and Collette would both go on to have long jazz careers. Neither had made a single recording session to date when they got the sideline spot at Columbia. How they got the job remains unknown. That each "plays" the appropriate instrument reveals yet again how sight and sound are scrupulously matched in Astaire's films.

Astaire's staging of "Bugle Call Rag" as an interracial encounter has important ramifications for the understanding of Astaire as a dancer primarily motivated by swing. Astaire assembled the music from historical and contemporary jazz practice after rejecting Porter's attempt at an original bugle call number. He turned "Bugle Call Rag" to his own purposes, borrowing a compendium of jazz tropes surrounding the standard from its time on the vaudeville stage to the present, when it was at the historic height of its popularity. While these tropes are not exclusively black or white, Astaire's contextualization of the dance as accompanied by a group of black musicians is significant in the same way that his dance to the Cugat small group in *You Were Never Lovelier* is full of self-consciously Latin steps and poses. Astaire's musical and choreographic choices locate this solo firmly within the jazz tradition. At a time when "Bugle Call Rag" suggested the "violent gyrations" of the jitterbug, Astaire worked against type, playing a modest sort of hoofer, underplaying his dance and enjoying the music, just hanging out with the band. "Bugle Call Rag" was a staple for jazz players in the late 1930s and early 1940s, when the number was often used to close out marathon public jam sessions, as Patrick Burke has shown in his study of 52nd Street. Every musician present sat in on these "Bugle Call Rag" finales, and anecdotal and photographic evidence "reveal a great deal of collaboration among black and white performers." Still, Burke continues, "Although 52nd Street's public jam sessions aspired toward racial integration, they never truly transcended notions of race."[20] The same can be said for Astaire's "Bugle Call Rag" and all his interracial numbers on film.

"Bugle Call Rag" dropped out of jazz practice right after the end of the war, with subsequent recordings all in a retrospective vein. Astaire, however, would periodically use the "Bugle Blues" form for another thirty years, the four-plus-eight division of the twelve-bar progression remaining central to his dance-making practice.

BOOGIE-WOOGIE BLUES

Unlike Astaire's preferred stride piano style, boogie-woogie was grounded in the twelve-bar blues. Pounded out in rural industrial contexts in the South—mostly at lumber and turpentine camps—in the early twentieth century, the boogie-woogie idiom made its way to Chicago a bit behind the northward journey of jazz.[21] The moniker "boogie-woogie" in commercial parlance dates to a 1928 recording, "Pinetop's Boogie Woogie." The music flourished in South Side settings, primarily as a solo piano music, for a decade, growing alongside an emerging and long-lasting Chicago blues style that was never embraced by the mass white audience. By contrast, the driving boogie-woogie aesthetic and its instantly recognizable eight-to-the-bar rhythm broke onto the national scene in a big way at the very end of the 1930s to become a key sound of the war years. It was heard in New York at the two "From Spirituals to Swing" concerts at Carnegie Hall (1938, 1939), and Barney Josephson's Café Society nightclubs served as a finishing school for the style, which burst on the pop music scene when white bands and vocal groups began to add it to their books. Boogie-woogie enjoyed a tremendous vogue during the early 1940s, only to flame out almost immediately after the end of the war.

Astaire played boogie-woogie piano to a limited extent, playing it on-screen only once, in the "Ad Lib Dance." Boogie-woogie as a rhythmic style occurs most prominently in Astaire's 1940s films made during the height of the boogie-woogie craze. His use of boogie-woogie rhythms and textures, almost always by way of the twelve-bar blues, was a transparent attempt to infuse his routines with a current popular music trend, a strategy evident in the work of other white musicians of the time (including classical pianist and unlikely movie star José Iturbi). Like many swing-oriented musicians, Astaire merged the eight-to-the-bar rhythmic matrix with his own style, but it is unlikely boogie-woogie made him dance in any particular way. His use of boogie-woogie has more to do with the logic of the popular music market and the expediencies of routine making than with any specifically musical inspiration.

Columbia's *You'll Never Get Rich* contains more boogie-woogie than most Hollywood musicals. Three of the film's six musical sequences reference boogie-woogie by name in the lyrics and/or use an eight-to-the-bar beat cued aurally by a prominent piano. The blues progression turns up in three numbers, "Bugle Call Rag" being one.

Astaire and Hayworth's new dancing partnership is put front and center in the first scene for both in the film, when Broadway dance director Astaire challenges chorus girl Hayworth's knowledge of a tap combination. They do the combination together to a boogie-woogie piano solo played by an offscreen pianist referred to as "Tommy," likely Astaire's 1940s rehearsal pianist Tommy Chambers. The brief but brilliant duet—"the second twenty-four bars," according to Astaire's spoken cue—re-creates Astaire's rehearsal room context and installs boogie-woogie as a key musical style in the film, while also introducing what one critic called the "tonic effect" of the Astaire-Hayworth combination.[22]

Satisfied with Hayworth's performance, Astaire continues the rehearsal with "Boogie Barcarolle," a big dance number that is mostly Robert Alton's work. (Kern and Mercer's rejected "Barrelhouse Beguine" for *You Were Never Lovelier* was perhaps working off this accepted double-B hybrid.) Porter expanded the twelve-bar blues chorus into a sixteen-bar strain. A driving boogie beat bumps up against a lush string melody in this battle between classical and boogie styles. A boogie beat works here because the eight-to-the-bar style instantly asserts itself. Actually playing through the twelve-bar blues is not strictly necessary to infuse a number with a boogie blues sensibility.

The production number "The Wedding Cake Walk" serves as the film's finale. The musical structure of this narratively and spatially complex number involves the insertion of boogie and swing blues choruses into a new thirty-two-bar song. Two precedents for combining the blues and an original song can be found in Astaire's routines from the previous several years: the "Drum Dance" in *A Damsel in Distress* and the concert dance finale from *Second Chorus,* the film Astaire made just before *You'll Never Get Rich.* What is new in "The Wedding Cake Walk" is the use of blues choruses in the boogie-woogie rhythmic matrix. The division of labor between Alton and Astaire is plain to see and hear. All the blues choruses accompany Astaire and Hayworth dancing a tap combination that Astaire likely created, with Alton responsible for the choreography and staging of the ensemble portions done to Porter's song.

"The Wedding Cake Walk" begins conventionally, with the verse and chorus of Porter's song introduced by uncredited girl singer Martha Tilton, best known at the time for singing with Goodman's band. Shortly after *You'll Never Get Rich,* Tilton was among the first singers signed by Capitol Records. Original audience members who knew Tilton would have shifted gears somewhat here: her unannounced appearance marks the film, for a moment, as a band pic. After the vocal portion—performed "in one" in front of a downstage curtain—Tilton departs and Hayworth as dancer becomes the center of attention. Transitional music employs Mendelssohn's traditional wedding recessional, followed by Porter's tune in triple meter, orchestrated for strings and unseen women's chorus as Hayworth swirls about surrounded by the bridal party. It's a romantic waltz down the aisle, all in service of Hayworth's ascendant star. (Alton puts the camera onstage in the midst of the dancers, a technique he uses in *Easter Parade*'s "Steppin' Out with My Baby," another parceled-out collaboration between Astaire and Alton.) Astaire first appears at the altar, appropriately deferring to Hayworth as both bride and Columbia starlet. In a sly plot point, his character has contrived to make the playacting of marriage vows into the real thing. Pronounced man and wife, Astaire and Hayworth whip around to face the audience and launch into a side-by-side tap routine to two boogie blues choruses that directly recalls the side-by-side rehearsal that opened the film. A chorus and a half of Porter's tune in a swing arrangement follows, with Astaire and Hayworth featured throughout. (The shift from blues to Porter's tune is garbled on both sound and image tracks, suggesting second thoughts in the editing room.) After Astaire, Hayworth, and company have danced in boogie and swing time—including slow-motion cakewalk kicks that reference Porter's title—the camera tracks forward through a series of curtains, taking the number into a different space by cinematic rather than theatrical means. This spatial transition is accompanied by a musical return to the boogie blues for one chorus. The number concludes with the full ensemble dancing on a huge tank-shaped, tiered wedding cake to swing riffs played above an eight-to-the-bar rhythm in the bass. Astaire and Alton's production number tells a conventional romantic story and uses a variety of musical styles to bring *You'll Never Get Rich* to a vigorous high-production finish. When Astaire is dancing, the beat is either boogie or swing and an eruption of the blues is always possible.

Five years later Astaire added some boogie blues choruses to Irving Berlin's "Heat Wave," a major production number in *Blue Skies*. Astaire came onto *Blue Skies* very late in the game: shooting had been underway for two weeks when he took the place of Paul Draper, the concert dancer unwisely signed for his first lead film role. Confronted with a production number that had already been worked out in its major points—Olga San Juan sings the vocal and Astaire's character falls from a high platform at the end, all in a brightly colored Caribbean setting—Astaire used the boogie blues as a means to quickly insert something personal. In the process he undermined whatever logic there had been to the "Heat Wave" production number.

During Astaire's first dance sequence in "Heat Wave," Berlin's tune is heard against a six-count tom-tom ostinato. Astaire, partnering San Juan, taps a counterrhythm throughout. Tap shoes are perhaps not the best footwear for Martinique: all the other men in the number go barefoot. As the tempo accelerates, Astaire pulls San Juan into dance position with a swing arm move common to his other lindy-ish dances. The exotic ostinato continues, giving the dance an appropriately intense quality. Caribbean-themed numbers were familiar fare in the 1940s, and the rather garish "Heat Wave" typifies this brand of Hollywood Technicolor exoticism. Then, all at once, the tropical conceit of the number falls away. Astaire twirls San Juan offscreen for no reason and the assembled company settles into a seated semicircle on the floor to watch Astaire dance six choruses of boogie-woogie blues. There is no preparation, musical or otherwise, for this sudden shift. Exotic production numbers like "Heat Wave" normally stay safely within their framing visual and musical conceit. This one does not. Astaire's boogie is the fly in the ointment.

Astaire was given composer credit on the *Blue Skies* cue sheet for this passage, which is listed as "Rhythmic Boogie Music (Heat Wave, Part 3)."[23] The studio system understood this as original material emanating from Astaire and not his rehearsal pianist, as was the case in similar situations. Perhaps Astaire improvised the music at the piano, quickly demonstrating what he wanted to orchestrator Van Cleave.

Connections to popular music are evident here as well, with a riff in Astaire's section referencing Gene Krupa's signature tune "Drum Boogie." Mueller notes that Astaire's "incongruously bright solo" borrows steps from *You'll Never Get Rich*, exceedingly unusual for a dance-maker who always sought fresh ideas.[24] On a musical level, the steps Astaire reused in his "Heat Wave" solo were originally danced to the boogie blues. Whether this was a musical connection or simple expediency is hard to tell, although Astaire's subsequent recycling of blues-based steps in his final television dances suggests a bit of both.

After Astaire's boogie-woogie incursion, San Juan returns, does a "he's my man" bit with a flower à la *Carmen*, and the Caribbean conceit resumes with a section marked "Tempo di Samba." General spinning, jumping, and energetic hand motions from the chorus spell Latin fire in the language of mid-1940s Hollywood. An entirely unmotivated climb up the stairway ensues for Astaire, with his melodramatic fall from a bridgelike structure bringing the curtain down and the number to a close. The central solo section—composed and choreographed by Astaire and built on the boogie blues—bears no connection to anything surrounding it.

At least one reviewer remembered the brief boogie-woogie solo from this long, musically overstuffed film. *Variety* noted, "The songs are pleasantly familiar to the World War I generation and, for the youngsters, they are refreshing and solid, especially as Berlin has modernized them." In particular, the reviewer highlighted "the modern boogie-woogie overtone to that corking arrangement in 'Heat Wave.'"[25] Berlin, of course, was uninvolved in the modernizing. Inserting some boogie blues into "Heat Wave" was Astaire's idea. He composed the music. Arranger Van Cleave created "that corking arrangement." And unlike "The Wedding Cake Walk," in which the boogie choruses punctuate the number's narrative and alternate meaningfully with Porter's tune, in "Heat Wave" Astaire stops both the show and the tune to solo in his chosen style on a blues base.

ROCK-AND-ROLL BLUES

Astaire's final studio-era solo was a rock-and-roll blues number by Cole Porter. Later audiences may stare in disbelief at "The Ritz Roll and Rock" from *Silk Stockings*—one of my students sighed and called the number "disappointing"—but the routine made eminent sense when it was created in late 1956 and early 1957 on the same lot where Elvis

Presley would shoot *Jailhouse Rock* just months later.[26] "The Ritz Roll and Rock" was an attempt to remain relevant, with the twelve-bar blues being one element of popular music continuity Astaire could hang on to.

Porter's song falls into the category of 1950s popular songs combining nascent rock-and-roll tropes with the craftsmanship associated with the thirty-two-bar song forms that had been the norm for half a century. Precedents for "The Ritz Roll and Rock" are plentiful, with several models close to hand. In 1953 the Fred Astaire Dance Studios briefly promoted a named-dance song called "The Creep" as the next thing for teenage couples. This AABA song by Andy Burton and Carl Sigman was published, like "Sluefoot," with dance illustrations and instructions included in the sheet music. Again, "many interesting variations" to "The Creep" could be learned at the Fred Astaire Dance Studios. MGM released a newsreel short promoting the dance, which showed couples dancing with their heads pressed together in good Carioca fashion.[27] The A phrases of "The Creep" are twelve-bar blues choruses. A standard-length eight-bar B phrase provides contrast. Porter's "The Ritz Roll and Rock" adopts exactly the same structure. Also from 1953, Anthony's "The Bunny Hop" was among the earliest pop hits of the postwar era built entirely on twelve-bar blues choruses. "The Bunny Hop" was a revision of an earlier Anthony instrumental, an aggressively swinging rhythm number called "Mr. Anthony's Boogie" recorded in late 1950.[28] The differences between these two recordings—the sharper "Boogie" groove and the sweeter "Bunny" sound—measure the shifting beat of the early 1950s, moving between one generation's slicked-up boogie-woogie and the next's sock-hop innocence. Both cuts were built solely on the twelve-bar blues. Finally, despite his later scathing denunciations of rock and roll—"[It] is the most brutal, ugly, desperate, vicious form of expression it has been my misfortune to hear"—Sinatra recorded two singles in the rock-and-roll vein for Capitol in March 1955, both using backup vocals echoing the previous year's surprise pop hit "Sh-Boom."[29] "Two Hearts, Two Kisses (Make One Love)" uses the blues progression for the A phrases and includes a honking saxophone solo. "From the Bottom to the Top" features piano triplets à la Fats Domino. Both anticipate arranger Skip Martin's try at a rock-and-roll sound in "The Ritz Roll and Rock."

A new song for Astaire's solo in *Silk Stockings* had always been in the works. Originally, Freed's writers had imagined Astaire doing a number at the start of the picture that showed him getting dressed in the "Royal Suite" of a fancy hotel.[30] This, to put it politely, had been done before. Instead, a nightclub number at the tail end of the picture was added late in the game.[31] It was quickly made and as timely as it could possibly be. Watchers of popular music and culture were observing the advance of rock and roll closely: was it just another dance craze, or would this novelty have lasting impact? Would Hollywood have to adjust to rock and roll as it had to swing a generation earlier? Perhaps the prudent move was to cautiously incorporate some references to rock and roll. One critic recognized this strategy of splitting the distance between old and new ways, noting "Mr. Astaire, too, has a bright solo (with chorus) to a new song. 'The Ritz Roll and Rock,' which, while synthetic, is not as inconsistent as it sounds."[32]

The Broadway version of *Silk Stockings,* which opened in February 1955, had just missed the explosion of rock and roll. The film, in development from mid-1956 on, did not. The year 1956 proved a transformative one for popular music on American television: Elvis was on all the time. He first appeared on the Dorsey Brothers' *Stage Show* in late January, with three more appearances in February and two in March. In April and June Elvis performed on *The Milton Berle Show* (telecast from California), and on 1 June the young man from Memphis visited *The Steve Allen Show.* This last appearance may have been the seed from which "The Ritz Roll and Rock" sprang. By the middle of 1956, Elvis's insinuating hips and astounding sales on RCA Victor could scarcely be ignored. In a bid to show he was just a nice boy, Elvis wore a top hat, white tie, and tails on Allen's show, singing "Hound Dog" to a hound dog that also donned a top hat. No rock-and-roll precedent for "The Ritz Roll and Rock" is quite so direct as the sight of Elvis dressed up like Astaire, a "synthetic" effect that, in this case, *was* as inconsistent as it sounds. The *New York Mirror* made the connection between Astaire and Elvis by inference in a June 1957 article on *Silk Stockings* titled "Look Who's All Shook Up: Fred Astaire Steps Up the Beat to Rock 'n' Roll." Reaching back to the earliest of Astaire's named dances, the article's author wrote of the dancer "putting his stamp of terpsichorean approval on every craze, from the 'Carioca' in 1933 to today's fantastic rock 'n' roll which has Freddie 'all shook up' in his newest musical, M-G-M's 'Silk Stockings.'"[33] Elvis's "All Shook Up" topped the charts in January 1957.

Musically speaking, "The Ritz Roll and Rock" follows Astaire's previous work with the blues closely. Rock and roll's use of the twelve-bar blues was one of the few aspects of the new style that could be understood by pop music professionals of the previous generation. Rock and roll was, in this respect, just a new spin on boogie-woogie and swing. As noted, Porter's tune follows the form of "The Creep" exactly: an AABA song with A phrases built on the twelve-bar blues and the B using a contrasting eight-bar idea. Porter might have been working from models sent his way by Pan or Astaire. Astaire's approach to Porter's blues-based tune is telling. During the danced instrumental sections, Astaire abandons Porter's melody and reverts to the four-plus-eight division of the blues typical of "Bugle Call Rag." This structural approach to the blues was fundamental to Astaire's creative work, as a look at his blues dances for television reveals.

MADE FOR TV BLUES

Astaire wrote his own blues-based popular song for his 1959 television special *Another Evening with Fred Astaire*. Words and music for "The Afterbeat" are credited to Astaire and Mercer, an unusual sharing of both elements. Astaire apparently began work alone, then turned to Mercer for help. Mercer's publishing company managed the song, which was never released as sheet music. Under the right circumstances, television could effectively launch a record or a new artist—the explosive success of Frankie Valli and the Four Seasons after an appearance on *American Bandstand* in 1962 is a classic example—but, unlike the film musical in earlier times, television was not a viable place to launch a new song. With the coming of rock and roll, song promotion gave way to record promotion, with performers appearing on television to lip-synch to their hit records, a live variant of the playback technique. In this new environment, "The Afterbeat" was a dinosaur.

"The Afterbeat" begins in old-fashioned style with a patterlike verse. The chorus, however, abandons the large-scale forms on which Astaire and Mercer had built their careers. The lead sheet consists of five blues choruses in C—each carefully numbered, with the melody unchanged and five sets of lyrics—and ends with a repeated vamp meant to fade out on applause.[34] In routining the song, Astaire (working with Pan and David Rose) made an effort to give this succession of blues choruses a larger shape. After the verse, the routine runs through twelve blues choruses divided into two six-chorus halves, each comprised of four sung, followed by two instrumental choruses. Astaire sings alone the first time through. The unseen Bill Thompson Singers take the vocal on the second pass. The four sung choruses are given the feel of an AABA popular song by harmonic means: the arrangement modulates up by a step before both the B and the final A phrases. "The Afterbeat" steals this modulating device from "The Bunny Hop," which occasionally rises by a step to give a larger shape to a series of pop blues choruses.[35]

As the song's title suggests, "The Afterbeat" is all about beats two and four, the offbeats that formed a central rhythmic difference between swing and rock-and-roll drumming. The drummer in Rose's orchestra plays the offbeats like a rock-and-roll drummer, with strong rim shots on his snare. Astaire initially snaps his fingers along with him, a subtle swinging gesture that could only work on television. The more violent hits of rock-and-roll drumming meet the sophisticated snaps of swing, and the fit is uncomfortable. Astaire and Mercer's lyric locates changing popular music style at the most fundamental level: in the drummer's hands. In good named-dance song fashion, the lyric works by comparison. This new beat is "like a back beat, or an echo beat": it is "not an oom-pah-pah, nor a cha-cha-cha." Mercer and Astaire also look for common ground between rock and roll, firmly installed by 1959, and their own rhythmic tradition, claiming that "a swingin' beat, and a dancin' beat, is the afterbeat." But fastidious grammar like "nor" and made-up terms like "echo beat" don't cut it. Some reference to Astaire's persona has to be inserted for the song to work. The satiric but knowing Ritz element, effectively deployed in Porter's song, is lacking. Everything rhymes with "beat" in this lyric that seems falsely simplistic. Chuck Berry could rhyme "beat" with "it" three lines running in the chorus to "Rock and Roll Music" (1958), but Mercer and Astaire could not. Neither Astaire nor Mercer had the youthful directness or fresh energy of rock and roll. "The Afterbeat" would be a spoof were it not for the straight-ahead routining it receives: parody was foreign to Astaire for the most part. His earnest embrace of rock and roll in "The Afterbeat" doesn't fly, and it's disingenuous to boot. After "The Afterbeat" the show moves to safer ground: to the adult pop of David Rose, and to the muted jazz of Jonah Jones.

Astaire and Pan's dance for "The Afterbeat" sits almost entirely on the offbeats. Placing almost every step on beats two and four makes for wooden dancing, compromising the broken rhythm aesthetic central to the pair's style. The rim shots on the snare reinforce each step, and the measured, moderate tempo is too slow. The boys and girls of the Hermes Pan Dancers enter by popping out one by one—on the offbeats, of course—from behind bits of scenery. A series of partner combinations in a stilted style follows. Astaire partners a different girl for each blues chorus, in front of a group of six couples doing the same moves. The whole takes on the quality of a dance demonstration. The steps are relatively easy, adaptable for social contexts and unfailingly proper. White gloves for the ladies would not be out of order. Each twelve-bar chorus demonstrates the same four-bar dance combination three times, and a seasoned social dancer might even be able to pick up some ideas. ("The Afterbeat" returns behind the special's closing credits, offering a second look.) There's no evidence the Fred Astaire Dance Studios taught "The Afterbeat," but the press obligingly reported that "Astaire thinks ["The Afterbeat"] could catch on as a new teen-age dance."[36]

For his 1960 special *Astaire Time,* Astaire adjusted his blues strategy to better match the role television was playing in popular music. He engaged the Count Basie Orchestra for the special and created an extended production number around Basie's featured singer Joe Williams, a pop singer and blues shouter riding the crest of a five-year partnership with the band. The Basie-Williams combination had broken through in 1955 with the hit blues tune "Every Day." As Stanley Dance has noted, "Trombonist Quentin Jackson once described the Basie band of the fifties as 'a sophisticated blues band.' With Joe Williams, the leader added a sophisticated blues singer to it, and then launched him with a song by Memphis Slim, a veteran but not unsophisticated blues artist himself. So evident a success was 'Every Day' that Basie's supporters promptly divided into two camps."[37] These two camps could be described as those who wanted Basie to preserve his historic jazz credentials (recycling his swing-era sound) and those who embraced Basie's effort to remain relevant (even if that meant accompanying Judy Garland and, later, making not one but two albums of Beatles' tunes). Always with his eye fixed on the business of show business, Basie succeeded in doing both. He understood that variety and appeals to youth could be a passport to ongoing success that would keep his outfit busy and profitable. As Gary Giddins writes of Basie's reinvention, "Basie had a jazz band, a commercial band, a singer's band, a dancer's band, a concert band—an institution."[38] The success of the Basie-Williams combination effectively launched Basie's revitalized band along with Williams's brief star turn. Before the success of "Every Day," Williams was more pop song stylist than blues shouter, and he always combined the two approaches during his Basie years, alternating blues albums with LPs of standards. Williams's deep, remarkably clear voice, impeccable diction, and debonair good looks combined to make him eminently promotable to adult pop audiences. Never a jazz singer per se, he perfectly matched Basie's effort to hold on to as large an audience as possible and stay in the pop-ular music game. Williams left Basie (with the leader's support) for a solo career in early 1961, so *Astaire Time* captures a partnership at its ripe end, a successful pop-jazz-blues formula at its creative limit.

Astaire's routine with Basie and Williams runs through sixteen blues choruses and pulls from four separate Basie-Williams blues tracks, most drawn from their most recent Roulette album *Everyday I Have the Blues.*[39] The well-known introduction and two instrumental cho-ruses of "Every Day" are heard as well, a nod toward the hit that started it all. For the 1960 audience this routine recapped the five-year run of a revitalized big band and an attractive African American singer who was not part of the onslaught of rock and roll. Astaire hitched his blues number to this aesthetic—which clearly inspired him—by building a dance on recorded music reperformed live, a television formula he turned to repeatedly.

Basie's group was, of course, brought onto the special to play live. But Astaire had worked out his routine from their recordings, and the necessity of Basie's group playing exactly as they had on the records caused problems. Basie's band didn't play the same piece the same way every time, so Astaire's danced response to their record was difficult to re-create when the band was actually there to play. Astaire exploited a technological loophole to address the problem. The Basie segments were prerecorded to accommodate the band's busy schedule and aired in sequence with live elements on the telecast. Astaire took advantage of this by cutting a portion of a Basie record into the soundtrack of the blues medley recorded especially for the television show, in effect doing some postproduction tinkering with a "live" performance.[40] The habits of film production died hard with Astaire, and he manipulated his sup-posedly live television specials to ensure maximum control over every element.

Basie's 1950s and 1960s bands—his "New Testament" outfit—inevitably looked back. In the era of the electric guitar, big bands were, by definition, old-fashioned, appealing to adults of a certain age. But the aging Astaire's dances with Basie (and Jonah Jones) made historical sense. The multigenerational television audience would have felt the rightness of these combinations even as they absorbed the novelty of black and white performers collaborating in new ways made possible by television and larger transformations in race relations (see chapter 9). However, Astaire persisted in his efforts to dance to genuinely new sounds, and his dance to the music of jazz organist Jimmy Smith provides a particularly successful case in point. It shows Astaire tapping into yet another syncopated blues-based idiom: soul jazz.

Jimmy Smith was a jazz phenomenon, creating a secure place in jazz for the Hammond B-3 organ with his sudden appearance on the scene in the mid-1950s. Self-taught on the organ, Smith remembered it was relatively easy to master the physical challenge of playing an independent bass line in the pedals: "In the earlier days I was a tap dancer so the transition to heel and toe playing was made without too much trouble."[41] Using his left hand for rhythmic and harmonic comping, Smith treated his right like a horn—trying, he said, to sound like saxophonist Charlie Parker. Together with this new instrumental voice, Smith brought together swing, bebop, blues, rhythm and blues, and gospel in an enduringly successful grooving formula that appealed strongly to the greater black audience, who were often turned off by modern jazz developments. As Kenny Mathieson notes, "The groove established the popular appeal of this music, and has kept it alive with successive generations of an audience which stretches well beyond the usual jazz crowd."[42] Smith laid down many recording sessions for Blue Note Records in the late 1950s, and the label released upward of twenty Smith LPs. Only two cracked the charts. Moving to Verve Records (no longer a Granz label) in 1962, Smith repackaged his grooving style for a wider audience, and pop success followed. "Walk on the Wild Side," a Smith organ solo sandwiched between big band passes through this jazzy movie theme, charted in the Top 40. Verve continued to package Smith in pop-oriented ways, and one of these projects led to an Astaire-Smith duet.

Astaire was responsible for Smith's appearance on the 2 October 1965 episode of *The Hollywood Palace,* and his introduction of the organist rang changes on familiar themes in Astaire's musical life. "As an admirer of the great recordings by our next artist, I prevailed on the producers to try and get him. Here he is, the fabulous jazz organist Jimmy Smith." The initial connection was made by way of Smith's records, which Astaire describes enthusiastically, and the dance Astaire made to Smith's music drew directly from his records, an approach typical for Astaire's TV dances. The show's finale is a dance by Astaire to Smith's "The Cat," from the eponymous LP pairing Smith's organ with a powerful all-brass big band arranged by Lalo Schifrin.[43] The album reached number twelve on the *Billboard* pop album chart in 1964, a strong showing for a jazz record during the Beatles' breakout year.

(Eight of Smith's Verve LPs charted between 1962 and 1966.) "The Cat" is a blues jam to a fast, driving beat with occasional interjections by the band. Smith could groove on the blues for long, long stretches. His Blue Note blues jams usually ran in the ten- to twenty-minute range. "The Cat," clocking in at three and a half minutes with a new-fangled long fade-out at the close, captures the energy of Smith's style in a pop-sized package. Expanding beyond his jazz base from the late 1950s, in the 1960s Smith offered hip music that effectively squared the circle, making popular jazz in the age of rock and roll. As jazz historian Alyn Shipton notes, Smith's "driving, powerful style continued to be a vital force in jazz until his death in 2005, and it is probably the only element of the hard-bop revolution to have remained current and popular for almost half a century."[44] This was exactly the kind of music Astaire had been dancing to his entire career: a highly syncopated style, incorporating jazz-based virtuosity, structured on the twelve-bar blues, and thoroughly popular in its reach. Because Smith's sound was so syncopated, so filled with broken rhythms, Astaire could tap into his own comfort zone, digging out his tap shoes in the mid-1960s when tap was dead just about everywhere else.

Astaire introduces "The Cat" as part of a monologue on his age. He notes that his own old movies regularly show up on the late show—"The later the show the younger I get"—then sets up the duet this way: "You're going to see a 119-year-old man dance—making like a cat, yet chasing a fly. I'll be accompanied by Jimmy Smith, my organist and personal physician." A shot of both Astaire and Smith in action assures the viewer that Smith is playing live. Astaire's live taps are occasionally audible as well. This dynamic, long, full-out solo works because Smith's rhythmic drive pushes all the buttons. Built on the live re-creation of a recorded jazz pop performance, music makes the dancer dance in a direct fashion grounded in Astaire's lifetime of work with jazz musicians. At almost three minutes in length, danced alone in direct interaction with the music and musicians, Astaire's "The Cat" reaches the level of inventiveness found in the great film solos. Smith's syncopated groove brings out old-school Astaire: following the music yields a rhythmically robust result.

And the audience loved it. At the end of the performance, Smith and Astaire are very comfortable physically with each other. Smith puts his arm around Astaire, who reciprocates; their mutual admiration is evident.

Astaire was always eager to offer "fresh ideas," but by the mid-1960s he started repeating himself. Reaching back to his earliest engagement with the blues in "Bugle Call Rag," he closed the 12 March 1966 episode of *The Hollywood Palace* this way.

> Dancers are often asked where they get the ideas for their routines. Well, most of the time we make up our own, but now and then we borrow a step from each other. Sort of like a library book: if it's good you forget to bring it back. One of my favorite steps is one I got years ago from that great dancer John Bubbles. He gave it to me for one of mine. I'm still using his step, but I don't know what he did with mine. I think he gave it to George Murphy [at the time a U.S. senator from California]. . . . I've been fooling around with an updated version of a favorite of mine: Bugle Call Rag. . . . Okay, Mitch, let's try it.

The dance that follows—six choruses in all—draws its musical and choreographic content directly from the guardhouse dance in *You'll Never Get Rich,* combining old ideas with a few new moves, including some freak poses and hip shaking. Mitchell Ayres's arrangement has a contemporary sound throughout, but the bugle calls are all recycled. Even "Yankee Doodle" turns up. The tempo change for the final chorus is initiated by a swing drum solo, and the number ends with a riff-based chorus and dissonant tutti chords straight out of earlier Astaire solos like "Puttin' on the Ritz." Far from fresh, this dance was made out of pieces of numbers from two decades in the past.

Astaire turned to the blues at the close of his performing career, dancing to the blues the final two times he danced on television. For the first of two appearances on *The Dick Cavett Show,* Astaire danced solo to three blues choruses. The dance begins with a hip contemporary beat—heavy on the afterbeats—led by a funky guitar. By the third chorus the beat grows jazzier, with brass in the mix and Astaire doing flash steps with a lot of movement. He ends with the final pose from "Puttin' on the Ritz." The *Cavett* blues from November 1970 was a shortened version of a dance from April of the same year, when Astaire reprised the "Music Makes Me" trope on the Academy Awards telecast. This time it was Oscar host Bob Hope who taunted Astaire into dancing.

> *Hope:* When you hear music doesn't the beat do something to you?
>
> *Astaire:* Nothing.
>
> *Hope:* Well, don't you miss dancing?
>
> *Astaire:* Oh sure, Bob, I sit in my rocking chair and cry all day long.
>
> *Hope:* But you've never danced on the Academy show.

Astaire: No.

Hope: And you're not going to tonight?

Astaire: No.

Hope: That's what you think.

Hope points to the pit and the music starts. It's the blues, of course, in a funky contemporary beat. Astaire restrains himself until the third measure, when he responds with a jolting full-body move. He launches himself into the dance by way of the Freak. After some comic moves and self-referential "What am I doing?" gestures, Astaire gets serious as the music moves into swing time. He starts tapping and ends with spinning flash steps, recapping crowd-pleasing strategies that had worked for decades. And, indeed, the fundamental trope from his first solo to "Music Makes Me" endures in this dance made and performed thirty-seven years later. Music—this time the twelve-bar blues—was still making him dance.

At the close of Astaire's "improvised" blues routine, the audience—as Oscar crowds do—rose to its feet and, unknowingly, applauded the end of several overlapping epochs in popular music history: the pop-blues period, the long swing era, and the age of Astaire.

CHAPTER 8

"Something that'll send me"

Astaire worked on a relatively small scale, trying always to stay within what he once called the "welcome limit."[1] But while he never showed an interest in making longer forms (such as dream ballets) or choreographing groups of dancers, Astaire's routines were more than miniatures. As he told an interviewer in 1937, "Working out the actual steps is a very complicated process—something like writing music. You must think of some step that flows into the next one, and the whole dance must have a pattern. If the dance is right, there shouldn't be a single superfluous movement. It should build to a climax and stop!"[2] Part of the task of routine making involved forging a unified, original structure that combined musical, choreographic, and cinematic choices into a satisfying whole. Astaire solved the question of cinematic unity by framing his dancing figure in its entirety, from head to toe, in a full shot and only rarely allowing cutaways from the dance. He stuck to this approach across his entire career and thereby made his routines legible, first and foremost, as dances. Use of a single song typically served to unify a routine musically, but as this study has shown again and again, it was by no means uncommon for Astaire to cut and restitch musical materials to get exactly the musical structure he desired. Manipulation of musical form lay at the heart of Astaire's approach to routine making.

On a choreographic level, his routines typically develop along a unified idea, cohering around the choice of setting, a prop, or a narrative conceit internal to the number, such as music making the dancer dance.

Usually Astaire's dances remain in one physically bounded, generally familiar space: nightclub dance floor, theater stage, or domestic interior. Astaire did not favor empty soundstages or stylized sets, as Kelly, for example, often did. When considered in the context of his decades of dance routines set in realistic furnished spaces, Astaire's dance up the walls and across the ceiling in *Royal Wedding* yields an extra measure of delight. What might have been a gimmick for others becomes a logical move for Astaire. Routines employing a change of scenery—"One for My Baby" visits three bars, and "Fated to Be Mated" ventures across three soundstages—travel for variety's sake, and matching shifts in the arrangement's musical style support each change of scene. Props could be central to choreographic unity as well. Canes define the choreography, visually and audibly, in "Top Hat, White Tie and Tails" and "Puttin' on the Ritz." The golf solo is, in essence, a dance with a golf club, and gymnasium equipment plus a coat rack unify "Sunday Jumps." Astaire's rehearsal pianist on *Funny Face* gave him the idea of using his raincoat as a bullfighter's cape, and the dance portion of "Let's Kiss and Make Up" came together around this Spanish conceit plus a dance with an umbrella, neither prop connected to Ira Gershwin's lyric or the plot of the film. On his 1958 television special Astaire did a prop dance without props, instead miming a series of objects he had danced with in his films, including a piano. Drummer Alvin Stoller provided the sound of these invisible props from off camera, showing how important the element of sound was in Astaire's prop-centered routines (not at all surprising, given Astaire's music-making approach to dance making). Typically built on mutually supportive cinematic, musical, and choreographic structures, most of Astaire's dance creations display a cohesion and inevitability that have contributed greatly to his critical reception as an artist of high caliber.

But not all of Astaire's routines hold together, and those showing signs of structural stress are worth examination. Frequently, production records and other sources reveal that Astaire was not completely in control of these less-than-unified routines.

"Bojangles of Harlem" *(Swing Time)* is a prime example of a long routine that does not hang together, with musical, lyrical, choreographic, and visual elements working at odds. Looking back on the number in 1973, Astaire let slip a revealing bit of information about this, his only performance in blackface: "Bill Robinson was well known at the time, and they thought it would be a good idea to have a takeoff on the Bojangles name."[3] That "they" is telling. Apparently, the salute to Robinson was not Astaire's idea. As noted, getting Kern to write a sufficiently syncopated song proved a struggle, and Astaire did not use Kern's tune for most of his own solo dance sections. Nor did he sing Dorothy Fields's lyric, which closely describes the content of "The Pied Piper of Harlem," a production number starring Robinson from *The Big Broadcast of 1936*.[4] (Fields's lyric describes the residents of Harlem running after Bojangles like rats, capturing the connection in direct if troubling language.) Astaire's dance with three large shadows, a long special effects sequence filling the second half of "Bojangles," was credited to chance by Pan, who said the idea came by way of three lights in the rehearsal hall casting similar shadows and sparking the visual concept. Nowhere in the routine does Astaire make an attempt to imitate Robinson's dancing style or persona, an odd choice given the tribute supposedly being made to the famous dancer. And so, while the title, lyric, and general conceit of the number point toward Robinson, very little of Astaire's contribution does. The highly sectionalized "Bojangles" doesn't hang together musically or choreographically. The join between Pan's choreography for the women's chorus and Astaire's dance with the shadows is arbitrary: the chorus just leaves, never to return. Even the soundtrack was divided between arranged sections for the orchestra and Borne's solo on a "jig piano," which apparently was never notated. In the end, "Bojangles" lacks coherence on all levels, perhaps one reason the number remains difficult to analyze.

The one element that should unify "Bojangles"—Astaire's blackface makeup—feels arbitrary. For most white Hollywood performers in the 1930s and '40s, donning blackface effected a fairly complete transformation of singing style and physical comportment. Judy Garland's blackface rendition of "Mr. Franklin D. Roosevelt Jones" from *Babes on Broadway* (1942) offers a typical example. But beyond his rather odd exit, wearing blackface effects no substantive change in Astaire's dancing. So why did Astaire do the number in blackface? "Bojangles" was among the last items added to and shot on *Swing Time*. The number is not listed in any budget and first appears in a script dated after shooting had already commenced.[5] Apparently, it was not part of Astaire's initial work on the dances for the film.[6] After all the book scenes had been completed, production closed down for a week of rehearsal on "Bojangles" and Astaire and Rogers's final dance to "Never Gonna Dance." Judging from their work patterns on other films, Astaire and Pan might have been making both routines at this late date. This may explain why "Never Gonna Dance" involves so much side-by-side walking and recycles steps from another number in the film. The song cue before and the dramatic scene after "Bojangles," both with Astaire in blackface, had been shot weeks earlier. Astaire was thus constrained by the demands of cinematic continuity when it came time to film "Bojangles," but he did not take his creative cues from the makeup he wore. In the end, the element of racial caricature, which under most circumstances would have shaped every element of the number, had little real effect on Astaire's contribution to an unsatisfactory whole.

In similar fashion, "Steppin' Out with My Baby" from *Easter Parade* betrays a sectional rather than unified structure. The number can be divided into two parts: 1) the opening through Astaire's partner combinations in turn with three women, each lasting for a full chorus of Berlin's tune, and 2) Astaire's two solo dance choruses, the second a special effects sequence juxtaposing Astaire in slow motion against a background of the chorus moving in real time. Astaire inherited "Steppin' Out" from Kelly and Alton, who were well along making the dance when Kelly was injured. Their plan included the dances with three partners, all of whom had already been cast. When Astaire came onto the film, one of the original three was replaced. Perhaps she was too tall. Astaire added the slow-motion sequence. It was an idea he had always wanted to try, and Metro had the technical means to make it happen and a desire to please this returning star who was saving the studio's investment in *Easter Parade*. Nothing connects the two parts of "Steppin' Out," and no larger idea binds the whole together. "Steppin' Out" is excessively busy and overly colored in visual and musical terms. Repeated viewing hints there might have been a continuing idea, particularly around the second woman Astaire dances with. Wearing a tight purple skirt with a high slit, she is featured again and again although the other two are not. She steals Astaire's cane and appears alone when others are partnered in the background during Alton's sections. In Astaire's special effects–driven section she disappears into the group. Like the boogie-woogie incursion in "Heat Wave," Astaire's slow-motion dance makes no reference to its surrounding context. Critics universally hailed the slow-motion dance as a highlight of the film. Their tendency to single out one element underlines the sectional nature of "Steppin' Out with My Baby," which does not hold together as routines completely in Astaire's control usually do.

The unity of musical, choreographic, and cinematic elements in a single routine is an important hallmark of Astaire's output and can be used as an index for his creative control. This chapter examines three extraordinarily unified routines from three successive films. Astaire created this triptych in an eighteen-month period spent working at two studios under three different production units. He is the consistent creative figure. Hermes Pan officially worked on two of the three. These standout dance numbers—none include singing—from *The Barkleys of Broadway* (1949), *Three Little Words* (1950), and *Let's Dance* (1950) all deal directly or indirectly with the jazz and popular music transition of the immediate postwar years. The jazz musicians heard and briefly seen in "Bouncin' the Blues" from *Barkleys* aptly represent a common career path among white swing musicians, who found work in the studios after the dance bands began to fold. Astaire created a routine that effectively used these players, a new creative resource on studio lots, to explore the rhythmic values of bebop, the cutting-edge jazz development of the day. In "Mr. and Mrs. Hoofer at Home," a stage-bound dance with the versatile Vera-Ellen from *Three Little Words,* Astaire used sharp shifts in musical style to tell a danced narrative. André Previn's score captures the precarious state of popular music in the film musical on the cusp of the 1950s and also taps into the young composer and pianist's still new exploration of jazz. The "Ad Lib Dance" from *Let's Dance* is a singular masterpiece among Astaire's solos, all but lost in a forgotten film (one of only four of Astaire's studio films yet to be released on DVD).[7] An unusual satirical number, the "Ad Lib Dance" deconstructs and destroys the musical, dramatic, and cinematic world of the band pic, for years a realm within which Astaire had moved with maximum freedom. Here he bids farewell to the nightclub in grand style by way of musical in-jokes and frequently violent actions. All three of these routines adopt a fairly radical strategy: none is built on a song. As a result, Astaire's firm grasp of musical form comes to the fore, showing the varied ways he could use musical means to make meaning within his primary creative realm, the filmed dance routine.

Charles Emge's *Down Beat* review of *The Barkleys of Broadway* ended with a section subtitled "Some Spark": "At one point the sound track comes briefly to life (the rehearsal sequence in the nearly empty theater) with spark supplied by a small group that included Mel Powell, piano; Gus Bivona, clarinet; Clyde Hurley, trumpet; and Frankie Carlson, drums. That, of course, is Frankie who practically co-stars (unseen) with Astaire in one number."[8] This routine—"Bouncin' the Blues"— demonstrates Astaire's knowledge of jazz music making in the late 1940s. Astaire created the dance in collaboration with experienced white jazz musicians on staff at Metro whose own careers add perspective to the routine. The rhythmic content hints at Astaire's conversance with bebop drumming developments. "Blues" in the title expands the range of meaning for that word in Astaire's work. And production file evidence shows that, as with "Swing Trot," Astaire made sure this number reflecting his musical values was a production priority on *Barkleys*.

"Bouncin' the Blues" and "They Can't Take That Away from Me" were the first two numbers Astaire and Rogers tackled in the rehearsal hall and in front of the cameras. Both were added to *Barkleys* when Rogers replaced Garland. Neither had been planned earlier. "They Can't Take That Away from Me" seems a commonsense addition, made to satisfy fans of the couple from the 1930s. Here was a romantic song about "the memory of all that" that had been sung by Astaire to Rogers in *Shall We Dance* but had never been danced by the pair. "Bouncin' the Blues" offered a different type of nostalgia. It has a clear precursor in "I'll Be Hard to Handle," the couple's duo from *Roberta* that, in Arlene Croce's view, is "the number in which 'Fred and Ginger' became fixed screen deities."[9] As in that earlier routine, in "Bouncin' the Blues" Astaire and Rogers wear rehearsal clothes (pants in Rogers's case); the context is a casual (but polished) rehearsal; collaborating jazz musicians are on hand to provide the music; and the substance of the dance is shared rhythm making for all.

"Bouncin'" comes early in the film, in the scene where the producers of Josh and Dinah Barkley's hit Broadway show initiate a plan to hire an understudy for Dinah to prevent any potential argument between the quarrelsome couple from curtailing a long run. In the Garland script, this scene included two complete musical auditions. First, a girl named Pinkie was to perform the Gershwin standard "I Got Rhythm" while doing an eccentric dance. Next, the character Shirlene, who would be tapped as Dinah's understudy, was to do her "Café Number," a routine contextualized as Dinah's own specialty in the show. Had this plan remained unchanged, Shirlene would have posed a more substantial threat to the Barkleys' marriage. It's also unlikely Gene Kelly would have used "I Got Rhythm" as a solo in *An American in Paris*. In the Rogers script, only Shirlene is up for the position as understudy, and she's hired on the spot. Dinah cuts off her singing audition after barely a measure, and Shirlene (Gale Robbins) never does more than speak in the film. With the plot point of engaging an understudy for Dinah neatly dispatched, the scene could now conclude with the added "Bouncin' the Blues."[10] Everyone else exits, leaving Josh and Dinah alone on the stage. Josh says, "Alright, let's go," and the four musicians waiting in the pit launch into the number. No explanation for how or when the musicians entered the theater is given. While this dramatically unconvincing scene may seem unsatisfactory from the perspective of character and plot development, for the purposes of the film a quick setup for the tap routine that is the real meat of *Barkleys* was all that mattered. The lead-in for Astaire's brainchild "Bouncin' the Blues" offers a perfect example of how film musical plots function as "hangers" for the musical numbers that are the essence of the genre.

The jazz players in the pit are hardly seen and go uncredited in the film, but Emge, in typical *Down Beat* fashion, entered their names into the historical record. His list, likely garnered from studio contacts, is not entirely accurate. The brief shot of the quartet in the pit includes a rhythm trio—drums, piano, and stand-up bass—with a fourth figure positioned with his back to camera. The soundtrack features drums, piano, and clarinet, with an unknown sax player briefly heard as well. Powell, Bivona, and Carlson are surely present on the soundtrack. How these jazz players found their way onto the Metro lot is worth recounting. All were white swing-era professionals of a similar age who, when faced with the drought of band work in the postwar era, found steady employment in Hollywood. *Down Beat* highlighted this trend in several articles around the time *Barkleys* was in production. The security of a studio job—union scale was about $7,000 annually, and there were about four hundred positions available, mostly for string players— proved attractive to some jazz musicians who had lived through the grueling era of the traveling name bands and had the connections to get the limited slots on offer.[11]

Like many swing players, pianist and arranger Mel Powell (born 1923) started his professional career while still very young. Already a veteran band musician, he joined the Goodman group at age eighteen and was often featured as soloist and arranger for two years. (Skip Martin and Powell were both playing and arranging for Goodman for several months of 1941.) During the war, Powell worked with Raymond Scott at CBS, played in Glenn Miller's Army Air Force Band, and recorded in Paris with Django Reinhardt, rejoining Goodman briefly in 1945. In the immediate postwar years, Powell spent some time at the Hollywood studios—where he played on "Bouncin' "—before heading back to school, studying composition at Yale with Paul Hindemith. Powell remained mostly in the realm of art music and music education until his death in 1998. Clarinet and saxophone player Gus Bivona (born 1915) had a similar career trajectory. A professional from his midteens, Bivona played with Bunny Berigan, Teddy Powell, Goodman, Jan Savitt, Les Brown, Tommy Dorsey, and Bob Crosby. He spent the war leading his own Naval Air Force Band. Bivona joined Metro's staff in 1947 and worked in Los Angeles, often with Steve Allen on television, for the remainder of his career. Frankie Carlson (born 1914) was the original drummer with Woody Herman's first band—the Band That Plays the Blues—from 1937 to 1942. After the war Carlson generally stayed around Los Angeles, playing in film, television, and record studios. He was a regular contributor to the jazz-heavy score for television's *Dr. Kildare,* played with Stan Kenton's experimental jazz groups in the 1960s, and even sat in with the Los Angeles Philharmonic. Powell, Bivona, and Carlson all had the opportunity to transition into reliable studio jobs, something their African American peers could not do. (Drummer Lee Young, with a contract at Columbia, was described in 1948 as "the brother of tenorman *[sic]* Lester and the only Negro musician to hold a staff ork [orchestra] job here in the movie business.")[12] White jazz veterans were on the lot and available to Astaire, who must have cast them as if they were contract players from the Metro pool. Carlson may have been the link. He knew Astaire from their recent collaboration on the soundtrack for "Drum Crazy." Given the complexity of "Bouncin' the Blues," it is unlikely Astaire assembled the number without serious rehearsal with the players, and Carlson in particular. Astaire was known at times to rehearse with drummers only, and the first third of "Bouncin' " is solely for drums and taps.

The earliest documentation for "Bouncin' the Blues" is a piano score by Harry Warren marked "instrumental medium bounce."[13] The number was never intended to have a lyric. Warren provided a thirty-two-bar AABA instrumental, with a bass line in the A phrases that resembles a walking boogie-woogie bass, perhaps the connection with "Blues" in the title. The chords in the bridge are quite sophisticated, especially for Warren. In the end Astaire used almost nothing from Warren's offering. All that survived in recognizable form was Warren's opening right-hand lick. Otherwise, the music is substantially reworked on every level. Table 4 diagrams the musical form of "Bouncin' the Blues," including the sounding contribution made by the dancers.

The unusual musical structure of "Bouncin' the Blues" is built on a series of eight-count phrases filled with rhythmic breaks as complex as anything Astaire ever made. The routine kicks off with an eight-count drum lead-in. A series of eight eight-count phrases ensues, most divided

TABLE 4 MUSICAL STRUCTURE OF "BOUNCIN' THE BLUES" (*The Barkleys of Broadway*)

		Counts 1–4	Drums on Count 4	Counts 5–8	Drums on Count 8
Intro		Drums only		Drums only	
	1	Ride cymbal/contrasting taps		Ride cymbal/contrasting taps	X
	2	Ride cymbal/contrasting taps		Tap break	X
	3	Ride cymbal/contrasting taps		Tap break	X
	4	Ride cymbal/contrasting taps		Tap break	X
	5	Syncopated pattern shared by drums and taps		Tap break	X
	6	Syncopated pattern in drums/contrasting taps		Tap break (alternating cramp rolls)	X
	7	Syncopated pattern shared by drums and taps (cowbell)	X	Tap break (rhythm x)	X
	8	Tap break (rhythm x)	X	Tap break (rhythm x as transition)/drums set up entrance of group	XX
Chorus 1	A	Piano w/melody in right hand		Tap break	X
	A	Piano comping chords		Tap break	XX
	B	Piano w/soloing right hand		Tap break	XX
				Tap break	XX

Section	Part	Description		
	A	Piano, clarinet play melody in unison	Tap break	R
Chorus 2	A	Clarinet on melody	Tap break	X
	A	Clarinet on melody	Tap break	R
	B	Clarinet, tenor sax, piano solo in Dixieland vein	Tap break	XX
	A	Clarinet, tenor sax, piano solo in Dixieland vein	Tap break	XX
		Larger band enters, continues to end		
Coda	1	Transition	Tap break	
	2	Riff y	Riff y	
	3	Riff y	Riff y	
	4	Riff z	Riff z	
	5	Riff z	X	

NOTE: Each row represents eight (dancer's) counts, divided into two groups of four. X = a single "bomb" dropped somewhere in the final count; XX = a double "bomb" dropped somewhere in final count; R = a press roll starts somewhere in final count, carrying over into start of next phrase.

into four-count pairs, all for Carlson on drums and Astaire and Rogers tapping (usually the same rhythms). This is the section Emge described as "Frankie co-star[ring] (unseen) with Astaire." Predictably, Emge ignores Rogers's presence, but his characterization gets to the heart of the creative matter nonetheless. There's an element of trading fours here, although no consistent call-and-response pattern emerges. Several rhythmic motifs running through the entire number are introduced in this opening section for drums and taps. Carlson's input must have been considerable, as many innovative rhythms are brought into Astaire's work for the first time here. Carlson uses a ride cymbal at the outset that projects a post-swing rhythmic drive associated with bebop drumming. Quite often taps and drums share identical, heavily syncopated patterns, often without any clear beat supporting the whole. This sort of discontinuous beat marks another element of bebop drumming incorporated into "Bouncin.'" Adding to the general lack of continuity is the persistent accenting, by drums and dancers alike, of the last beat in each eight count. These bombs—to use contemporary bebop parlance—are actually placed just after the final beat, before the downbeat: they are not square but swing. Similarly placed bombs prove an important rhythmic element to the end. Later in the number Carlson embellishes his bombs with added hits and short, tense rolls. Most of the time, the dancers' rhythmic figures come to a close on the final beat bombs, leaving a brief silence after them and chopping up the rhythm considerably. Astaire and Rogers dance side by side in complete unison throughout the opening section (with one brief exception for some alternating cramp rolls). In fact, until the midpoint of the second chorus, when the couple moves into closed partner position for some swing moves, the dance they do together could easily have been done by Astaire alone.

After the long first section of nothing but rhythm, the other members of the small ensemble make their entrances. No tune per se is heard, although the melodic idea used in the A phrases finds its origin in Warren's tune, which must have been circulating among the players as a starting point of sorts. A sixty-four-bar AABA chorus is played twice, the second time modulating upward a step. Despite what on the surface might appear to be a standard form, only close, repeated, analytical listening reveals the structure of these choruses behind the onrush of the music. It would have been uncatchable by a theater audience in 1949, accustomed as they were to dance numbers in film musicals being built on recognizable tunes. "Bouncin' the Blues" makes no concessions to the need for a tune at all. Bebop players took the form and harmonic changes from known popular songs, such as "I Got Rhythm," and built new, less audibly apparent structures above them, in the process sometimes obscuring the comfortable patterns of popular song form that had organized most music making in the swing era. The musical structure of "Bouncin' the Blues" is similarly opaque. The first chorus uses mainly piano, with the flighty little tune tossed off like an improvisation. Powell doesn't bother repeating it for the second A phrase—he comps chords for four then lays out for a tap break—so it never sticks in the ear. Bivona doubles with Powell in octaves on the melody for the final A of the first chorus, to a pseudo-bebop effect. The group breaks out in some pseudo-Dixieland during the second half of the second chorus, with Bivona playing an embellished line in the upper register and the unknown tenor sax player taking the tune for the longest stretch without a tap break (during which Astaire and Rogers do their partnering swing moves).

The unlikely sound and style of "Bouncin' the Blues" suggest a particular jazz analogue: a recording from April 1947 called "Boppin' the Blues" by Lucky Thompson and His Lucky Seven, an interracial group that captures the multifaceted nature of jazz in Los Angeles in the late 1940s. Several musicians heard on "Boppin' the Blues" had already or would eventually come into contact with Astaire: Lee Young, who played on the soundtrack for "One for My Baby," on drums; Neal Hefti on trumpet; and Barney Kessel on guitar. Beyond the obvious connection at the level of title, "Boppin'" and "Bouncin'" are for similarly small groups, begin with short drum solos, ride on cymbal-centered "modern" beats, include rippling, single-line piano solos in a bop idiom, and end on an unexpected bomb. The similar opening drum solos even hint at a modeling of the film routine on the just released record (see example 6). At the same session Thompson and his players recorded a track called "From Dixieland to Bop," which, like "Bouncin' the Blues," begins with a stuttering drum solo and, as the title suggests, moves between the traditional sounds of Dixieland and the modern approach of bop, adapting the same melodic material to both sensibilities. "Bouncin'" does this as well. While no direct connection can be drawn between the players on "Bouncin'" and Thompson's group, all these jazzmen were circulating in Hollywood in the late 1940s. Astaire's "Bouncin' the Blues" finds its jazz context in this same small combo milieu.[14]

The bulk of "Bouncin' the Blues" uses a drastically pared-down sound for an MGM musical, and at the coda a larger swing band makes its perhaps obligatory entrance. Using a jazz combo for a major musical

EXAMPLE 6. Drum solo openings of "Bouncin' the Blues" and "Boppin' the Blues."

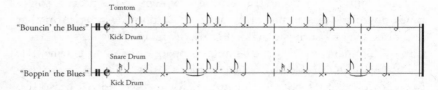

number decidedly went against the grain at a studio where musical tastes ran toward the "colossally gigantically tremendous," as the record reviewer in *Down Beat* opined of a contemporary MGM score.[15] Still, the brief big band coda in a riff-based swing style doesn't succeed in wiping out the tight, casual, modern sound that dominates the arrangement. After "Bouncin' the Blues" was filmed, the option of altering the soundtrack was discussed. An undated document gives specific instructions to the music department: "Music: Sweeten 'BOUNCIN' THE BLUES' from entrance of Band on."[16] As there are no violins heard in "Bouncin' the Blues" and no record of a second scoring session on the number, efforts to alter the arrangement were apparently scrapped.

Unexpected accents and a discontinuous beat were central aspects of bop drumming. Astaire works this rhythmic sensibility into the abrupt close of the routine. Astaire and Rogers take their time exiting, combining baby steps forward with a cutesy pose as they gradually move toward the edge of the proscenium. On the final bump from the band, Rogers reaches out and yanks the curtain to cover them both. All at once the dance is done. This sharp move falls on count four—that same beat before the downbeat where Carlson kept dropping bombs—shutting the number off in the middle of an eight-count phrase, yet another unexpected aspect of Astaire's bop routine "Bouncin' the Blues."

If "Bouncin' the Blues" explored postwar jazz changes, "Mr. and Mrs. Hoofer at Home" took up the popular music quandary facing Hollywood musicals at the close of the 1940s. The genre of the musical had always drawn on popular music, but with the long dominance of the swing bands clearly over and no trends for the future evident, where was the sound of the present to be found? A genuine irony attending all the musical choices in *Three Little Words* was the setting of this biopic about songwriters Kalmar and Ruby in a historical vacuum, where neither of the World Wars nor the Depression troubles the rise of the team across what can only be assumed to be the first half of the century. For a historical film *Three Little Words* is laughably vague about history. "Mr. and Mrs. Hoofer" is supposedly a vaudeville act performed for President Woodrow Wilson, placing the scene somewhere between 1913 and 1920, and yet the stage set for the number sports all the ruffles and prints of the late 1940s. Vera-Ellen's costume, hair, makeup, and silhouette are also à la mode for the film's release date. (With Astaire fashion doesn't matter so much; he wore similar clothing for fifty years.)

"Mr. and Mrs. Hoofer" tells a simple story. After a husband returns home to his wife, they quarrel, make up, eat dinner, briefly play football with their baby, and then exit for a night on the town, twirling offstage through a paper wall instead of using the door. It's a brilliant routine that lets both dancers be themselves. Vera-Ellen does some acrobatic flips and extra-high kicks, Astaire does a nifty prop trick lassoing an old-style telephone, and there's plenty of tap dancing along the way. The tone is relentlessly upbeat, almost hyperactive at times. Musically, "Mr. and Mrs. Hoofer" offers up a compendium of style options for the Hollywood musical, and since the four-minute routine is not tied to any tune, composer André Previn was free to work with Astaire and Pan, creating a series of melodies—most in generic song forms—that expressed the simple narrative of the scene. Previn, who was twenty at the time, also did the orchestration, which demonstrates his precocious mastery of the Hollywood and pop idioms of the day. Reviewing the musical styles heard in "Mr. and Mrs. Hoofer" here serves useful as a control of sorts for the "Ad Lib Dance," which Astaire made for his next film. Several of the musical tropes heard in the former are included in the latter, which takes a decidedly less earnest tone. The musical structure of "Mr. and Mrs. Hoofer at Home" is outlined below.

20 counts   Introduction

Her (studio orchestra, strings, and flutes)

16 counts	A
16 counts	A
16 counts	B
8 counts	A (interrupted by Astaire's entrance)

Him (big band, swinging)

16 counts	a + a
8 counts	vamp
16 counts	b + b
16 counts	c

| 16 counts | d + d |
| 20 counts | Transition |

Rumba Phone Call (four 8 counts)
Her (as at start)

16 counts	A
16 counts	A
16 counts	B
8 counts	Transition

Her (in waltz time, strings only)

8 bars	A
8 bars	A
8 bars	A

Boogie-woogie Dinner (three 12-bar blues choruses)

| 16 counts | Transition (unaccompanied tap break initiating faster tempo) |

Them (driving swing, tune for BB phrase borrowed from the "Jukebox Dance" in *Broadway Melody of 1940*)

16 counts	AA
16 counts	AA
16 counts	BB
16 counts	AA
16 counts	AA
16 counts	BB
28 counts	AA and close

"Mr. and Mrs. Hoofer" opens with Vera-Ellen alone, straightening up the house. She dances to an AABA melody I call "Her." (There are almost no archival materials for this film.) Scored for strings, flutes, and a solo trumpet, this is studio orchestra music, a delicate and feminine sound that nonetheless matches Vera-Ellen's full-out style. The conventional song form is audible immediately even if the melody is instrumentally rather than vocally conceived. Previn was chiefly a composer rather than a songwriter, and it shows throughout this routine. His melodic ideas deploy various instruments idiomatically and hint at his recent engagement with jazz piano.

Previn was almost surely Astaire's rehearsal pianist on this project. Una Rasey, MGM staff trumpeter, told Levinson that Astaire was especially picky on *Three Little Words,* going through five rehearsal pianists in two weeks.[17] Perhaps Astaire's dissatisfaction was twofold, with the pianists MGM had to offer and with the Kalmar and Ruby song catalog. Previn was still a boy wonder on the lot, and *Three Little Words* was his first musical as music director. Astaire ended up dancing more to new music by Previn than to the old songs that were purportedly the reason for the film.

The final A phrase of "Her" is interrupted by the entrance of Astaire to a new tune—"Him"—scored for a swinging big band. There's no song form here, just a string of eight-count melodic ideas, some drawing on "Her," but they come and go so freely that the connections do not stand out. The change in orchestration, particularly the prominent rhythm section, marks the entrance of the masculine half of the couple.

After both dancers have been introduced by way of contrasting tunes and instrumental forces, the phone rings (with a Mahler-esque trumpet fanfare from Previn to boot). Astaire answers and the sound of an exotic rumba insinuates any number of possibilities about who may be on the line. Previn sits on one chord, building up a texture of Latin percussion and a snaky flute. Vera-Ellen eavesdrops on the call, Latin motion in her hips signaling jealously or just suspicion. The long rumba craze—sent up in the 1940 hit tune "Six Lessons from Madame La Zonga" and still current enough to provide a running joke in the 1948 film *A Date with Judy*—is evoked, then cut off when Vera-Ellen abruptly disconnects the call. This brand of Latin sensuality would soon be a relic with the arrival of the hotter rhythms of the mambo in the early 1950s and the cha-cha-cha in the late 1950s. (Astaire included a raucous cha-cha-cha in "Too Bad" from *Silk Stockings,* the first time he partnered with Barrie Chase.)

A brief quarrel follows, with the music mickey mousing the couple's mimed anger. They reconcile to three successive A phrases of "Her" played in waltz time by a mass of strings, the sound of the future. Waltzes would return in the 1950s after the virtual disappearance of triple meter in the swing era, and the sound of sweet pop strings would find a permanent place in popular arranging with the work of Weston and others. The romantic dance Astaire and Vera-Ellen fall into carries not a trace of parody, sentimentality, or, it must be said, sensuality.

Having made up, the couple sits down to eat to the sound of three boogie-woogie blues choruses. The shift from waltz to boogie-woogie is immediate, again without a trace of parody. Previn cleverly matches the action at the dinner table—such as Vera-Ellen throwing a sugar cube into Astaire's coffee cup—while sustaining the driving energy of the boogie-woogie beat and texture. The flexibility of this style is put on brilliant display, but, like the rumba, it was a music whose time was past in 1950. And despite all the fun Astaire and Vera-Ellen have adding more rhythmic layers with their silverware, this dip into boogie-woogie would have sounded out of date to original audiences.

The boogie-woogie dinner ends with an unaccompanied side-by-side tap passage that accelerates the tempo—a strategy reaching back to *The Gay Divorcee*—and sets up a final musical style. Previn contributes yet another new tune—"Them"—which is, again, built on readily heard song forms, a sixty-four-bar AABA chorus that modulates up a step on the repeat. The B phrase quotes directly from the music for the "Jukebox Dance," a similarly virtuoso tap routine.[18] Using the snippet here, in a roughly analogous situation with a similarly skilled partner, was likely Astaire's idea. He was the only collaborator on "Mr. and Mrs. Hoofer" who had also worked on the "Jukebox Dance," and it would be just like him to demonstrate the B phrase at the piano in the heat of the creative process. Previn was just getting into jazz at the time but had already experienced notable success. The A phrase of "Them" is reminiscent of Previn's contemporary jazz compositions "California Clipper" and "Mulholland Drive," both among his earliest recordings as a pianist and combo leader.[19] All these Previn compositions favor abstract, busy, complicated lines, and it's not difficult to imagine the piano original behind Previn's brilliantly orchestrated "Them." Previn's early and formative model was Art Tatum, but his playing also betrayed modern trends that reveal an interest in the advanced harmonic and melodic flights of bebop. The speed and gestural quality of "Them" suggests that Previn brought these varied musical passions into the rehearsal hall where he worked with (and for) Astaire.

"Mr. and Mrs. Hoofer at Home" demanded wide stylistic range from the dancers and exploited the versatility of its composer/orchestrator, whose original score is a particularly rich exploration of popular music and jazz styles. Although no single tune holds it all together, music and dance combine to tell the story, with various musical styles, old and new, used as transparent signifiers. The routine is a virtuoso package: fast-paced, good-natured, and professionally—indeed, flawlessly—made. Previn said of *Three Little Words*, "The finished film was pleasant and mild, and it made money."[20] In studio terms, the product sold. "Mr. and Mrs. Hoofer" takes no risks: it's designed only to please. In the more experimental "Ad Lib Dance," Astaire employed many of these same musical styles in a reflexive manner for a solo routine that is markedly less regular in its musical forms, in the process exploring both how music activates the dancer and the current state of the nightclub culture that had supported popular music and dance for the preceding several decades.

Let's Dance opened at the Paramount Theater in New York City on 29 November 1950 for a three-week stand with a stage show featuring the Jimmy Dorsey Orchestra, headliner Nat "King" Cole, and, as added attractions, comedian Mickey Deems and the Tong Brothers dance team.[21] None of this could have hoped to upstage Astaire's standout solo in this forgotten film. *Variety* described the number tersely: "Astaire spotlights a rhythm dance around a piano for his terp topper."[22] Bosley Crowther in the *New York Times* was a bit more specific: "Mr. Astaire, who is the greatest dancer on the screen, does a solo exhibition of terpsichorean gymnastics in a night club sequence that is just incredible. With effortless grace he glides all over a piano and over the backs of chairs. . . . Altogether Mr. Astaire is a fascinating artist."[23]

Few Astaire solos reveal his mastery of musical form and allusion so completely. As was the case for a handful of his routines, Astaire shared the composer credit on the "Ad Lib Dance" with those closest to his creative process: his rehearsal pianist Tommy Chambers, who appears on-screen and is called by name in the scene, and orchestrator Van Cleave, who was available to Astaire because the film was a Paramount product. Van Cleave first worked with Astaire on "Puttin' on the Ritz" for Paramount's *Blue Skies.* At the dancer's request, Metro negotiated a one-week loan-out so the arranger could do "Steppin' Out with My Baby" in *Easter Parade,* more evidence that Astaire had strong feelings about arrangers. The credited songwriter on *Let's Dance* was sidestepped entirely: Frank Loesser's musical input on the number was apparently nil. The musical structure of the "Ad Lib Dance" is outlined below. (Mueller calls this routine "Piano Dance," but Paramount production files use the title "Ad Lib Dance.")

Intro	10 bars	piano
Waltz chorus	8 bars	piano
Waltz chorus	8 bars + 2-bar extension	+ strings
Bluesy Stride	Four 16-bar choruses (Astaire dances on, around, and in grand piano)	

Transition	8 bars (Four big chords from band matching Astaire's poses on lid of grand piano, glissando from Chambers matches Astaire's move to upright piano)	
Piano Boogie	Four 12-bar choruses (Astaire solos on upright piano)	
Riff chorus [A]	16 bars	
Riff chorus [B]	16 bars	
Tiger Rag	16 bars (Astaire plays seven descending glissandos on keyboard with his right foot, ends with release of cats from inside the piano)	
Riff chorus [C]	16 bars	1st chair fall (glissando in band matches each chair)
Riff chorus	16 bars	2nd and 3rd chairs [A1, C2]
Extension	6 bars	4th chair [C2, A1]
Exit [D]	8 bars	exits on 5th chair

The "Ad Lib Dance" begins with Astaire's request for "something that'll send me." His nightclub boss looks to the pianist and says, "Tommy, send him," and Chambers proceeds to play a waltz. Incredulous, Astaire cries out, "Oh no, no, not that . . . a waltz!" But Chambers plays on. Astaire goes to the piano as if called to ballet class and executes a string of ballet moves as if at the barre. The parodic tone of the "Ad Lib Dance" starts here: Astaire's first two ballet moves—an arabesque and a grand plié—are done with mock winces of pain, completely unprecedented in Astaire's work. He had never before made reference to his body in this way: it's the first suggestion he might be mortal. Soupy strings, the only nondiegetic instruments heard in the arrangement, enter the soundtrack during the waltz section as well. But then Chambers drops into a medium-tempo bluesy groove on the piano, with a stride left hand and tremolos in the right. Astaire responds physically and facially, expressing delight. Piece by piece a big band, briefly seen early on, amplifies Chambers's piano lead. This is the music that "sends" Astaire. The juxtaposition of musical opposites provides an early key to the nature of this routine: lush strings playing a sweet waltz cue a parody of ballet moves; Chambers and the band playing a bluesy sixteen-bar chorus give Astaire the chance to make some rhythm in the breaks or lay out while Chambers takes a solo. Once silenced, the strings are never heard from again: those ten bars were expensive to record given how little the twenty-two string players called on the session actually played.[24] The slow stride groove grows in strength with the addition, chorus by chorus, of characteristic big band sounds: low-register clarinet, growling trumpets, then the full band. As the texture thickens, Astaire's actions grow more and more surprising. He uses the four stride choruses to methodically explore all sides and surfaces of the grand piano Chambers is playing. He slides his legs and lower torso underneath the instrument, hits the curved case wall, then leaps *into* the instrument, suspending himself between lid and soundboard, playing bumps on the bass strings with his foot and screaming with pleasure. It's a bizarre moment in Astaire's work. The craziness continues as the camera angle changes and Astaire suspends himself upside down, his legs thrown over the curved part of the raised lid like a gymnast on a bar. The only space left to explore is the top of the open lid. Astaire swings himself up and over, dancing a short tap break where the piano's music desk would be. A series of exaggerated poses follow, all suggesting this is all meant to be a big joke. Astaire indulges in a broadly stated silliness quite unusual for his solo numbers. But the silliness is over once he slides down the piano lid—to an accompanying glissando from Chambers—and moves to an upright piano located to screen left of the grand.

At the upright Astaire launches into a piano solo, his first in a decade. (The last time he played piano in a film was *Broadway Melody of 1940*.) Taking up the already passé boogie-woogie style for the first time on-screen, Astaire performs a solo that is interesting on two levels: as a display of his keyboard technique in an unexpected idiom and as an example of piano playing as a cinematic subject. Many 1940s films featured keyboard players, from Hazel Scott and José Iturbi to Oscar Levant and even Gracie Allen, who played with a one-finger technique. An array of framing options was developed to inject visual variety into a static instrument and highlight the player's hands and body. Astaire, as always, keeps it simple, emphasizing the authenticity of his performance, even holding his hands up to the camera before striking the keys as if to say, "Yes, I'm actually playing." His solo contrasts a serious act of musical skill with the preceding, decidedly silly dance beside, under, in, and on a piano. The embracing theme of this routine—"Piano Dance" is a good name for it—is explored from a new angle in Astaire's piano solo, where playing the piano can be read as dancing and the showmanship of popular musicianship is again thrown into relief.

The next and final section of the dance returns to the unpredictable spirit of the opening with an added edge of violence. Having played one piano and danced all over another, Astaire proceeds to mistreat both. The upright comes in for abuse first. The board covering the strings has been removed, and to fill an empty break Astaire grabs the damper bar and pounds out a syncopated fill on the strings. Getting the desired effect on the soundtrack was, no doubt, a tricky piece of sound engineering. Astaire then proceeds to kick the instrument—he'd done this before but here he does it with ferocity—and slam the lid. Violence was not normally part of Astaire's persona. Throughout the "Ad Lib Dance" he takes positive glee in mistreating the materials of music making that had served him for decades. It's among the few times Astaire let what Cagney called "the hoodlum in him" into his dancing. While standing atop the upright, Astaire does a parodic time step (a generic tap step he almost never used) and daintily raises his pant legs a bit (a joking move taken from black male lindy hoppers).

Moving to the grand, rudely pushing Chambers out of the way, Astaire stands on the music desk and plays a downward glissando with his right foot. The band, getting the reference without missing a beat, launches into "Tiger Rag," one of the best-known jazz tunes of the time. Crawford and Magee rank it second among pre-1942 jazz standards on record, but it was a relic by 1950. Astaire follows the band's lead and plays a total of seven smears with his foot. By this point audience members who knew syncopated dance music—virtually anyone who had lived through the war years and listened to popular music—would have been roaring with laughter. Paramount paid for the joke: the royalty for "Tiger Rag" amounted to $2,500.[25] Astaire, trapped by the music and making funny faces, finally just stops playing the smear. The resulting silence is filled with the terrified meows of a small group of cats, domesticated tigers who come roaring out of the piano itself, running between Astaire's legs and offscreen to God knows where (see figure 17).

If we didn't think this was a parody before, we now know it is, and from this point on the real destruction begins. Astaire kicks the piano stick out from under the lid. It drops with a bang. He flips over the remaining lid piece and leaps to the bench and then the floor. These acts

FIGURE 17. Cats come roaring out of the piano at the climax of "Tiger Rag" in the "Ad Lib Dance" from *Let's Dance*.

of brutality—no musician treats an instrument this way—occur in startlingly empty breaks where he would normally tap out sophisticated broken rhythms. The effect is as crude as Astaire ever allowed himself to be. Upon reaching the floor he immediately drops to his knees as the band plays more and more loudly. Astaire mounts an armless dining chair, one foot on its back, and slowly rides the chair to the floor. The chair bit, like every move Astaire ever made, is timed precisely. He seems to be in control of how fast objects, himself included, fall to earth. (Pan remembered the chair fall as his idea.[26] An identical move occurs in the 1948 Bing Crosby film *The Emperor Waltz* during a similarly parodic, and very funny, dance.) When Astaire does the chair move—it happens a total of five times—the band plays a smear referencing those just heard in "Tiger Rag." Physical action (falling chairs), musical gesture (downward smears), and jazz history ("Tiger Rag") come together in this final section of the "Ad Lib Dance," a sequence devoted to leaving the place a wreck and exiting in style. The old showbiz imperative to "kill the people" comes to mind. Astaire tops himself again and again in this routine, designed, as it is, to elicit continually mounting reactions from the audience.

But, crucially, this is not the anarchic destruction of the Marx Brothers. Rather, it is a skilled professional who is aggressively, even gleefully, smashing up the tools of his trade. Everything Astaire attacks—the pianos, the well-known tune, the nightclub itself—represents the world of popular music as he had known it during his creative life as a dancemaker. Obviously there's nothing ad-libbed about the "Ad Lib Dance." The structure of the music, especially in the final section, is finely matched to each physical action. It's the content of these actions that stand out from Astaire's other work. At the core of the "Ad Lib Dance" lies an ambivalent attitude toward the very music and dance materials that had sustained Astaire's work to this point. Structural patterns in both music and dance are subtly unpredictable. For example, the smears in "Tiger Rag" and the smears for the falling chairs are placed similarly in rhythmic terms within the bar, but they follow different logics. The former follow the tune, while the latter are dictated by the space of the set and the placement of the chairs. The audible logic of the routine's sixteen-bar strains—organized usually in AABA patterns—is regular at first and then breaks down near the end, where a single confusing six-bar phrase leads into a quick exit of just eight bars. Riff-based swing choruses are usually regular in their phrasing. Consistent organizing patterns—like AABA song form or the twelve-bar blues—help players, dancers, and listeners alike in their analogous roles as the makers and active or passive consumers of swing. Here, in a specialty routine, the unfolding of musical events is anything but predictable, and the content on every level is continually surprising.

Running through the entire "Ad Lib Dance" is a simultaneously tongue-in-cheek and desperate attitude toward jazz history, jazz spaces, and the piano as a jazz instrument. (Substituting "swing" or "dance" for "jazz" in the preceding sentence also works.) Cats escaping from a piano on which a dancer plays "Tiger Rag" with his foot is straight out of vaudeville, but Astaire isn't a comedian; he's a serious dancemaker. The overexcited, overstimulated tone of the whole routine—from his primal scream inside the piano onward—suggests creative exhaustion, reaching for new ideas in a well-worn environment at a time when musical forces external to the filmmaking process were no longer providing stimulus for dance making. As shown in the previous chapter on the twelve-bar blues, Astaire consistently renewed the musical content of his dances by drawing on new trends in popular music and jazz. In the "Ad Lib Dance" there are no such new sources to draw upon. Instead, all the references are to the past, with Astaire casting each aside as he proceeds to knock over the nightclub and close up the pianos. Perhaps the anxiety of the immediate post-swing era is driving some of the fury of the "Ad Lib Dance." The background for *Let's Dance* was increasingly disappearing from the real world and Hollywood alike. Elaborate nightclub floorshows were a rarity by 1949 when this scene was made. The introduction of a 30 percent entertainment tax in 1944 and the postwar downturn in nightlife generally, spurred on by the arrival of television, spelled the end of lavish nightclub entertainment. Smaller, cheaper cabaret acts filled the void left by dancing chorus girls and big bands.[27] *Let's Dance* was among the last Hollywood films set in this disappearing nightclub world. Tellingly, Astaire and Hutton's comical cowboy nightclub routine "Oh, Them Dudes" is set in a Western bar where they see city folk doing square dances on a television. The pair begin their dance by drawing their guns and shooting out the picture tube.

On the level of the production process, the "Ad Lib Dance" squarely fits the pattern of Astaire's earlier work. Three major routines for Astaire were in the works for *Let's Dance*. He took up the "Ad Lib Dance" first, and it was the only one to be fully realized. The other two—an elaborate fairy tale number and a partner routine involving special effects—were ambitious, expensive ideas that made it into the film only in drastically reduced forms. Concerns about cost are evident everywhere in the production files for *Let's Dance*. Paramount wanted to make this Technicolor film as efficiently as they could, investing as little as possible in the sets and effects while still creating a first-class picture. The "Ad Lib Dance" was the sort of routine designed to succeed in this budgetary environment. The solo was neatly shaped around a set used for multiple purposes in the film, similar to the satisfying solos Astaire created in his two films for Columbia, where he also used spaces built for book scenes as a place for dance making. The "Ad Lib Dance" required three days' rehearsal on the set, followed by three days' filming. Initial budgets provided two days of rehearsal and two days to shoot, and there was some concern about the two extra days Astaire used. However, his privileged place in the production hierarchy provided for a reasonable amount of extra time, and Paramount executives knew from experience that Astaire was a reliable and efficient filmmaker. The "Ad Lib Dance" exemplifies how Astaire's creative methods and interests fit comfortably into a variety of studio contexts, and suggests that numbers like this one reveal Astaire's core identity as a creator most directly.

"Bouncin' the Blues," "Mr. and Mrs. Hoofer at Home," and the "Ad Lib Dance" were screened in succession at the 1973 Film Society of Lincoln Center tribute to Astaire. (Astaire helped select the routines shown at the event.) All three reveal Astaire's skill at making complex music-oriented dances without the structural net of a song. All three also exemplify studio-era musical filmmaking at its best: quickly and efficiently made from the collaboration of skilled individuals, the films are polished in every technical and aesthetic aspect and continually entertaining for the viewer. And behind the trio lurks the unanswered question of where popular music, jazz, and the film musical might go in the dynamic postwar era.

CHAPTER 9

"You play and I'll dance"

In 1935 Astaire gave an interview to *The Chicago Defender,* an African American newspaper with national reach. Like all black newspapers, the *Defender* followed entertainment news closely: it was an area where black individuals excelled on the national stage. Prominent use of black performers in "The Carioca" suggested to some in the African American community that Astaire's future films might provide further openings for black song-and-dance talent on the big screen. Going to the source, the *Defender*'s reporter wanted to know if Astaire's ascendant star promised more possibilities for "Race" performers.

FRED ASTAIRE TELLS RACE DANCERS TO BE ORIGINAL

"Flying Down to Rio," RKO's big 1933 sensation, did two things for the Race. It gave Etta Moten her big chance as the singer of "Carioca" and showed that Race dancers could not only master Fred Astaire's most intricate steps but add considerable individuality to them. Although sepia steppers did not get an opportunity to do the "Continental" in his recent *Gay Divorcee,* he declares that in some future film he will again include them. Incidentally, he advises Race dance acts to create rather than fall into the ruts.

"Eternal practice and constant creative work is the price of success in dancing," according to Fred Astaire, the wing-footed star currently appearing in RKO-Radio Pictures musical romance, *Roberta,* with Irene Dunne and Ginger Rogers.

Astaire has been dancing for more than 20 years, and he works harder today than ever he has before. Harder, because each achievement gives him something to top.

"One cannot stand still, either literally or figuratively, and stay at the pinnacle as a dancer," Astaire states emphatically. "And to go backward is to start the swift toboggan that leads to oblivion. There is only one direction to go—forward. And that means constant creative work.

"One simply can't get to the top or stay there just by mastering a lot of intricate steps and routines," Astaire said earnestly. "You have to create. To think up new stuff and perfect it. I wouldn't last long in pictures, or on the stage, if I kept doing the same dances over and over again.

"The creative work is the most difficult, as well as the most interesting phase of dancing. Naturally, it is woven in with the practice so it helps to keep that part of the work from becoming routine drudgery. I mean that new steps are evolved from experimenting in practice and the regular workouts stimulate fresh ideas."[1]

Astaire comes off as surprisingly voluble in this, his only known interview with the black press. His emphasis on creation and practice reinforce the image of Astaire presented in the previous chapters as a disciplined maker of dances, obsessed with finding "fresh ideas." But the advice he gives could hardly be taken at face value by aspiring black dancers in Hollywood. Opportunities were too few and too far between: there was never a chance for a black Fred Astaire to emerge in the studio era. Astaire surely understood this, but by adopting an upbeat tone he emphasized that creativity would find its way in the world. Hopeful black dancers and musicians who carved out professional careers had to have believed the same. Astaire's personal views about race remain opaque, although the article suggests he viewed black performers as his creative peers. (Around this time Astaire met the Nicholas Brothers on the lot at RKO. Silent home movies capture some danced clowning around by the threesome.)[2]

The only news in the *Defender* interview was a promise "that in some future film [Astaire] will again include" African American dancers. Astaire kept his word—sort of. He brought a black dancer into a film routine only once after "The Carioca." Made almost twenty years later, "A Shine on Your Shoes" in *The Band Wagon* featured LeRoy Daniels, an African American shoe shiner whose downtown Los Angeles stand was a familiar landmark to the makers of the film. Daniels was not a professional performer. He danced with Astaire during part of the routine but did not sing. The sounds of his brushes and rags were dubbed in by others, and possibly by Astaire himself. "A Shine on Your Shoes" stands outside the norms of Astaire's routines, not fitting into any larger pattern in his work. The black performers Astaire did bring into his numbers were not dancers but musicians: singers and players from popular music and jazz who appeared beside Astaire periodically in his films and regularly on his television shows. This chapter considers five interracial routines Astaire made with African American musicians.

Astaire featured black musicians—in both cases, singers—in two studio-era films. His solos "Slap That Bass" from *Shall We Dance* and "Since I Kissed My Baby Goodbye" from *You'll Never Get Rich* both include the sound of black male vocal harmony groups, a common presence on the radio and records. (*You'll Never Get Rich* also used a group of black musicians as sideline players for the "Bugle Call Rag" routine discussed in chapter 7.) On television, Astaire danced with famous black jazz players, some of whom also sang, on five separate occasions. This body of consistent if widely spaced work with black musicians, increasing in frequency across the decades, forms another aspect of Astaire's uniqueness among Hollywood musical stars. Astaire's unusually large number of interracial routines stands in contrast to Gene Kelly, who created two interracial numbers with black dancers (not musicians): the acrobatic clown routine with the Nicholas Brothers sans their tap shoes in *The Pirate* and an old-fashioned buck-and-wing with boxer Sugar Ray Robinson on Kelly's 1958 special *Dancing: A Man's Game* (a quite amazing piece of television). However, relative to the talents and presence of black performers in the world of show business, Astaire's list of interracial numbers is paltry. Any student of the Hollywood musical feels this lack even when celebrating the careers of black musical stars.

The challenges facing African American performers of any kind in the studio era are well described by Jill Watts in her biography of Hattie McDaniel, the first African American actor to win the Oscar and the most visible black presence in Hollywood during Astaire's career.[3] (McDaniel made one brief appearance in an Astaire film as Rogers's maid in *Carefree*.) Watts writes, "The white studios' back lots were simply microcosms of the racism that dominated American society at large. Although Hollywood was home to a number of progressive whites, the studio system perpetuated American racism both before and behind the cameras."[4] Watts continues, "Black characters became props, manipulated by white filmmakers to signal specific messages regarding white social position and racial ideology."[5] Certainly this happened in the musical, but in the performance-oriented context of the musical, individual African American performers with careers outside film could propose alternative types, giving the lie to the submissive servitude, "comic" mental dullness, or excessive sexuality typically ascribed to black characters. In the musical, black performers could demonstrate skill, assert talent, mark their central place within popular culture, and move audiences to applaud.[6] All the African American musical stars who gained access to the screen musical—among them Bill "Bojangles" Robinson, Ethel Waters, Lena Horne, Hazel Scott, and the Nicholas Brothers—presented alternatives to the standard Hollywood narratives about African Americans, even as their numbers had to function within the Hollywood imaginary. Thus, the musical as a genre had the potential—not always realized—to make a potent counterstatement to mainstream American racial ideology.

Habitual Hollywood practice and fear of protests from Southern distributors normally prevented blacks and whites from getting too close to each other on-screen.[7] Watts quotes white film star Martha Raye: "Hollywood rules called for a stipulated distance separating the white performers from the Negroes while they were before the cameras."[8] As will be shown below, Astaire tried to minimize that "stipulated distance" on several occasions, often finessing the composition of cinematic space in the process. But little real change in racial representation is evident across the thirty-year history of the studio-era musical. Racial limitations on black performance remained in place and progress was isolated: short breakthroughs by individual performers did not effect any lasting change on the genre. The high point for black performers in the musical came during the war, when the federal government and civil rights groups waged backdoor and public campaigns to expand the presence of blacks on-screen and to improve the image of African Americans in Hollywood products. Opportunities for black performers in the postwar color and widescreen era contracted sharply, and industry investment in black-cast musical films remained an anomaly at any time.[9]

And yet Astaire managed to create isolated interracial dance numbers during the studio era. After his move to television, interracial routines became a regular component of Astaire's work. The social transformations of the postwar civil rights movement, in which television played no small part, facilitated both more and new sorts of routines for Astaire with black musicians. Astaire did things on television he never could have done on film, but what he did in both mediums is, inevitably, connected. The seeds of his television dances with well-known black jazz players are to be found in his more limited film dances with anonymous black musicians. The most basic pattern to be found across these interracial routines is Astaire's persistent desire to dance to music made by African American musicians, who were pictured making music while he danced. Making connections with black musicians was, in itself, a theme running across these numbers, all of which feature Astaire at first listening closely to black players or singers, then joining in, adding his own tapped musical line. The persistent theme in Astaire's work of syncopated music making the dancer dance is thus intensified by explicit racial boundary crossing in all his routines with black musicians.

Before looking closely at the numbers Astaire made with black musicians, some ideas for interracial routines that were rejected are worth a brief examination. Culled from the archives, these imagined routines afford a glimpse of routines that didn't get made. Differences between Astaire and his screenwriters are again apparent. On several occasions scriptwriters conceived of Astaire doing a musical number with a young black boy. The following ideas were persistently posed but all put aside. The writers of *Top Hat* wanted to open the film with a danced interracial encounter between Astaire, on his way to perform at a West End theater, and a "negro boy" street performer who would challenge Astaire to a dance. As late as mid-March 1935—Astaire had already reported for rehearsals—an estimating script for *Top Hat* began with a "Tap Dance—Fred and Negro Boy."[10] Added late in the process, the film's comically quiet opening at the very English, very old, very elite Thackeray Club is the opposite of this original idea in almost every particular, establishing Astaire's American credentials by way of noisy contrast with the English rather than rhythmic sympathy with an African American. In the original treatment for *Carefree*, Marian Ainslee and Guy Endore envisioned a street number for Astaire and Rogers precisely located at "a dead-end off Madison Street, abutting on the East River" that would include "A Negro boy [sitting] there dangling his legs and blowing on a mouth organ." After listening a bit, Astaire and Rogers begin to dance to the boy's playing, and other "little boys gather and try to imitate them."[11] Astaire did dance to a harmonica in *Carefree*, but the scene with the "Negro boy" was cut. And it wasn't only at RKO that screenwriters imagined Astaire interacting with black children. In the opening scene of Paramount's *Holiday Inn,* the trio of boys hoofing and playing harmonica that Astaire encounters outside a club that "might be on 52nd Street in New York" were originally described as black. They were supposed to inspire the Salvation Army Santa nearby to start ringing his bell in swing time like a "poor man's Gene Krupa."[12] In the filmed version, the black boys became a trio of white boys and Astaire starts the syncopated bell ringing. Indeed, in one of the earliest treatments for *Holiday Inn,* a text summarizing story conferences between Irving Berlin and Mark Sandrich, Astaire was imagined "exchanging steps with the little pickaninnies," children of the black cook at the inn.[13] Astaire would have been responsible for the dance and musical content of these proposed numbers, and he must have been in on the process that eliminated them. None of the numbers could be made without his creative engagement. The contrast with "A Shine on Your Shoes" is telling. In that street number with a shoe shiner, Astaire invites the dance by directly addressing a song to a black man who is not a professional dancer or street musician. Astaire starts the singing and dancing and spends much of the number directly engaging his black counterpart. The internal narrative of a white dancer imitating or joining a black dancer is markedly absent.

The interracial numbers Astaire made all involved adult black male musicians, one reason that a missed opportunity from the late 1930s stands out as historically significant. The RKO script files contain a version of a film that did not get made that informs our understanding of the version that did. In 1937, Oscar Hammerstein II was brought in by RKO to write what would be the last Astaire-Rogers picture of the decade, *The Story of Vernon and Irene Castle.* Four years older than Astaire, Hammerstein was closely attuned to popular culture. He had lived through the dance craze that helped usher the Castles to prominence, and he had worked on Broadway as a lyricist and book writer throughout the 1920s and '30s. His signal triumph as of 1937 was *Show Boat,* the 1927 musical that brought the normally separate strands of black and white Broadway together on the same stage.[14] Hammerstein had recently scripted the 1936 Universal film version of *Show Boat.* He now wanted to offer a balanced view of the Castles in his high-profile assignment at RKO, an Astaire-Rogers film about the dancing couple most Americans would have said were Astaire and Rogers's obvious precursors and perhaps only historical peers.

From the earliest drafts, Hammerstein envisioned several on-screen appearances by a "colored orchestra," and not just any black dance band, but James Reese Europe's "Society Orchestra," a historically important ensemble that audiences of Hammerstein's and Astaire's generation likely remembered well, if distantly. (The group's ragtime sound had long since gone out of fashion.) The Castles are seminal figures in American social dance history: they created respectable venues for modern social dance where middle- and upper-class white dancers were taught to incorporate black moves and black rhythms in acceptably moderated forms.[15] The Castles made a point of dancing to the music of black bands like Europe's. Hammerstein's "First Draft Continuity" script from December 1937 was very specific about who was in Europe's band: "And FADING IN and OUT of these shots, the Castles dance, and richly dressed audiences applaud. Jim Europe's Society Orchestra bangs out dance rhythms as only colored men can. Feature Jim Europe, the conductor, and Buddy, the drummer."[16] Buddy Gilmore was a close collaborator of Vernon Castle's. They performed alternating "acrobatic drum solos" during the Castles' 1914 national tour, and after it at the New York Tempo Club in 1915.[17] Gilmore was highly visible at Vernon's funeral. One newspaper memorialized Vernon as "the champion trap drummer of the United States," adding "and Buddy Gilmore had taught him how."[18] In her 1919 book *My Husband,* Irene Castle mentions twice that Gilmore "trained" Vernon in drumming and drum showmanship, exactly the sort of stick throwing that Astaire incorporated in his own drum dances.[19] (Astaire's "Drum Dance" in *A Damsel in Distress* was in production while Hammerstein was writing his *Castles* script.) Hammerstein knew all this history from personal experience—the Castles, Europe, and Gilmore had played Hammerstein's grandfather's rooftop nightclub when Oscar was in his late teens—and he saw the inclusion of black musicians as essential to the film's reconstruction of the Castles' story and America in their time. Hammerstein even imagined an elaborate closing montage that brought the film into the present, with brief appearances by real black and white swing bands and clips from Astaire and Rogers's earlier films presented as the legacy of the Castles' and Europe's earlier collaboration.

But RKO set Hammerstein's script aside and handed the project to Dorothy Yost, who eliminated Europe and his band and added the sentimental tear-jerking scene that ends the picture, a direct steal from Jeanette MacDonald and Nelson Eddy's *Maytime,* a top-grossing film of the previous year. As will be shown, Astaire was always eager to dance with black musicians, and the promise held out by Hammerstein's script can be read as the single greatest missed opportunity in Astaire's career. Astaire named Vernon Castle as a role model and saw Castle's work with Europe and other black musicians in his youth. How he might have translated this personal history onto film at the height of the swing era remains a mystery. Hammerstein's idea for the Castle film was a tale of interracial music and dance making that Hollywood was not prepared to tell.

The sight of black and white performers making music and dance in the same shot was unusual at any time in the studio era, and Astaire's two film routines with black singers raise similar questions about how a Hollywood musical might arrive at such a moment. "Slap That Bass" from *Shall We Dance* begins with a cluster of unusual cinematic choices. Anomalies in musical and visual style at the opening set this interracial routine apart from all Astaire's earlier solos, and even the song cue is without precedent. In his previous four films (*Roberta, Top Hat, Follow the Fleet,* and *Swing Time*), Astaire's solo turn had been a fully staged public performance for an on-screen audience. "Slap That Bass" is cued by a bit of dialogue that does not include Astaire and is set in a different physical location from the routine to come. The content of the spoken exchange hints that Astaire's character may be doing something better left unseen. Edward Everett Horton's ballet company is traveling from France to America on an ocean liner. Up on the main deck, Horton asks a steward to locate his lead dancer, Petrov (Astaire). The steward reports that the dancer cannot be found and suggests he may be in a stranger's stateroom doing something "entirely up to him." This mildly titillating lead-in offers no clue where the film might go next. Indeed, a 1930s audience would not have taken the exchange for a song cue. When the film dissolves from the sunny deck to the depths of the ship, and an engine room that could only have been imagined in Hollywood, the audience would have been surprised, and perhaps relieved, that the first full-fledged musical number in *Shall We Dance* was beginning.

"Slap That Bass" opens with the relatively common film trope of black men singing while they work. Black men had been seen doing this in the handful of sound films featuring groups of African Americans, most notably *Hallelujah* (1929) and *Show Boat* (1936). But the black men in *Shall We Dance* are not hoeing fields or rolling cotton bales. Instead, they are polishing a streamlined, chrome-plated showplace of modern technology. The men, fifteen in all, are dressed identically in white T-shirts and light dress pants, with tidy white handkerchiefs knotted around their throats and equally bright white shoes on their feet. Machines make up the rhythm section during the introduction, and the beat they lay down—lines A and C in example 7—supports several layers of rhythmically varied musical gestures sung by the black men, each added in turn. The engines powering the ship set the tempo, and the character of the music added by the black workers links black musical expression to the cutting edge of modern life. Near the end of the routine, during Astaire's dance solo, the swing band on the soundtrack falls silent while he taps furiously to nothing but the rhythm of machines. His black-derived tap style is similarly linked to a machine-made beat. "Slap That Bass" coheres

EXAMPLE 7. Layered introduction to "Slap That Bass" *(Shall We Dance)*. The texture builds up from the bottom at start of the number, each new idea heard twice before the next enters. Line F, not transcribed here, is the only melodic rather than rhythmic idea.

around a specific idea, a common trait of Astaire's best work. Pan remembered the number as inspired by a cement mixer Astaire encountered on the RKO lot.[20] The rhythms of the mixer cued the dance and, reportedly, planted the seeds of the solo. The addition of a black men's chorus fell within established links between modernity and black-derived rhythms. As Joel Dinerstein has pointed out, the connection was seen as vital and forward looking in the 1930s.[21] Ira Gershwin tuned his lyric to this larger theme as well, with rhythm offering "aid" in a chaotic world situation and the use of coded words like "misery" and "milk and honey" putting a mark of blackness into the song text itself.[22]

The tracking crane shot that initiates the viewer into the surprising world of "Slap That Bass" is the most virtuoso single shot in *Shall We Dance* and one of the most complex camera moves in the entire Astaire-Rogers cycle. Director Mark Sandrich used complicated tracking crane shots sparingly. Here, the elaborate shot required the requisition of a small crane and an additional $1,000 to "Narrow ramp, move walls, and raise height of [the] set."[23] The opening of "Slap That Bass" should be read in production context as a special effect.

The vocal texture builds in complexity as the introduction unfolds. As the camera pulls back, more machines and men appear, and as each new group of workers is revealed, another layer is added to the vocal texture. The sound/image match is scrupulously maintained. The style of the musical introduction stands out sharply from the sound world of the Astaire-Rogers pictures. It is not the sound of a studio orchestra or choir, nor is it a texture common to white jazz bands, sweet or hot. These are black musicians singing in an identifiably black idiom. Black vocal groups, descendants of the jubilee quartets that broke off from spiritual-singing black choirs, had been popular on records and radio from the mid-1920s.[24] The arrangement recalls the Mills Brothers, particularly their 1934 rendition of "Limehouse Blues," which begins with a layered vocal texture topped by a sung growling trumpet solo. The combination of pulsating accompaniment and speaking trumpet imitation (line F) is also reminiscent of the opening to Duke Ellington's "East St. Louis Toodle-Oo." This music is heavily coded as black.

The sung introduction and tracking crane shot end with an establishing image that brings all the participants in the number together for the first time. Pictured left to right are: Astaire seated on a stool, the bass player, some backup singers, an open space showing the extreme depth and height of the set, a further group of singers, and, on the side opposite from Astaire and also seated, two sideline musicians, one holding a saxophone and the other a trumpet, both pretending to play in time to the nondiegetic orchestra that sneaks into the soundtrack just as they are revealed on-screen. This image of the entire company holds the screen for a few seconds and then cuts to Astaire alone in a point-of-view shot from the perspective of the black singers. This shift of perspective disrupts the "'180°' or 'axis of action' system of spatial editing" operative in classical Hollywood film. As described by David Bordwell, filmic space in the studio era relied on "the assumption . . . that shots will be filmed and cut together so as to position the spectator always on the same side of the story action."[25] The engine room wall behind Astaire alone is never seen again. It is, technically, outside the narrow space of the set and is never seen in context. (The shot may have been set up much farther back on the screen left side of the set, where a wall and short stairway similar to those seen behind Astaire are visible.) Furthermore, the reverse angle shot is mapped onto the soundtrack in an unusual way. The cut to Astaire occurs in the middle of a brass gesture leading into the sung verse, performed solo by the uncredited Dudley Dickerson, one among the singers standing to screen right. Dickerson's voice is heard before the viewer sees him, and he has not been singled out in conventional terms to this point. The entrance of his voice is slightly jarring. Sandrich, the cutter, or Astaire (who was around for the editing of musical numbers) chose to highlight Astaire's reaction over Dickerson's performance. All these decisions had to have been made during shooting in any event, as a separate setup done to playback to get Astaire's reaction to the music was necessary. Only after the four "zooms" that start the verse have been sung does the image cut to Dickerson, again in the middle of a musical phrase.

Changing a shot midphrase—let alone twice in quick succession—and failing to show the start of a featured singer's solo are both breaches of common practice. The cutaway to Astaire suggests early on that "Slap That Bass" will likely feature Astaire, but for the first-time viewer it is not all that clear what kind of musical number this will be. The elaborate crane shot and extravagant set designate a scene of some importance, but Astaire—the star, after all—begins the number in a triply subordinate position: he's seated, he's at the margin of the frame rather than at the center, and he's playing the part of the audience, attentive but passive, listening but not singing.[26] Astaire gives over the singing of the verse to an anonymous performer, who, like a black alter ego, is backed up by a similarly dressed all-male chorus, just as Astaire had been in his solos in *Top Hat* and *Follow the Fleet*. From just the opening frames of "Slap That Bass," spectators knew they were in for a highly unusual encounter. It was equally unusual for the production staff making the number at RKO.

The earliest shooting schedule for *Shall We Dance* lists the number as "Ship's Engine Room. Freddie Dance 'Slap That Bass' Colored Chorus?"[27] The question mark after "Colored Chorus" persisted on all subsequent shooting schedules, only one indication of the production challenges inherent in such a number. Where, after all, could a "colored chorus" be found in the overwhelmingly white world of a Hollywood studio like RKO? In the first treatment for *Shall We Dance*, typed about the same time as the shooting schedule, the larger outline of "Slap That Bass" is described:

> The mammoth engine room of the Normandie in its clean, bright, meticulous modernity is where Freddie has been hiding out. He has discovered a small group of negro oilers who have improvised a swing band below ship utilizing the boiler and the whistle for the rhythm. Freddie, enthralled, joins them as they vocalize in "Slap That Base *[sic]*." As the number gets hotter, Freddie's feet get itchier and finally to the steady beat of the engine's throb

he goes into a rhythm routine as he mounts the little steel platforms of which
a boiler room is compiled. We discover the shaft of the other machines beating out a counter tempo to the other motors. Freddie, whose sense of rhythm
predominates in his make-up, utilizes this. The rhythm becomes hotter and
faster as he mounts the levels of the ship's boiler room.[28]

The treatment uses familiar language to describe Astaire's dancing, but
with "negro oilers" in the scene, the links between black musicians, hot
rhythm, and Astaire's own rhythmic "make-up" can be explicitly
stated—in the script, at least. In the film, these connections were im-
plied for the original audience.

A quite specific description of "Slap That Bass" was incorporated
into the screenplay. It differs from the film.

INT. SHIP'S ENGINE ROOM—DAY

MUSIC: CLOSE SHOT of Petroff as he sits on an old box. Over the scene can be
heard improvised music. The CAMERA PULLS BACK to disclose the mammoth
engines, which are clean, bright and shiny. A group of Negro Oilers have
utilised various parts of the huge engine as musical instruments, and now
slap away rhythmically as they and Petroff vocalize: "Slap That Bass."[29]

Sandrich, of course, did not begin the number with a close-up of Astaire.
Instead, he created the elaborate crane shot that ended with Astaire at
the edge of a frame crowded with black men. Perhaps the tracking crane
shot was inspired by the layered nature of the introduction, with the
music here making not only the dancer dance but also the camera move.

The "Colored Chorus?" started work on 21 February 1937. It is unclear how they were hired, but they were paid as freelancers through
the music department. The group rehearsed together over four consecu-
tive days, led by Meyer Alexander, a low man on the music department
totem pole, whose pay stubs described his tasks during these days as
"Chorusmaster for Singers" and "Working with Singers on Set."[30] Alexander was also paid $50 for the vocal arrangement of "Slap That Bass."
Most likely he worked with the black men, and together they shaped
the many-layered introduction to the song. There is no other explanation for why it took four days of rehearsal to pull the group together. If
Alexander had actually authored the vocal arrangement, then rehearsal
would have been briefer (and cheaper), perhaps occurring during the
recording session itself. In this sense, the black chorus's introduction
was "improvised music," as called for in both treatment and script. The
demands of the playback system necessitated that improvisation be limited to the preparation period of the number, but the creation of the

vocal arrangement did entail an investment of time and money on the part of RKO—specifically, four unbudgeted days of vocal rehearsal. Astaire, it should be noted, does not dance to any of the music made by the black chorus. There was apparently no interaction between the black singers and Astaire during the dance-making process, although they worked together during recording and shooting.

On 24 February, the final day of vocal rehearsals, the soundtrack for "Slap That Bass" was prerecorded so that Astaire, Dickerson, and the black chorus could lip-synch to it during photography the next day. Two copyists were rushing out parts for vocal and dance arrangements all day long. The recording session started after 8 P.M. and ran past midnight, well outside normal working hours at RKO. As noted earlier, twelve players from the Jimmy Dorsey band were brought in to play on the soundtrack, collaborating with the twelve black men hired to sing. And so the concept spelled out in the earliest treatment—"negro oilers improvising a swing band"—was to some degree realized, at least to the extent possible at RKO, where the very idea of a colored chorus came with a question mark attached. "Slap That Bass" took four days to shoot (25 and 26 February and 1 and 2 March). Fifteen black singers, including the soloist Dickerson, were paid on these days for "sideline photography." The overwhelming majority of the men seen in the number are also heard on the soundtrack. The black vocalists in "Slap That Bass" were thus paid for eight full days of work, plus an extra half day for the late-night recording session. Standard pay was $10 a day, with Dickerson receiving $12.50. RKO thus made an effort to have the musical content of "Slap That Bass" genuinely reflect the black performers shown on-screen performing it. This may also have been the simplest way to meet the casting requirements of the scene. To a surprising extent, sight matches sound in this, Astaire's first dance to the music of black musicians.

The interracial encounter at the core of "Slap That Bass" begins when Astaire actively steps into the number. This moment bears examination from both cinematic and musical perspectives as Astaire is crossing a line, eliminating the "stipulated distance" required by the visual practice of racial segregation in studio-era Hollywood. An abrupt musical transition into Astaire's sung chorus subtly invokes his identity as a dancer activated by syncopated music, and his impatience to join the black singers casts a specifically racial light on this, the central trope of Astaire's persona. As noted above, Astaire begins in a subordinate position. For the first minute and twelve seconds of the five-minute number, he remains seated, listening to music being made by a group of black men. For the first-time viewer, the nature of "Slap That Bass" remains unclear for as long as Astaire just listens. Is this an engine room specialty for some black performers (a number that Astaire will simply observe), or is this an Astaire solo (and if so, then why isn't he singing)? When the sung verse ends, the multilayered vocal texture from the start of the number returns. The camera cuts to the bass player, then back to the unusual reverse shot of Astaire described earlier, recapping the order of images at the start of the verse. Astaire's eyes dart back and forth between two offscreen positions (understood to be Dickerson and the bass player). He is clearly contemplating some action, framed in musical terms as an impulse that won't be denied. The black men's sung introduction is reintroduced layer by layer and, as at the start, each layer is heard twice before the next is added. The texture unfolds in four-bar segments. But when the growling trumpet enters, it is heard for only two bars before Astaire launches into the chorus. The transition is thus ten bars long instead of the expected twelve. Astaire comes in early. He jumps the gun. The creative decision to have Astaire enter early in musical terms was made in rehearsal, part of the process of crafting this dance before recording the music or filming the action. In this case, one that was not at all unusual for Astaire, the musical structure works to characterize Astaire as a screen figure in racially coded musical terms.

Eye contact between Astaire and the black chorus is crucial in the early part of the routine. However, once Astaire rises to sing, the character of "Slap That Bass" changes a bit and the limits on interracial music making come into view. This is no song-and-dance utopia. Astaire sings the chorus while standing in the middle of the half circle made by the black chorus. He has his back to most of them. He sings the first half of the AABA chorus mostly to the bass player. For the second half, Astaire shifts his focus away from the bass player and seems to be singing to no one. "Slap That Bass" briefly adopts a presentational setup: soloist in front, facing front; chorus behind, also looking forward. Eye contact between Astaire and the black singers becomes impossible, and any sense of shared music making disappears. What was initially framed as an informal musical encounter begins to look like a performed theatrical number. Due to its interracial content, "Slap That Bass" could not have been contextualized as a theatrical performance for an audience pictured within the film, and yet for half of the sung chorus the positions of Astaire and the chorus echo the visual tropes of theatrical numbers. In-film audiences could serve an important function, as Jane Feuer has noted. "In order to get a direct response from the film audience, Hollywood musicalmakers had to place in their path another, spectral audience," one task of the internal audience being to cue applause at the end of a number, a new movie audience behavior several have said occurred for the first time with Astaire's films.[31] The lack of an on-screen audience sets the sung chorus of "Slap That Bass" within an awkward silence, capturing the incompleteness of this interracial number, a lack carried over into Astaire's other dances with black musicians on film. These are not idealistic moments transcending all-too-real racial divides. Astaire might resist the limits on interracial encounters on the musical screen, but the visual conventions of the genre constrain him and the black musicians he employed. And even though he and the black singers have clearly bonded musically, their bond is untranslatable above deck, whether understood literally as the boat itself—the black workers disappear after "Slap That Bass"—or figuratively as American society, where the image of a white man making music with a group of black men was simply not part of public culture in the 1930s. When Astaire dances with black musicians on television twenty years later, the audible response of a live studio audience makes the act of interracial performance into an unambiguously public act, something it could not be in the studio era.

At the end of his sung chorus, Astaire reinitiates visual contact with the black men behind him, and the group is reinstated as the primary reference point for the routine. Astaire moves to the top of the semicircle and looks from one side of the group to the other. He is going to dance, and his expression suggests that now it is his turn to show them what he can do. As Astaire begins to tap the men lean forward, eager to watch and listen. (The "colored chorus" is, of course, taking direction here.) A cut is made at this point—the start of the dance proper—and the black workers are not seen again until the final shot of "Slap That Bass," where they clap and cheer. They turn out to be the internal audience for the number, inviting the film's audience to join them in their appreciation of Astaire's dancing. However, throughout the first section of the dance, while Astaire remains on the lower level of the engine room, he makes constant eye contact with the black chorus, who are still understood to be watching by way of the convention of the eyeline match (where the image of an actor looking offscreen was followed by an image of what he was looking at). Astaire avoided cutaways from his dances, so only his side of the eyeline match is shown—the watching black chorus must be inferred by the viewer. Astaire plays a ballet dancer in *Shall We Dance,* and several times in "Slap That Bass" he uses pseudoballet arms as if by reflex. In one instance Astaire looks at his arms, held before him in a forward port de bras, as if they belonged to someone else. With a purposeful shrug he relaxes his arms, tossing off the ballet gesture in favor of the loose-limbed freedom of the tapper. At the same moment he sends a meaningful smile toward the black workers watching offscreen left. Astaire maintains the black workers as his primary focus for much of his solo. He is dancing principally for them. As noted above, the production file confirms that the African American ensemble members were on set during all four days of filming.

"Slap That Bass" begins with a strange song cue, spoken in another space by characters unconnected to the number: indeed, they never know it occurs. By setting the song cue above deck, the film skirts the need to explain how Astaire and the black workers met and came to share and trade music and dance in the first place. The local narrative initiating the number in the engine room is omitted, perhaps because it's difficult to imagine how Astaire might have started a conversation with these black men while remaining within the conventions of Hollywood film. Astaire did not overhear the "Negro oilers" making music, then wander in and watch unobserved. His character, known from earlier scenes to secretly dance to jazz records, went looking for the real thing and negotiated a way to hear it. At some unseen point, after unheard verbal exchanges, he pulled up a stool and the black men started singing for him. That's when the film audience shows up, ushered into the scene by a special effects crane shot that calls attention to itself rather than the incongruous scene it reveals. Any exchange of words between Astaire and the black singers lay outside the racial imagination of Hollywood and America at the time. Only the shared song and dance of this interracial encounter could be committed to film, in part because the pleasures of listening and watching distract the viewer from asking too many questions about how the film got to this moment in the first place. This problem with the setup for an interracial number—at once a narrative, verbal, and spatial challenge—continued in Astaire's next studio-era dance to the sound of black singers, made just four years later.

Astaire's dance to the Cole Porter song "Since I Kissed My Baby Good-bye" introduces the guardhouse setting in *You'll Never Get Rich,* site of

Astaire's solo to "Bugle Call Rag" discussed earlier. Like "Slap That Bass," "Since I Kissed" uses the popular sound of black male vocal harmony, but unlike the anonymous group assembled as a one-time "colored chorus" at RKO, Columbia engaged a known ensemble for *You'll Never Get Rich,* the four members of the Four Tones plus a fifth singer (likely added so that this group would match the different set of black men—jazz players—who are seen to accompany "Bugle Call Rag.") In "Since I Kissed," the introduction of a filmic space where interracial music and dance is permissible comes not by way of an elaborate set and virtuoso crane shot but rather by a breach of normal Hollywood framing and editing practices, suppressing the viewer's sense for the space, counting on the attraction of Astaire's tap dancing to carry the story into a visually mundane but narratively fantastic, socially impossible locale.

As in *Shall We Dance,* the choice of setting and the construction of cinematic space prove important aspects of Astaire's collaboration with black singers in *You'll Never Get Rich.* Columbia went to great lengths to get the visuals of an Army training camp just right, sending set designers to Camp Haan in nearby Riverside and re-creating portions of the camp to exact specifications on the studio's back lot. The only structure that was altered was the guardhouse, which was enlarged to accommodate Astaire's dance solos.[32] Settings, especially those destined to play an important part in a film's story, were typically presented to the viewer in a logical fashion in classical Hollywood. Establishing shots set the context for action, and, as Bordwell notes, "The classical scene must immediately reveal two things about the characters: their relative spatial positions and their states of mind. The establishing shots should, while exposing the surroundings, also indicate where everyone is."[33] The presentation of the guardhouse slyly avoids common practice, likely because what is going on in this musical military lockup is an interracial exchange of song and dance that lay outside the limits of normal racial practices in the Hollywood dreamscape and American reality.

The dialogue cue for "Since I Kissed" is an exchange between Hayworth and a military sentry. Hayworth has arrived at the base to visit her fiancé, an officer. Sitting in a car with her fiancé's mother, she hears the blues-tinged sound of guitar and fiddle floating on the evening air. Hayworth asks the sentry, "Where's the music coming from?" He replies, "From the guardhouse, ma'am." The film's next destination having been named, the image cuts from Hayworth to a view inside the guardhouse. The music continues as a connecting element. Contrary to usual practice, the first shot of the interior does not orient the viewer to the space as a whole. The guardhouse will prove an important locale for the remainder of the film—*You'll Never Get Rich* ends there—but the way the locale is introduced does not suggest this. As with "Slap That Bass," the characters who speak the song cue are physically removed from the scene of the song to come. However, unlike Horton and the steward in "Slap That Bass," Hayworth and the sentry can hear the music of the black performers who unexpectedly intrude upon this otherwise all-white film. The sound of this music, together with Astaire's added tap line, will draw Hayworth into the scene, and her arrival will have important musical ramifications.

The "relative spatial position" of Hayworth vis-à-vis the guardhouse is suggested sonically at the outset. Initially heard in the distance, the music gets appropriately louder with the move into the guardhouse. But once the viewer is inside, visual confirmation of the relationship between Astaire and the Four Tones is withheld until the very end of the dance. The fact that black and white soldiers are sharing the same lockup is suppressed by both the framing and the editing of the scene. Table 5 diagrams the relationship of musical form, cinematic space, and shot structure in "Since I Kissed My Baby Goodbye."

The first shot inside the guardhouse shows the Four Tones from an oblique angle. The room is quite dark and the other prisoners, seen in the foreground of a relatively deep composition, are completely still and largely in shadow. The five members of the Four Tones are visible in a corner, one wall of which will never be seen again in the film. This first shot violates the "axis of action" rule as it will be applied to the rest of the scenes in the guardhouse. The viewer's first glimpse of the guardhouse is disorienting. The second shot—a frontally positioned setup—frames the Four Tones in an artfully arranged pose. They wear work uniforms (topstitched denim pants and jackets) and hold instruments (two guitars, a clarinet, and a fiddle). Framing, pose, costumes, and props combine to reproduce visual tropes of the blues, similarly evoked in the contemporary film *Blues in the Night* (1941, originally titled *Hot Nocturne*), which featured members of the Jimmy Lunceford band in an analogous situation. In *Blues in the Night,* a group of white band musicians listens to a group of black men—Dudley Dickerson from "Slap That Bass" among them—in an adjacent jail cell singing the title song by Harold Arlen and Johnny Mercer. Barriers of jail bars articulate

TABLE 5 MUSIC, DANCE, AND SHOT CONTENT OF "SINCE I KISSED MY BABY GOODBYE" (*You'll Never Get Rich*)

Song Form	Shot	Soundtrack	Dance
Introduction	Hayworth and sentry	Violin and guitar only	
A (16 bars)	Shot 1: the Four Tones from oblique angle, white onlookers watch from the shadows; shot 2: The Four Tones in artful pose (cut occurs at the halfway point in the musical phrase)	Vocal	
A (16 bars)	Shot 3: begins on Astaire's feet, widens to include his entire body, entire shot framed against wall flat to the camera	Vocal	Astaire lying on bunk.
Bridge (16 bars)	Shot 3 continues, widening as needed	Vocal	Astaire sits up, rises to his feet at the halfway point of the bridge, but remains near the bunk.
A1 (16 bars)	Shot 4: dynamic view of Astaire in the guardhouse	Vocal	Astaire moves freely within the guardhouse, circling around three of the four posts.
Bridge (16 bars)	Shot 4 continues, moving with Astaire within the guardhouse, ending with Astaire and the Four Tones framed together	Vocal	Astaire continues to move freely throughout the guardhouse, with the unaccompanied break ending the bridge pulling him forward into a shot that finally locates the Four Tones relative to Astaire and the guardhouse itself. Hayworth's voice cuts off dance in midstep.
A1 (16 bars)	Shot 5: cut to Hayworth at the window; shot 6: brief cut back to shot 4 setup of Astaire with the Four Tones; shot 7: Hayworth and Astaire at the window for short dialogue scene	No vocal; tune taken by violin	

the space in a series of powerfully framed images: black singers behind bars, white musicians looking longingly at them through bars. The sound of the black singers, heard without instrumental accompaniment, inspires the whites to form a band, committing themselves to jazz rather than commercial pop music. The black singers in *Blues in the Night* serve a crucial plot function, initiating the white band's restless search for authenticity, which the film explicitly locates among African Americans in the South. *Blues in the Night* scrupulously maintains a physical separation between black and white, a commonsensical aspect of the jail setting and the visual embodiment of a segregated nation. By contrast, where the musical soldiers in *You'll Never Get Rich* come from and what they are doing in the guardhouse at this particular military base in 1941 are questions *You'll Never Get Rich* neither asks nor answers. Once Astaire enters the scene, the presence of the Four Tones is explained by simple association with the star of the film. It's a dance specialty and nothing more (or less).

Shot three, beginning with the second A phrase in this AABA song, opens on Astaire lying on his bunk. The musicians disappear but the sound of their singing continues. At first, only Astaire's feet and legs are visible. They move easily, irresistibly, to the music. As in so many of his solos, the dance begins only after the music has already begun, and the sight of Astaire's legs is the first indication this will be a danced routine for Astaire rather than a specialty for the singers. The frame opens up smoothly to include Astaire's full body, continuing to pull back as he rises from his cot to a standing position. This kind of changing shot composition is unusual in Astaire's work: among his solos, it is unique. "Since I Kissed" is the only Astaire solo to begin by framing just his feet, emphasizing their (in this case, silent) response to music heard within the diegesis of the film. (A similar framing of Bill Robinson's feet responding to diegetic music being played nearby occurs in the 1943 film *Stormy Weather*. Like Astaire, Robinson rises from his bunk and starts dancing to the music of a small group of black musicians.) Throughout shot three, while lying on the bunk Astaire looks to screen right as if that is where the music is coming from.

The question of physical proximity is primary. What is the spatial relationship between the Four Tones' corner and Astaire's bunk? Astaire is pictured in a relatively shallow, evenly lit composition against a wall of wooden planks; the musicians were seen in a more complex space, with jail bars and shadows. Lacking an establishing shot of the guardhouse interior, the film audience has no way of connecting the musicians and Astaire outside the continuity of the soundtrack, which betrays nothing in terms of changes in auditory perspective once inside the guardhouse. Are the Four Tones and Astaire in the same room? The question is left unanswered except by inference. The United States was a segregated society in 1941. The film's original audience probably would *not* have assumed that the Four Tones and Astaire were sharing a cell, especially since no black men are seen in any other shot in the army camp and military units were segregated at the time. The absence of a normal succession of establishing shots and eyeline matches suggests that director Sidney Lanfield and Astaire wanted to keep the question open for as long as possible.

In this rhythm-oriented solo Astaire goes to great lengths to create a dance that appears to be improvised and for no one in particular. It is, fundamentally, for the dancer himself. His feet and legs bounce freely; his hands pat his body and rap on the wall; during a pause to light a cigarette the dance seems to stop, until Astaire strikes a match in time to the music and starts using the matchbox as a rhythm instrument. The ambiguous start-stop opening on the bunk is, again, unique in Astaire's work. In contrast to his other "improvised" solos in *The Gay Divorcee, Shall We Dance, Holiday Inn,* and *Let's Dance,* the music Astaire dances to in the guardhouse is unrelated to him. He is not dancing to a record or to a band in a nightclub. He is not in the privacy of his own room. For the first and only time in his solos, Astaire reacts to music over which he has no control and to which he has no apparent connection—music he is overhearing coming from a live source in a still-undefined proximity to him. Unlike in "Slap That Bass," Astaire is not seated in the circle with the black musicians he is listening to. They are not performing for him. Astaire's solo has no dramatic motivation outside the dancer's urge to dance, an urge constructed here, again, as activated by music.

As his dance builds in speed and volume, the music continues on its own relaxed way. The Four Tones never alter the mellow surface of their vocal harmony. Astaire's tap rhythms are structured as a crescendo of activity, building over a chorus and a half of the song. His exploration of the environment's rhythmic possibilities grows noisier and noisier as the dance unfolds. Mueller perceives a disconnect between the "pain and depression" of the lyric and Astaire's "noisy crashing tap dance."[34] Within African American practice, the disjunction is not so

great. It may even be central. As Albert Murray noted in his seminal
Stompin' the Blues, "Blues music regardless of its lyrics almost always
induces dance movement that is the direct opposite of resignation, retreat or defeat," and "With all its preoccupation with the most disturbing aspects of life, [the blues] is something contrived specifically to be
performed as entertainment."[35] Cole Porter's lyrics express generic blues
sentiments, language by a white songwriter—not particularly known for
such songs—and handed off to be sung by black singers with no say in
the matter. But the stylish and polished way the Four Tones sing the
song is their own, betraying their identities as professional pop singers.
Astaire's reaction, in turn, lies well within the practices of black musicians and dancers outlined by Murray. The blues transcend sorrow in a
burst of creative expression. This tradition was not Astaire's: it was
something he (literally) tapped into, and his stature within the Hollywood system granted him the power to bring all these elements together. And while his position of power is indisputable, at the very least,
as in the jail scene in *Blues in the Night,* Astaire's absurdly integrated
guardhouse admits the theft, acknowledges the debt, and tries to bridge
that "stipulated distance" that defined racial relationships in Hollywood film.

The spatial relationship between black singers and white dancer in
"Since I Kissed" is not suppressed entirely. By the start of the half chorus Astaire is making a lot of noise, due in part to his greater mobility.
The dance climaxes with a rapid, noisy move forward, filling the unaccompanied eight-count break at the end of the bridge. Astaire travels
quite a bit—perhaps ten feet—and by the end of the break the physical
relationship between dancer and musicians is, at long last, visually established. Astaire's break takes him to a new area of the guardhouse,
landing him squarely in front of the Four Tones. Dancer and musicians
are in the same room. For the first time this fact of the film's diegesis is
confessed. At exactly this moment of revelation, the dance—but not the
music—is brought to an abrupt halt. Hayworth's hard voice stops
Astaire midstep with the warning, "Say, soldier!" The image cuts to Hayworth standing outside the guardhouse, framed by the widely spaced
bars in one of its large windows. She critiques his dancing—"You're a
beat off!"—and the image cuts back to Astaire, standing as before in
front of the musicians who continue to play. While Astaire pauses to toss
his cigarette to the floor and stamp it out, the physical relationship of
Astaire and the five black musicians is again briefly confirmed.

The interracial encounter at the heart of "Since I Kissed My Baby Goodbye" is visually deemphasized by a subtle undermining of the normal rules for laying out cinematic space. The musical connection, of course, is evident throughout. The viewer knows who is making the music that is activating Astaire's dance but they do not know, until the very end, how Astaire is coming into contact with that music. The high interest of Astaire's dance distracts the viewer from the missing information that is normally provided within the syntax of classical Hollywood cinema. This gives Astaire the room he needs to improvise to music being made by black musicians. The Four Tones' only acknowledgment that they are serving the purposes of a scene in a film comes when they stop singing the lyrics during the last sixteen bars of the chorus while Astaire and Hayworth talk at the window. Smoothly adjusting to their shift in status, the Four Tones go from featured musical collaborators to providers of diegetic underscoring. As a result, Astaire's solo ends, uncharacteristically, without applause.

Comparison with a famous jazz film from three years later helps contextualize the guardhouse in *You'll Never Get Rich,* underlining the innovative nature of both of Astaire's interracial dances there. *Jammin' the Blues,* a musical short filmed and released in 1944, was the brainchild of jazz promoter and activist Norman Granz. *Life* magazine photographer Gjon Mili, famous for his images of jazz musicians, directed this visually inventive film. Jazz and film scholar Arthur Knight discusses *Jammin' the Blues* at length in his book *Disintegrating the Musical,* and his conclusions are well worth considering beside Astaire's guardhouse dances. Knight situates *Jammin' the Blues* within the history of interracial jazz performance across the 1930s and early 1940s. He discusses the important difference between interracial groups on record and those same groups in live performance and on film. He also includes an informal list of interracial musical performances in films. Knight does not, however, include the Astaire solos discussed in this book. In limiting his discussion to filmed performances that look like jazz—when "guests" from the world of jazz visit Hollywood films and perform (i.e., improvise) in formal contexts—Knight omits the important role popular music and jazz played in many Hollywood musicals, particularly those starring Astaire. Knight also undervalues jazz as dance music and tap dancers as jazzmakers.[36]

Jammin' the Blues lasts ten minutes, time enough for three separate musical numbers. In the first, tenor saxophonist Lester Young is featured with an all-black rhythm section: drums (Sid Catlett), piano (Marlowe Morris), and string bass (Red Callender). For the second, African American singer Marie Bryant and white guitarist Barney Kessel join the group in a rendition of "On the Sunny Side of the Street." On the third selection, John Simmons takes over on bass and Jo Jones steps in on drums. Catlett tosses Jones one of his sticks and Jones gets his own beat going without Catlett's beat ever ceasing. It's a visually oriented bit of stick-tossing showmanship, ubiquitous in American showbiz, and even the self-consciously artistic *Jammin' the Blues* makes some space for a modest flash move for the drumming pair. To get the best sound, the film was shot to playback. There's nothing improvised about the image track, and the soundtrack would have been recorded with the knowledge that any and all musical decisions would have to be reproduced exactly during filming. The drum handoff between Catlett and Jones is as meticulously choreographed as any dance Astaire ever made. In addition to the change of drummer and bassist, the ensemble is enlarged to include black jazzmen Harry Edison on trumpet and Illinois Jacquet on tenor sax.

Kessel is the lone white player in this session. While it was not unknown for a single African American jazz musician to appear among the ranks of a white big band in a Hollywood film in the early 1940s, it was without precedent for a black ensemble to include a single white player.[37] In this regard, *Jammin' the Blues* broke new ground for interracial performance on film, albeit in the noncommercial world of shorts. As Knight notes, Kessel's presence is mediated and minimized in four ways: 1) by effacing his image completely (during "Sunny Side of the Street" he can be heard on the soundtrack but is not visible on-screen), 2) by placing him in a partially obscured position in shots of the entire group during the third number, 3) by limiting the image to his hands on his guitar during his solo, and 4) by doubling his image in a distorting, art photography manner for the only shot of Kessel's head and upper body.[38] The second strategy—employing an oblique camera angle and deep shadow to deemphasize the presence of black and white subjects in the same frame—resembles the framing of the Four Tones and white soldiers lying on their bunks in shot one of "Since I Kissed My Baby Goodbye." The fact that blacks and whites share the frame is finessed by means of surprisingly similar shot composition and lighting in these two films.

Knight comments insightfully on the question of venue: "The setting [of *Jammin' the Blues*] never intrudes because there is none—only apparently limitless blackness or whiteness surrounding the players. *Jammin' the Blues* rejects the architectures of both professional and 'folk' musical performance—theaters, bars, levees, barns—common to Hollywood films."[39] In similar fashion, Astaire's interracial musical numbers reject genre-bound settings in favor of unusual spaces: a fantastic engine room and a fantastically integrated guardhouse. Location proves crucial to Astaire's dances with black musicians. But because he remains within the genre of the narrative musical, these unusual settings must be worked into a larger world. The interracial guardhouse was, of course, a complete fiction, as some noted at the time and later.[40] But however absurd the setting in realistic terms, neither solo could be cut when *You'll Never Get Rich* played in the South. Astaire's integration of black musicians into two solos speaks for the importance of *You'll Never Get Rich* as a film musical that pushed against the racial limits of the genre in the interest of Astaire making visible exactly who was making the music that made him dance.

Finally, contra Knight, the jazz content of Astaire's guardhouse solos must be emphasized. Astaire's masterful rhythm tap to "Since I Kissed My Baby Goodbye" and the compendium-like nature of his "Bugle Call Rag" locates both routines squarely in the realm of jazz at the time, just as much a part of the swing mainstream as Marie Bryant's dance to the pop tune "On the Sunny Side of the Street" in *Jammin' the Blues*. Solo rhythm tap was jazz, and in the narrow confines of the guardhouse Astaire comes close to being a simple hoofer. And just like the jazz players in *Jammin' the Blues*, Astaire is dancing to playback. Recognizing this context for Astaire's work is essential to viewing the Hollywood musical—at least in Astaire's creative hands—as a place where the disciplines of jazz could find a particular sort of home on the big screen.

But, it must be noted, the black singers and musicians in *You'll Never Get Rich* remain anonymous. Like the black chorus in "Slap That Bass," they have no larger role in the film and go uncredited in the print. The Four Tones received screen credit in their all-black films with singing cowboy Herb Jeffries: Columbia hired them but did not acknowledge their contribution by name. Indeed, the shift of personnel between "Since I Kissed" and "Bugle Call Rag" goes entirely unacknowledged. It's assumed the viewer will register a group of blacks rather than individual men, and in neither case are the black men making music in the guardhouse presented as skilled professionals. They are just black men who happen to be musicians, an unremarkable equation in Hollywood's view of things.

A decidedly abstract film, *Jammin' the Blues* unfolds without an audience. Astaire's interracial guardhouse, of necessity, includes a scattered group of silent white onlookers. During "Since I Kissed My Baby Goodbye," they remain motionless in the shadows. During "Bugle Call Rag," the white soldiers inside the guardhouse and the white sentries outside watch and applaud. A curious stillness overtakes the screen at the end of Astaire's "Bugle Call Rag." As in so many of his solos, onscreen onlookers clap and cheer, providing the film audience with the chance to do so as well. Astaire normally breaks his final pose and bows in acknowledgment of such applause. Here he remains oddly frozen. After "Bugle Call Rag," Astaire acknowledges neither the white soldiers and guards behind him nor the black musicians to his right. He holds perfectly still, as if there were no way to break out of the pose that concludes this interracial number. The screen goes dark on his slightly uncomfortable grin. Astaire had to wait until his television specials, created seventeen years and an ongoing civil rights revolution later, to dance to the music of black musicians and call them to his side at the end for a shared bow before a live studio and nationwide television audience.

Astaire's primary creative outlet simply disappeared in the late 1950s when the studio production units devoted to the expensive genre of the musical closed up shop. After the commercially disappointing widescreen musical ran its four-year course—time enough for Astaire and Kelly to make only three films each in the new format—the genre that had hosted Astaire's creative work for a quarter century folded. Faithful adaptations of Broadway musicals, Elvis pictures, and rock-and-roll beach parties filled the void. In truth, Astaire the dance creator seems hardly to have noticed. He transitioned seamlessly onto television, his first special airing just five months after his last studio musical was released. Astaire took to television with a creative fervor registered by everyone in the industry. *An Evening with Fred Astaire* swept the Emmys in 1959 and was rebroadcast as late as 1964. The creative discipline of routine making continued to inspire Astaire and still had a place in American mass media. The difference on television was the lack of a framing narrative. Astaire could be himself and, unsurprisingly, his most distinctive television work involved dancing with black jazz musicians to that same story of music making the dancer dance.

Relatively speaking, there was a fair amount of room for black performers on television.[41] Variety shows of this era were in constant need of talent, and nationally recognized black singers and musicians found a place in a medium that was still aimed principally at adults in prime time. But the appearance of black performers was not without controversy. In February 1952 on *The Colgate Comedy Hour,* host Eddie Cantor mopped the perspiration from guest star Sammy Davis Jr.'s forehead and "vicious, racist mail poured in to NBC." Cantor brought Davis back on his next episode.[42] As the decade advanced, black jazz performers appeared more and more often. One precedent-setting show was NBC's *Tonight* hosted by Steve Allen beginning in September 1954, just months after the Supreme Court's landmark civil rights decision *Brown v. Board of Education.* Allen was a jazz pianist who looked to black players like Teddy Wilson and Errol Garner as his models. He consistently brought jazz guests, black and white alike, onto his show and often jammed with them. Jazz was so prominent that one historian has dubbed *Tonight* "a living jazz museum."[43] During a visit to the show by Lena Horne in 1955, Allen greeted her with a kiss on the cheek. An outraged viewer sent Allen a letter decrying the kiss, after which Allen proceeded to read the letter on the air, calling the viewer "an absolute bigot" and suggesting he "should go to a hospital."[44] In an article for *Ebony,* Allen explained why he featured so many black jazz and popular music artists on his show.

> Talent is color-blind. It's a gift not a commodity, and those who have it ought to be treated as the VIP's they really are. On my television show I use a lot of talent and it is all talent that, to me, has no color tag. It just so happens that a pretty high percentage of the guest performers on my show are Negroes. It's not a planned thing. I don't suppose I could be called a crusader. With me, it's basically a question of my accidentally doing what I guess is the right thing. I just hire the best singers and piano players and trumpet players and it just happens that a very high percentage of them are Negroes. It's about that simple. Of course, I have special tastes in music, singers and musicians, and these tastes have a lot to do with the artists I have on my show.[45]

Elsewhere in the article Allen expresses great enthusiasm that his position on television allowed him "to meet, and have on the show and also know socially" some of his musical idols. Allen provided a signal example of how a white musician with control over his own television show might use this power to both spotlight and make music with prominent black jazz musicians in the still-new medium.

Astaire was surely aware of Allen's model. His own specials were filled with black jazz players who were invited to play for a national audience on their own, then for and with Astaire. Like Allen, Astaire also developed personal relationships with several of his African American guest stars. Collaboration between guests and host entailed a complicated production process: the guest didn't just show up and do their own material but instead worked creatively with the host on special material for that telecast. Astaire found ways to streamline the process, such as building his dances on recordings by his guest stars that could be re-created live. As has been shown, this could cause problems when working with jazz players who didn't play a given number the same way every time. Astaire's working methods made ample room for guest and host to collaborate. Defying common practice in the industry, Astaire insisted on weeks and weeks of rehearsal, just as he had while making films. The press regularly highlighted this aspect of Astaire's specials, and their superior finish was chalked up to Astaire's perfectionism and investment in rehearsal.

Astaire's blues-based television numbers with Basie and Williams and Smith were considered from a musical perspective in chapter 7. Here, Astaire's collaborations with two generations of black jazz players on television are explored within the context of his work with black musicians on film in *Shall We Dance* and *You'll Never Get Rich*. The most notable difference on television was Astaire's ability to collaborate with famous black musicians rather than anonymous groups of black singers. Astaire had specific jazz tastes: he liked melodically oriented jazz players who were successfully reaching broad popular music audiences. Swing veterans and members of the younger generation alike were doing this, and Astaire brought both onto his specials. His dances with the old-timers opened the door for new experiences: Astaire admitted to improvising a majority of his solo dance with Count Basie's band, and he deepened the connection between a black singing voice and his own white dancing body while working with Jonah Jones. Astaire's dances with younger players followed old patterns both in his own work and in jazz as a showman's art. Making a dance on the fly with the Young-Holt Unlimited soul jazz trio allowed Astaire to explore some of the fundamental themes of his dance-making career one last time. With no need to finesse the fact of interracial music making, Astaire could bring a more personal tone to his television dances with black musicians than the restrictive limits on the film musical had allowed. Evidence for the larger social changes enabling his dances with black jazz players is captured in a 1959 comedy sketch with Jones, a scripted exchange that hinted at how interracial song and dance might participate in the ongoing story of racial reconciliation playing out on American television at the time.

On *Astaire Time,* his third special, Astaire introduced Basie with the words "And now, Count Basie," as if everyone in the audience already knew who he was. This was 1960, and Basie had made relatively few television appearances. Many more would follow, but Basie mentions only this one in his 1985 autobiography, which also includes a photo of Basie and Astaire. (Oscar Peterson similarly included a picture with Astaire in his autobiography. In all the many illustrated books on Astaire, these two pictures appear only in these two jazz memoirs.)[46] The Basie band's first number on *Astaire Time* was a blues called "Not Now, I'll Tell You When," which features a lot of solo time for the leader and a series of false endings—a favorite Basie gimmick—that refer to the title (itself reaching back to "The Hucklebuck," a 1949 hit for R&B singer and honking sax player Paul Williams). During the applause, Astaire approaches Basie at the piano. Basie remains seated and they share a quick exchange.

> *Astaire:* Hi, Count.
>
> *Basie:* Hi, Fred.
>
> *Astaire:* I'm mighty proud to have you here. You know, I've been dying to dance to your music.
>
> *Basie:* And I've been dying to play for you, too.
>
> *Astaire:* Oh, that's fine. Well, I guess there's nothing else to do but just get at it, then.
>
> *Basie:* I guess we should start.
>
> *Astaire:* Alright. You play and I'll dance.
>
> *Basie:* No, you dance and I'll play.
>
> *Astaire:* Oh, that's better yet. "Sweet Georgia Brown"?
>
> *Basie:* Crazy.

Astaire taps an introduction, making eye contact with Basie, the drummer Sonny Payne, and the band in general. Astaire greets the first full chord from the Basie players with a full-body gesture, throwing his arms out as if he could fly. With his back to the camera, his response to the band is shared with the band (rather than the audience), and the rest of the number involves much comic miming with individual players. The number ends with a series of knee drops, Astaire reaching toward the band in general and Basie in particular. Astaire and Basie share a long handshake at the close, and on this image the screen fades to black and the show goes to commercial. The choice of song—a jazz standard first recorded in 1922—adds to the retrospective feel of the dance. Astaire plays a hoofer with the Basie band, recalling a lost world of tap dancers who performed with bands, a part Astaire had played in a few of his films, but never with a black band.

Astaire used this dance with Basie to do something he had never allowed himself to do on film or television before: improvise. In a 1961 interview Astaire reflected on the fun of working with Basie and the opportunities television provided. "And in the last show I worked with Count Basie, which I had wanted to do for a long time. We did 'Sweet Georgia Brown' and made it up as we went along. It's not always easy to ad lib, but I was inspired by him. And I did a dance number in which I improvised about 75 percent of it on camera. Those are things I could never do in films, and they were fun."[47] Not only did the playback system of the film musical discourage genuine improvisation, but studio practices also stood in the way of interracial numbers. For these technical and social reasons, playing the hoofer with the Basie band was impossible in Astaire's studio days. Television opened the door to both improvisation and interracial dance making with a coequal star. In Astaire's experience, both were "things [he] could never do in films."

On his 1958 and 1959 specials Astaire featured only one musical guest: Jonah Jones, a jazz trumpeter and singer with roots in the swing era.[48] Born in 1909 in Louisville, Kentucky, Jones followed a career path that echoed that of Louis Armstrong. He picked up the horn in a local boy's marching band, found early work on Mississippi riverboats, joined black dance bands based in the North, and then embarked on a career as a soloist who played and sang. Jones enjoyed enduring success across the popular marketplace. In the late 1930s, he teamed up with violinist Stuff Smith for a long-running crowd-pleasing gig at the Onyx Club on New York's 52nd Street. When Jones joined Cab Calloway's outfit in 1941, Calloway added a specialty called "Jonah Joins the Cab." The connection with Calloway lasted over a decade, ending with a stint in the pit for the early 1950s Broadway revival of *Porgy and Bess*. Jones embodied a combination of musicianship and showmanship typical of many swing players who never took the path of modern jazz. As Jones told an interviewer in 1979, his career-long goal had been "to entertain people and get some kicks out if it. . . . My audience knows they're going to get some melody along with the jazz. You've got to remember not everybody's a musician."[49] Like Basie and Williams around the same time, Jones hit on a winning commercial formula in the latter 1950s. Recording as a quartet leader for Capitol Records under producer Dave Cavanaugh (who was working with Sinatra and Nat "King" Cole as well), between 1957 and 1963 Jones enjoyed substantial success with a brand of muted trumpet jazz and growling, good-natured vocals that was accessible to nonjazz audiences and drew on contemporary popular and Broadway songs. No fewer than three of Jones's albums reached the *Billboard* Top 40 albums chart in 1958. Jones's status as the only musical guest on Astaire's first two specials made good sense, coming at a time when Jones was enjoying dramatic national success. *Newsweek* profiled Jones in 1959. The trumpeter said of his successful new sound, "A lot of people say far-out music sounds pretty good, but they don't know what's being played. People also get bored with things that are too simple. I reach a happy medium—right down the middle. I play standard and show tunes, and then turn around and swing it. I definitely try to let people know what I'm playing."[50]

Before Jones's first appearance on the 1958 special, Astaire explained the jazz trumpeter's presence in personal and general terms: "When I first heard a Jonah Jones album, it did something to me. It knocked me out just like it did everybody else." (Astaire wasn't kidding. In a photo spread for *Life* magazine, photographer Ralph Crane caught Astaire at home playing the drums with a console stereo nearby. On the floor lay the cover for Jones's LP *Jumpin' with Jonah*.[51] See the cover photo of this volume.) Jones and his quartet appear on-screen and play two tunes in succession: "Baubles, Bangles, and Beads" and "Mack the Knife." As Jones sings the latter tune, the camera zooms in closer and closer until his face almost fills the screen. The urbane, understated Jones showed a real knack for television; his reserve and cool approachability, similar to Astaire's, played well in the medium. After the second number, Astaire appeared on a different part of the soundstage and said, "That was it Jonah, yes sir, that was *it*. We're gonna get together on the show before the evening's over, believe me." The pleasure Astaire takes introducing Jones to a national television audience can be felt in their next exchange. Astaire brings Jones out for some friendly banter. When Jones enters, Astaire shakes his hand and holds it, eventually standing with his other hand on the black man's shoulder. Their mutual respect and physical comfort with each other is everywhere evident. The two begin a rather unfunny shtick where they try to "talk" by way of music, Jones with his horn and Astaire with his taps. It ends with Jones putting his foot on Astaire's feet and Astaire stuffing his handkerchief in Jones's horn. They part as friends and the shared number Astaire promised earlier in the broadcast, a version of the jazz standard "St. James Infirmary," begins. In the original sketch, Astaire was to narrate a potted history of jazz, with Jones refusing to play along. In answer to Astaire's romantic notions of the music's history, Jones was to offer ironic asides emphasizing the jazz musician's more mundane search for a livelihood.[52] All this talk of jazz history was cut in favor of the conceit of horn and taps talking. Once again, Astaire avoided musical labels or explanations in favor of letting music alone make the point.

For the special, Jones re-created his version of "St. James Infirmary" from the 1957 album *Muted Jazz*.[53] His five-minute rendition begins with a cadenza, segueing into a down-and-dirty delivery of the melody, sparingly accompanied by his rhythm section. The single played verse is followed by five sung verses delivered in a passionate but clipped and cool style. Taking up the persona of the lyric, Jones sings as a man who finds his lover dead on "a long white table" at a New Orleans hospital morgue. In the third and fourth verses the singer turns to a description of his own death and the procession at his funeral, which will feature a "red hot jazz band." The final verse rounds out the story, closing with the singer in a bar calling for more booze. After this narrative, accompanied by a hauntingly spare bass ostinato, Jones goes into another trumpet verse and cadenza, which brings the number to an indeterminate halt just shy of four minutes. In the remaining minute of this dramatically conceived jazz record, the drums join in and Jones starts a minor-mode, in-time solo to an upbeat groove, perhaps evoking a second-line jazz band after the funeral. He quotes the hoochie-coochie melody and the up-tempo section closes with yet a third flourish. A slow, rising minor arpeggio from the piano brings Jones's moody recording to a close.

Producing his own television special allowed Astaire to make a dance to Jones's evocative vision of the song and to share the screen with Jones in new ways that move beyond his earlier dances with unnamed black musicians on film. Jones's performance has a lonely stylishness, effectively realizing an old song in an idiom at once dramatic, popular, and contemporary. Astaire could never have delivered the lyric with Jones's passion and authority. Astaire's vocals stayed on the lighter side, self-effacing and understated. He needed to borrow both Jones's voice and trumpet to get the right mood—a new mood for him—and Astaire

made it clear to the television audience that Jones was playing and singing while he was dancing. He says as much in his spoken introduction,
but he reinforces the point visually by way of specific framing and
movement choices. At the start of the number, Jones is shown playing
his opening flourish and the camera pans right to find Chase as the dead
lover literally "stretched out on a long white table." (She rises from the
dead to dance with Astaire during the closing up-tempo section.) When
Astaire enters, he pantomimes to Jones's vocal. Jones is shown on one
side of the screen singing, while Astaire is seen on the other side dancing. At the lyric "She'll never find another sweetman like me," Astaire
and Jones perform identical hand gestures, polishing their nails. For a
moment, dancer and singer do the same moves. In his earlier dances
with black singers, Astaire never suggested this sort of ventriloquism,
opting instead to make the visible and audible point that black performers were performing with him. Astaire's contribution comple-
mented their preexisting performance. But with Jones on television, the
connection is much closer. Astaire acts the part as Jones delivers the
lines. In the process, Astaire acts out his love for Jones's performance, a
love born of private listening that he shares with his audience on the
largest of public levels.

At the end of "St. James Infirmary," Astaire and Chase break out of
their final pose and approach the camera and the studio audience to
acknowledge the applause. Jones joins them from his position just off
camera and all three bow together. This was a pattern Astaire continued
in later shows. At the conclusion of the blues medley from the 1960
special, Astaire, Chase, Basie, and Williams all acknowledge the applause together, standing in a line with Astaire and Chase holding
hands. Interracial bows are all but unknown in musical film, where interracial numbers set in public performance contexts are extremely
rare, Gene Kelly and the Nicholas Brothers' quick bow at the end of
their interracial dance in *The Pirate* being the exception that proves the
rule. But television variety shows, modeled on vaudeville, always had a
live audience, and applause at the end of the number, acknowledged by
the performers, was customary. In the context of the civil rights movement, the interracial bows on Astaire's specials spoke for larger shifts in
the culture. The image of black musicians and white dancers coming
together to create dramatic dance numbers around identifiably black
musical idioms on national television provided a potent visual symbol
in the late 1950s and early 1960s. These interracial routines and curtain
calls transgressed on a fundamental level an American musico-dramatic

convention—as old as minstrelsy—that blacks and whites should appear onstage one race at a time. Here black and white bow as equals, with music and dance sharing the credit.

Verbal introductions of guest stars, standard practice on variety television for almost two decades, were omitted on Astaire's 1968 special *The Fred Astaire Show*. Instead, an especially bountiful array of musical guests simply appeared and did their bit. The Young-Holt Unlimited came on second, after Astaire and Chase's initial number together. This was a prime spot, filled on all Astaire's specials by African American jazz musicians. The Young-Holt Unlimited—a trio with Eldee Young (born 1936) on bass, Isaac "Red" Holt (born 1932) on drums, and Don Walker on piano—had one genuine hit to their name in February 1968. Their blues jam "Wack Wack" held the bottommost spot on the Top 40 chart for two weeks in January 1967. Two-thirds of the trio—Young and Holt—were just coming off a successful run with pianist Ramsey Lewis, highlighted by their 1965 number-five hit "The 'In' Crowd." Young-Holt Unlimited followed Lewis's lead, sustaining a place in pop music for the piano jazz trio. They would chart a second time in December 1968, reaching number three with "Soulful Strut."

Young, Holt, and Walker wisely began their five and a half minutes on national television with "Wack Wack," their pop calling card. Placed on a simple set, the group was arranged so they could interact visually while playing. Their regular repetition of the title words were intentionally not miked, but left for the general microphone setup to catch as it could. An aura of genuine performance prevails: this was not lip-synched as so much of variety television was during the 1960s. During the fifth and last chorus each player takes a short solo in turn, each solo beginning with a shot of the soloing player's black shoes, tapping in time to the music. Three pairs of black shoes are followed by a cut to a pair of white shoes—Astaire's—tapping along with the music, raising and lowering his heel in a heavy beat, just as he did in his first film solo to "Music Makes Me" in *Flying Down to Rio* more than thirty years earlier. Here, of course, Astaire is tapping along to a black jazz trio rather than a white jazz combo, but the beat in both cases is syncopated, popular, and jazz-based.

Near the end of "Wack Wack," Astaire is visually brought into the number as an engaged listener, echoing his positioning during the introduction and verse to "Slap That Bass." After the applause, enthusiastically led by Astaire, the dancer approaches the musicians as if to talk. He pulls a chair up to Young, who is busy checking the tuning on his

FIGURE 18. Astaire in motion at age sixty-nine, improvising with the Young-Holt Unlimited. Bassist Eldee Young is visible directly behind Astaire.

bass. The almost mimelike conceit of the special prevails. No one says a word; the music says it all. Young plays a new idea, an upward glissando of about an octave. Astaire likes this and makes a move to match. Matching gestures—musical and physical—are traded back and forth. The piano starts in and soon a second number has begun, this time for Young-Holt and Astaire together (see figure 18). The content of this dance involves a series of direct dance and music connections between Astaire and each member of the group. It ends with Astaire dancing all the way around the threesome and exiting by sliding out on his back along the floor, looking back at the musicians who wave to him while the audience laughs. The whole thing was put together in a single day's rehearsal—very quick work by Astaire's standards. Early on, while sitting with his legs crossed, Astaire switches his legs in time to Holt's drum rolls. Holt watches closely. Eye contact initiates further sound-and-movement jokes, such as a series of kicks Holt reinforces with rim shots. After establishing a pattern Astaire prepares to kick but doesn't follow through. Holt is hung out to dry, providing a rim shot for an unexecuted kick. The two exchange a "gotcha" look. Later, Astaire stands over the drums and points out which ones Holt should play. Holt complies but surprises Astaire with a rim shot that seems to nip the dancer's outstretched finger. Turnabout is fair play in this interracial encounter. The comic trick where Astaire fools Holt by not kicking is followed by an exactly synchronized, quite complicated combination between drummer and dancer, clearly the result of rehearsal. Astaire is not wearing taps—they were difficult to mike on television—and so Holt, in effect, dubs in the sounds Astaire's feet would have made (or that Astaire would have dubbed in himself in postproduction if this dance were for film and not performed live for a studio audience). The entire exchange plays on earlier themes of dance moves being under-lined by drumbeats or body parts making actual contact with drums and thus generating sound. The roots of Astaire's dance ideas reach back to his many film drum dances. Drummer Holt remembered Astaire saying, "'Catch me, man, catch me.' It was all impromptu—no choreographer was involved. It was all about what he felt."[54] The Young-Holt musicians are, in essence, a small vaudeville pit band, playing for the star's specialty, catching his falls and making sophisticated jokes on the practice of visual/aural coordination between dancer and drummer, all while sustaining a swinging beat. The practice reaches far back in American entertainment history, probably beyond the beginnings of Astaire's career as a child in vaudeville.

On the level of musical content, Astaire's dance with Young-Holt is true to form for both dancer and musicians. It takes a while to register, but the tune they are grooving to is Scottish rocker Donovan's 1966 hit "Mellow Yellow," perhaps an unlikely candidate for jazz treatment. But covering pop rock tunes was central to Young-Holt's repertory. Their 1969 album titled *Just a Melody* typified an approach to song selection embracing everything from The Doors' "Light My Fire" to Glen Campbell's "By the Time I Get to Phoenix" to the French chanson "I Wish You Love."[55] Young-Holt assumed a jazz trio still had something to say about the melodies of the moment. Astaire's specials, especially the final one, show a similar willingness to meet the audience partway and take on the tunes of the times. Even in 1968, Astaire was still trying to keep up with the pop music moment in a way that stayed true to the syncopated roots of his style.

Perhaps Astaire's most extraordinary interracial routine was a short comedy sketch with Jonah Jones preceding the number "Night Train" in the 1959 special *Another Evening with Fred Astaire*. As before, initially Jones and his group did two numbers without Astaire: Jones sang and played "My Blue Heaven" and "A Gal in Calico," old pop standards. On the first he traded fours with bass, piano, and drums in turn, offering hot improvisation in a tuneful context, a solid example of swing showbiz values. After these two featured numbers, Astaire appears and calls Jones over to him. The two men greet each other warmly and shake hands for a long time, Astaire puts his arm around Jones, and then they sit side by side on two tall stools. Astaire turns to address the audience. Jones interrupts him, saying, "I think you have my stool." Astaire, ever the gentleman, switches stools and turns back to the audience. Jones remains uncomfortable and puts his hand on Astaire's shoulder. Jones says, with a smile, "I was wrong," and they trade stools again. Astaire starts to speak but turns back to Jones, who smiles, and, without a word, they trade yet again. After this third exchange, Astaire calls for a marker and writes "yours" on the seat of Jones's stool and "mine" on the seat of his own stool. The two men sit. After a beat, Jones taps Astaire on the shoulder and says, "You've got mine." Jones is right: Astaire has the stool labeled "mine." They trade. The audience laughs. Astaire starts the intro again but after a few words stops himself. He turns to Jones, the light of revelation in his eyes, and says, "I've got yours," which, of course, he does. "So you have . . . so you have," says Jones, as they trade stools one more time and the audience laughs yet again. The stools sketch is predicated on Jones demanding, in the politest of ways, that he get the right stool, that he be comfortable. After Astaire labels the stools "yours" and "mine," Jones could use the inherent instability of these possessives to turn the idea of possession against Astaire to comic effect. The stools sketch can be read as a civil rights–era "Who's on first?" routine, where confusion about language has a resonance that goes beyond humor. The "yours" and "mine" language game is no trivial contest. Possession is the issue, stools are the contested objects, and the black man is demanding a choice the white man comes to see involves him in a matter of responsibility toward his fellow man.

Another Evening with Fred Astaire first aired on 4 November 1959. On 1 February 1960, less than three months later, four African

American men—Ezell Blair Jr. (Jibreel Khazan), David Richmond, Joseph McNeil, and Franklin McCain—initiated the sit-in movement by seating themselves on stools at the lunch counter of the Elm Street Woolworth's in Greensboro, North Carolina. The four men ordered coffee, were refused service, and themselves refused to leave until the store closed a half hour later. Within three days, the effort to integrate lunch counters went interracial, with the addition of white students from the local women's college. Within two months, sit-ins were occurring in nine states and fifty-four cities. Astaire's special, with its pointed "that's my stool" routine, was rebroadcast on 9 May 1960, when the lunch counter sit-ins were filling the nightly news. Two sorts of interracial encounters—Astaire and Jones's comic sketch about stools and multiple acts of political activism at lunch counter stools—aired in the same time frame on the same national stage: network television.

Arthur Kempton has described the interaction between the civil rights movement and network television this way:

> In [black gospel singer] Mahalia [Jackson]'s time the civil rights movement unfolded on television in serial snippets at the dinner hour. Nightly news shows were the national stage for repertory companies of real people performing a scene a day from several simultaneous productions. Some players and some plays came and went quickly, while others stayed on and on. The campaign against racial segregation in the South made good television for ten years. It had arresting visuals, a simple, uplifting story line, dramatic conflict, a big climax, and a happy ending.[56]

Astaire and Jones's stools sketch—like Cantor's mopping of Davis's brow or Allen's on-camera talk back to a racist viewer—was part of the civil rights "serial," Kempton posits. In the context of Astaire's long career, the exchange with Jones formed one in a series of interracial encounters reaching back to "Slap That Bass" in the 1930s. The continuing viability of jazz music making in popular contexts supported the coming together of black and white across all these decades, and Astaire's interracial numbers consistently found the cutting edge of the changing possibilities.

As the laughter for the stools shtick dies down, Astaire turns to the camera and starts the introduction for the next number. He says, "You know, with a show like this it's fun to do things that you've always wanted to do but never had an opportunity to do for some reason or other." This statement could apply to the sketch just finished, or the number that follows, which begins with Astaire and Jones singing and playing the tune "Night Train" in unison, otherwise unaccompanied. Jones fills the breaks. The intimacy of the shared musical moment is heightened by the memory of the black man and the white man having shared a pointed joke just before. It's the quietest, most personal of Astaire's many numbers with black musicians, and it came at a moment when personal, as well as casual public, interactions between black and white Americans were much on the mind of the nation as a whole. On the small screen—an improvisatory, less regulated space than studio film, a space without a history, where filling airtime was always a challenge—Astaire could dance to the music of famous black jazz musicians and then talk to them, casually and with his natural enthusiasm. The sketch with Jones is good-natured, well timed, and completely unnecessary. Astaire, executive producer of the special, went out of his way to allow Jones to do more than just entertain the crowd by singing and playing. He effectively presented Jones on national television as more than just an entertainer: Jones is shown to be a person with talents, rights, and a sense of humor. In the process, the stools sketch indirectly anticipated a controversy that would engage the national media and national attention soon after.

The sit-in movement asked a simple question: could black and white Americans share the same row of stools, drink from the same coffee cups, and enjoy a sociable environment in a public place? In short, could they have a nonmusical, nondramatic, everyday interracial encounter in the public arena? Astaire's television specials demonstrated that, indeed, they could. Astaire may not have intended this effect—there is no way to assess his positions on the racial issues of the time—but the length and breadth of his career gives evidence that, for him, interracial sociability was a foregone conclusion, particularly around the act of music making and dancing. He did what he could on several occasions to incorporate black performers into his dance numbers in contexts where interracial performance was unusual. He showed an eagerness to create routines that celebrated his admiration for the black musicians who inspired his work as a song-and-dance man working in popular music and jazz. And the progression of musical numbers discussed in this chapter shows that the mild comedy of Astaire and Jones trading stools had precedents in Astaire's film work reaching back to the 1930s, where he first listened to a group of African American men while seated on a stool. The stools sketch forges another link in the chain of interracial encounters with black jazz musicians that comprise a vital part of Astaire's creative life, a singular and important progression in his work where Astaire demonstrated two things: first, that jazz made him dance, and second, that the jazz that did it best was frequently made by black Americans.

Conclusion

Jazz records had a meaningful place in Astaire's musical life. More than just a means to play drums with a big band at home or a shortcut to collaboration with his television guest stars, jazz records could goad Astaire on as a dance creator, as shown by his oft-told story of why he came out of retirement in 1948. Astaire announced his retirement in 1946, symbolically ending his career with a solo dance to "Puttin' on the Ritz" in *Blue Skies*. But after a year spent traveling, watching his racehorse Triplicate rack up wins, and launching the Fred Astaire Dance Studios, Astaire was ready to return to creative life making dance routines on film. At that time and later, he repeated the same music-centered story to explain why he was heading back to work. At the center of this tale was a jazz record that posed rhythmic challenges Astaire found irresistible. Columnist Hedda Hopper quoted Astaire in 1948, around the time *Easter Parade* was released: "One morning while loafing about the house I played one of Lionel Hampton's records, 'Jack the Bell Boy *[sic]*.' The music began to send me. I jumped to my feet and started dancing. So when Gene Kelly broke his ankle and I was asked to take over *Easter Parade* I didn't hesitate. You might say I went back to work to get a rest."[1] In his 1959 autobiography Astaire repeated the story, again using the verb *to send:* "Home in Beverly Hills a few months later, I was playing a record of Lionel Hampton's 'Jack the Bell Boy *[sic]*' one day and it 'sent' me right through the ceiling. I thought to myself, 'I might as well be doing this someplace where it counts.' The urge and inspiration to go back to work had hit me."[2] As noted earlier, Astaire used the verb *send* in the revised song cue to the "Ad Lib Dance," where he tells Tommy Chambers to play "something that'll send me." Using the same verb to describe Hampton's "Jack the Bellboy," Astaire constructs his return to work as a physical imperative to meet a musical stimulus with a danced response and, importantly, to take that response into the public sphere of musical film, "where it counts." (Astaire's story fits with the facts. He declared an interest in returning to the screen two months before Kelly's injury brought him back to Metro for *Easter Parade*.)[3] Astaire's description of a significant turning point in his career in musical terms affords further evidence, of a more personal kind, that music came first with him, in this case, a virtuoso sort of jazz that never lost sight of the swing musician's imperative to entertain.

Hampton's "Jack the Bellboy" is a fast and wild ride, an extended drum solo recorded on 9 May 1940 with Hampton on drums, Nat "King" Cole on piano, Oscar Moore on guitar, and Wesley Prince on string bass.[4] It's easy to hear why Astaire loved the record, a driving rhythm section feature. Even though it prefigures the faster tempos and extreme virtuosity of bebop, "Jack the Bellboy" indulges in lighthearted sounds and gestures that speak to the uninitiated. Hampton sports a masterful mix of technique and showmanship not too far from Astaire's own blend of sophistication and accessibility. As an extended drum solo, the record celebrates the performer's absolute control of physical space, a theme that resonated with Astaire on many levels.

Lionel Hampton was born in Louisville, Kentucky, in 1908. Among the most visible African American jazz musicians of the swing era, he achieved national prominence in the mid-1930s when he joined the Benny Goodman quartet. Although not the first jazz player to play vibraharp—as he called it—Hampton gave the vibraphone a solid jazz identity. He also played piano (in his own two-fingered style) and drums and sang. Hampton also composed songs, mostly without lyrics, including his theme song, the jazz standard "Flying Home." With a savvy wife who managed his career, Hampton adapted to meet the changing popular music and jazz market, making recordings and fronting small groups and big bands until his death in 2002. He negotiated the change from swing to bebop by staying in touch with the most popular modern jazz players, such as Oscar Peterson (with whom he recorded widely) and moving closer to rhythm and blues. Hampton appeared on television often in the 1960s, whether jamming with the host (who played vibes) on *The Steve Allen Show* or playing *The Hollywood*

Palace (the same season Astaire did), where he was introduced as "one of the legendary names in American music."[5] He was a crowd-pleasing performer known for his showmanship—a favorite word of Hampton's—for well over fifty years.[6]

Hampton initially rose to national fame in an interracial context as a member of the Benny Goodman Quartet. This foursome of two whites (Goodman on clarinet, Gene Krupa on drums) and two blacks (Hampton on vibes, Teddy Wilson on piano) not only helped create small-group swing, but it was also the first interracial ensemble to play nationally. They were captured on film in one of the earliest band pix, *Hollywood Hotel*. The inclusion in the film of the quartet, which had already begun recording together and playing on the radio, made visually manifest the interracial nature of their music making. Like several other sidemen from the breakthrough Goodman band, Hampton quickly made himself a leader. Between 1937 and 1941 he organized twenty-three sessions for the Bluebird record label.[7] The personnel for each session changed, with a total of eighty-eight musicians participating. A quarter of the players Hampton called for the sessions, many from the Goodman band, were white. On the vast majority of the recording dates—about four out of five—Hampton assembled an interracial combo.

"Jack the Bellboy" was recorded during one of these small-group sessions, and Astaire may have been hanging around the studio. At another session that same Thursday in 1940, Astaire joined the Benny Goodman Orchestra for two numbers: the Gershwins' "Who Cares?" with Astaire on the vocal and a version of Astaire's own "Just Like Taking Candy from a Baby."[8] Hampton played on the latter. These discs do not stand out from Goodman's massive recorded output beyond the unfamiliar presence of a singing and dancing movie star. The two Goodman-Astaire sides do, however, stand out from Astaire's recording activity to this point. In the 1930s, Astaire regularly made pop records of the new songs from his RKO films with either the Leo Reisman or Johnny Green Orchestra.[9] These arrangements tend toward the sweet side: most appear to have been made in conjunction with Astaire's short-lived radio program. Neither Reisman nor Green cultivated a particularly hot sound, and Astaire's tapping is the only improvised element. Several songs receive a novelty treatment, taking a film song out of its context and building a new comic narrative for Astaire to play out on the disc. For example, "Pick Yourself Up" from *Swing Time* becomes a little scene, with Astaire attempting a complicated tap step, failing—the beat actually stops—then, with verbal encouragement from the band, getting it in the end. Astaire is the center of attention on all these records, which were made within the logic of what Irving Berlin called effective "exploitation" of a new song. Astaire's recordings with the Goodman band differ in both commercial intent and musical content. It is unclear why Astaire made the session with Goodman, his only work with an established name band on recordings that had no links to his film projects. The two sides point toward Astaire's ongoing ambition to be a hit songwriter and to personal connections between Astaire and the band scene. Well outside his normal context, Astaire effortlessly integrated himself into a group closely attuned to his own musical tastes.

Goodman chose the popular songs his band promoted and he must have liked Astaire's "Just Like Taking Candy from a Baby," for he had his principal arranger, Fletcher Henderson, make an arrangement. At the session, Henderson's chart was used on the first chorus only, with the bulk of the record mapped out in the recording studio as a shared improvisatory excursion for Astaire, Goodman, and Hampton.[10] After the band plays the first chorus, the second chorus shifts to the sound world of the Goodman and Hampton small groups. Astaire sings while Hampton and Goodman both solo around him, all with the support of the rhythm section only. After a brief transition using the full band, the small group returns for the third chorus, with Astaire now tapping instead of singing while Hampton and Goodman play, shifting between arranged or agreed-upon riffs and freer solo passages. Astaire is integrated into the band by having Hampton and Goodman accompany him throughout his sung and tapped solos: the lighter texture allows Astaire's taps to be heard in a balanced relationship to all other elements. The fourth chorus shifts among a variety of textures: the full band with clarinet and tenor sax soloing above it; the delicate triple-solo combination of Astaire, Hampton, and Goodman; and a final exchange between Astaire and Nick Fatool on drums. This is jazz for listening, not dancing. The levels of musical activity are many and varied. The Goodman version of "Just Like Taking Candy from a Baby" puts Astaire squarely into a hot swing context, and does so without making the record into an Astaire solo. The disc features Astaire without emphasizing him to the exclusion of the other players. His presence does not upset the group aesthetic. He is at once boy singer and jazz tap sideman. Astaire steps back from the spotlight, becoming a featured member of the band in a way that his film solos and the star-driven genre of the musical simply could not accommodate. The weight of Astaire's stardom inevitably made all his film solos about *him,* and the spectacle of an Astaire solo on film inevitably centers on Astaire's dancing body. On records Astaire could take a more modest role. As a result, on his jazz records the aural relationship between Astaire as a hoofer and jazz of the swing variety can be heard with great immediacy.

The postwar decline of the swing bands and the rise of bebop might have severed Astaire's connection to the ongoing history of jazz. The film musical lost touch with jazz when dance bands ceased to be Hollywood attractions and developments in modern jazz proved a tough sell in the popular marketplace. As has been shown, in the late 1950s and in the 1960s, Astaire reconnected with jazz, bringing popular jazz artists onto his television shows in a greatly altered popular music landscape. What about the years in between? How did Astaire stay in touch with jazz between 1945 and 1958? As earlier chapters have shown, in 1949 Astaire made a routine with white jazz players on staff at Metro ("Bouncin' the Blues"), and in 1955 he brought Ray Anthony's band into the last of the big band pix *(Daddy Long Legs)*. But far and away the most directly jazz-oriented project of these years was not Astaire's idea at all. He had to be cajoled into participating, but once convinced he entered in fully and never forgot the experience.

In 1952 jazz producer and entrepreneur Norman Granz asked Astaire to be part of a boldly conceived set of recordings that would allow the singer and dancer to renew his interaction with jazz players in a modern idiom. Granz claimed Astaire had not known who he was at first and initially said no when Granz described the project over the phone. That same evening, however, Granz ran into Astaire with his sixteen-year-old son, Fred Jr., at a Duke Ellington concert in Los Angeles. Fred Jr. had some Jazz at the Philharmonic discs, which Astaire had heard and liked, and this connection through his son made Astaire willing to go forward with Granz's plan, which took Astaire outside the closely controlled environment of the Hollywood studios.[11] Granz's vision for how Astaire might find a place in postwar recorded jazz brings this book to a close by refocusing on the paired terms in my subtitle: "Fred Astaire" and "jazz." None of Astaire's work has elicited consideration as jazz by jazz critics as has the result of these sessions, *The Astaire Story,* a four-record set that brought Astaire together with a group of Jazz at the Philharmonic players. In the context of this book, the resonance of *The Astaire Story* grows, as themes and patterns evident in Astaire's film and television work find a comfortable place among jazz players in the recording studio.[12]

Interracial music making was par for the course for most top jazz players in the swing years. White players like Benny Goodman and Artie Shaw brought black soloists into their bands because they wanted to play with the best, and they were not about to let race get in the way. For the times, that alone was a fairly progressive position. Granz shared the goal of bringing the best together in a color-blind context. But Granz also articulated a strong antisegregation agenda, and he understood interracial jazz performance as a powerful tool to effect change both nationally and globally. Granz's Jazz at the Philharmonic (JATP)—a successful but controversial combination of concert tours and recordings—had the express purpose of challenging bans on interracial seating in auditoriums across the nation. Press coverage of Granz invariably brought music and social action together. And while Granz's musical values and choices were grounded in the swing past, he had, in Alyn Shipton's view, "a radical impact on the climate for jazz in the 1940s and 1950s," helping to "heal some of the more damaging aspects of the 'modern' verses 'trad' split of the 1940s."[13]

Astaire recorded the thirty-eight tracks of *The Astaire Story* over a series of thirteen sessions in December 1952. He was making *The Band Wagon* at the time. It's not clear how he found the time to do both, but he did. Black jazz pianist Oscar Peterson, still in the early stages of his career, was joined for the sessions by members of the trio Granz had recently assembled around him: Barney Kessel, the white guitarist who appeared in *Jammin' the Blues,* and Ray Brown, an African American bassist.[14] Peterson's trio, like Hampton and Goodman's small groups and Artie Shaw's Gramercy Five in the late 1930s, was a consistent site of racially integrated music making. The Oscar Peterson Trio had recorded and toured widely in 1952 and did not normally work with a drummer. For the Astaire sessions, Granz added white drummer Alvin Stoller, whose creative connection with Astaire would continue to his television specials. (Astaire and Stoller would go on to create drum-centered routines for the 1958 and 1959 shows; see frontispiece.) Two regular JATP sidemen augmented the interracial Peterson quartet: white saxophonist Flip Phillips and black trumpeter Charlie Shavers. Phillips was a rare white jazz player who had been a sideman in a black band, playing with Frankie Newton's combination on 52nd Street in the early 1940s. Shavers was an influential improviser with many years' experience playing for white leaders such as Tommy Dorsey. Everyone involved, including Astaire, had had significant interracial jazz experience.

The Granz sessions put Astaire into the middle of a jazz milieu that was markedly different from the one he shared with Goodman and Hampton just over a decade earlier, but again he was cast as a combination singer and jazz tap sideman. The small-group jazz of JATP—what Barry Kernfeld calls "swing-bop combos"—was stylistically distinct from the big band swing of Astaire's Goodman records and the majority of his film solos.[15] JATP specialized in a sound that "the English critic Stanley Dance has called 'mainstream'—the kind of swing-playing that survived into the 1950s and which absorbed much of the more accessible elements of bebop harmony and melodic improvisation."[16] Astaire's easy integration into a context where his talents were not at the center expands the notion of Astaire as a dancer trying to find a place in the music as a jazz musician might. *The Astaire Story* affords a glimpse of Fred Astaire as a JATP All Star, a member of a team rather than a Hollywood star. Granz's strategy was—and, in retrospect, remains—daring: bringing a musical film star into a concert jazz combo context that was, in some ways, Granz's own invention and was by no means universally accepted as good for jazz among critics at the time or since.[17] Still, the project falls logically within Granz's larger goals: to increase the audience for and the public visibility of jazz and to challenge racial segregation on stage and in the popular music audience. The possible commercial success of linking JATP to a movie star like Astaire was certainly not lost on Granz either.

This would be the first time Astaire rerecorded a whole group of older material, and Granz was the first to recognize the commercial viability of Astaire redoing material the public associated with him. (Such trips to "nostalgiaville"—Astaire's word—formed a regular part of Astaire's television specials, always scheduled just before the close.) But the repertoire on *The Astaire Story* reached beyond tunes introduced by Astaire. The set includes songs and musical forms linked to both Astaire's jazz tastes and the developing practices of postwar jazz, a story Granz himself was trying to shape. Introducing a tap improvisation to a twelve-bar blues jam, Astaire says, "You know this album is a kind of a jazz album too, and jazz means the blues." As chapter 7 has shown, Astaire knew jazz history and he knew the blues. While introducing a track titled "Jam Session," Astaire steps aside completely: "The fellows are going to step out on their own here and do some jamming. I'll sit this one out." The "Jam Session" lasts six and a half minutes, the longest track of the set. Astaire's introduction inserts him into the scene as a listener, a position he was never uncomfortable with, whether at home listening to records like "Jack the Bellboy," on-screen in "Slap That Bass," or on television while the Young-Holt Unlimited played "Wack Wack."

Recording with a coterie of jazz musicians in an improvisatory situation with real consequences placed Astaire outside his comfort zone: the (still relatively new) tape was rolling. At the JATP sessions Astaire showed up and sang songs he already knew with musicians who already knew each other well. The arrangements were done on the spot, a point Granz emphasized in an interview with Leonard Feather for *Down Beat*. The primary task of the early sessions was getting used to playing together. "'S Wonderful," the fourth song recorded, offers a good example. Peterson and Kessel trade ideas they employed on a trio recording of the same tune made around the same time. Astaire's vocal is an added, not entirely necessary, layer. His performance is casual and self-effacing, projecting the singer's knowledge that this exercise in collaboration was not about him. Modesty, not typically associated with Hollywood legends, was one of Astaire's primary character traits, and here it is exercised as a form of jazz etiquette, his stepping back before the music and musicians a testament to his deepest creative values.

At the last sessions Astaire and the rhythm section recorded three dance numbers in a row. These were Granz's idea, and each was named by its relative tempo: "Fast Dances," "Medium Dances," and "Slow Dances." Astaire sets up the "Fast Dances" this way in one of several spoken introductions on the discs: "You know, I've always felt that dancing for records wasn't too effective as far as my stuff was concerned because I get off the floor a great deal and there may be a lot of empty spots for me. But I'd like to take a stab at it. I'll tell you what . . . I'll step in and ad lib with the boys. If you hear some strange noises out there, remember that's me. All right, let's go."

On this cue, Peterson launches into a version of the "Rhythm changes," a ubiquitous scaffold for improvisation drawing on Gershwin's "I Got Rhythm."[18] Peterson's trio recorded a twelve-minute improvisation using this same thirty-two-bar progression at the identical tempo the preceding February. The long cut was titled "The Astaire Blues," a nice irony considering the formal structure of the improvisation matches that of an AABA popular song and not the expected twelve-bar blues. The out chorus of "Fast Dances" sports rapid-fire rhythmic trade-offs between Stoller and Astaire, a noteworthy example of Astaire integrating himself into a modern jazz rhythmic sensibility. They are not exactly trading twos or fours here. Ideas thrown down by one are taken up and spun off by the other in a pattern that lies atop a discontinuous beat. The *Astaire Story* dances were an extra dividend, a product of the musical, professional, and personal relationships forged between Astaire and the JATP jazzmen during their month together in the studio. They are among the most convincing tracks in the set. Astaire sometimes sounds uncomfortable with the often very slow tempos while singing, but in the dances he integrates his rhythmic talents into interracial postwar jazz with complete success. It's ironic that during the height of the swing era, when tap was pervasive, Astaire had only one opportunity to tap in an improvisatory recorded jazz context, with the Goodman-Hampton collaboration on "Just Like Taking Candy from a Baby." A decade-plus later, at a time when tap was passé and jazz and popular music were heading in different directions, Granz opened the way for the most thoroughgoing jazz encounter of Astaire's professional life, sessions far removed from the MGM musicals Astaire was making simultaneously. In his television specials, unburdened as they were by character or setting and generically welcoming to a shared spotlight between host and musical guest star, Astaire was able to follow up on the experience of integrating his dancing with a genuine jazz context.

Arthur Knight describes *Jammin' the Blues* as "the first national advertisement for the JATP ideology of oppositional inclusion and progressive consumerism."[19] *The Astaire Story,* coming eight years later, on the other side of the shift from swing to bebop, worked as another innovative product in the same campaign to bring interracial, small-group jazz as art music to a wider audience, an audience Granz hoped would be attracted by Astaire, who experienced a resurgence of popularity after *Easter Parade. The Astaire Story* was packaged and marketed in deluxe fashion and issued in two formats: four twelve-inch LPs, sold separately at $5.95 apiece, and a limited edition box set of all four discs with additional printed matter, priced at $50.[20] The latter connected sound to image on two levels: documentary photos of the sessions by jazz photographer Gjon Mili and evocative line drawings by David Stone Martin, a regular JATP graphic artist whose spare style was closely identified with modern jazz for mainstream audiences. These visual components have the effect of transferring Astaire's physical presence into Granz's jazz scene in a palpable way. Looking at the photos and drawings while listening induces a bit of jazz and popular music vertigo: what is this movie star doing in the jazz world? Granz managed to promote the high-profile release on multiple levels in the 28 January

1953 issue of *Down Beat*. A broadly smiling Astaire in straw hat—he wore one into the late 1950s—and loosened tie was pictured on the cover (see figure 19); an interview with Granz about the genesis of the set appeared on page one; and the discs were favorably reviewed further on in the issue as well. The unsigned review, which bestowed the highest rating on the set, was three to four times the length of the average capsule review. It addressed the seemingly divided market for the discs with separate paragraphs beginning, "If you're an Astaire fan . . ." and "If you're a jazz fan . . ." The distance separating these two groups changed over the course of Astaire's career. Clearly, Astaire hoped this distance would always be bridgeable, for his audience and for himself.

The Astaire Story has never gone out of print, and several jazz critics have said positive things about the experiment. In 1979, Whitney Balliett wrote, "The notion of recording Astaire with jazz musicians was a good one, and it is a pleasure to hear him unfettered by visual images and a large orchestra."[21] Nat Hentoff praised the set in 2002, highlighting how Astaire, "without any guideposts but his own instincts and imagination, became one of the swinging improvisers on the date. . . . What comes through is the spontaneous pleasure of the musicians and Astaire as they kept finding a common groove, using space as an integral moving part of each number."[22] Writing in 1980, Richard Sudhalter identified enduring value in the set and used it to locate Astaire within the realm of jazz musicians.

> Among the many distinctions Fred Astaire has won in his 80 years, one of the most notable is the respect he commands among jazz musicians. He's not a jazzman himself in any strict sense. Even his dancing, at its peak, was an echo—albeit a highly elegant one—of precedents established by Bill (Bojangles) Robinson, Honi Coles, Baby Laurence and the other legendary hoofers. Yet whether dancing, singing, or acting, Astaire is a natural. His feeling for phrase is faultless, his time impeccable. . . . Astaire and his accompanists seem to have established an easy working rapport right from the start. They glide easily and with consummate taste through familiar territory. . . . It is an indispensable addition to the library of any jazz lover, regardless of stylistic persuasion.[23]

Sudhalter, like Marshall Stearns, remains suspicious of Astaire's hoofer credentials, implicitly downgrading Astaire's rhythmic prowess as a dancemaker by calling him a highly elegant "echo" of black tappers like Coles (born 1911) and Laurence (born 1921). But the comparison doesn't work: Coles was twelve and Laurence twenty-two years younger than Astaire. How could Astaire's rhythm tap—captured on

FIGURE 19. Granz gets Astaire onto the cover of *Down Beat* for 28 January 1953.

record as early as 1926, on film in 1933—be an echo of either man's style? Astaire can be compared to Robinson, but the differences outweigh the similarities. If elegant means refined, then Robinson wins on that score. Astaire's flat-footed, stamping, broken-rhythm jazz tap style contrasts sharply with Robinson's delicate, on the toes, less-accented approach, which has the evenness of "elementary drum paradiddles" expertly played.[24] Surprisingly, Sudhalter doesn't mention John Bubbles (born 1902), who was Astaire's contemporary and whose rhythm-tap style Astaire drew upon most directly and spoke of with admiration. Still, Sudhalter evaluates Astaire as if he were a jazz musician and not a movie legend, a valuable perspective and one that I hope the preceding chapters have rendered more complex and more richly explained.

Who, in the end, is a "jazzman" in the "strict sense"? Astaire's career with jazz, in jazz, and as a jazzmaker challenges any easy answer to the question. Critic Stanley Crouch contributes a more expansive view of jazz and Astaire's accomplishment in the context of American culture writ large.

> Astaire was so good that he is equally as large in American dance as Louis Armstrong is in American music. Astaire was like Armstrong because his confidence changed the art form in which he worked. . . . Astaire, who well understood swing, was one of Armstrong's children.
>
> Astaire's innovations came along at the right time, just as Armstrong's had, and were charismatic for exactly the same reasons: Astaire was incomparable. There may have been greater tap dancers than Astaire in some Harlem somewhere in America. Or, Astaire may have been right when he supposedly said that Bill Robinson was the greatest dancer he had ever seen. Even so, we can't be sure: What a genius sees when experiencing someone else working within his idiom is usually not only what is going on but what is *implied*. As it stands, taking into consideration all of the racist limitations that meant there could be no black leading men in the 1930s, we have to recognize Astaire for what he was. Not, as Honi Coles observed, the greatest tap dancer but the greatest American dancer, because Astaire was a master of blending and invention, as all truly superior domestic artists must be.
>
> The biggest difference between Armstrong and Astaire was that everything stopped with Astaire, while Armstrong opened up a new world of individuality that made it possible for many giants to follow in his wake.[25]

It is my hope that *Music Makes Me: Fred Astaire and Jazz* makes clear in concrete historical terms why Astaire appeared when he did and why he had no followers. His medium was too complex in technological terms and too industrial in its base. The historical window for his kind of creative work was ultimately quite narrow, and he threaded the needle perfectly. In this sense, Astaire's timing was unbelievably right and, it must be said, the fact he was white made it all possible. Astaire caught an unrepeatable historical beat and stayed with it as long as he could. That beat hasn't been there for anyone since, and it's now gone for good. All that remains are Astaire's creations—his routines—perfect confections of sound and image that endure not as echoes, but as pieces of the past to be experienced anew in the present (for fortunate viewers on the big screen).

It's tempting at this point to reverse the terms of my subtitle. What about jazz and Fred Astaire? Throughout this book I have used jazz to shine a new light on Astaire. How might Astaire's admittedly idiosyncratic career serve to illuminate the span of jazz history that coincided with his time on the big and small screens? I suggest three larger conclusions, a sketch of jazz history as captured on film and television. First, the Hollywood studios and early television made room for jazz when the music was attracting a mass audience or when powerful individuals brought jazz players into their films or television shows. Jazz in the studio era appears more often as a matter of context (nightclubs and bands) than content (improvisation). The technical requirements of audiovisual media put certain limits on jazz expression, but there was plenty of room for certain kinds of jazz artists (in particular, arrangers) to do solid work. Second, powerful white creative players could circumvent the racism and segregation endemic to the industry and the nation and make interracial jazz encounters. Astaire was not alone in doing this, but he had among the most empowered positions within the industry to bridge the distance between black and white. It was consistently his desire to do so, and the way Astaire expressed this desire changed and grew with the times. Third, jazz practices and traditions could inform the structure of film musical numbers when a given filmmaker had the requisite interest, skills, and clout. Knowledge of jazz history has been shown to illuminate Astaire's routines again and again in this book. Some of this knowledge was common coin for Astaire's original audiences. They saw and heard Astaire's work differently because of the surrounding jazz and popular music context. My analysis of Astaire's routines has endeavored to make such a contextual reading possible for present-day audiences as well.

Fred Astaire was incomparable. Those he worked with remembered him as such and often shared their stories. After his death, reporter

Sarah Giles traveled the world asking Astaire's friends and collaborators to share their reminiscences for the book *Fred Astaire: His Friends Talk*. Giles was amazed to find that no one had a single negative word to say about the man. Missing from Giles's list of interviewees was Oscar Peterson (indeed, it did not include any jazz figure). In Gene Lees's 1988 biography *Oscar Peterson: The Will to Swing*, the pianist recalled a time when Astaire remembered him.

> Oscar said, "When we made that album with Fred Astaire, Fred gave us all ID bracelets, Charlie Shavers, Flip Phillips, Barney Kessel, Ray Brown and Alvin Stoller. Ray's was stolen, somebody else lost his. On it he had engraved 'With Thanks, Fred A.' I became a friend of Fred's."
>
> "All these years later, when Sinatra invited us up to the house, and I walked in, I saw Fred and Gene Kelly standing together by a little bar. Fred said, 'How are you, Oscar, it's so good to see you.' And he introduced me to Gene Kelly. Then he grabbed my wrist, and said, 'You've *still* got it, you've still got it!' I said, 'Of course I do, I wear it all the time.' He said, 'I know, I've seen you on television, and I see it.' He was so enamored that I wore it, and I said, 'Except now and then, when I'm fishing or something, I never take it off.' He was amazed that I always wore it. Fred Astaire."[26]

Peterson's use of the verb *enamored* is resonant, evoking an enduring trope of jazz history: the white man in love with the musical power of black men. But Astaire was enamored with what the bracelet represented: the creative time Peterson, Astaire, and a group of jazzmakers had shared in the recording studio. My primary goal has been to understand as completely as possible the creative work Astaire undertook in the rehearsal halls, recording studios, and soundstages where he spent his long career in recorded media. Peterson's story—which closes with a poignant reiteration of Astaire's name—reminds us these were all places where Astaire's collaborators came into contact with a creative artist who was a perfectionist, a musician, a relentless searcher for "fresh ideas," a lover of jazz, and a modest human being.

Introducing the blues-based "Slow Dances" on *The Astaire Story*, Astaire said, "This album is a kind of jazz album." Kind of? There he sat in a recording studio with cutting-edge jazz players, a thoroughly modern pickup group with one of the best-paying, highest-profile gigs around, making a record destined for promotion on the cover of *Down Beat,* and yet Astaire qualified the proceedings. His other equivocations—"That isn't jazz," "Something that'll send me," "I just dance"—echo around that "kind of." Perhaps Astaire—always leery of musical code words, as we have seen—was just too shy to call what he did by the name jazz.

Certainly many others have struggled to define both Astaire and jazz. Both sit astride the categories of high and low, entertainment and art, technique and technology, virtuosity and vision. Both are deeply American. As Martin Williams noted in his perceptive essay on Astaire from 1992, "If Fred Astaire had been any less modest and a lot more pretentious about himself and his work . . . he would have been written up regularly in our major newspapers and magazines as a great American artist. Astaire simply became a great American artist not by announcing that he was one but by becoming one, and by leading and instructing his audiences, if not always his critics."[27]

On *The Astaire Story* Astaire introduced a jam to the Gershwin song "Oh, Lady Be Good" this way:

> Before I started doing pictures, my sister Adele and I were a very active part of the New York and London stage, and all points east and west, I might add. Oh, we covered a lot of territory. One of the most important of our shows was *Lady, Be Good!* George Gershwin did that score, of course. I don't think George ever dreamed that the title song was destined to become a jazz classic, but it has become just that. In the show it was performed as a plot song, sort of slow and straight. How it ever developed into a standard jam session number I'll never know. Nevertheless it has. I always love to hear it.

"Oh, Lady Be Good" wasn't really an Astaire tune—he had never sung it before this—but it was something of a JATP theme song. Astaire's spoken introduction situates the song in two musical worlds: Astaire's world of musical comedy and popular song, and the JATP world of modern jazz jam sessions. Astaire's "I'll never know" acknowledges the tenuous connection between the two worlds. Of course, on a larger level he did know how Broadway and Hollywood songs might turn into something called jazz. The practical details of his own career—the bands he worked with, the arrangers he hired, the cinematic scenes he danced in, the rhythms he made—held the answer. This book—a long response to Astaire's "I'll never know"—demonstrates that the links between Fred Astaire and jazz are many, and provides manifold and meaningful evidence for a rethinking of this unique creator's lifetime making music and dance in the racially segregated, but sometimes integrated, world of American popular culture.

Notes

ABBREVIATIONS USED IN NOTES
Archival Collections

AFSO   American Film Scripts Online, www.alexanderstreet2.com/
            afsolive

AMPAS   Academy of Motion Picture Arts and Sciences Script Collections,
            Margaret Herrick Library, Los Angeles

Baker   Herbert Baker Papers 1939–1978, UCLA Special Collections

Berlin   Irving Berlin Collection, Library of Congress, Washington, D.C.

Berman   Pandro S. Berman Papers, Wisconsin Historical Society, Madison

Davis   Interview with Astaire conducted by Ronald L. Davis, 31 July
            1976, Southern Methodist University Oral History Project,
            number 88, SMU Oral History Collection

Diamond   I.A.L. Diamond Papers, Wisconsin Historical Society, Madison

Edens   Roger Edens Collection, USC Cinematic Arts Library, Los Angeles

Fox   Twentieth Century-Fox Collection, USC Cinematic Arts Library,
            Los Angeles

Freed   Arthur Freed Collection, USC Cinematic Arts Library, Los
            Angeles

Gallup   *Gallup Looks at the Movies: Audience Research Reports,
            1940–1950* (microfilm collection), Scholarly Resources, Inc.,
            Wilmington, Delaware, 1979

McBride   Joseph McBride Papers, Wisconsin Historical Society, Madison

Mercer	Johnny Mercer Papers, Georgia State University Library, Atlanta
MGM	MGM Music Department Papers, USC Cinematic Arts Library, Los Angeles
Paramount	Paramount Collection, Margaret Herrick Library, Los Angeles
Porter	Cole Porter Collection, Irving S. Gilmore Music Library of Yale University, New Haven, Connecticut
Rennolds	John and Seymour Rennolds Collection, Georgia State University, Atlanta
RKO	RKO Collection, Arts Special Collections, UCLA
Sandrich	Mark Sandrich Collection, Margaret Herrick Library, Los Angeles
UCLA	UCLA Film and Television Archive
Warners	Warner Bros. Script Collection, Wisconsin Historical Society, Madison

Film Titles

BB	*The Barkleys of Broadway*
BS	*Blue Skies*
BW	*The Band Wagon*
C	*Carefree*
DID	*A Damsel in Distress*
DLL	*Daddy Long Legs*
FDR	*Flying Down to Rio*
FTF	*Follow the Fleet*
GD	*The Gay Divorcee*
HI	*Holiday Inn*
LD	*Let's Dance*
R	*Roberta*
RW	*Royal Wedding*
SC	*Second Chorus*
SS	*Silk Stockings*
ST	*Swing Time*
SWD	*Shall We Dance*
TH	*Top Hat*
TLW	*Three Little Words*
YT	*Yolanda and the Thief*
ZF	*Ziegfeld Follies*

Newspapers and Magazines

DB   *Down Beat*

NYT   *New York Times*

INTRODUCTION

1. *FDR* review, *Variety*, 26 December 1933.
2. AFSO, *FDR* shooting script.
3. Wierzbicki 2009, chapter 7.
4. Astaire only abandoned the practice of live music on set with *Top Hat*.
5. Tuba player Barsby recorded with two important bands in the early 1920s: Ferde Grofe's Virginians and Paul Whiteman's group. The tuba disappeared as the bass instrument of choice in the electronic microphone era (after 1925 or so), but low brass, which recorded particularly well, hung on at the studios into the mid-thirties, when further improvements in recording technology allowed for more subtle instruments to take over the bottom part. Using a tuba here, in a self-consciously jazz-oriented context, gave a slightly retro quality to Astaire's "Music Makes Me." Trumpeter La Franiere would record with Louis Prima's band in 1936, and Sharpe would play reeds on many Astaire films at RKO in the thirties, as well as make several arrangements for these films meant to mimic the sounds of contemporary dance bands.
6. RKO M/768.
7. Compare Venuti's recordings of "Sensation" (recorded 27 September 1928, Okeh 41144) and "Vibraphonia" (recorded 8 May 1933, Columbia 2782) to the hot sounds of the sextet assembled on the set to play for Astaire.
8. Giddins 1981, 81–82.
9. "Four String Joe" (recorded 15 November 1927, Okeh 40947) is one example of Venuti's approach.
10. Feuer 1993, 114–15.
11. Berliner 1994, 150, 172.
12. Balliett 2000, 545–46.
13. Paramount, *HI* production files. She apparently did not know that the minuet is danced in triple meter. Gavotte is a more accurate characterization of Astaire and Reynolds's classically inspired dance.
14. "Service Parties Easy to Arrange," *NYT*, 7 September 1943.
15. Astaire's television work has never been released commercially in any recorded format. Excerpts on YouTube and pirated copies for sale sometimes turn up on the Internet. While the shows remain difficult to view today outside of archival collections at UCLA and the Paley Center, the soundtracks for Astaire's first three specials were released as promotional LPs by Chrysler, Astaire's sponsor, and rereleased together in a box set by DRG Records (Astaire 1980).
16. Daniels 1983.
17. Astaire (book) 1959, Green and Goldblatt 1973, Freedland 1976, Thomas 1984, Satchell 1987, and Levinson 2009. Billman 1997b is a reference work.
18. Mueller 1985, 3–35.
19. McBride 93/3, interview with Fred Astaire, 6 January 1981.

CHAPTER 1

1. "Audit of Marquee Values" reports, prepared by George Gallup's Audience Research Institute in the 1940s, consistently put Astaire in a very small group of male stars appealing to men and women equally. See Gallup.

2. *R* review, *Variety*, 13 March 1935.

3. Davis 2005, 43.

4. Frank 1994, 56–59.

5. *Footlight Parade* (1933), *Something to Sing About* (1937), *Yankee Doodle Dandy* (1942), *The West Point Story* (1950). Cagney was in the musicals *Love Me or Leave Me* (1955) and *Starlift* (1951) but did not sing or dance in either. He does one duet in *Never Steal Anything Small* (1958) and dances briefly in *The Seven Little Foys* (1955), reprising his signature musical role as Cohan.

6. McGilligan 1979, 71.

7. Astaire 1951, 89.

8. Yablonsky 1974, 20.

9. Bosley Crowther's review of *Blue Skies* uses the word "hanger" to describe the function of the plot relative to musical numbers (*NYT,* 17 October 1946, 36).

10. Gilvey 2005.

11. Hirschhorn 1984, 114 ff. discusses Kelly's contract career.

12. Robert Montgomery's experimental *Lady in the Lake* (1947) is a very rare exception.

13. Dick 2007.

14. Giddins 2001.

15. Santopietro 2008.

16. Friedwald 1995, 20.

17. Friedwald 1995, 41.

18. Friedwald 1995 and Granata 1999 detail Sinatra's process in the recording studio.

19. Astaire (book) 1959, 242.

20. Basinger 2007, 20–36; Schultz 1994.

21. Hill 2000.

22. Some African American dance directors did work unofficially, such as Willie Covan, who helped create Ann Miller's "I Gotta Hear That Beat" from *Small Town Girl* (MGM, 1953). Busby Berkeley received screen credit for the number. Billman 1997a cites anecdotal evidence that Covan and other African Americans were working behind the scenes.

23. *Down Argentine Way* (1940), *Tin Pan Alley* (1940), *Sun Valley Serenade* (1941), *The Great American Broadcast* (1941), *Orchestra Wives* (1942), *Stormy Weather* (1943), and *The Pirate* (1948). All but the last, a Freed MGM musical, were done during the Nicholas Brothers' brief time under contract at Twentieth Century-Fox. Short features in *Kid Millions* (1934) and *The Big Broadcast of 1936* preceded their run at Fox.

24. Haskins and Mitgang 1988.

25. LeGon relates this story in the television documentary *Jeni LeGon: Living in a Great Big Way* (1999, dir. Grant Greschuk, Film Board of Canada).

26. Bogle 2001.
27. Eyman 2005, 76.
28. *Varsity Show* (1937) at Warners; *I Dood It* and *Cabin in the Sky* (both 1943) at MGM; and *A Song is Born* (1948) for Samuel Goldwyn.
29. Hill 2010, 2.
30. Hill 2010, 79.
31. Goldberg 1978.
32. Hill raises an important issue when she queries, "Was Ginger Rogers a tap dancer, if Hermes Pan choreographed all her routines with Astaire, rehearsed them for her, and dubbed the taps in postproduction?" (Hill 2010, 116).
33. Stearns and Stearns 1968, 224.
34. Kelly 1948.
35. Hill 2010, 201.
36. Hill 2010, 89.
37. Mueller 1985, 3–4.
38. Gibbons 2008.
39. Pollock 2005, 74–80.
40. Peterson 2002, 206.
41. Sidney Skolsky, "Hollywood is My Beat," *New York Post,* 24 April 1955.
42. Bill Davidson, "Fred Astaire: Just Beginning to Live," *Look Magazine,* 10 November 1959, 39–40.
43. Susan Lydon, "My Affaire with Fred Astaire," *Rolling Stone,* 6 December 1973, 62.
44. Korall 1990, 21.
45. See Krupa in *George White's Scandals* (1945), Robinson in *Stormy Weather* (1943), and Powell and Rich in *Ship Ahoy* (1942).
46. Charles Emge, "*Easter Parade* Product of Thorough Teamwork," *DB,* 22 September 1948, 8.
47. Freed, *YT* undated clipping, "Astaire, Composer and Harp Player."
48. Letter to the editor, *DB,* 1 August 1941, 9.
49. Tucker 2000.
50. Torme 1991; Meriwether 1998.
51. Eichenbaum 2008, 14.

CHAPTER 2

1. Fred Astaire, *Steps in Time* manuscript, USC Cinematic Arts Library, Los Angeles.
2. Kathleen Carroll, "Astaire: The Amiable Hoofer," *Sunday News,* 6 May 1973.
3. Lahr 1996, 244.
4. The Gershwin brothers also wrote a few songs for the Astaires in *For Goodness Sake* (1922).
5. Goldberg 1978; Giles 1988, 5; Pollock 2005, 74–80. In Gershwin's case, see also the memories of Thomas "Fats" Waller as recounted to his manager and biographer Ed Kirkeby in Kirkeby 1966, 53.
6. Floyd 1990, 32.

7. Lederer 1973, 56.

8. English Columbia 5173.

9. English Columbia 3969.

10. Perlis and Van Cleve 2005, 219.

11. Astaire and Mercer, together with composer Richard Myers, collaborated on a song, now lost, called "More and More" in 1930.

12. Mercer II-3/4, condolence note, Astaire to Ginger Mercer, 28 June 1976.

13. Furia 2003, 147.

14. Lederer 1973, 57. Berlin even had a spy of sorts at Paramount, whose regular reports on the making of *Holiday Inn* can be found in Berlin 324.

15. Youmans wrote five songs for Astaire and his sister on Broadway in *Smiles* (1930).

16. Kendis Rochlen, "Candid Kendis," *Mirror-News*, 2 May 1955.

17. Mueller 1985, 410.

18. Davis.

19. *Variety*, 17 June 1942.

20. Crawford 2001, x.

21. Ephron 1977, 133.

22. Mueller disagrees. See Mueller 1985, 23, 26.

23. Thomson 2004, 371–72.

24. Steiner's three-stave short score for this sequence survives (currently misfiled with the *Carefree* materials in RKO M/665). In a margin note to his arranger Maurice DePackh, Steiner wrote, "From the new material on—I'd like a feeling of '*Drama*' but still keeping a little rhythm going—My idea is to have this somewhat like a symphonic 'Paul Whiteman' arrangement."

25. AFSO, *FTF* shooting script.

26. Paramount, *LD* script, 23 March 1949.

27. Paramount, *LD* script, 4 April 1949.

28. Paramount, *LD* script, 25 April 1949.

29. Near the end of this eight-year absence from Hollywood, Mamoulian did some uncredited direction for David O. Selznick's *The Wild Heart* (a radical remaking of Powell and Pressberger's *Gone to Earth*).

30. Freed, *SS* script memos, July 1956.

31. Mueller 1985, 393–94.

32. Freed, *SS* production file.

33. Freed, *BW* memo, 9 December 1952.

34. Available on *The Band Wagon* 1996.

35. Eleanor Powell said as much about her and Astaire's similar approaches to making dance numbers. McBride, taped interview with Eleanor Powell, 3 March 1981.

36. Fields told the story at a Lyrics and Lyricists evening at the 92nd Street Y (New York City) in 1972, released on Fields 1988.

37. Croce 1972b, 57.

38. Banfield 2006, 286.

39. Analogues for this practice of lengthening breaks occur in swing band arrangements, such as Edwin Wilcox's version of "I'm Nuts about Screwy Music," recorded by the Jimmie Lunceford Orchestra in December 1935.

40. RKO P/79, *DID* production file.

41. Mueller 1985, 357; Levinson 2009, 187; MGM, *BW* prerecording schedule.

42. On a late 1952 recording made while *The Band Wagon* was in production, Jo Stafford sang the start of the second half of "Dancing in the Dark" an octave higher than the first, but she inevitably drops back down to the original octave soon after. No singer could sing the song in two different octave ranges.

43. Garber 2010 discusses the important dialogue between printed sheet music and performers making songs their own, a dynamic at work in several of Astaire's routines.

44. Dan Georgakas, "The Man Behind Fred and Ginger: An Interview with Hermes Pan," *Cinéaste* 12, no. 4 (1983): 26.

45. Croce 1972b, 51.

46. RKO M/34.

47. *Life,* 25 August 1941.

48. *Variety,* 24 November 1937.

49. Giles 1988, 9.

50. Thomas 1984, 98, 100.

51. Frank 1994, 81–82.

52. Joe Niemeyer, "Take It from His Stand-in!" *Silver Screen,* July 1948, 24–25, 60–62.

53. See, for example, Fordin 1996 [1975] and Silverman 1996.

54. In Davis, an interview almost forty years after *Yolanda* was made, Astaire emphasizes repeatedly that the choreography for the ballet was entirely Loring's work.

55. The chaotic situation on *Blue Skies,* which Astaire joined after production had already commenced, and the death of director Mark Sandrich were likely contributing factors as well.

56. Levinson 2009, 190.

57. Levinson 2009, 187.

58. McBride, taped interview with Gene Kelly, 19 February 1981.

59. Freed, *ZF,* "Proposed Order," 21 January 1944, and "Running Order for Show," 18 February 1944.

60. "Babbitt" was recorded on 12 May and shot soon after, strongly suggesting the number was made well after Alton's 31 March scenario was submitted. Astaire was making and shooting "If Swing Goes, I Go Too" through 17 April.

61. McBride, taped interview with Eleanor Powell, 3 March 1981.

62. *Broadway Melody of 1940* 2003.

63. Paramount, *HI* production file.

64. Freed, *RW* production file.

65. Goldmark 2005, 148.

CHAPTER 3

1. B.R. Crisler, "Mr. Selznick Does an Encore," *NYT,* 31 March 1940.

2. Altman 1987 and Feuer 1993 (first published in 1982) have been touchstones of film musical scholarship for the past generation. Altman sorts the genre

into three plot types (fairy tale, show, and folk) that are unrelated to industry terminology, and he seldom addresses questions of music or dance content or style. Feuer, leaning heavily on Metro and specifically Freed musicals, similarly reads musical films as wholes rather than assemblages of parts. The aspirational view of American screen and stage musical history as a movement toward greater integration of music, dance, and narrative has been a powerful one. Mueller 1985 asserts a place for Astaire in this historiographic stream. Taking a distinctive approach more in line with this study, Rubin 1993 approaches the work of Busby Berkeley by way of musical numbers rather than musical films.

3. Basinger 2007, 35.

4. Peretti 2007 offers a history of New York nightclub culture and politics across Astaire's career. See Erenberg 1981 for a prehistory of the nightlife pictured in Astaire's films. Waggoner 2001 provides a visually stimulating introduction to the post-Prohibition resurgence, and Malnig 1992 covers the nightclub era through the careers of exhibition ballroom dancers.

5. See Irwin 2010, part 3.

6. Charles Emge, "Movies Grab Name Bands," *DB*, 15 September 1940, 12.

7. Simosko 2000, 75.

8. White 2004, 100–101. A surviving partial draft of the script at AMPAS confirms Shaw's description.

9. Mercer and Hanighen's 1937 hit "Bob White"—about a bird who's got a "corny trill" and needs to learn to swing—imagines a similar dilemma in less acerbic terms. Furia 2003, 99.

10. Paramount, *SC* press book.

11. *Variety,* 7 October 1942.

12. When Regan's group appears they play their radio theme song, Arthur Freed and Nacio Herb Brown's "You Are My Lucky Star." It's the only tune heard in this biopic that's not written by Kalmar or Ruby, the songwriting duo being profiled. Early scripts imagined Whiteman's band filling this slot. Freed, *TLW* script file.

13. Fox, "CONFERENCE NOTES ON Daddy Long Legs," 7 September 1951.

14. Diamond 5/12, *DLL* memo, 22 July 1953.

15. Ephron 1977.

16. Fox, *DLL* "Writer's Working Script," 11 May 1954.

17. Rogers 1991, 79.

18. RKO S/424, Erwin Gelsey and Dorothy Yost, "*I Won't Dance* First Draft Screen Play," 141–42.

19. Clum 1999, 94–100.

20. Recorded 15 February 1935. Duchin recorded versions of most songs from the Astaire-Rogers cycle.

21. Barnet and Dance 1984, 43.

22. Hal Holly, "Music in Movies," *DB*, 1 December 1941. Ray Bauduc and Bob Haggart, members of Crosby's group, are, however, visible during the Washington's birthday number.

23. Hal Holly, "Music in Movies," *DB,* 15 December 1941.

CHAPTER 4

1. Giles 1988, 20.
2. AFSO, *FDR* shooting script.
3. AFSO, *FTF* shooting script.
4. AFSO, *DID* shooting script.
5. Paramount, *LD* script, 4 April 1949.
6. *The Fred Astaire Top Hat Dance Album and The Fred Astaire Dance Album,* both 1936.
7. Bindas 2001.
8. Warners, *Hollywood Hotel* script files.
9. RKO S/447, *SWD* treatment, 11 November 1936.
10. RKO S/446, *SWD* script, 3 December 1936.
11. RKO S/446, *SWD* script, 30 November 1936.
12. RKO S/447, *SWD* script, 23 December 1936 (white pages).
13. Perhaps Scott was still around. His daughter Pippa told Levinson, "For my dad, dialogue was absolutely his thing. He was always on the set. He not only had to be there, but Mark Sandrich wanted him there because they always improvised lines." Levinson 2009, 102.
14. RKO S/447, *SWD* script, 23 December 1936 (blue pages dated 6 January 1937).
15. Astaire 1951.
16. *SWD* review, *Variety,* 2 May 1937.
17. McLean 2008 explores the ballet side of *Shall We Dance* relative to other studio-era depictions of the male ballet dancer.
18. Cohan 1993, 55.
19. Cohan 1993, 63.
20. Freed, *BB* list of musical numbers, undated.
21. Phil Harris, bandleader on the enormously popular Jack Benny radio show, often used "Hiya, Jackson" as a greeting. Astaire's use of the phrase here may be a reference to Harris.
22. Paramount, *LD* script, 23 March 1949.
23. Freed, *BW* symposium transcript, 12 July 1953.
24. Edens, *BW* script, "Private Eye," 16 December 1952.
25. Mueller reads the dance as "notable for its strained efforts at hard sell, its ersatz sexiness, and its lack of musical wit and sophistication—qualities that suggest Astaire had little to do with the choreography." Mueller 1985, 361.
26. Fox, *DLL* script, 11 May 1954.
27. Mercer IV-18–3, *DLL* script, 3 September 1954.
28. Mueller 1985, 369.
29. Fox, *DLL* "Notes on Final Script of 8/3/54."

CHAPTER 5

1. Kay Thompson, vocal arranger and coach at Metro's Freed Unit, and Audray Granville, music editor at Selznick International Pictures, are noteworthy exceptions. See Irwin 2010, part 2, and Platte 2010, 194–229.

2. Van de Leur 2002; Magee 2005; Determeyer 2006.

3. Ferencz 1999; Suskin 2009.

4. There is no entry for George Gershwin in the *Grove Dictionary of Jazz.* Townsend 2007 addresses this question in the context of the early 1940s.

5. The bound conductor's score for *Blue Skies,* for example, reveals that jazz arranger Sy Oliver did a section of the production number "Everybody Step." Berlin 73.

6. McLean 2004, ix.

7. Mueller 1985, 172.

8. Astaire used the move a final time with Rogers in "They Can't Take That Away From Me" *(Barkleys of Broadway),* a fluid dance in which foot sounds are similarly suppressed.

9. Murphy 1937, 16.

10. Cugat 1948, 178.

11. Cugat 1948, 141. The alternate spellings "Cugie" and "Cugi" show up on occasion in other sources.

12. RKO M/664 and 666.

13. RKO M/666.

14. Ferencz 1999, 37.

15. Available on *The Band Wagon* 1996.

16. Freed, *BW* symposium transcript, 12 July 1953.

17. MGM, *BW* music department logs.

18. Balio 1993 defines the studio production system as a "group effort involving a strict division of labor" (10). Balio hardly mentions the music departments, but they operated on exactly the same organizational model as other departments and the studio as a whole.

19. Giles 1988, 192.

20. *Hollywood Reporter,* 30 January 1942, 3.

21. Berlin 351/7, 4 February 1942; Sandrich, 4 February 1942. Melnick 1999 addresses the "colored boy story" in Berlin's biography.

22. Berlin 356/10, 10 February 1942.

23. Berlin 351/7, 5 February 1942.

24. Berlin 351/7, 6 February 1942.

25. Berlin 351/7, 7 February 1942.

26. Berlin 256/13, *HI* cue sheet.

27. The sixth was the short instrumental introduction to Crosby's "Song of Freedom."

28. Paramount, *HI* recording programs, 29 November 1941.

29. The two versions were recorded within weeks of each other in late 1952: Stafford and Weston's on 12 September, Astaire and Franklyn's on 8 October. Stafford's LP wasn't released until August 1954 (Stafford 1954).

30. Bogle 1997, 165.

31. Anderson: recording as Ivie Anderson and Her Boys from Dixie on Variety VA-591, 8 June 1937. Garland: with Georgie Stoll and His Orchestra on Decca 1432 B, September 1937.

32. Bogle 1997, 166.

33. Server 2006, 217–18.

34. Barry Ulanov, "Phil Moore Five Paved Way for Race in Exclusive Gotham Spot," *California Eagle*, 25 October 1945, 13.

35. Bogle 1997, 167.

36. RKO M/352.

37. RKO M/351.

38. Charles Emge, "Movie Music," *DB*, 1 October 1943.

39. Jackson's career as described in this paragraph is taken from scrapbooks on recent graduates preserved in the Julliard archives. Most of the clippings came from black newspapers.

40. Leonard Feather column, *DB*, 15 May 1940.

41. Sherk 2007.

42. MGM, Calvin Jackson personnel file. Special thanks to Ned Comstock for this source.

43. Previn 1991, 5.

44. MGM, Calvin Jackson personnel file, memo, Arthur Bergh to Izzy Friedman, 22 November 1943.

45. "Calvin Jackson to Play Sunday," *California Eagle*, 26 July 1945, 13.

46. Freed, *ZF* "Recording Programs."

47. Available on *Ziegfeld Follies* 1995. Astaire's taps are, of course, lost.

48. Freed, *ZF* AD reports.

49. Edens 14.

50. Stoll 1947.

51. RKO M/61

52. Fordin 1996, 301–2.

53. MGM, Calvin Jackson personnel file.

54. Feather 1961.

55. Newquist 1966 includes an interview with Jackson where he describes his creatively satisfying musical life as a pianist and composer.

56. Jackson 1958.

57. Feather 1961.

58. The selections described in this paragraph were reissued together on Verve Records' Popular 2000 series of jazz LPs. See Moore 1955.

59. Basie 1985, 192.

60. Barnet and Dance 1984, 85–86.

61. Martin did at least one arrangement for Sinatra, his 1962 version of "I've Got a Right to Sing the Blues."

62. Martin contributed to five big band jazz albums for the Somerset label in 1959 alone: *The Video All-Stars Play TV Jazz Themes: A Brilliant Program of TV Jazz Themes Scored, Arranged and Played by the Leading West Coast Men who have created this new medium of television background scores*, SF-8800; *Skip Martin's Scheherajazz for Symphony and Jazz Band*, SF-9700; *Let's Dance to Swingin' Things from Can-Can*, SF-12400; *Sounds and Songs from the Era of the Untouchables*, SF-12900; and *Swingin' with Prince Igor and Tannhäuser*, SF-1170.

63. Mercer 1958.

64. Mueller 1985, 355.

65. Brown 1953.

66. Privately held archival document, *DLL* cue sheet. Special thanks to Chris Bamberger for facilitating my access to this document.

67. Astaire 1952.

68. Basie released Beatles albums in 1966 and 1969. Ellington played a Beatles medley for *The Ed Sullivan Show* in 1970.

69. Alba 2005, 194.

70. Ayres 1966 provides a sample of the sound of *The Hollywood Palace*.

71. Hefti 1962.

CHAPTER 6

1. Wald 2009.

2. Balio 1993, 170–71.

3. *FDR* review, *NYT,* 22 December 1933.

4. Dolores del Rio, star of *Flying Down to Rio,* embodied this Hollywood type at its most proper extreme. In "The Carioca," the type lets its hair down a bit. See Rodríguez 2008, 53–61.

5. R.T. Galvao provided the studio with samples from Radio Sociedade Record Sao Paulo. RKO M/558.

6. Gil-Montero (1989, 54–58) describes the *baiana* archetype Miranda drew upon. Gil-Montero mistakenly claims that Dolores del Rio, the romantic lead in *Flying Down to Rio,* appears costumed as a *baiana.* Del Rio's sophisticated and Continental screen persona would never permit such a descent in social status. She does not visit the Carioca nightclub. Astaire and Rogers, *Flying Down to Rio*'s thoroughly American second couple, are, however, eager to join in the fun as led by Moten's hot *baiana.*

7. Harrison 1999, 44–45.

8. Willis 2009, 52.

9. Croce 1972a, 85.

10. John Lonergan, "Let Yourself Go! A Double Tap Routine," *American Dancer* (April 1936), 15.

11. Harrison 1999, 47.

12. Malnig 1995, 125.

13. Rogers claimed the eight leaps over Astaire's leg to end the dance were her idea (Rogers 1991, 201). Mueller credits the move to Pan (Mueller 1985, 145). Astaire, working with Pan, reused the move with Vera-Ellen in "Mr. and Mrs. Hoofer" from *Three Little Words.*

14. Sandrich, 16 November 1937.

15. Manning and Millman 2007, 153.

16. The initial lines of this verse date to a 1931 unpublished song called "Any Love Today?" (Kimball and Emmet 2001, 296).

17. Manning and Millman 2007, 103.

18. *Life,* 22 August 1938.

19. Berman 28/8, C publicity materials.

20. Brunswick 8190. Berlin 90 contains scores and parts.

21. *Dance,* November 1938, 26.

22. The *New York Times* noted the arrival of the Lambeth Walk in a demonstration at a dance teacher's convention in late July 1938. "The Yam" had been shot a month earlier. Murray added the dance as a special supplement to his 1938 book.

23. Murray 1938, 175.

24. Murray 1938, 188.

25. Murray 1938, 197.

26. Arlene Croce defined the "Big White Set" in Croce 1972a.

27. Wilbur Morse Jr., "Memoir from a Dancing Master," *Picture Play,* May 1940.

28. Mueller 1985, 181.

29. "Meet Swing Music Master; His Middle Name Is 'Umph'," *Detroit Free Press,* 2 March 1939.

30. "This Is the 'Dig It'," *NYT,* 17 November 1940, 135.

31. Paramount, *SC* press book.

32. Paramount, *SC* press book.

33. Stearns and Stearns 1968, 324.

34. James never recorded Basie's "Shorty George," but radio transcriptions from 1943 capture his band's version. Unrelated blues songs using "Shorty George" as the title were recorded by Sippie Wallace in 1923 and Huddie Ledbetter (Lead Belly) in 1935.

35. Frank 1994, 82.

36. Croce 1972b, 57.

37. Ferencz 1999, 159.

38. White and White 1998.

39. Kay Kyser, Paul Whiteman, Bob Crosby, and Benny Goodman all recorded the tune.

40. This soundie can often be found on YouTube.

41. Segrave 2002, 156–57.

42. "Astaire Dances with Hayworth," *Life,* 9 November 1942, 64.

43. This short can often be found on YouTube.

44. Manning and Millman 2007, 153.

45. Cue titles and credits for this scene are taken from the *DLL* cue sheet, a privately held source.

46. Anthony 1953.

47. Anthony 1951; Champion and Champion 1954 (published in conjunction with a dance instruction book); Whiteman 1955.

48. Murray 1955; Anthony 1956.

49. "New Pop Records," *Time,* 26 January 1953.

50. Mueller 1985, 370.

51. Helen Dzhermoijnska, "Swingtime on Park Avenue," *Dance* (April 1947), 25; Fred Astaire Dance Studios, *Ballroom Manual: Gold Standard* (1959).

52. "The Astaire: The New Swing-Trot Ballroom Dance Created by Fred Astaire," music by Cy Walter, lyrics by Andrew Rosenthal, published by Leo Feist.

53. Engel 1962, chapter 24.

54. Freed, "Musical Numbers for Barkleys of Broadway," 7 June 1948.
55. Freed, "Musical Numbers for Barkleys of Broadway," 19 June 1948.
56. Freed, "Musical Numbers for Barkleys of Broadway," 21 July 1948.
57. Wall 2009.

CHAPTER 7

1. Charles Emge, "Why *Tempo* Sold Out to *Down Beat*," *DB*, 15 May 1940, 10.
2. Charles Emge, "*Barkleys* Good Boxoffice *[sic]* But Can't Figure Out Why," *DB*, 29 July 1949, 9.
3. Robert Russell Bennett's first try was rejected. The scores for "Loch Lomond" are preserved in RKO M/665 and 666.
4. Goldmark 2005, 20.
5. Handy 1926 offers a good measure of the meaning of the word "blues" in the broader popular music scene of the 1920s. Handy includes sheet music for the Gershwin tune "The Half of It, Dearie, Blues," written for Astaire to introduce in *Lady Be Good!*
6. Gushee 2005.
7. Porter I 34/229.
8. AFSO, *FTF* shooting script.
9. ASFO, *GD* script.
10. RKO P/50, *GD* partial script, 6 June 1934.
11. AFSO, *FTF* shooting script.
12. Mueller 1985, 70.
13. Crawford and Magee 1992, x.
14. The following is a list of "Bugle Call Rag" recordings surveyed. The names of the leaders are followed with the tempo, in quarter notes per minute, in parentheses. An * denotes recordings beginning with the bugle call to assembly.

1922: New Orleans Rhythm Kings (235)

1923: Abe Lyman Orchestra (192)

1926: Ted Lewis (246)

1927: Cannon's Jug Stompers (175), Red Nichols and his Five Pennies (203)

1928: Mills' Musical Clowns (194), The Washingtonians [Duke Ellington] (244)

1929: Jack Pettis (196*), Reuben "River" Reeves (138), Ed Lang (220*)

1930: Chocolate Dandies (199*)

1931: Cab Calloway (237*)

1932: Duke Ellington (195*), Mills Brothers (250), Billy Banks, with Eddie Condon and Pee Wee Reese (242*), "Test for Victor Young," with Tommy Dorsey (264*)

1933: Jack Hylton (228*), Benny Carter (244*), Harry Roy (239*)

1934: Benny Goodman (286*, 244), Joe Venuti (242)

1935: KXYZ Novelty Band (285*), Zutty Singleton (216), Ray Noble (243*)

1936: Casa Loma Orchestra (247*), Goodman (247*, 244*), Don Redman (245), Benny Carter with Kai Ewans (243)

1937: Roly's Tap-Room Gang, with Jonah Jones and Adrian Rollini (205), Goodman (325*), Cab Calloway (268*), Django Reinhardt (200*)

1938: Fletcher Henderson (239)

1939: Bobby Hackett (205); Duke Ellington's "The Sergeant Was Shy" (192) is an especially sophisticated version

1940: George Wettling (202), Rex Stewart's Big Seven (196)

1941: Metronome All-Stars (228*)

15. The sheet music includes a melody seldom heard on any recording, and no recording surveyed (even the vocal version by the Mills Brothers) includes the lyrics as printed in the 1923 sheet music.

16. The Ray Noble version from 1935 takes quotation to an extreme. Folk songs, national anthems ("La Marseillaise"), classical themes (Ravel's *Bolero*), and the hoochie-coochie song are inserted into opening breaks that are artificially extended to make room for longer, and presumably funnier, quotations. This thoroughly arranged version allows the novelty song aspect of "Bugle Call Rag" to overtake its utility as a venue for improvisation.

17. Three other tunes were recorded at the 23 July 1940 session where Rex Stewart's Big Seven recorded "Bugle Call Rag": "Solid Rock" (a blues), "Cherry," and "Diga Diga Doo." Except for the out chorus on "Cherry," all three are played in a thoroughly contemporary swing idiom. The throwback to New Orleans–style collective improvisation for "Bugle Call Rag" was perhaps an exercise in nostalgia or conscious emulation of a past style. White drummer Dave Tough joined an otherwise all-black ensemble.

18. Stearns and Stearns 1968, 190.

19. Levinson 2009, 126.

20. Burke 2008, 151.

21. Silvester 2009.

22. Thompson 1970, 73.

23. Berlin 73, *BS* conductor's score.

24. Mueller 1985, 273.

25. *Variety,* 25 September 1946.

26. "The Ritz Roll and Rock" was created in December 1956 and recorded and shot in early January 1957. Freed, *SS* production file.

27. *News of the Day* 25, no. 241 (15 January 1954).

28. "Mr. Anthony's Boogie" (Capitol 1280); "Bunny Hop" (Capitol 2251).

29. Guralnick 1994, 437.

30. Freed, *SS* "Temporary Layout for Musical Numbers," 2 August 1956.

31. Freed, *SS* recording schedule, 12 November 1956.

32. *SS* review, *NYT,* 19 July 1957, 11.

33. George J. Rosenberg, *New York Mirror Magazine,* 30 June 1957, 10.

34. Rennolds V/6, "The Afterbeat" lead sheet.

35. "The Afterbeat" can be heard on the 1959 album *Now* (Astaire's only entry in the late-1950s LP market dominated by Sinatra on Capitol) and a pro-

342 | Notes to Chapters 7 and 8

motional soundtrack LP of *Another Evening with Fred Astaire* distributed free by Chrysler, sponsor of the special (Astaire [recordings] 1959a and 1959b). Astaire 1980 also includes the number as heard on television.

36. "Astaire Tries for a Topper," unidentified clipping, Astaire clippings file, Wisconsin Historical Society, Madison.

37. Dance 1980, 199.

38. Giddins 1998, 183.

39. Basie and Williams 1959.

40. Levinson 2009, 275–76; Sheridan 1986, 563. Certain segments of Astaire's specials were prerecorded, then shown interleaved with live segments, a daring decision at a time when color videotape was still in its early development. Astaire was pushing the technology—trying, perhaps, to make the inherently risky context of live television more like the controlled filmmaking process. See Meisel 1988.

41. Mathieson 2002, 54.

42. Mathieson 2002, 61.

43. Smith 1964.

44. Shipton 2007, 503.

CHAPTER 8

1. Davis.

2. Eustis 1937, 110.

3. Lederer 1973, 58.

4. Robinson also appeared in a number in the Broadway production of *George White's Scandals* (1936) called "Brother Sublime and His Pied Piper of Harlem."

5. RKO P/67 and S/425, ST production and script files.

6. Much rehearsal time was spent on a long vaudeville act to the song "It's Not in the Cards." The routine was filmed, but virtually all of it was cut from the film.

7. *Let's Dance* was released in VHS format, as were all of Astaire's musical films.

8. Charles Emge, "'Barkleys' Good Boxoffice [sic] But Can't Figure out Why," *DB*, 29 July 1949, 9.

9. Croce 1972a, 47.

10. The Garland and Rogers versions of *Barkleys* are in Freed.

11. By the close of the 1950s all the studio orchestras had been dismantled and the studio music departments that supported Astaire's creativity, together with the studios themselves, were gone.

12. Charles Emge, "Studio Job Scramble Subsiding," *DB*, 20 October 1948. Young was leaving Columbia when this article was published. He noted, "There was no race pressure in my leaving."

13. MGM. The "Bouncin'" lead sheet is dated 23 June, a full three weeks before Garland was cut and Rogers put in her place. "Bouncin'" appears for the first time on a musical breakdown for the film immediately after Rogers came

aboard. Perhaps Astaire requested the number thinking it might serve as an alternate solo should "Shoes with Wings On" not pan out.

14. The Thompson session took place 22 April 1947. Saxophonist Benny Carter, recently featured at MGM with Lena Horne in *Ziegfeld Follies,* is credited as arranger and composer on both "Boppin' the Blues" and "From Dixieland to Bop."

15. "Diggin' the Discs" review of *Till the Clouds Roll By, DB,* 7 May 1947.

16. Freed, *BB* production file.

17. Levinson 2009, 168–69.

18. Special thanks to Christine Bamberger, who alerted me to this borrowing.

19. Both recorded 13 October 1945, with Previn at the piano, Dave Barbour on guitar, and John Simmons on bass.

20. Previn 1991, 139.

21. Stockdale 1999, 506.

22. *LD* review, *Variety,* 9 August 1950.

23. Bosley Crowther, *LD* review, *NYT,* 30 November 1950.

24. Paramount, *LD* music department records. Recorded 17 June 1949, Robert Emmett Dolan, conductor. The instruments used here are fourteen violins, four violas, four cellos, one bass, seven saxes, four trumpets, four trombones, one guitar, one piano, and one drum set, "2nd Channel: 2 Specialty Pianos"

25. Paramount, *LD* final production budget, 18 July 1949.

26. Giles 1988, 10.

27. Gavin 1991.

CHAPTER 9

1. *Chicago Defender,* 2 February 1935, 7.

2. UCLA, "Home Movies. The Nicholas Brothers. Tapes 1 and 2."

3. Other sources on African Americans in studio-era Hollywood include the work of Thomas Cripps and Donald Bogle.

4. Watts 2005, 112. Bogle 2005 offers a panorama of black Hollywood in the studio era.

5. Watts 2005, 82.

6. Bogle 2001, 117–35.

7. The practice of cutting out black specialty numbers is often assumed in the literature. Regester 2002, a valuable survey of the entertainment coverage in four black newspapers before 1950, provides solid evidence for the practice.

8. Watts 2005, 113. Raye did a blackface number backed up by a black chorus and Louis Armstrong in the film *Artists and Models* (1937), an extremely rare combination of interracial and blackface performance. Eddie Cantor in blackface shared a brief exchange with The Nicholas Brothers in *Kid Millions* (1934).

9. Knight 2002.

10. Sandrich, *TH* "Estimating Script FOOTAGE of MUSIC & DANCE NUMBERS," 15 March 1935.

11. RKO S/598, C treatment, 27 July 1937.

12. Berlin 106/5, *HI* script, 24 November 1941.

13. Berlin 106/2, "Notes on conference between Mr. Berlin, Mr. Sandrich and Mr. Myers," 28 April 1941.

14. See part one of my dissertation (Decker 2007) and my forthcoming book *Show Boat: Race and the Making and Re-making of an American Musical* (Oxford University Press).

15. Badger 1995; Malnig 1995; Cook 1998; Golden 2007.

16. RKO S/585, Oscar Hammerstein II, "*The Castles* First Draft Continuity," 13 December 1937.

17. Badger 1995, 104.

18. Badger 1995, 177.

19. Castle 1919, 58

20. Mueller 1985, 120.

21. Dinerstein 2003.

22. Graham Wood notes the juxtaposition of "urban modernity and outdoor work songs" at the outset of "Slap That Bass" (Wood 2002, 228).

23. RKO P/73, *SWD* production file. These details suggest the tracking shot was Sandrich's idea.

24. The Mills Brothers pioneered this sound in the popular music marketplace in the mid-1920s. See Southern 1997, 513; and Maultsby 2005, 252–53.

25. Bordwell et al. 1985, 56.

26. The extravagance of the set can be appreciated by comparison with other Art Moderne sets from the period. See Mandelbaum and Myers 2001.

27. RKO P/73, *SWD* shooting schedule, 13 November 1936.

28. RKO S/447, *Watch Your Step* treatment, 11 November 1936.

29. RKO S/447, Allan Scott and Ernest Pagano, *SWD* "First Draft Screenplay," 30 November 1936.

30. This section draws throughout on RKO P/73, *SWD* production files.

31. Feuer 1993, 26.

32. Green and Goldblatt 1973, 226.

33. Bordwell et al. 1985, 63–64.

34. Mueller 1985, 192.

35. Murray 1976, 45.

36. Knight 2002 shows an ahistorical bias against swing bands, calling Cab Calloway's group "commercial jazz" and dismissing the Nicholas Brothers as merely "dancers" (224). In 1944 all recorded jazz was issued under commercial auspices, and the jam session, pictured in *Jammin' the Blues,* was still a relatively new phenomenon for the mass audience, something that needed to be named and described.

37. For example, Roy Eldridge appears as a featured member of Gene Krupa's band in *Ball of Fire* (1941).

38. Knight 2002, 227–29.

39. Knight 2002, 218. Knight uses genre categories from Altman 1987.

40. John Martin, "The Dance: Fred Astaire A Distinguished Art in an Unpretentious Medium," *NYT,* 2 November 1941; Green and Goldblatt 1973, 228.

41. Morgenstern 2004, 637–56. Morgenstern mentions Jonah Jones's appearances on Astaire's first special, which is described as "another essentially non-jazz show" (649).

42. Goldman 1997, 277–78.
43. Alba 2005, 93.
44. Alba 2005, 103.
45. Steve Allen, "Talent Is Color-Blind," *Ebony,* September 1955, 41.
46. Basie 1985, 335–36; Peterson 2002, 204–7.
47. "It Was Fun for Astaire, Too," *New York Herald Tribune,* 19 February 1961.
48. Dance 1974, 161–75; Burke 2008, chapter 3.
49. Josephson 2009, 51–52.
50. "Jonah on the Trumpet," *Newsweek,* 23 November 1959, 108.
51. Jones 1958.
52. Baker, *An Evening with Fred Astaire* draft scripts.
53. Jones 1957.
54. Levinson 2009, 280.
55. Young-Holt Unlimited 1969.
56. Kempton 2003, 55.

CONCLUSION

1. Hedda Hopper, "Fred Astaire Comes Out of Retirement to Rest Up," *Los Angeles Times,* 18 April 1948, C1.
2. Astaire (book) 1959, 290.
3. A.H. Weiler, "By Way of Report," *NYT,* 17 August 1947. Kelly's injury was sustained on 12 October.
4. Victor 26652. At the same session Hampton and his small group recorded "House of Morgan" and "Central Avenue Breakdown." White singer Helen Forrest, a regular part of Goodman's band, joined Hampton's group for "I'd Be Lost Without You."
5. *The Steve Allen Show* aired 16 January 1964; *Hollywood Palace* aired 6 November 1965.
6. Hampton and Haskins 1989.
7. These sessions were reissued collectively as Hampton 1976.
8. Columbia 35517.
9. Release of film soundtracks on record only began in the late 1940s. *Easter Parade* was the first Astaire film to be released in this manner.
10. Magee 2005, 256.
11. Leonard Feather, "*The Astaire Story* Another Milestone in Granz' Career," *DB,* 28 January 1953, 1.
12. Astaire and the Jazz at the Philharmonic All Stars 1953.
13. Shipton 2007, 465.
14. Kessel would remain with Peterson only one year. Brown first worked with Peterson at a JATP concert in 1949, and the pair collaborated into the mid-1960s.
15. Kernfeld 1991, 349–64.
16. Shipton 2007, 465.
17. On Granz, see Balliett 1959; Feather, 1972; Horricks 1991; and Shipton 2007.

18. See Crawford 1993, chapter 7, for a discussion of this Gershwin tune and its career as a basis for jazz improvisation.

19. Knight 2002, 212.

20. The complete set, reissued repeatedly in LP and CD formats, has never gone out of print.

21. Balliett 2000, 546.

22. Hentoff 2004, 29.

23. Richard M. Sudhalter, "Fred Astaire Makes an Impression on New Disc," *NY Post,* 22 March 1980.

24. Fell and Vinding 1999, 1–2.

25. Crouch 2006.

26. Lees 1988 [2000], 181.

27. Williams 1992, 11–12.

References

BOOKS AND SCHOLARLY ARTICLES

Newspaper and magazine articles referenced only once appear solely in the endnotes.

Alba, Ben. 2005. *Inventing Late Night: Steve Allen and the Original Tonight Show.* Amherst, New York: Prometheus Books.

Altman, Rick. 1987. *The American Film Musical.* Bloomington: Indiana University Press.

Astaire, Fred. 1951. "Long Live the Beat." *Esquire,* December, 88–89, 190.

———. 1959. *Steps in Time.* New York: Harper and Brothers.

Badger, Reid. 1995. *A Life in Ragtime: A Biography of James Reese Europe.* New York: Oxford University Press.

Balio, Tino. 1993. *Grand Design: Hollywood as a Modern Business Enterprise, 1930–1939.* Berkeley: University of California Press.

Balliett, Whitney. 1959. "Pandemonium Pays Off." In *The Sound of Surprise: 46 Pieces on Jazz.* New York: E.P. Dutton. First published in *The Saturday Review* (1954).

———. 2000. *Collected Works: A Journal of Jazz, 1954–2000.* New York: St. Martin's Griffin.

Banfield, Stephen. 2006. *Jerome Kern.* New Haven, CT: Yale University Press.

Barnet, Charlie, with Stanley Dance. 1984. *Those Swinging Years: The Autobiography of Charlie Barnet.* New York: Da Capo Press.

Basie, Count. 1985. *Good Morning, Blues: The Autobiography of Count Basie as Told to Albert Murray.* New York: Random House.

Basinger, Jeanine. 2007. *The Star Machine.* New York: Vintage.

Berliner, Paul F. 1994. *Thinking in Jazz: The Infinite Art of Improvisation.* Chicago: University of Chicago Press.

Billman, Larry. 1997a. *Film Choreographers and Dance Directors*. Jefferson, NC: McFarland & Co.

———. 1997b. *Fred Astaire: A Bio-Bibliography*. Westport, CT: Greenwood Press.

Bindas, Kenneth J. 2001. *Swing, That Modern Sound*. Jackson: University Press of Mississippi.

Bogle, Donald. 1997. *Dorothy Dandridge: A Biography*. New York: Boulevard Books.

———. 2001. *Toms, Coons, Mulattoes, Mammies, and Bucks: An Interpretive History of Blacks in American Films*. 4th ed. London: Continuum.

———. 2005. *Bright Boulevards, Bold Dreams: The Story of Black Hollywood*. New York: Ballantine Books.

Bordwell, David, Janet Staiger, and Kristin Thompson. 1985. *The Classical Hollywood Cinema: Film Style and Mode of Production to 1960*. New York: Columbia University Press.

Burke, Patrick. 2008. *Come In and Hear the Truth: Jazz and Race on 52nd Street*. Chicago: University of Chicago Press.

Castle, Irene. 1919. *My Husband*. New York: Charles Scribner's Sons.

Clum, John M. 1999. *Something for the Boys: Musical Theater and Gay Culture*. New York: St. Martin's Press.

Cohan, Steven. 1993. "'Feminizing' the Song-and-Dance Man: Fred Astaire and the Spectacle of Masculinity in the Hollywood Musical." In *Screening the Male: Exploring Masculinities in Hollywood Cinema,* ed. Steven Cohan and Ina Rae Hark. New York: Routledge.

Cook, Susan C. 1998. "Passionless Dancing and Passionate Reform: Respectability, Modernism, and the Social Dancing of Irene and Vernon Castle." In *The Passion of Music and Dance: Body, Gender and Sexuality,* ed. William Washabaugh. New York: Berg.

Crawford, Richard. 1993. *The American Musical Landscape*. Berkeley: University of California Press.

———. 2001. *America's Musical Life*. New York: Norton.

Crawford, Richard, and Jeffrey Magee. 1992. *Jazz Standards on Record, 1900–1942: A Core Repertory*. Chicago: Center for Black Music Research.

Croce, Arlene. 1972a. *The Fred Astaire and Ginger Rogers Book*. New York: Galahad Press.

———. 1972b. "Music for Astaire and Rogers: A Conversation with Hal Borne." *Ballet Review* 4, no. 3: 50–60.

Crouch, Stanley. 2006. "Brothers-in-Arts: The Unique Talent that Links Fred Astaire and Louis Armstrong." Available at www.slate.com.id/2136738 (accessed 11 November 2010).

Cugat, Xavier. 1948. *Rumba Is My Life*. New York: Didier.

Dance, Stanley. 1974. *The World of Swing: An Oral History of Big Band Jazz*. New York: Da Capo Press.

———. 1980. *The World of Count Basie*. New York: Charles Scribner's Sons.

Daniels, Don. 1983. "Astaire on the Air." In *Fred Astaire: The Television Years*. Museum of Broadcasting exhibit brochure, 6 December 1983–28 January 1984.

Davis, Ronald L. 2005. *Just Making Movies: Company Directors on the Studio System*. Jackson: University Press of Mississippi.

Decker, Todd. 2007. "Black/White Encounters on the American Musical Stage and Screen (1924–2005)." Ph.D. diss., University of Michigan, Ann Arbor.

Determeyer, Eddy. 2006. *Rhythm Is Our Business: Jimmie Lunceford and the Harlem Express*. Ann Arbor: University of Michigan Press.

Dick, Bernard F. 2007. "Crosby at Paramount: From Crooner to Actor." In *Going My Way: Bing Crosby and American Culture*, ed. Ruth Prigozy and Walter Raubicheck, 87–98. Rochester, NY: University of Rochester Press.

Dinerstein, Joel. 2003. *Swinging the Machine: Modernity, Technology, and African American Culture Between the World Wars*. Amherst: University of Massachusetts Press.

Eichenbaum, Rose. 2008. *The Dancer Within: Intimate Conversations with Great Dancers*. Middletown, CT: Wesleyan University Press.

Engel, Lyle Kenyon. 1962. *The Fred Astaire Dance Book: The Fred Astaire Dance Studio Method*. New York: Cornerstone Library.

Ephron, Henry. 1977. *We Thought We Could Do Anything: The Life of Screenwriters Phoebe and Henry Ephron*. New York: Norton.

Erenberg, Lewis A. 1981. *Steppin' Out: New York Nightlife and the Transformation of American Culture, 1890–1930*. Chicago: University of Chicago Press.

Eyman, Scott. 2005. *Lion of Hollywood: The Life and Legend of Louis B. Mayer*. New York: Simon and Schuster.

Eustis, Morton. 1937. *Players at Work*. New York: Blom.

Feather, Leonard. 1961. Liner note for *Calvin Jackson: Jazz Variations on Movie Themes*, Reprise Records R-2007.

———. 1972. "The Granzwagon." In *From Satchmo to Miles*. New York: Da Capo Press.

Fell, John L., and Terkild Vinding. 1999. *Stride!: Fats, Jimmy, Lion, Lamb and All the Other Ticklers*. Lanham, MD: Scarecrow Press.

Ferencz, George, ed. 1999. *"The Broadway Sound": The Autobiography and Selected Essays of Robert Russell Bennett*. Rochester, NY: University of Rochester Press.

Feuer, Jane. 1993. *The Hollywood Musical*. 2nd ed. Bloomington: Indiana University Press.

Floyd, Samuel A., Jr. 1990. "Music in the Harlem Renaissance: An Overview." In *Black Music in the Harlem Renaissance: A Reader*, ed. Samuel A. Floyd Jr. New York: Greenwood Press.

Fordin, Hugh. 1996. *MGM's Greatest Musicals: The Arthur Freed Unit*. New York: Da Capo Press. Originally published in 1975 as *The World of Entertainment: Hollywood's Greatest Musicals*. New York: Doubleday.

Frank, Rusty E. 1994. *Tap!: The Greatest Tap Dance Stars and Their Stories, 1900–1955*. New York: Da Capo Press.

The Fred Astaire Dance Album: Ginger Rogers and Fred Astaire in "Follow the Fleet." 1936. London: Queensway Press.

The Fred Astaire Top Hat Dance Album: A Comprehensive Compendium on Ballroom Dancing, Second Edition. 1936. London: Queensway Press

Freedland, Michael. 1976. *Fred Astaire*. New York: Grosset and Dunlap.

Friedwald, Will. 1995. *Sinatra! The Song is You: A Singer's Art*. New York: Scribner.

Furia, Philip. 2003. *Skylark: The Life and Times of Johnny Mercer*. New York: St. Martin's Press.

Garber, Michael. 2010. "'Some of These Days' and the Study of the Great American Songbook." *Journal of the Society for American Music* 4, no. 2 (May); 175–214.

Gavin, James. 1991. *Intimate Nights: The Golden Age of New York Cabaret.* New York: Grove Weidenfeld.

Gibbons, Jack. 2008. Lecture recital at Fred Astaire: The Conference, 24 June 2008, Oriel College, Oxford, UK.

Giddins, Gary. 1981. *Riding on a Blue Note: Jazz and American Pop*. New York: Oxford University Press.

———. 1998. *Visions of Jazz: The First Century*. New York: Oxford University Press.

———. 2001. *Bing Crosby: A Pocketful of Dreams, The Early Years 1903–1940*. New York: Little, Brown.

Giles, Sarah. 1988. *Fred Astaire: His Friends Talk*. New York: Doubleday.

Gil-Montero, Martha. 1989. *Brazilian Bombshell: The Biography of Carmen Miranda*. New York: Donald I. Fine.

Gilvey, John Anthony. 2005. *Before the Parade Passes By: Gower Champion and the Glorious American Musical*. New York: St. Martin's Press.

Goldberg, Jane. 1978. "John Bubbles: A Hoofer's Homage." *The Village Voice*, 4 December, 112.

Golden, Eve. 2007. *Vernon and Irene Castle's Ragtime Revolution*. Lexington: University Press of Kentucky.

Goldman, Herbert G. 1997. *Banjo Eyes: Eddie Cantor and the Birth of Modern Stardom*. New York: Oxford University Press.

Goldmark, Daniel. 2005. *Tunes for 'Toons: Music and the Hollywood Cartoon*. Berkeley: University of California Press.

Granata, Charles L. 1999. *Sessions with Sinatra: Frank Sinatra and the Art of Recording*. Chicago: A Cappella.

Green, Stanley, and Burt Goldblatt. 1973. *Starring Fred Astaire*. New York: Dodd, Mead and Co.

Guralnick, Peter 1994. *Last Train to Memphis: The Rise of Elvis Presley.* New York: Little, Brown and Co.

Gushee, Lawrence. 2005. *Pioneers of Jazz: The Story of the Creole Band*. New York: Oxford University Press.

Hampton, Lionel, with James Haskins. 1989. *Hamp: An Autobiography.* New York: Warner Books.

Handy, W.C., ed. 1926. *Blues: An Anthology.* New York: Albert and Charles Boni.

Harrison, Mary-Kathryn. 1999. *Fred Astaire's Contribution to American Freestyle Competition Ballroom Dancing*. M.A. thesis, Dept. of Theater and Dance, University of New Mexico, Albuquerque..

Haskins, Jim, and N.R. Mitgang. 1988. *Mr. Bojangles: The Biography of Bill Robinson*. New York: William Morrow.

Hentoff, Nat. 2004. *American Music Is*. New York: Da Capo Press.

Hill, Constance Valis. 2000. *Brotherhood in Rhythm: The Jazz Tap Dancing of the Nicholas Brothers*. New York: Oxford University Press.

———. 2010. *Tap Dancing America: A Cultural History*. New York: Oxford University Press.

Hirschhorn, Clive. 1984. *Gene Kelly: A Biography*. New York: St. Martin's Press.

Horricks, Raymond. 1991. "Clef/Verve: A Company Report." In *Profiles in Jazz: From Sidney Bechet to John Coltrane*. New Brunswick, NJ: Transaction Publishers.

Irwin, Sam. 2010. *Kay Thompson: From Funny Face to Eloise*. New York: Simon & Schuster.

Josephson, Sanford. 2009. *Jazz Notes: Interviews Across the Generations*. Santa Barbara, CA: ABC-CLIO.

Kempton, Arthur. 2003. *Boogaloo: The Quintessence of American Popular Music*. New York: Pantheon Books.

Kernfeld, Barry. 1991. "Swing-Bop Combos." In *The Blackwell Guide to Recorded Jazz,* ed. Barry Kernfeld. Oxford: Basil Blackwell.

Kimball, Robert, and Linda Emmet. 2001. *The Complete Lyrics of Irving Berlin*. New York: Alfred A. Knopf.

Kirkeby, Ed. 1966. *Ain't Misbehavin': The Story of Fats Waller*. New York: Dodd, Mead & Co.

Knight, Arthur. 2002. *Disintegrating the Musical: Black Performance and American Musical Film*. Durham, NC: Duke University Press.

Korall, Burt. 1990. *Drummin' Men: The Heartbeat of Jazz, the Swing Years*. New York: Schirmer Books.

Lahr, John. 1996. *Light Fantastic: Adventures in Theatre*. New York: Dial Press.

Lederer, Joseph. 1973. "Fred Astaire Remembers . . . Gershwin, Porter, Berlin, Kern and Youmans." *After Dark* (October), 55–59.

Lees, Gene. 1988 [2000]. *Oscar Peterson: The Will to Swing*. Updated ed. New York: Cooper Square Press.

Levinson, Peter. J. 2009. *Puttin' on the Ritz: Fred Astaire and the Fine Art of Panache*. New York: St. Martin's Press.

Magee, Jeffrey. 2005. *The Uncrowned King of Swing: Fletcher Henderson and Big Band Jazz*. New York: Oxford University Press.

Malnig, Julie. 1995. *Dancing Till Dawn: A Century of Exhibition Ballroom Dance*. New York: NYU Press.

Mandelbaum, Howard, and Eric Myers. 2001. *Screen Deco: A Celebration of High Style in Hollywood*. New York: Hennessey & Ingalls.

Manning, Frankie, and Cynthia Millman. 2007. *Frankie Manning: Ambassador of Lindy Hop*. Philadelphia, PA: Temple University Press.

Mathieson, Kenny. 2002. *Cookin': Hard Bop and Soul Jazz, 1954–65*. Edinburgh: Canongate.

Maultsby, Portia K. 2005. "Rhythm and Blues." In *African-American Music: An Introduction,* ed. Mellonee V. Burnim and Portia K. Maultsby. New York: Routledge.

McGilligan, Patrick. 1979. *Cagney: The Actor as Auteur*. New York: Da Capo.

McLean, Adrienne L. 2004. *Being Rita Hayworth: Labor, Identity and Hollywood Stardom*. New Brunswick, NJ: Rutgers University Press.

————. 2008. *Dying Swans and Madmen: Ballet, the Body and Narrative Cinema.* New Brunswick, NJ: Rutgers University Press.

Meisel, Myron. 1988. "Some Enchanted Evenings." *American Film Magazine,* May, 17, 52–53.

Melnick, Jeffrey. 1999. *A Right to Sing the Blues: African Americans, Jews and American Popular Song.* Cambridge, MA: Harvard University Press.

Mercer, Johnny. 1958. Liner notes for *8 Brass 5 Sax 4 Rhythm.* MGM Records, E3743.

Meriwether, Doug. 1998. *Mister, I Am the Band!: Buddy Rich—His Life and Travels.* North Bellmore, NY: National Drum Association.

Morgenstern, Dan. 2004. *Living With Jazz.* New York: Pantheon Books.

Mueller, John. 1985. *Astaire Dancing: The Musical Films.* New York: Wings Books.

Murphy, Lyle "Spud." 1937. *Spud Murphy's Swing Arranging Method.* New York: Robbins Music.

Murray, Albert. 1976. *Stompin' the Blues.* New York: McGraw-Hill.

Murray, Arthur. 1938. *How to Become a Good Dancer.* New York: Simon and Schuster.

Newquist, Roy. 1966. *Showcase.* New York: William Morrow.

Peretti, Burton W. 2007 *Nightclub City: Politics and Amusement in Manhattan.* Philadelphia: University of Pennsylvania Press.

Perlis, Vivian, and Libby Van Cleve. 2005. *Composer's Voices from Ives to Ellington: an Oral History of American Music.* New Haven, CT: Yale University Press.

Peterson, Oscar. 2002. *A Jazz Odyssey: My Life in Jazz.* New York: Continuum.

Platte, Nathan R. 2010. "Musical Collaboration in the Films of David O. Selznick, 1932–1957." Ph.D. diss., University of Michigan, Ann Arbor.

Pollock, Howard. 2005. *George Gershwin: His Life and Work.* Berkeley: University of California Press.

Previn, Andre. 1991. *No Minor Chords: My Days in Hollywood.* New York: Doubleday.

Regester, Charlene B. 2002. *Black Entertainers in African American Newspaper Articles.* Jefferson, NC: McFarland.

Rodríguez, Clara E. 2008. *Heroes, Lovers and Others: The Story of Latinos in Hollywood.* New York: Oxford University Press.

Rogers, Ginger. 1991. *Ginger: My Story.* New York: Harper Collins.

Rubin, Martin. 1993. *Showstoppers: Busby Berkeley and the Tradition of Spectacle.* New York: Columbia University Press.

Santopietro, Tom. 2008. *Sinatra in Hollywood.* New York: Thomas Dunne Books.

Satchell, Tim. 1987. *Astaire: The Biography.* London: Hutchinson.

Schultz, Margie. 1994. *Eleanor Powell: A Bio-Bibliography.* Westport, CT: Greenwood Press.

Segrave, Kerry. 2002. *Jukeboxes: an American Social History.* Jefferson, NC: McFarland.

Server, Lee. 2006. *Ava Gardner: "Love IS Nothing."* New York: St. Martin's Press.

Sheridan, Chris. 1986. *Count Basie: A Bio-discography.* New York: Greenwood Press.

Sherk, Warren M. 2007, "Fascinating Rhythms: Dimitri Tiomkin, African American Music, and Early Jazz." Available at www.dimitritiomkin.com (accessed 28 March 2009).

Shipton, Alyn. 2007. *A New History of Jazz*. Revised and updated ed. New York: Continuum.

Silverman, Stephen M. 1996. *Dancing on the Ceiling: Stanley Donen and His Movies*. New York: Knopf.

Silvester, Peter J. 2009 [1989]. *The Story of Boogie-Woogie: A Left Hand Like God*. Rev. ed. Latham, MD: Scarecrow Press.

Simosko, Vladimir. 2000. *Artie Shaw: A Musical Biography and Discography*. Lanham, MD: Scarecrow Press.

Southern, Eileen. 1997. *The Music of Black Americans: A History*. 3rd ed. New York: Norton.

Stearns, Marshall, and Jean Stearns. 1968. *Jazz Dance: The Story of American Vernacular Dance*. New York: Macmillan.

Stockdale, Robert J. 1999. *Jimmy Dorsey: A Study in Contrasts*. Lanham, MD: Scarecrow Press.

Suskin, Steven. 2009. *The Sound of Broadway Music: A Book of Orchestrators and Orchestrations*. New York: Oxford University Press.

Thomas, Bob. 1984. *Astaire: The Man, the Dancer*. New York: St. Martin's Press.

Thompson, Howard. 1970. *Fred Astaire: A Pictorial Treasury of his Films*. New York: Falcon.

Thomson, David. 2004. *The Whole Equation: A History of Hollywood*. New York: Knopf.

Torme, Mel. 1991. *Traps the Drum Wonder: The Life of Buddy Rich*. New York: Oxford University Press.

Townsend, Peter. 2007. *Pearl Harbor Jazz: Change in Popular Music in the Early 1940s*. Oxford: University Press of Mississippi.

Tucker, Sherrie. 2000. *Swing Shift: "All-Girl" Bands of the 1940s*. Durham, NC: Duke University Press.

Van de Leur, Walter. 2002. *Something to Live For: The Music of Billy Strayhorn*. New York: Oxford.

Waggoner, Susan. 2001. *Nightclub Nights: Art, Legend and Style, 1920–1960*. New York: Rizzoli.

Wald, Elijah. 2009. *How the Beatles Destroyed Rock 'n' Roll: An Alternative History of American Popular Music*. New York: Oxford University Press.

Wall, Tim. 2009. "Rocking Around the Clock: Teenage Dance Fads from 1955 to 1965." In *Ballroom, Boogie, Shimmy Sham, Shake: A Social and Popular Dance Reader*, ed. Julie Malnig. Chicago: University of Illinois Press.

Watts, Jill. 2005. *Hattie McDaniel: Black Ambition, White Hollywood*. New York: Amistad.

White, John. 2004. *Artie Shaw*. New York: Continuum.

White, Shane, and Graham White. 1998. *Stylin': African American Expressive Culture from Its Beginnings to the Zoot Suit*. Ithaca, NY: Cornell University Press.

Wierzbicki, James. 2009. *Film Music: A History*. New York: Routledge.

Williams, Martin. 1992. *Hidden in Plain Sight: An Examination of the American Arts.* New York: Oxford University Press.

Willis, Corin. 2009. "Blackface Minstrelsy and Jazz Signification in Hollywood's Early Sound Era." In *Thriving on a Riff: Jazz and Blues Influences in African American Literature and Film,* ed. Graham Lock and David Murray, 40–61. New York: Oxford University Press.

Wood, Graham. 2002. "Distant Cousin or Fraternal Twin?: Analytical Approaches to the Film Musical." In *The Cambridge Companion to the Musical,* ed. William A. Everett and Paul R. Laird, 212–30. New York: Cambridge University Press.

Yablonsky, Lewis. 1974. *George Raft.* New York: McGraw Hill.

DISCOGRAPHY

Anthony, Ray. 1951. *Houseparty Hop.* Capitol T292.

———. 1953. *Arthur Murray: Swing Fox Trots.* Capitol T546.

———. 1956. *Ray Anthony Plays for Dream Dancing.* Capitol T723.

Astaire, Fred. 1952. *Fred Astaire's Music for Tap Dancing.* Capitol L341.

———. 1959a. *Another Evening with Fred Astaire* (television soundtrack). Chrysler Corp K80-P-1087–8.

———. 1959b. *Now.* Kapp 1165/3049.

———. 1980. *Three Evenings with Fred Astaire.* DRG S3L 5181.

Astaire, Fred, with the Jazz at the Philharmonic All Stars. 1953. *The Astaire Story.* Clef MGC 1001–4.

Ayres, Mitchell. 1966. *The Hollywood Palace Starring Mitchell Ayres and His Orchestra.* Command Records RS 33–902.

The Band Wagon (original motion picture soundtrack). 1996. Rhino Movie Music R2 72253.

Basie, Count, and Joe Williams. 1959. *Everyday I Have the Blues.* Roulette Birdland R52033.

Broadway Melody of 1940 (original motion picture soundtrack). 2003. Rhino Handmade RHM2 7601/Turner Classic Movies 1433.

Brown, Les, and His Orchestra. 1953. *Concert at the Palladium, vols. 1 and 2.* Coral CRL 57000–01.

Champion, Marge, and Gower Champion. 1954. *Let's Dance with Marge and Gower Champion.* Columbia CL 605.

Fields, Dorothy. 1988. *An Evening with Dorothy Fields.* DRG 5167.

Hampton, Lionel. 1976 *The Complete Lionel Hampton: 1937–1941.* RCA AXM6–5536.

Hefti, Neal. 1962. *Jazz Pops: Neal Hefti and His Jazz Pops Orchestra.* Reprise R-6039.

Jackson, Calvin. 1958. *Calvin Jackson and His Orchestra: Jazz Variations on Gershwin's Rhapsody in Blue.* Liberty LRP-3071.

———. 1961. *Calvin Jackson: Jazz Variations on Movie Themes.* Reprise R-2007.

Jones, Jonah. 1957. *Muted Jazz.* Capitol T839.

———. 1958. *Jumpin' with Jonah.* Capitol T1039.

Kelly, Gene. 1948. *The Song and Dance Man*. MGM E30.

Martin, Skip, and His Orchestra. 1958. *8 Brass 5 Sax 4 Rhythm*. MGM E3743.

Moore, Phil. 1955. *Fantasy for Girl and Orchestra*. Verve MGV-2005.

Murray, Arthur. 1955. *Arthur Murray Presents Dance and Dream Time*. Capitol T641.

Smith, Jimmy. 1964. *The Cat . . . The incredible Jimmy Smith, Arranged and Conducted by Lalo Schifrin*. Verve V6–8587.

Stafford, Jo, with Paul Weston and His Orchestra. 1954. *Jo Stafford Sings Broadway's Best*. Columbia CL 584.

Stoll, Georgie, and His Orchestra. 1947. *Hollywood Melodies*. MGM 11.

Whiteman, Paul. 1955. *Cavalcade of Dance*. Coral CRL 57005.

Young-Holt Unlimited. 1969. *Just a Melody*. Brunswick BL754150.

Ziegfeld Follies (original motion picture soundtrack). 1995. Rhino Movie Music R2 71959.

Acknowledgments

I am beholden to many libraries and librarians. My home library at Washington University in St. Louis—and the music librarian Brad Short and the Interlibrary Loan department in particular—were indispensable. The archivists at the Wisconsin Historical Society in Madison and the New York Public Library for the Performing Arts were always helpful. Mark Horowitz and the staff of the Music Division of the Library of Congress proved invaluable again and again. Los Angeles is a great city for film research, and I drew many times on the expertise of Edward Comstock at the Cinematic Arts Library at the University of Southern California, Lauren Buisson at UCLA Arts Special Collections, and the staff at the Margaret Herrick Library of the Academy of Motion Picture Arts and Sciences. Branches of The Paley Center for Media in Beverly Hills and Manhattan were equally important. Kevin Fleming at the Georgia State University Library Popular Music and Culture Collection, Roberta Staats of the Cole Porter Trust, and Jeni Dahmus at The Julliard School all helped as well. Bruce Pomahac, music director at the Rodgers and Hammerstein Organization, facilitated my research again and again with helpful emails. Joseph McBride and Richard D. Zanuck kindly granted permission to reproduce archival materials.

The vitality of popular music and film studies is evidenced by the many opportunities I had to share parts of this book as a work in progress. My research and writing benefited from public vetting at many scholarly meetings, including the annual conferences of the Society for

American Music (2007, 2010), the Society of Dance History Scholars (2009), and the American Musicological Society (2010), as well as three special gatherings: Fred Astaire: The Conference (organized by Christine Bamberger and Kathleen Riley at Oxford, 2008), the Musicological Film Studies Conference (chaired by Michael Pisani and William H. Rosar at USC, 2009), and Popular Music in the Mercer Era, 1910–1970 (sponsored by the Johnny Mercer Foundation and organized by the Georgia State University Library in Atlanta, 2009).

Generous research funds from the Washington University School of Arts and Sciences, under Deans Ed Macias, Ralph Quatrano, and Gary Wihl, made possible my many journeys to archives and conferences. A subvention from the Claire and Barry S. Brook Endowment Fund of the American Musicological Society assisted with production costs. Support such as this sustains scholarship in the humanities and expands the story scholars can tell about the American experience.

I started thinking and writing about Astaire in my first doctoral seminar, a course on George Gershwin taught by Richard Crawford in his final year before retiring from the University of Michigan. Rich generously served as co-chair of my dissertation committee, and his mentoring and friendship are deeply important to me. One-third of my dissertation concerned Astaire's dances with African American musicians. My committee—Steven Whiting (co-chair), with Paul Anderson, Mark Clague, and Beth Genné—was a great help in moving me forward as a scholar. Beth, in particular, urged me to think broadly about Astaire's place in American dance and cheered me on when it counted. Others at Michigan who made a lasting impact on my thinking and writing include Ellwood Derr, Charles Hiroshi Garrett, Edward Parmentier, and Louise Stein.

A year spent teaching at UCLA brought me into the welcoming circle of the musicology department there, helping me find my way to the University of California Press in the process. Lunches and conversations with Raymond Knapp, Mitchell Morris, and Susan McClary challenged my knowledge of Hollywood film and broadened my outlook on what musicology could embrace as a discipline.

Washington University in St. Louis has been my scholarly home while writing this book. My colleagues in musicology and theory—chair Dolores Pesce, Craig Monson, Hugh MacDonald, Seth Carlin, Robert Snarrenberg, Peter Schmelz, John Turci-Escobar, Patrick Burke, Martin Kennedy, and Bruce Durazzi—have been tremendously supportive of my work in popular and film music. The Film and Media Studies faculty—chair Gaylyn Studlar, William Paul, and Philip Sewell—has been another important part of the intellectual community at Washington. Voice faculty Christine Armistead shared her love of Astaire on many informal occasions. The terrific students in my American Musical Film courses watched countless Astaire routines and helped me think anew about the musical as a genre.

Dafydd Foster Evans and Renaud Seligmann provided hospitality in New York and Washington, D.C. on many research trips. Nathan Platte read the whole book and listened to me work through ideas over many a gin and tonic. My parents, Ron and Linda Decker, followed my progress on the book from start to finish.

My anonymous readers for University of California Press offered much helpful advice and encouragement. Pointed input from the Faculty Editorial Committee improved the book in the final stages. Project editor Suzanne Knott, manuscript editor Sharron Wood, and Eric Schmidt made the book better as it moved down the home stretch.

My editor Mary Francis has been a true joy to work with. Her belief in the book and willingness to talk baseball moved things forward again and again. She was a perfect fit for this project.

Music Makes Me owes a tremendous debt to Christine Bamberger, co-moderator of an international Astaire discussion list on Yahoo, co-chair of the Astaire conference at Oxford, and advocate for Astaire's place in contemporary culture. Chris read the entire manuscript closely, at times challenging my readings and pointing me toward details I had missed. Chris cares about Astaire, shares that love with others, and, in the process, enlarges the audience for scholarly work such as this.

This is my first book, and I dedicate it to my sons, David and James, and to my wife, Kelly. David watched every one of Astaire's musicals with me—*Follow the Fleet* is his favorite (a solid choice). Sharing classical Hollywood cinema with him has been one of the early blessings of becoming a film scholar. James was born too late to get in on our family Astaire marathons, but he has followed the writing process by trying, again and again, to interrupt it. Jamie was always a good excuse to take a break. Kelly has been a constant help, watching the films, reading the manuscript, sharing her opinions, and listening patiently while I worked out my ideas and frustrations at any time of the day or night. I can't imagine writing this book or living life without her.

Permissions

Top Hat, White Tie and Tails

The Yam

Dig It

The Shorty George

These Orchids

Index

TEXT
10/13 Sabon

DISPLAY
Sabon (Open Type)

COMPOSITOR
Westchester Book Group

PRINTER AND BINDER
Maple-Vail Book Manufacturing Group